579-1743

THE
OLD TESTAMENT
STORY

JOHN TULLOCK

Belmont College

PRENTICE-HALL, INC.
Englewood Cliffs, New Jersey   07632

Library of Congress Cataloging in Publication Data

TULLOCK, JOHN H. (date)
  The Old Testament story.

  Bibliography: p.
  Includes index.
  1. Bible. O.T.—History of Biblical events.
2. Bible. O.T.—History of contemporary events.
3. Bible. O.T.—Introductions. I. Title.
BS1197.T78   221.6'1   80-16766
ISBN 0-13-633941-7

Excerpts from "Akkadian Myths and Epics," trans. by
E. A. Speiser; "The Code of Hammurabi,"
trans. by Theophile J. Meek; and "Palestinian
Inscriptions," trans. by W. F. Albright in
*The Ancient Near East: An Anthology of
Texts and Pictures,* by James B. Pritchard
(ed.) (Copyright © 1958 by Princeton University Press), pp. 70, 165, and 213. Reprinted
by permission of Princeton University Press.

©1981 by John H. Tullock

Printed in the United States of America

10 9 8 7 6 5 4 3 2 1

Editorial/production supervision and interior design
    by Barbara Alexander
Cover design by Frederick Charles Ltd.
Manufacturing buyer: Harry P. Baisley

PRENTICE-HALL INTERNATIONAL, INC., *London*
PRENTICE-HALL OF AUSTRALIA PTY. LIMITED, *Sydney*
PRENTICE-HALL OF CANADA, LTD., *Toronto*
PRENTICE-HALL OF INDIA PRIVATE LIMITED, *New Delhi*
PRENTICE-HALL OF JAPAN, INC., *Tokyo*
PRENTICE-HALL OF SOUTHEAST ASIA PTE. LTD., *Singapore*
WHITEHALL BOOKS LIMITED, *Wellington, New Zealand*

To Helen,
the love of my life;
faithful fan for over thirty years;
whose loving support has made
telling the story a joy.

Contents

CHAPTER SIX

Israel Confused: The Period of the Judges   **114**

CHAPTER SEVEN

Israel Gains a King: The United Monarchy   **129**

CHAPTER EIGHT

Israel Becomes Two: Israel and Judah
to the Fall of Israel   **176**

Preface

There is one overriding purpose in writing this book: To help college students, particularly freshmen, and interested laypersons to understand what the Old Testament contains. It is not aimed at the more advanced students, since there is already a wealth of excellent introductory texts to fill that need. I have made a conscious attempt to use simple language and a variety of illustrations to accomplish my purpose. As regards the critical issues raised in the past century by biblical scholars, I have given them the attention that I thought was appropriate for this level of study. Enough discussion is given, it is hoped, so that a student will not be totally mystified if issues are raised on any point. It is assumed that those students who have enough interest to take more advanced biblical courses will get a more than adequate exposure to such matters. I believe that before one can deal intelligently with the critical questions, that person should first know the material being considered, not just what someone says about it. Nothing simplifies a biblical discussion more than knowing what the Bible says.

A word needs to be said about the arrangement of materials. Though I realize that there are valid reasons for starting with the history of Israel and thus with the book of Exodus, nevertheless, I believe there will be less confusion for the beginning student if the traditional order is followed, with Genesis studied first. Beyond the first five books (the Pentateuch or Torah), when one comes to the study of the monarchy, a more historical order is followed by blending the historical books (1, 2 Samuel; 1, 2 Kings) with the books of the prophets to see the prophets in the context of their times. The one exception to this is the book of Jonah, which is seen as a part of an important debate about Israel's world responsibility in the postexilic period. The Writings, plus Jonah, then, are discussed separately for two reasons: (1) They reached their final form in about the same time—the postexilic period; and (2) because of the diverse times from which the materials that many of them contain come, they are not so easily fitted into a historical scheme as are the prophets.

Footnotes are kept to a minimum. When they are used, they, like the short bibliographies that appear at the end of each chapter, are more often used to indicate sources for further study. For this reason, the books and periodicals cited in the footnotes are not repeated in the bibliographies, except in rare instances. Where possible, more readily available paperback editions were cited.

To make the book more relevant to students, it has been tested in introductory Old Testament history classes at Belmont College, Nashville, Tennessee. Some 800 students, mostly college freshmen, have used it already and have been asked to react to it. They have been the first and foremost critics of it. On the basis of their reactions, the suggestions of my colleagues at Belmont, the special help of Page Kelley of The Southern Baptist Theological Seminary, and reviewers chosen by the publisher, revisions have been made which I hope have improved and strengthened this work.

Except for a few phrases from *The Bible in Today's English Version* (TEV) © 1966, 1971 © 1976 by the American Bible Society and the King James Version (KJV), all scripture quotations are from the Revised Standard Version of the Bible, 1946, 1952, © 1971, 1973 by the Division of Christian Education of the National Council of the Churches of Christ in the United States of America, and are used by permission.

Special words of thanks need to be given to President Herbert C. Gabhart and Dean Glen Kelley of Belmont College, who gave me a lighter teaching load to give me time for writing; to those special friends and colleagues in the Department of Religion and Philosophy of Belmont College, who not only made helpful suggestions but who actually insisted that I write the text in the first place; to Carol Poston, my hard-working and efficient secretary, who labored long and hard to turn my scratchings into a legible typescript, even after Master Seth Rhodes Poston made his appearance in the world; to Mary Ruth Brew and Bill Latta for valuable editorial suggestions and help in getting illustrations; and to Dale Brown, Prentice-Hall's Nashville area representative, who first insisted that I submit my work to Prentice-Hall and who has been helpful in ways too numerous to count.

TO THE STUDENT

I welcome you to the study of what to me is the world's most fascinating book or collection of books—the Bible. I hope this introductory journey through the Old Testament will whet your appetite for the study of this Book of Books that has been so influential through the ages.

JOHN H. TULLOCK

CHAPTER ONE

The Book
and Those Who Study It

Storytelling is one of the ways in which humanity has expressed its understanding of society. The story of ancient Israel took many forms: the accounts of the creation of the universe and man; the sagas of its ancestors, the explanations of its beginnings as a people, including its legal system; and the oracles of its prophets, the songs of its singers, and the wisdom of its wise men. And all these are a part of the Old Testament story.

The Old Testament: What Is It?

DEFINITION

The Old Testament is a collection of thirty-nine books, differing widely in their nature and content. It was produced during nearly 1000 years (1200–200 B.C.) by the people known first as Hebrews, or Israelites, and later as Jews. Before they became the Old Testament, these writings were the Hebrew Bible. Even to the early church it was the Bible, both in Hebrew and in the Greek version. Only after some Christian literature became looked upon as Scripture did it become known as the Old Testament to Christians. The Old Testament, then, is the story of God's dealings with a people, Israel, and is the accumulation of the literature that grew out of Israel's experiences with God. It is one of the world's literary treasures and, to those who consider it sacred Scripture, it contains the message of God to man.

INSPIRATION

The Old Testament, then, began as a collection of the sacred literature of the Jews. It grew up in the context of the history of the nation of Israel. It is viewed by both Jew and Christian as "inspired," or sacred, literature. How the Bible is inspired is subject to a number of interpretations. There are those who hold that every word in the original text was virtually dictated by God to men whose only function was to write it down in the idiom of their time. Others view inspiration as a process in which men encounter the Divine in their everyday living and write out of their reaction to that Divine encounter. Some say simply that the Old Testament is written by persons inspired in the same way that all great literature is inspired—it flows from the wellspring of human genius.

For devout Jews and Christians the last possibility is not enough to explain the sense of the sacred they find in the Bible. The view taken in this book is as follows: God's power is unlimited and this must surely include His power to reveal Himself. Inspiration is man's reaction to God's making Himself known to man. However, man's power to understand what God is revealing is definitely limited, and this limitation of man's understanding is reflected in what he writes about what God has done or is doing in the world. The Old Testament mirrors the strengths and weaknesses of those men whose experiences are portrayed, including their understandings and misunderstandings of God and His will for their lives. For this reason, a biblical character's understanding of God's will in his historical situation might be quite different from our understanding of God's will in our contemporary situation. For instance, the Christian apostle Paul accepted slavery as a part of his world and gave instructions about how slaves were to behave. Today we do not accept nor do we believe that God approves of slavery. What has changed, God's will about slavery or man's understanding? Most would answer that our understanding of what God's will is concerning slavery has changed. God was not wrong—it was man's understanding of God that was wrong. But even in this realization that a biblical character could misunderstand God's will, we learn one of the great lessons of faith—that we, too, are prone to error but can still be effective servants of God. As William Neil has observed, "The Bible is essentially a book about our human situation in a bewildering and perplexing universe."[1]

[1]William Neil, *The Rediscovery of the Bible* (London: Hodder and Stoughton Ltd.), 1954, p. 9.

BEGINNINGS

As it now stands, the Old Testament starts at the beginning of all things—the creation—but this order is probably not how the story of Israel actually developed. All through the Old Testament, the one theme which continually appears is the Exodus. This was the supreme event in Israelite history. Israel became a people through this event and those which followed. Thus it is commemorated in song and story (Exodus–Deuteronomy) and in numerous references in Psalms (e.g., 66:6; 68:7-18; 78:11-55; 114; 135:8-12; 136:10-22) as well as in other places in the Bible. A classic summary is found in Deuteronomy 26:5-9:

> And you shall make response before the Lord your God, "A wandering Aramean was my father; and he went down into Egypt and sojourned there, few in number; and there he became a nation, great, mighty, and populous. And the Egyptians treated us harshly, and afflicted us, and laid upon us hard bondage. Then we cried to the Lord the God of our fathers, and the Lord heard our voice, and saw our affliction, our toil, and our oppression; and the Lord brought us out of Egypt with a mighty hand and an outstretched arm, with great terror, with signs and wonders; and He brought us into this place and gave us this land, a land flowing with milk and honey."

The Exodus event made Israel aware of itself as a group of people with common experiences that united them. Just as a baby first notices his hands, his toes, and parts of himself, so Israel was first aware of itself as a people. But as the child grows he becomes aware of others and begins to ask questions, "Who am I?" "Where did I come from?"

When a people begin to ask these kinds of questions, they begin to look at their history—so Israel, in times of literary activity, had historians who gathered together the memories and traditions of the people and began to weave them into a story. In this story they explained not only their own origins in the Exodus but also carried that explanation back through the patriarchs to the origin of the human race, and even of the universe itself. As the nation grew, the history was expanded, either in written or oral form. Then when the tragedy of the Babylonian Exile struck and it looked as though not only historical materials but the words of the prophets, the wisdom materials, and the songs of the people might be lost, a concerted effort was made to gather together and preserve the literary heritage.

THE TWO CANONS

Since this literature was looked upon by Israel as being the result of God's dealings with them as a people, it was said to be viewed as sacred writings or scripture. These writings became scripture by a process known as *canonization.* To "canonize" means to establish a standard. Thus these books, through their usage and *because they spoke God's message to men,* came to be considered as the standard for human religious conduct.

The Hebrew canon.   Though the process of canonization took place over a long period of time, the Hebrew canon is usually spoken of as evolving as follows:

1. 400 B.C. The *Torah* (Genesis–Deuteronomy), or Law, was considered sacred by this time.
2. 200 B.C. The *Nebi'im* or Prophets were canonical. There was a twofold division of the Prophets.
   (a) The former prophets. The books of Joshua; Judges; 1, 2 Samuel; 1, 2 Kings.
   (b) The latter prophets. Isaiah, Jeremiah, Ezekiel, and the Twelve, generally known to Christians as the Minor Prophets.
3. A.D. 100. According to a widely held view, the rabbis at the Council of Jamnia declared the canon of Hebrew Scripture closed, recognizing those books known as the *Kethubi'im,* or Writings. These include Psalms; Job; Proverbs; Ruth; Song of Songs; Ecclesiastes; Lamentations; Esther; Daniel; Ezra; Nehemiah; 1, 2 Chronicles.

The question might legitimately be asked, "Why these books and not others?" That there were others is an established fact, for many religious writings have survived from biblical times which are not now considered to be scripture. Basically two tests determined what books were to be included in the Old Testament canon. First, was the test of time and usage. The literature, oral or written, that survived the tests of time and continued to speak to the needs of the users was judged to have the breath of the Divine about it.

According to a widely held view, a second test was established by the rabbis of Jamnia around A.D. 100. Although there were still strong centers of Judaism outside Palestine, especially in Babylon and in Alexandria, Egypt, Palestinian Judaism's lamp was almost blown out with the fall of Jerusalem in A.D. 70. Johanan ben Zakkai, a leading rabbi of the time, escaped the doomed city, and after pledging to the Romans that he would cause them no trouble, established a rabbinic school at Jamnia, near the site of the present city of Tel Aviv. The move toward canonization that dated back at least to the time of Ezra in the fifth century B.C., climaxed in the period following Jerusalem's fall in A.D. 70. The threat of Hellenistic influences that were centered in Alexandria; the extreme positions taken by apocalyptic groups, who chose certain books that could be interpreted in line with their radical views; and the rise of the fledgling Christian community, with its claims of scriptural status for certain of its writings, all had their effects on the final form the Old Testament took. The most generally accepted view is that the rabbis of Jamnia established the principle that inspiration ceased with Ezra. Following this, they are said to have established the final listing of those books considered sacred by the Jews of Palestine.

The Alexandrian canon.   Not all Jews accepted this canon, however. The Jews of Alexandria in Egypt had ideas of their own about which books should be in the canon. Both groups agreed on the *Torah* (Law) and *Nebi'im* (Prophets). The disagreement came over books to be included in the *Kethubi'im* (Writings). As a result, the Alexandrian Jews introduced an extra fifteen books in their canon: 1, 2 Esdras; Tobit; Judith; the additions to the Book of Esther; The Wisdom of Solomon; Ecclesiasticus, or the Wisdom of Jesus the Son of Sirach; Baruch; The Letter of Jeremiah; The Prayer of Azariah and the Song of the Three Young Men; Susanna; Bel and the Dragon; The Prayer of Manasseh; and 1, 2 Maccabees. This Alexandrian canon is called the Septuagint, or LXX.

The Alexandrian canon influenced the great fourth-century Catholic scholar Jerome in his Vulgate translation, which became the standard Latin version of the Bible for many centuries. Thus, today the Roman Catholic versions include the extra books which we know as the *Apocrypha*. Protestant translations are based on the canon established at Jamnia and therefore do not contain the Apocryphal books since they are not accepted among Protestant Christians as being Scripture.

How It Began

How did the Old Testament come to be written? Did someone just suddenly decide, "I'm going to write the Old Testament"? Or, was it a more complicated process?

To answer the first question with certainty is impossible. A New Testament writer for whom the Old Testament was the Bible spoke of how "holy men of old wrote as they were moved by the Spirit of God." Yet, even that statement, setting forth the conviction that God was the initiator of the process that led to the writing, also suggests that the development of the Old Testament was a historical process. The following is a suggested scheme of how the Old Testament may have been developed.

FIRST THE EVENT

Nothing happens without a cause, something that triggers it. The Old Testament grew out of the events and circumstances of the life of the people of Israel. While the Exodus and the circumstances surrounding it first stimulated the men of old to record God's dealings with Israel, many events before and after contributed to the material resources from which the Old Testament was constructed.

THEN THE STORY

First, things happened. The persons to whom they happened told others about what had happened to them. Just as every family has a fund of stories about various relatives, many of the stories that eventually were to be a part of the Old Testament came from the oral tradition of the people who were to be known as Israel. Not all the stories, however, were based on actual events. Some stories, called *aetiologies,* for example, were created to answer "why" questions. Other stories, like Jotham's fable about the trees (Judges 9:7-15) or Samson's riddle (Judges 14:14), were told to make a point. Telling the stories over the centuries also had its effects on their nature and their subsequent interpretation.

THEN THE INTERPRETATION

When things happen to us we usually take them as part of the natural flow of life. Later, however, as we look back at our lives, we may interpret a particular event in an entirely different light than we did at the time it happened. Time and circumstances may have given us a different insight into its significance for us. For instance, we may well consider something which happens to us as a disaster immediately after it happens. Later we may look upon it as something very positive and meaningful for us.

AND THEN THE HISTORY

The Old Testament grew from such hindsight. At some point in the life of Israel as a people, someone, or a number of someones, looked back at the past and concluded that God had been at work in the lives of the people—calling their ancestors out of paganism, making himself known to them, leading them from the Tigris–Euphrates River valleys to Palestine and eventually into Egypt and bondage. But even that bondage, a disaster by most normal standards, was God's way of preserving the Israelites as a people. He raised up a leader, Moses, and prepared him, as the adopted son of the Egyptian princess and as a Midianite shepherd, for the difficult job of leading a band of slaves and a mixed multitude of others into the Sinai desert, there to weld this motley group into a people, united in covenant with him.

Furthermore, God led them to a land—a land he had promised to their ancestors, Abraham, Isaac, and Jacob. After a long and difficult period, the land became theirs. But their troubles were not over. After more than 200 years of struggles to achieve some kind of national unity, they finally settled on a monarchy as the kind of government they would have. Although it had a sputtering start with Saul, the monarchy took off with an earth-shaking roar under David, reaching its greatest territorial limits and enabling it to withstand any challenge to its territory by any outside power. This thrust was continued under Solomon; but when Solomon's son Rehoboam came to the throne, the kingdom fell apart because the young king miscalculated the depth of the people's discontent over the unwise policies of his father.

For two centuries, the two parts of the once-proud kingdom of David limped along—sometimes as enemies—sometimes as friends. At times in their periods of friendship, they combined forces to bring a measure of prosperity to their people, but for most of the time they were like pawns, toyed with by the great powers of the time—Egypt and Assyria. Finally, in 721 B.C., Israel, the northern kingdom, was blotted out of existence by the Assyrian giant who destroyed its cities and deported all that was left of its upper classes, replacing them with foreigners who were to intermarry with the poor people of the land, producing the Samaritans.

Judah, the southern kingdom, struggled on for just over a century, but it too fell, this time to Babylonia, the nation which had succeeded Assyria as the terror of the Near East.

Although Judah's surviving leadership was deported, as Israel's had also been, different factors had been at work there which caused the people to keep their identity. The prophets had warned that such an occurrence was likely if Judah persisted in its wrongdoing. Seemingly, also, the stability of the government in the south gave the people a greater sense of unity, which helped them to hold together in the time of national disaster. Then, too, the Babylonians seemed to have contributed to the situation by settling the people in communities where they could follow the advice of the prophet Jeremiah and live as normal a life as possible (Jeremiah 29).

In response to the trauma of the Exile and the threat of annihilation, Jewish scholars began in earnest to collect and to create the literature of the people. History was written, poetry was collected, and the words of the great prophets were arranged and preserved. Much of the Old Testament as we now know it took shape during the Exile and immediately afterward.

With the people now convinced of the importance of the preservation of their traditions, the period following the Exile, while not a time of national glory, was a time of collection, preservation, and interpretation which reached its climax in the final canonization of the Old Testament early in the Christian era.

How It Developed

THE PROCESS

But did the process of forming the literature of the Old Testament begin in the Exile? The answer most certainly is "No." Theories vary considerably about the mechanics of that process, but they may be divided into two basic views: (1) that the creation of the literature had its beginnings with Moses, who, according to this view, wrote the Pentateuch; and (2) that the literature is the result of a more complex pattern of development, a view that is the product of modern biblical scholarship. This latter theory goes beyond the Pentateuch and involves the whole of the Old Testament.

The development of the Old Testament may be compared to a river and its tributaries. A river does not begin full-sized. Rather it is a combination of dozens of smaller streams which have joined together to form the river. So it was with the Old Testament. Some quickly point out that it began with God. Even so, God worked through human agents, and it is the work of these human agents that we are discussing.

The first tiny streams were the oral traditions: the poems of victory; the stories of the ancestors; and the memories of great events, which were treasured, gathered, and passed on by word of mouth for many generations. At shrines where clans (i.e., the extended families) gathered for worship, the stories were combined into larger units to form cycles of tradition. Finally someone conceived the idea, by what religious men call inspiration, that the stories of God's dealings in history with his people needed to be written down or put into a complete story so they could be preserved.

MOSAIC AUTHORSHIP

When this story was written is one of the points of the debate about authorship, especially as it related to the Pentateuch or Torah. Scholars of a more conservative bent say Moses wrote the Pentateuch, and it was he who joined the many tiny streams of tradition into a major tributary. Even here there is variation, some saying that Moses used available traditions and others advocating that Moses received the totality of the material through divine revelation. As evidence of Mosaic authorship, they cite the long Jewish tradition that Moses was the author of these books. To support this view, they cite numerous Old Testament passages, some of which are Deuteronomy 31:9,24; 1 Kings 2:3; 2 Kings 23:25; Malachi 4:4; Joshua 8:31; 2 Kings 14:6; Nehemiah 8:1; and 2 Chronicles 25:4, 35:12. Jesus' statements in Luke 24:27,44 are also cited as evidence for Mosaic authorship. Differences in writing style in the text are explained by saying that

Moses used different scribes, giving to them the sense of what was to be said and the scribes putting it in their own idiom.[2]

DOCUMENTARY HYPOTHESIS

Scholars of a less traditional persuasion see the smaller streams of tradition continuing in oral or written form until the time of the kingships of David and Solomon. They say it is during this period that the first attempts were made to write a history of Israel. This view extends beyond the Pentateuch or Torah and embraces all the major historical books: Joshua–2 Kings; as well as Ezra; Nehemiah; and 1, 2 Chronicles.

According to this view, that stream of tradition which began with the Exodus stories was chosen as the main stream. To it were added the stories of the patriarchs and stories of the creation. This first edition of the history of Israel (characterized by the designation of God by the personal name Yahweh) was made up largely of materials from the southern part of Israel. It flowed on for a hundred years or so, until it was joined by another stream of materials from the northern part of the country, identified by the fact that it used a more general or "family" name for God—Elohim. There materials started with stories about Abraham, but they became so mingled with the main stream that it is difficult now to determine just how much they contributed to the total volume.

The next major tributary was of such volume and force that it became dominant in the historical materials. In the reign of Josiah, King of Judah (640–609 B.C.), "the book of the law" was found in the temple when repairs were being made (2 Kings 22:8). Scholars conclude, on the basis of the religious reforms which followed and which seemed to be based on the contents of the book of the law, that this book was essentially the book of Deuteronomy. Some argue that it was written not more than 100 years before its discovery. Yet, it is usually agreed that a major part of the materials it contains are from a much earlier time.

Like a river whose whole character is changed by the joining of a major tributary, so the character of the presentation of the history of Israel is changed by the reform growing out of the discovery of the Deuteronomic materials. Beginning particularly with the book of Judges, Israel's history is interpreted in a distinct fashion. It is viewed as following a cycle: Israel *sins; judgment* comes through the oppression of an enemy; Israel *repents;* God raises up a leader to *deliver* the people from their enemies. This pattern is especially clear in the book of Judges (3:7-11),

[2]For a concise discussion of the traditional view see G. Herbert Livingston, *The Pentateuch in Its Cultural Environment* (Grand Rapids: Baker Book House, 1974), pp. 218–220.

but is not so obvious in the history of the monarchy (1, 2 Samuel; 1, 2 Kings).

The exile in Babylon and the years following saw a tremendous flood of materials enter the stream. Because the danger of the extinction of the people brought a new reverence for the sacred traditions and a zeal for preserving the sacred literature, the people established a unifying symbol which led to the preservation of the preservers. Torah, now expanded to mean not only the Pentateuch but also the history and sayings of the great prophets, the wisdom of the sages, and the sacred songs of the people, gave the people a sense of unity and purpose which was to enable them to survive many centuries of adversity.

Just as today, when the dangers of losing the natural beauty has led to governmental action to preserve some streams as scenic rivers, so the Jews moved to preserve their most meaningful literature by designating it as sacred. The final contributors to this literary river were the priests in the exilic and postexilic periods. They gave the material its final form through an editorial process and through collecting those books known as the Writings, including the last edition of the history of Israel as found in Ezra–Nehemiah, plus 1, 2 Chronicles. All that remained was the final act in the process of canonization by the rabbis of Jamnia. So, as the river finally reaches the ocean, so the Hebrew Bible became the possession of the world through the Jewish community and its major offspring, Christianity.

The Work of Scholars

How do we know that the Old Testament developed in this or any other way? The fact that it exists is ample evidence that it developed somehow, somewhere, and at some time. Since there are no time machines to transport us back through the ages to watch the Bible being written, we must depend upon those scholars who can discover and interpret clues about its beginnings and growth.

But the questions arise, "Why go to all that trouble?" "Why not just accept it as it is?" Those who would ask such questions would probably insist, however, that one needs to understand the Old Testament—or the Bible as a whole, for that matter—as well as possible. Just as we can understand others better if we understand their background, so we can understand the Bible better if we understand its background. If we study the results of their efforts, all varieties of biblical scholars can contribute to our understanding of the Bible, whether they are textual specialist or theologian; form critic or archaeologist; literary historian or redaction critic. We need then to describe briefly some of those kinds of scholarship that are used to aid in understanding and interpreting the Bible.

TEXTUAL CRITICISM

First are those scholars whose concern is the biblical text itself. Nobody possesses a single original copy of any book of the Bible, either in the Old or New Testaments. The oldest complete copy of any single book in the Old Testament is a copy of the Book of Isaiah, found among the Dead Sea Scrolls in 1947 and dating from about the time of Christ. This means that the original copy of the book of Isaiah, as we now know it, was written several hundred years before the Dead Sea Scroll Isaiah was copied.

On the other hand, there are more copies of biblical manuscripts than of any other kinds of ancient manuscripts. There is far more manuscript evidence for the prophets of Israel than there is for Plato and Aristotle. That such a profusion of manuscripts exists creates something of a problem, however, in that they differ in places. This is where the talents of the textual scholar are put to work. Through a vast knowledge of the ancient languages, the textual specialist is able to compare the various manuscripts and thus bring us closer to what the original copies said. It should be pointed out that most of the variants in the text involve only about five percent of the total material.

LITERARY AND HISTORICAL STUDIES

In the second place, there are scholars who study the text from a literary and historical standpoint. They are concerned with an analysis of the text to determine its sources and to trace the development of the present books from those sources. Among other things, they study the Old Testament itself, the literature of Israel's neighbors, and the results of archaeology to find evidence concerning these matters. From the evidence they gather they form hypotheses to try to explain what they find.

Documentary hypothesis. Such a view is the documentary hypothesis known as the JEDP Hypothesis. It was developed gradually in the nineteenth century by a number of scholars, but was stated in its classic form by Julius Wellhausen, a nineteenth-century German Old Testament scholar. Wellhausen had been greatly influenced by Darwin's theory of evolution and saw an evolutionary pattern in the development of the literature of the Pentateuch. Wellhausen saw four major stages in the development of the Pentateuch: (1) A history of Israel which was written in the time of Solomon and which was characterized by the use of Yahweh, God's personal name. The letter J was used to designate this Yahwistic history. (2) A second edition, characterized by the use of Elohim to speak of God, came into being in the eighth century B.C. The letter E represents the Elohistic history. (3) The book of Deuteronomy was discovered in the Temple in Jerusalem during the time of Josiah in 621 B.C. It, in turn, influenced later history writing. This version of the history is called the Deuteronomic history. (4) Finally, all this was brought together and edited by the priests around 450 B.C., who wrote their own version of the history, adding to it the legal materials in Exodus, Leviticus, and Numbers. This priestly history is designated by P. For Wellhausen, each of these separate histories reflect the time in which they were written; in other words, the contents of each of them was largely the creation of the author or authors.

Oral tradition. The rigid evolutionary view of Wellhausen was greatly modified by those who became interested in what happened before any history was written down. Led by another German Old Testament scholar, Hermann Gunkel, and greatly expanded by scholars from the Scandinavian countries, a thorough investigation was made of the Old Testament from the standpoint of its oral development. These scholars have shown that while it might have been true that Israel's history was written down in stages somewhat as Wellhausen suggested, the materials used in writing—i.e., the stories, laws, and songs—were much older. Furthermore, they have suggested that even the so-called histories themselves might have been passed down in oral rather than written forms.

FORM CRITICISM

This has led to other fields of biblical study. One is form criticism. In an earlier time in our history, rural women made butter. Each farm wife had a wooden mold into which she packed the fresh butter. When it came out of the mold, it had a distinctive shape and a distinctive mark so that others could recognize "Mrs. Smith's butter" or "Mrs. Jones's butter." Form critics look for those distinctive types of speech patterns that characterize a certain type of literature. A good example is the discovery that the prophets often used the language of the court system to describe God's judgment on the people. In Micah 6:1-8 there is an indictment (6:1-2), the evidence against the defendant (6:3-5), the defense (6:6-7), and the judgment (6:8). Today, we can often tell what a person does or what his interests are by the pattern of his speech.

REDACTION CRITICISM

Another scholarly discipline is called redaction criticism. An editor is one who determines what stories are selected for inclusion in the newspaper. A book editor suggests to the writer what needs to be left out and what should be changed. Redaction criticism studies how the books of the Old Testament have been edited by the redactor, who was both editor and author. For example, the story of David's life is found in 1 Samuel 16-1 Kings 2:12, and in 1 Chronicles 10:1-29:30. The materials in both versions of David's life are largely identical. Yet there are some very important omissions in the Chronicler's history, particularly the story of David's sin with Bathsheba. By the Chronicler's time, after the Babylonian Exile, David was looked upon as the ideal king, so much so that the Israelites envisioned a day when a new David, the Messiah, would come to deliver Israel from its enemies. So the redactor, or editor, did not feel it would do any good to bring up David's indiscretions with Bathsheba. The editor was not just a compiler of materials but was more of a theologian with a message which he shaped by the materials he selected to tell the story.

A word should be said about the terms "critic" or "criticism." Too often we give a negative meaning to these words. Here, however, they mean "one who analyzes" or the "analysis of" the materials for the purpose of coming to a better understanding of them.

While other scholars are concerned with the text and its history, these examples are sufficient to show how complex the matter of biblical study can be. The scholars who attempt to make use of the products of all this scholarly work are the biblical theologians. They try to take the results, interpret the text in the light of those results, and communicate its meaning to those who are interested. Whatever approach one takes to the Bible, whether to study it as part of the world's great literature or to study it as a sacred book, all can profit from these efforts in gaining new insights into its meaning. This does not mean, however, that an individual who reads the Bible unaided can have no understanding of it. Rather, it is the hope of the biblical scholar that he can help the average Bible reader to have a better understanding of what he reads.

Archaeology as a Tool for Understanding

The discovery in Syria of the remains of an ancient city destroyed nearly 4300 years ago was announced in 1976. A library of more than 16,000 clay tablets, which will take many years to translate, was found. Estimates are that as many as 30,000 tablets may be found when the excavations are completed. Fortunately, Paleo-Canaanite, the language on some of the tablets, is closely related to biblical Hebrew, thereby greatly aiding the process of translation. Already it seems evident that when the tablets are deciphered, they will tell us of a new group of people who occupied the biblical area hundreds of years before the time of Abraham.[3]

[3]See "News from the Field," *Biblical Archaeologist*, XXXIX (March, 1976), p. 4.

This discovery was the work of archaeologists who have been digging at this site for more than ten years. One may ask, "What is archaeology?" "How does an archaeologist know where to dig?" "What value is archaeology?"

DEFINITIONS

Some people think of an archaeologist as a person who digs in a likely spot, and one who puts anything that he finds into a museum, into his personal trophy case, or sells it to an antique dealer for whatever he can get for it. Others think of the archaeologist as a person who sets out to prove that the Bible is true. There is an element of truth in each of these ideas. The archaeologist does dig, and often what he finds does end up in a museum. It is also true that the net result of the work of archaeologists has been to substantiate and to clarify many things in the Bible, but the main purpose of archaeology is neither to furnish museum pieces nor to substantiate a particular biblical event. In fact, not all archaeology is biblical in its interest.

Archaeologists investigate many cultures, including the Indian cultures in our own country. The archaeologist is a scientist who is searching for truth by excavating ancient sites as carefully and as systematically as possible, using any scientific tool or discipline to assist him in discovering everything he can about the site he is studying. Those disciplines may include chemistry, metallurgy, the plant sciences, geology, engineering, photography, and radiocarbon dating. Thus the purpose of all archaeology, including biblical archaeology, is to understand ancient cultures, not to prove or disprove anything. In this quest for understanding, all kinds of materials have been discovered, including extensive written materials.

SITE SELECTION

How does an archaeologist who is interested in biblical sites know where to dig? With the Bible as his geography book, he tries to determine the approximate area where a particular city was located. Then he looks for what is called a *tell*, an artificial hill built up in a layer-cake fashion over many centuries of occupation. Since Palestine, as well as much of the ancient Near East, is relatively dry, this limited the number of places where cities could be built. Thus, when a city was destroyed, it would not be unusual for some other group of people to come along in ten, fifty, or a hundred years and build another city upon the ruins of the one that had been destroyed, often using whatever remained, such as foundations, in building the new city. In some tells this process was repeated as many as twenty times.

Figure 1–1. Cultural or archaeological ages of the past in Palestine. This illustration shows how a *tell* was built up by layers, over the centuries, as cities were built and destroyed.

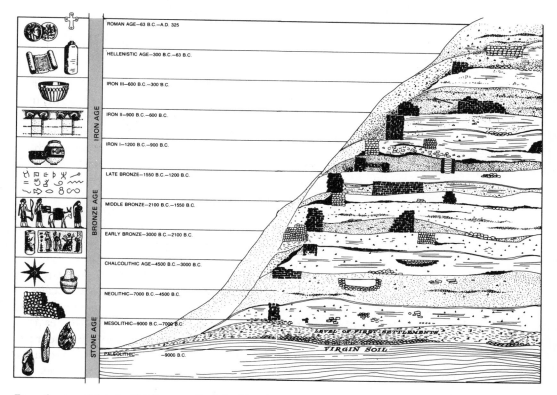

From *Compass Points for Old Testament Study* by Marc H. Lovelace. Copyright © 1972 by Abingdon Press. Used by permission.

DATING

When a city was destroyed, many things were left behind. The most common remains were the everyday utensils, largely clay pottery. Because of the work of men like Sir Flinders Petrie and W. F. Albright, it has been discovered that pottery styles changed from century to century, just as clothing styles or automobiles change today. One does not have to be an expert to recognize the differences between a Model A and a Thunderbird. Experts discovered that the patterns in pottery were much the same over much of the ancient world. If one finds in southern Palestine a piece of pottery which was of the same style as pottery found in northern Syria, it can be assumed that they came from approximately the same time in history.

The discovery of what is known as radiocarbon dating has also been applied in archaeology. When charred wood from a burned building is discovered, it can be tested for radioactivity and an approximate date for the destruction of the city can be determined. One of the ways that the date of the Dead Sea Scrolls was determined was by burning a small piece of the linen wrappings from the scrolls and testing it by the radiocarbon process.

DIGGING

How does the archaeologist proceed once he has decided where to dig? A common method is to survey the site and divide it into squares 5 meters by 5 meters. After the surface dirt in a square has been removed, excavation is done very carefully, taking off no more than a few inches of soil at a time over the whole area. The chief tools for this slow, careful excavation are hand picks, trowels, and brushes. All pottery and other small objects are kept and carefully marked as to the level from which they came. Once the entire square has had a layer of dirt taken off, it is brushed carefully, and any changes in the color of the surface from one part of the square to another are noted. This procedure is necessary because many ancient buildings were built of mud brick that can be seen only when the surface is smooth and dry. Discovery of rocks may indicate that there is a wall. Even the city's household garbage pits hold valuable information in the form of animal bones that give indications about the diet of the people. One of the fascinating aspects of archaeology is that our knowledge of past cultures depends in large measure upon what the people threw away. The study of all this requires careful work, accurate record-keeping, liberal use of photography, and the analytical skills of the archaeologists as well as other experts.

VALUE

What is the value of all this work? First, archaeology has taken the outlines sketched for us by the Bible and has painted in the backgrounds. Today, because of the work of archaeologists, we know what the biblical people ate, what kind of houses they lived in, what their customs were, what languages they spoke, what animals they had, what kind of jewelry they wore, and even how they made out deeds for property.

Furthermore, we are far richer in the number of biblical texts available to us today than ever before, thanks to the archaeologists. In addition, our ability to understand those texts is far greater because of archaeological discoveries. This can be illustrated by a brief description of some of the most prominent archaeological discoveries.

Figure 1–2. The early stages of an excavation, showing the squares with the dirt balks that separate them. The balks can be removed as the excavation progresses.

Photograph by John H. Tullock.

IMPORTANT DISCOVERIES

These are but a few of the many examples that can be given.

The Rosetta Stone. Discovered in Egypt in 1801 by an engineer in Napoleon's army, this trilingual inscription was written in Greek, demotic, and hieroglyphics, the ancient Egyptian form of picture writing. By means of this inscription, Champollion was able to read hieroglyphic writing for the first time. This, in turn, made possible the reading of thousands of ancient Egyptian inscriptions which before had been untranslatable. The knowledge of early Egyptian history was immeasurably increased. The Rosetta Stone is now in the British Museum.

The Behistun Stone. When the Persian ruler Darius I had his exploits recorded on a mountainside in Persia (modern Iran) in the sixth century B.C., he could not have realized that the inscription—written in Babylonian, Elamite, and Persian—would furnish the key for modern scholars to decipher the records of the Babylonians. When the inscription was translated in the nineteenth century by Sir Henry Rawlinson, it revealed the meaning of Babylonian and other cuneiform writings, which previously had been unidentified marks on clay tablets, and gave a new dimension to our understanding of Old Testament background.

The Ugaritic materials.   In the late 1920s a Syrian farmer turned up some clay tablets in his field, which led to the discovery by French archaeologists of the ancient city of Ugarit. In the royal archives were found numerous clay tablets, containing, among other things, religious texts that greatly increased our knowledge of Canaanite religions, which the Israelite prophets had so strongly opposed. These texts shed new light on numerous biblical texts that previously had been obscure.

The Dead Sea Scrolls.   A Bedouin boy searching for a lost goat made this important discovery in a cave near the Dead Sea. The first manuscripts fortunately fell into the hands of experts who realized their value. This, in turn, initiated a systematic examination of other caves in the area, leading to the discovery of a veritable treasury of biblical and nonbiblical manuscripts. As a consequence, there are now available manuscripts for portions of the Old Testament that are 1000 years older than any

Figure 1–3.   Cave Four at Qumran where many of the Dead Sea Scrolls were found.

Photograph by John H. Tullock.

previously known manuscripts. Today, some thirty years after the initial discovery, the materials are still being examined.

The Mari tablets.   These tablets were discovered at Mari, the capital city of a Semitic state located in northern Mesopotamia. These pre-Abrahamic ancestors of the Israelites had many customs which were the same or similar to those of the Hebrew patriarchs, Abraham, Isaac, and Jacob.

The Bar Kochba Letters.   Found also in the area around the Dead Sea, these letters do not relate directly to the Old Testament. They do, however, shed new light on a rather obscure period in Jewish history—the Bar Kochba revolt of A.D. 132–135. The letters are dispatches sent by Simon Bar Kochba, the leader of the revolt, to his commanders in the field.

The Ebla discoveries.   In northern Syria archaeologists have discovered the capital city of a previously unknown empire that existed around 2500 B.C. It is too early to measure the importance of this discovery, but it promises to rival the Dead Sea Scrolls in its impact on Old Testament studies.

Archaeology has shed new light on the background of both the Old and New Testaments, not only in historical events, but also in the everyday life of the ordinary Palestinians and other Near Eastern peoples. It has added to the increasing store of biblical manuscripts, furthermore, and in so doing, has helped us to move close to the goal of discovering what the manuscripts of the Bible mean.

STUDY QUESTIONS

1. What does it mean to say that the Old Testament (or Hebrew Bible) is inspired?
2. Why did the Israelites begin their story with the Exodus? *signified when Israel become a people*
3. Why were there at least two canons or lists of books for the Old Testament? *because Jews didn't accept Hebrew, wanted changes made to it*
4. How were the early traditions about Israel developed and passed along from generation to generation? *orally*
5. Identify and define two major ideas on how the Pentateuch was written. *Moses wrote it / complex development - by word of mouth*
6. How does each of the kinds of scholarship defined by the text contribute to our understanding of the Old Testament? *textual - brings us closer to actual writings*
7. How does archaeology illuminate biblical backgrounds?

8. Learn at least one important fact about each of the archaeological examples given.

FOR FURTHER STUDY

Biblical Archaeology

Biblical Archaeologist. A quarterly publication of the American Schools of Oriental Research whose purpose is "to provide the general reader . . . with an interpretation of the meaning of new archaeological discoveries for the biblical heritage of the West."

Biblical Archaeology Review. A quarterly magazine published by the Biblical Archaeology Society. It has more of a popular magazine format.

CORNFELD, GAALYAH and DAVID NOEL FREEDMAN, editors. *Archaeology of the Bible: Book by Book.* New York: Harper & Row, 1976. This work takes the Bible book by book and tells of archaeological discoveries that relate to that book.

WRIGHT, GEORGE ERNEST. *Biblical Archaeology.* Revised and expanded edition. Philadelphia: Westminister Press, 1962. An interesting, well-written book that relates archaeological discoveries to both Old and New Testament history.

Biblical Criticism

The first four books are in the *Guides to Biblical Scholarship Series,* edited by Gene M. Tucker, and are designed for the beginning student.

HABEL, NORMAN C. *Literary Criticism of the Old Testament.* Philadelphia: Fortress Press, 1971.

KRENTZ, EDGAR. *Textual Criticism of the Old Testament: From the LXX to Qumran.* Philadelphia: Fortress Press, 1971.

RAST, WALTER E. *Tradition History and the Old Testament.* Philadelphia: Fortress Press, 1971.

TUCKER, GENE M. *Form Criticism of the Old Testament.* Philadelphia: Fortress Press, 1971.

BRIGHT, JOHN. *The Authority of the Old Testament.* New York: Abingdon, 1967. An excellent discussion on the relevance of the Old Testament for modern life.

HAYES, JOHN H., ed. *Old Testament Form Criticism.* San Antonio: Trinity University Press, 1974. A book that applies the principles of form criticism to parts of the Old Testament.

JEFFREY, ARTHUR, "The Canon of the Old Testament" in *Interpreter's Bible,*
I. New York: Abingdon, 1952, pp. 32–45.
TORRO, JAMES C., and RAYMOND E. BROWN, "Canonicity" in *The Jerome
Biblical Commentary,* pp. 515–534.

Extrabiblical Texts

CROSS, FRANK M. *The Ancient Library of Qumran and Modern Biblical Studies.*
Garden City, N.Y.: Doubleday, 1961. An in-depth treatment of the
Dead Sea Scrolls. Paperback.
GASTER, T. H. *The Dead Sea Scriptures,* rev. ed. Garden City, N.Y.: Double-
day, 1964. The best available collection of the nonbiblical materials
from Qumran. Paperback.
J. B. PRITCHARD, ed. *Ancient Near Eastern Texts Relating to the Old Testament,*
3rd ed. with supplements. Princeton: Princeton University Press,
1969. The best collection of extrabiblical texts available in English.
————· *The Ancient Near East in Pictures Relating to the Old Testament.*
Princeton: Princeton University Press, 1954.
————· *The Ancient Near East: An Anthology of Texts and Pictures.* Princeton:
Princeton University Press, 1965. This is a paperback condensation
of Pritchard's two longer works and is more available to the average
reader.

CHAPTER TWO

The Geographical and Historical Setting for the Old Testament Prior to 1200 B.C.

In a remarkable photograph taken from the Gemini XI spacecraft in 1966, the biblical world from Egypt to Mesopotamia is captured in one magnificent view. One is struck by the dry, barren look that characterizes much of this area, called the Near East. And dry it is. Deserts abound—the Arabian Desert is on the east, the desert of the Sinai Peninsula is to the south, and the great Sahara Desert in North Africa pushes its way right up to the banks of the Nile River in Egypt. Only where there were rivers was there settled life in early times. These rivers furnished water to drink and for the irrigation that made possible the development of agriculture. Other regions might have in the occasional oasis enough water for nomadic herdsmen, but these oases were so far apart that desert travel was limited until the domestication of the camel. Nomads in the prepatriarchal era traveled by ass or donkey and thus were limited in their range.

The Fertile Crescent

The watered areas of the Near East form a rough crescent-shaped pattern known as the Fertile Crescent. This fertile strip of land begins on the east at the Persian Gulf and runs northwestward, taking in the valleys of the Tigris and Euphrates rivers. North of this region high mountains form a barrier between the rivers and what we know today as southern Russia. Mesopotamia, the name given to this region, means literally "in

Figure 2–1. The Fertile Crescent from Gemini XI.

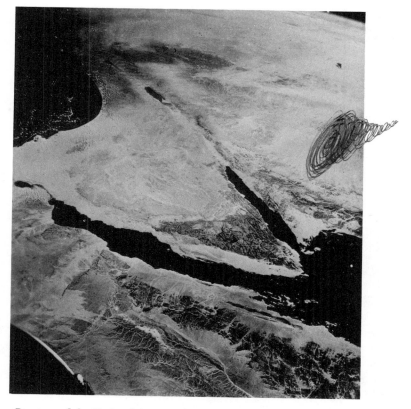

Courtesy of the National Aeronautics and Space Administration.

the midst of, or between rivers." These mountains continue in the northwest, separating Mesopotamia from Asia Minor and the Mediterranean Sea.

The center of the Fertile Crescent was Syria-Palestine, a narrow band of fertile land caught in a vise between the Arabian Desert and the Mediterranean Sea. All the major roads from Africa to Asia passed through this narrow strip of land, thus making it a prize to be seized by the great world powers of the time.

The southern end of the crescent was Egypt, the land of the Nile. Isolated from other major civilizations by deserts and distance, it developed one of the earliest and most powerful civilizations.

Figure 2–2. The Fertile Crescent.

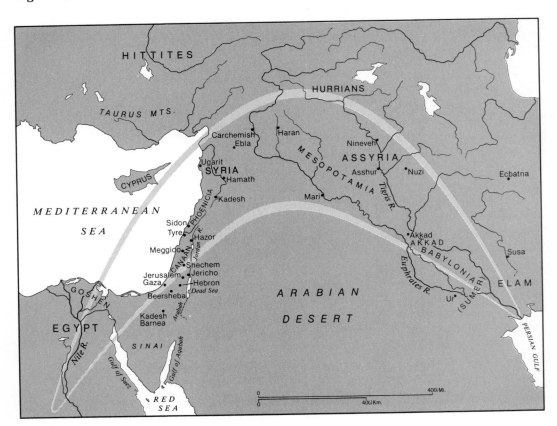

Mesopotamia

3000–2000 B.C.

The Sumerians. These people, named for their chief city, Sumer, occupied a number of city-states that dominated the lower Mesopotamian region from 3150 to 2350 B.C. and again from 2060 to 1950 B.C. In this later period, Ur, one of the truly great cities of the ancient world, was dominant. The Sumerians were finally conquered by people known as the Elamites.

The Akkadians. The first empire builder was Sargon of Akkad, who interrupted the Sumerian dominance of Mesopotamia from 2350 to 2060 B.C. The Akkadians were Semites, the race from which the later Israelites came. These people moved northwest into Mesopotamia from the Arabian Peninsula. The Akkadians had a strong influence on the area. Their literature was adapted and passed on by the Babylonians. Through archaeology it has come to us, and it furnishes a wealth of knowledge about the religious and cultural life of the Mesopotamian region.

2000–1500 B.C.

The Amorites (Arameans).   These people, known as "Westerners," were originally seminomadic tribesmen from Arabia. In the 200 years after 2000 B.C., they appeared all over the Fertile Crescent, causing great disruptions. Some areas, particularly the area east of the Jordan River, were deserted for several hundred years after their raids. In other areas, they settled down, building new towns in northern and western Palestine and establishing two strong states in Mesopotamia around 1800 B.C.— Mari, located in the northwest, and Babylonia, in south-central Mesopotamia. Babylonia's most famous king was Hammurabi, best known for his famous law codes. From Mari we have the Mari tablets, which clarify many patriarchal customs.

Like the Akkadians, the Amorites were Semitic people. Their invasion of the Fertile Crescent was during the same general time of the Hebrew patriarchs Abraham, Isaac, and Jacob. What has been learned about them through archaeology fits in remarkably with the descriptions of the lifestyle of the patriarchs.

The Hurrians.   The Amorite states also passed away, being succeeded by the Hurrians, or Horites as the Old Testament calls them. They absorbed the Amorite population into a state called Mitanni, and they also absorbed much of the Amorite culture. Fortunately, many of their writings were preserved on clay tablets at Nuzi, one of their major cities. The discovery of these tablets has helped clear up many obscure passages in the Old Testament.

1500–1000 B.C.

Arameans and Habiru.   Again, as it had happened 500 years before, the Fertile Crescent was overrun by seminomads from Arabia. Among them were people referred to as *Apiru* or *Habiru*. Many pages have been written to try to answer the question, "Who were the Habiru?" They appeared in many roles—as outlaws; as hired soldiers, or mercenaries; as slaves; as seminomadic wanderers. The similarity of their name to the word Hebrew makes it tempting to say they were the Hebrews. However, references to them come from places all over the Fertile Crescent, so they cannot be one and the same. *Habiru* refers to a much broader range of people. On the other hand, the Hebrews seem to have belonged to the same class of people. In other words, not all *Habiru* were Hebrews, but the Hebrews seem to have been *Habiru*.

Asia Minor

The Hittites.   While it actually lay outside the bounds of the Fertile Crescent, Asia Minor was to play a very influential role in biblical history, especially in the Christian era. For many years, however, it was thought that it had little or no role in Old Testament history. Now we know that central Asia Minor was the center of the Hittite Empire. The Hittites were known in the Old Testament as the "Sons of Heth." Their capital was Hattusa. They pushed down from Asia into what is now Lebanon and Syria around 1400 B.C., having won the area from the Mitanni. Their greatest threat was to the power of Egypt, who controlled Palestine during that time.

Egypt

3000–2000 B.C.

The part of Egypt comprising the fertile area—a narrow strip of land along the Nile River—looks like a crooked tree with a fan-shaped top representing the Nile delta. There the river breaks up into many branches before entering the Mediterranean Sea. This delta region was a tempting target for hungry nomads throughout biblical history, for its well-watered lands produced food and pasture in abundance when other areas were devastated by drought.

At the same time, Egypt's separation from the rest of the Fertile Crescent by the land bridge of Palestine and the Sinai Desert enabled its civilization to develop with a minimum of interruption from outside forces. This early period, before 2000 B.C., was the time of the building of the great pyramids.

Figure 2–3. The Great Pyramid of Gizeh, symbol of Egypt's magnificent past.

Photograph by Roy A. Helton, Sr.

2000–1000 B.C.

Genesis 12:10-20 contains the story of Abram (Abraham) taking his family to Egypt. This kind of emigration was a common practice of that time. It also came at the time when the Fertile Crescent was experiencing the invasions by the Amorites, the Semitic tribesmen from Arabia.

From 1720 to 1570 B.C., Egypt was ruled by the Hyksos, or "foreign-ers." Hyksos were the people who developed the use of chariots and cavalry units for warfare. They also built cities that had a distinctive kind of protective wall. These walls had a steep slope, or *glacis*, extending out from the base of the wall, which made it difficult for aggressors to attack the wall. Their kingdom included both Egypt and Palestine.

The Hyksos were overthrown by the eighteenth Egyptian dynasty, founded by Ahmose I. In the centuries which followed, the Egyptians dominated Palestine. Their rule there was opposed by the Hurrian (Horite) kingdom of Mitanni, or *Naharin*. Later, the Hittites took control of the Hurrian empire, but Egypt was still able to control Palestine proper until late in the 1200s B.C. Egypt's last great rulers were Seti I (1308–1290 B.C.) and Ramses II (1290–1224 B.C.). These were probably the pharaohs whose policies led the Hebrew exodus from Egypt.

Syria-Phoenicia

3000–2000 B.C.

Syria, bounded on the west by the Mediterranean Sea and on the east by the Arabian Desert, is the northern portion of the land bridge connecting Mesopotamia, Asia Minor, and Egypt. Its southern boundaries during the period of the Israelite kingdoms varied from period to period but generally were marked by Mt. Hermon, whose melting snows furnish water for the major sources of the Jordan River.

As part of the corridor connecting the continents, Syria's population varied with each new outbreak of migration and conquest. Until recently, no major civilization was known to have existed in Syria before 2000 B.C. Now, however, there have been discovered at Tell-Mardikh-Ebla in northern Syria more than 16,000 clay tablets of a previously unknown empire that existed from 2400 to 2250 B.C. It was a major rival of the kingdom of Sargon of Akkad, which was the first great Near Eastern empire. Ebla, the capital city, was finally destroyed by fire by the Akkadian ruler Naram-Sin. These tablets are of vital interest to biblical scholars because the language is closer to biblical Hebrew than any previously discovered prebiblical language. It will be some years before the total impact of these discoveries can be assessed.[1]

2000–1000 B.C.

The southwestern coastal area of Syria, known in biblical times as Phoenicia and Lebanon, was one of the major strongholds of the Canaanite populations so frequently mentioned in the Old Testament. Possessing the finest natural harbors in the eastern end of the Mediterranean Sea, coupled with an abundance of fine timber and a lack of agricultural land, its economy was based on the sea. The Phoenicians developed a merchant fleet that became, in effect, the navy and merchant fleet of the Israelite kings David, Solomon, Omri, and Ahab, who had trade agreements with the local kings, especially the kings of Tyre. In addition, Israelite building programs used Phoenician architects, craftsmen, and vast quantities of the famous "cedars of Lebanon."

Farther north lay the city of Ugarit, center of Canaanite culture and learning around 1400 B.C. Here were discovered the Ras Shamra texts,

---

[1] G. Pettinato, "The Royal Archives of Tell-Mardikh-Ebla," *Biblical Archaeologist*, 39, 2 (May, 1976), 44.

which, like the discoveries at Ebla and the Dead Sea Scrolls, opened up whole new areas of understanding in Old Testament studies.

The most famous of all Syrian cities was and is Damascus, which was already an old city in the time of the patriarchs. Through it passed the traders, wanderers, and armies of the ancient world on their way to everywhere.

Palestine

ITS IMPORTANCE

Possibly no geographical area in the Western world holds a greater fascination for more people than does Palestine. For three major religions it is the "Holy Land." Its strategic location made it the object of a continual tug-of-war between the ancient empires. Each one coveted its territory, not because it possessed vast lands or rich resources, but simply because one going anywhere north or south in the ancient East had to cross Palestine to get there. On the west the barrier was the Mediterranean Sea. Although some small ships sailed its waters, it was not a major means of travel for many centuries. To the east lay the vast reaches of the Arabian Desert, virtually impassable to the donkey-riding traders of early times. The famous ship of the desert, the camel, did not come into common use until after 1000 B.C. Thus, if one traveled through from Egypt northward or from Mesopotamia or Asia Minor southward one had to pass through Palestine.

GEOGRAPHICAL FEATURES

As one moves eastward from the Mediterranean coastal area, four major divisions of the land are evident. First is the coastal plain itself. The plain, broader in the southern region, becomes more narrow, generally speaking, as one goes northward. In the south it is known as the Plain of Philistia after its most famous conquerors, the Philistines, a sea-faring people who took control of it in the twelfth century B.C. after being repulsed by the Egyptians. Here they had five major cities—Gaza, Ashdod, Ashkelon, Ekron, and Gath. Not until David's time was the area under Israelite control.

The northern border of the Philistine territory was the Yarkon River, one of the few free-flowing streams in Palestine. From the Yarkon north

Figure 2–4. The major divisions of Palestine.

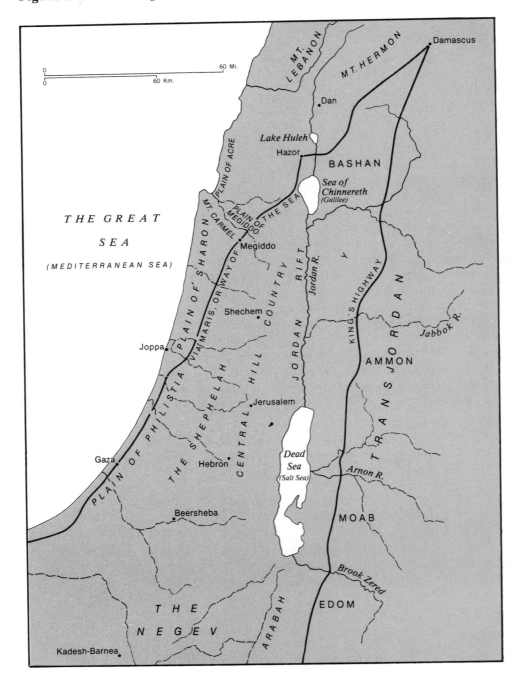

Figure 2–5. Coral reefs such as these and a lack of deep water effectively prevented the Israelites from developing seaports.

Courtesy of George L. Kelm.

to Mt. Carmel was the Plain of Sharon, covered in biblical times by forests. It, too, came under Israelite control rather late.

Mount Carmel, a major landmark jutting out into the Mediterranean, divides the Plain of Sharon from the Plain of Acco, or Acre, a much smaller plain extending northward to the "Ladder of Tyre," where once again the mountains meet the sea. This latter feature marked the boundary at times between Israel and its northern neighbors. While the Plain of Acco was controlled by David, Solomon had to give up much of it to pay his building debts to Hiram, King of Tyre.

The second major division as one moves eastward is the central hill country. In the north, the hills of upper Galilee vary in heights from 2000 to 3000 feet, whereas lower Galilee farther south has hills of 2000 feet or less. Separating the Galilee hills and the Carmel range is the flat triangular plain known as the Plain of Megiddo. On this plain stood the powerful city of Megiddo, one of the great cities of the ancient Near East.

As one moves southward, the mountains become progressively higher, pierced occasionally by valleys, running west to east. This region was known as the hill country of Ephraim in much of biblical history. Further south it becomes the hill country of Judah before beginning to decrease

Figure 2–6. A view of the rough terrain of the central hill country of Palestine.

Photograph by John H. Tullock.

in altitude. In the south is the Negev, an area of rather flat land, primarily suited to the raising of sheep and to agriculture on a limited scale. Beyond the Negev lies the Sinai desert.

The third division, the Jordan Rift, is a deep scar in the earth which stretches from the base of Mount Hermon in the north all the way through Palestine and eventually even into East Africa. In Palestine it is the channel for the Jordan River; the Sea of Galilee, its only large body of fresh water; and the Dead Sea, one of the world's most unusual lakes.

The Jordan, appropriately named the "down-rusher," is formed from a number of smaller sources, the primary ones being the Dan and Banias rivers, which rise near Mt. Hermon. In earlier times it flowed into a rather swampy area called Lake Huleh, before dropping rather rapidly into the Sea of Galilee. Lake Huleh has been drained in recent years to make farm land. By the time the Jordan reaches the Sea of Galilee it is already more than 600 feet below the level of the Mediterranean. Leaving the Sea of Galilee, it continues its winding, twisting descent through the great rift valley until it comes to the Dead Sea, whose surface lies more than 1290 feet below sea level. The Dead Sea is a taker, giving up nothing without a struggle. As a result it has such a high concentration of natural pollution that very little life can exist in its waters.

South of the Dead Sea the rift valley is known as the Arabah. Rising gradually from the Dead Sea, it eventually begins to slope downward again until it reaches the Gulf of Aqabah, an arm of the Red Sea.

The fourth division of the land is the Transjordan Plateau. To the north opposite the Huleh Valley and the Sea of Galilee was the region known in biblical times as Bashan. The ownership of Bashan, known for its fine cattle, was under constant dispute between the Israelite kingdoms and Syria. It has been in the newspaper headlines in recent years under its modern name, the Golan Heights.

Across the Jordan from the hill country of Ephraim lay the territory of Gilead. Through it ran another major tributary of the Jordan, the Jabbok River. It was at one of the fords of the Jabbok that Jacob had his famous wrestling match (Genesis 32:22-32).

The hilly country in Gilead descends to form a broad plateau area.

Figure 2–7. The Negev, lying between the sown land and the desert, was the home of pastoral groups such as the Amalekites.

Photograph by John H. Tullock.

Figure 2–8. An aerial view of the Jordan River as it follows a serpentine path toward the Dead Sea.

Courtesy of George L. Kelm.

Traditionally called Moab, it bordered the Dead Sea and was ideal sheep country. Its broad, flat plains are broken only by an occasional stream, the chief one being the Arnon River.

The Brook Zered, which enters the Arabah at the southern end of the Dead Sea, was the traditional boundary between Moab and Edom. The Edomite territory was more rugged and less suited to pastoral or agricultural development than the other parts of Transjordan. This area often went for long periods with no major settlements. Those who did settle there were famous as traders and merchants.

MAJOR ROADS

The chief value of Palestine to the ancient world powers lay in two roads which crossed its territory. Of first importance was the road called "the way of the Philistines," "the Way of the Sea"; in Roman times, the *Via Maris*. As its name suggests, it followed the seacoast as it ran northeastward from Egypt, passing through the important Philistine cities of Gaza and

Ashdod. As it neared the northern boundaries of Philistine territory, it had to swing eastward toward the foothills to avoid the swamps caused by the blockage of the Yarkon River by shifting sands. Proceeding northward, it passed through the Carmel range near Megiddo and across the plain, skirting the Sea of Galilee and crossing the Jordan near Hazor, the largest city in ancient Palestine. From there it continued northeastward through Damascus and on to Mesopotamia.

The desire to control this road was motivated by two things—power and money. It was the major invasion route followed by armies from Mesopotamia, Egypt, and Asia Minor. A nation controlling the road beyond its borders could expect greater safety for its empire. Furthermore, the caravans which traveled over it were made to pay for that privilege, thus providing a rich source of revenue for the country which controlled it.

To a lesser degree the same thing was true of the major north-south route east of the Jordan River—the King's Highway. Beginning with a

Figure 2–9. "We will not pass through field or vineyard . . . we will go along the King's Highway" (Num. 20:17). The King's Highway approaches Madaba (Biblical Medeba) on the ancient border between Moab and Ammon. Today a modern road follows the ancient caravan route.

Photograph by Ken Touchton.

major trans-Sinai route from Egypt to Edom, the King's Highway proceeded northward until it, too, came to Damascus. It was this route which Israel followed in part as it came out of the desert to invade Palestine.

While not of international importance like the Via Maris and the King's Highway, a number of secondary roads were of importance for travel within the land. Perhaps the most significant of these was the route which ran through the hill country, connecting such strategic points as Shechem, Bethel, Jerusalem, Hebron, and Beersheba. A major cross-country route ran from the Plain of Acre through Megiddo and on to the Jordan River via the Valley of Jezreel. In the South, routes into the central hill country followed the valleys of Aijalon and Elah.

STUDY QUESTIONS

1. Why is this area known as the Fertile Crescent?
2. Identify the major powers who controlled Mesopotamia from 3000 to 1000 B.C., and note at least one distinctive accomplishment of each.
3. What relationship do the terms Amorite, Aramean, and Habiru have to each other?
4. How was Egypt unique among the major areas of the Fertile Crescent?
5. What two major archaeological discoveries have been made in Syria, and how do they relate to biblical studies?
6. Why was Palestine such an important part of the Fertile Crescent?
7. Palestine has a wide variety of climates within a small area. How would its geography contribute to this characteristic?
8. Why were the roads in Palestine important?

FOR FURTHER STUDY

Bible Atlases

AHARONI, YOHANAN, and MICHAEL AVI-YONAH. *The Macmillan Bible Atlas.* New York: The Macmillan Company, 1968. An atlas that emphasizes the military aspects of Old Testament history using clear maps and appropriate archaeological illustrations.

MAY, HERBERT G., ed. *Oxford Bible Atlas.* New York: Oxford University Press, 1974. A good Bible atlas that is available in an inexpensive paperback edition.

WRIGHT, G. ERNEST, and FLOYD V. FILSON, eds. *The Westminster Historical*

Atlas to the Bible, rev. ed. Philadelphia: Westminster, 1956. This has long been a standard work in this field.

Geography

AHARONI, YOHANAN. *The Land of the Bible.* Trans. by Anson F. Rainey. Philadelphia: Westminster, 1967. A detailed historical geography.
BALY, DENNIS. *The Geography of the Bible.* New York: Harper & Row, 1974. A thorough study of all aspects of the geography of Palestine.

CHAPTER THREE

Israel Looks at the Beginnings

The Beginnings

THE PRIMEVAL HISTORY

The primeval history, as Genesis 1–11 is often called, is a different kind of history. It is different, first of all, because it is based on oral traditions passed along over a long period of time. It is different also because of the way it speaks of God's direct relationship to man, unlike the style of a modern historian. After all, there was no television newsman with his cameraman filming the events of creation for the 6 o'clock news.

The nature of this material then is theological—that is, it speaks of God's activity in creation. It is the product of Israel's thoughts about how the world came into being, expressed in the oral traditions that were a part of Israel's heritage.

But Israel's neighbors also had creation stories. One of the most famous goes back to the Akkadians, who dominated Mesopotamia from 2350 to 2060 B.C. Because it comes to us through the Babylonians, it is called the Babylonian creation epic, or *Enuma elish,* after the opening words in the text.

ENUMA ELISH

This myth describes how the gods were the offspring of Tiamat and Apsu in chaos. Later, there is warfare among the gods and goddesses, caused by the fact that Apsu (the lover of Tiamat, the mother goddess) had been killed. Tiamat vowed to get revenge on Ea, who had killed Apsu. He trembled in fear at the possibility. He pleaded with Anshar, his father, for advice. It was decided that Marduk, the strong man of the gods, would meet Tiamat in battle. He, however, demanded first ranking among the gods as the price for fighting Tiamat. Anshar, mortally afraid of Tiamat, agreed.

Taking along the four winds to help him, Marduk went out to meet Tiamat. She came out at him with her mouth open, intending to devour him. That was her fatal mistake. Marduk turned loose the four winds, who entered her mouth, blowing her up like a balloon. Then, Marduk took his sword and sliced her into halves like a grapefruit. The upper half of her body he used for the dome of the heavens, and the lower half he used to create the earth. He then killed her latest lover, Kingu, and made man out of his blood.[1]

THE ISRAELITE UNDERSTANDING OF CREATION

The Old Testament is filled with references to creation. Such is the case of Psalm 104:2-8, where God is described as one

> who coverest thyself with light as with a garment,
> who hast stretched out the heavens like a tent,
> who hast laid the beams of thy chambers on the waters,
> who makest the clouds thy chariot,
> who ridest on the wings of the wind,
> who makest the winds thy messengers,
>   fire and flame are thy ministers.
> Thou didst set the earth on its foundations,
>   so that it should never be shaken.
> Thou didst cover it with the deep as a garment;
>   the waters stood above the mountains.
> At thy rebuke they fled;
> at the sound of thy thunder they took to flight.
> The mountains rose, the valleys sank down
>   to the place which thou didst appoint for them.
> Thou didst set a bound which they could not pass,
> So that they might not again cover the earth.

The concepts used by the psalmist reflect images present in his world.

The influence of Israel's world can best be seen, however, in the Genesis creation stories. Both Genesis 1:1–2:4a and the *Enuma elish* speak of the watery chaos, covered by darkness, which precedes the work of

---

[1]For all the gory details, see James B. Pritchard, ed. *The Ancient Near East: An Anthology of Texts and Pictures* (Princeton: Princeton University Press, 1958), pp. 30-39.

creation; they follow something of the same order of creation—firmament, land, sun and moon, man—and in each, the creator rests after his work is finished. But as often is true, agreement in detail many times is not nearly so significant as the differences. After all, all humans are similar. Their differences make them unique.

GENESIS 1:1–2:4a

This account of creation, the product of centuries of theological reflection, was put into its final form by the priestly theologians of Israel. Well aware of other creation stories, they expressed their conviction that the God of Israel was the only God and creator of the visible universe.[2] In the myths, the gods arose out of the creative process. This was not so for Israel. God did not arise from creation—He was Creator! There is no speculation about God's beginning; Israel assumed that God was and had always been.

"In the beginning, God created the heavens and the earth" (1:1) is a summary statement of all that is to follow. God (called *Elohim*) is transcendent (separated from the material universe) and powerful (he speaks and things come into being). There is no struggle to bring order out of chaos, but God in his majesty calls things into existence. Like the notes of a symphony, certain phrases appear and reappear: "and God said" . . ."God called (named)" . . ."God saw that it was good" . . ."God made" . . ."And there was evening, and there was morning."

There seems to be a conscious effort to counter the Near Eastern creation myths. In contrast to the struggle waged between Marduk and Tiamat, God is in complete control of creation. The heavenly bodies, the sun, the moon, and the stars (1:14-19), worshiped as gods by Israel's neighbors, are created (1:14). They get their light from God, not from their own powers. The earth, furthermore, looked upon as the mother goddess by many ancient people, has no power to give life except as God commands (1:21). Finally, man, the crown of creation, is made in God's image and is commissioned by God to be the caretaker of creation (1:26-27).

The statement, "Let *us* make man in our image and after *our* likeness" (1:26) is one which has drawn much attention for two reasons: (1) because of the personal pronouns "us" and "our" and (2) because of the meaning of the "image of God."

Three possible explanations of the use of the plural pronouns are advanced. (1) Since the word for God (*Elohim*) is a plural form expressing God's majesty, the use of the plural pronoun is to be expected. The

---

[2]Compare the view of God found here to that found in Isaiah 40:12-31.

problem with this explanation is that *Elohim* is used at other places with the singular pronoun. (2) It is simply the equivalent of "Let's do it" as if to say, "I will do it" (Isa. 6:8). (3) God is pictured as a king, addressing a heavenly court of council, expressing what he wants done to those who serve him.[3]

The meaning of the expression "the image of God" has caused much ink to be used. That the ancient Hebrews thought of God as having certain physical traits cannot be denied since numerous references are made to such in the Old Testament. The temptation is to see "image" and "likeness" in these terms, but it surely goes more deeply than a physical image. One aspect of the image seems to lie in the fact that man, like God who is the ruler over all creation, is given power to rule over the earth. The privilege of naming the animals signifies power over them. Another aspect of the image of God must lie in man's intelligence and power of creativity which he shares with God.

GENESIS 2:4b–2:24

In reading this version of Israel's creation stories, the first thing to notice is that God is now referred to as the "LORD God" (2:4) (Hebrew: *Yahweh Elohim*). Some would call this the Yahwistic version of creation since it uses Israel's personal name for God, *Yahweh*. Its simplicity and directness indicate that it is much older than the more highly developed account in 1:1–2:4*a*. The main interest is the creation of man, which is placed first. The creation of the world is already assumed to have taken place.

The patterned kind of story found in 1:1–2:4*a* is missing in this account. Furthermore, God's creative acts are described in human terms. To say that "the Lord God *formed* man of dust" . . . "*breathed* into his nostrils the breath of life" . . . "*planted* a garden" . . . "*took* the man and *put* him in the garden" is to speak in what is called "anthropomorphic language;" that is, "to describe God in human terms." God is pictured as acting in human ways as he made man, talked with him, and, like a concerned father, disciplined him when he did wrong (Gen. 3).

Just as the exalted view of God in Genesis 1:1–2:4*a* (which theologians call transcendence) is needed so that he will be held in reverence and respect by the worshiper, so a more personal view of God (which theologians speak of as his immanence) is needed to emphasize his nearness and concern for the worshiper. If the exalted view of God is

---

[3]See 1 Kings 22:19-23; Zechariah 3:1-2; Job 1-2. For a good discussion of this problem see Bruce Vawter, *On Genesis: A New Reading* (Garden City: Doubleday and Company, Inc., 1977), p. 53ff.

overemphasized, there is the danger that he will become looked upon as the God who is so far removed from man that he has no real interest in man. On the other hand, a "humanized" God can lead to overfamiliarity—with the result that he becomes a "big Daddy" or "the man upstairs." A balance between the two extremes more nearly represents the biblical view.

Man, created by God from the dust of the earth and given life by the breath of God, is not created for idleness. Instead, he is placed in a garden that the LORD God has "planted" and is given the responsibility for its cultivation (2:15). As tenant he has privileges, but he also has responsibilities. Man, from the first, has his "do's" and "do not's," and the major "do not" is "Do not eat of the tree of the knowledge of good and evil" (2:17). He is given power over the animals, symbolized by the privilege of naming them (2:19-20); but power does not satisfy the basic human need for companionship. So woman is created, and man is complete (2:23). Made for each other, they have nothing to hide (2:25).

THE FALL (GEN. 3:1-24)

Man's glory is also his undoing. Created in God's image, he soon wants to take God's place. The serpent's appeal to the woman is that if she eats of the forbidden fruit, she will "be like God, knowing good and evil" (3:5). The ancient storyteller had a marvelous understanding of human nature. His description of the forbidden fruit's appeal to Eve's appetite ("good for food"), to her sense of beauty ("a delight to the eyes"), and to her sense of pride ("the desire to make one wise," 3:6), shows how well he understood the nature of temptation. If he lived today he probably could make a fortune in advertising.

The woman falls for the serpent's line so quickly that she was hooked before she realized what was happening. The man, no less gullible than the woman, falls for the same line. Suddenly, they are ashamed of what they see of each other. And so they try to cover their nakedness with clothing made of leaves (3:7).

Discovery of man's disobedience brings God's displeasure. Since man wants to be like God, he has to take the responsibility for his action. It has already created a barrier between him and his wife. Now, he hides from God, who created him and gave him paradise (3:10). As a further result of his disobedience, he is banished from the garden and separated from God. Work becomes a burden, and life loses much of its joy (3:17-20).

The biblical writer here has given his view of man's basic problem in relation to God. Adam (mankind) wants to be God, but the Creator cannot and will not yield his unlimited authority to his creation. Man has been given as much power as he can handle wisely. To give him more would be disastrous for him, so limits have to be established (3:24).

CAIN AND ABEL (GEN. 4:1-26)

As a large stone dropped in a calm body of water begins a series of ever widening circles that do not stop until they reach the shore, so the first sin is described as creating even more disastrous consequences as its influence passes from generation to generation. Guilt and suspicion between husband and wife pay off in brother killing brother in the next generation. The murder was instigated by jealousy on the part of Cain over Abel's more acceptable sacrifice. Sin so alienated Cain from Abel that personal feelings had greater value than human life. But murder will not stay hidden. The ancients believed that when a body was not properly buried, as would be usual in the case of murder, that the blood of the victim which contained the life would cry to God until justice was done (4:10). So try as he may, Cain could not escape the consequences of his sin (4:13). Even so, God showed mercy by giving Cain a protective mark (4:15).

But Cain's murder of Abel was only a beginning. By the time of Lamech, human life was so worthless that Lamech could brag:

> I have slain a man for wounding me,
> a young man for striking me (4:23).

ADAM'S DESCENDANTS

After indicating the passage of a long period of time by "the book of the generations of Adam" (Gen. 5), the narrator continues his account with the story of the great flood.

FLOOD STORIES AND THE FLOOD (GEN. 5:32–9:19)

Flood stories are a part of the traditions of many peoples. The biblical flood story (which properly begins with the introduction of Noah and his sons in 5:32), shares common features with two accounts of a great flood from Mesopotamia—the Gilgamesh Epic and the Atrahasis Epic.

The Gilgamesh Epic. Gilgamesh, the hero, seeks the secret of eternal life. He goes to Utnapishtim, who tells him how the gods tried to destroy mankind with the great flood. Ea, one of the gods, had warned Utnapishtim, who escaped by building an ark. The flood was so great that even the gods themselves thought they were going to be destroyed.

When the waters receded a bit, the ark landed on Mount Nisir.

Utnapishtim sent out a dove and a raven to see if the waters had receded sufficiently for him to leave the ark. When the flood was over, he made a sacrifice:

> The gods smelled the sweet savor,
> The gods crowded like flies about the sacrificer.[4]

The Atrahasis Epic.   This epic, first published in English in 1969, also comes from the Babylonians. Like the biblical account, it starts with a creation story. The people are so numerous and noisy that the gods decide to destroy them. A number of solutions are tried—plague, drought, famine—but none are satisfactory. Finally, a flood is called for, after which a new kind of world will appear, in which various means will be used to prevent overpopulation.[5]

The flood (Gen. 5:32–8:22).   The story of the marriage of the "sons of God" and the "daughters of men" (6:1-4) serves as the background for the biblical account of the flood because it illustrates the conclusion reached in 6:5:

> The LORD saw that the wickedness of man was great in the earth, and that every imagination of the thoughts of his heart was on evil continually.

The reference to the "sons of God" reflects an ancient belief that marriage between divine men and human women produced a race of giants (6:4). For the priestly theologians it was used to illustrate the depths of human sinfulness which resulted from the Fall, so much so that it involved members of the heavenly court.

That Israel also had at least two different flood traditions can be seen when one separates the passages using LORD from those using God.[6] Each series of passages tells a story of the flood. The two have been blended without regard to duplications.[7] Numerous attempts have been made to confirm the flood story by archaeology. None of these attempts has been conclusive, including well-publicized attempts to find the ark.[8] The importance of the flood story does not depend upon the archaeologist,

---

[4]Pritchard, *The Ancient Near East,* p. 70.

[5]Wilford G. Lambert and A. R. Millard, *Atrahasis: The Babylonian Story of the Flood* (New York: Oxford University Press, 1969).

[6]God (Priestly version) 6:1-4, 9-22; 7:11 to 8:5; 13-19. Lord (Yahwist version) 6:5-8; 7:1-10; 8:6-12; 20-22.

[7]See Vawter, *On Genesis,* p. 115, for a list of duplications.

[8]For a sane discussion of wood samples from Mount Ararat, see Lloyd R. Bailey, "Wood from 'Mount Ararat': Noah's Ark?," *The Biblical Archaeologist,* 40, 4 (December, 1977), 137–146.

or anyone else for that matter. The ancient storyteller did not let variations in the traditions he received deter him from his purpose of weaving these materials together to say what he wanted to say about God. For him the story of Noah is a vehicle to tell about (1) God's judgment upon sin, which had so infected his creation; (2) God's concern to preserve what he has begun in creation; and (3) God's reaching out to man in covenant.

Unlike the Atrahasis Epic, in which man had become so numerous and noisy that the gods decided to destroy him, Israel's theologians see destruction resulting from the corruption that arises from man's abuse of the created order. The covenant brings law and structure to society where such as not existed before. The shedding of blood especially is singled out as a taboo.

It seems that for the priestly theologians this polluting of the land by the shedding of human blood may well have been the "wickedness" which led to the desire by God to start anew with man.[9]

The covenant (Gen. 9:1-17).   Noah represented a new beginning. Like Adam, he was told to "be fruitful and multiply and fill the earth" (9:1,7). But earth was no longer a paradise where man and beast lived in harmony—the beasts feared man, who was made master over them. Man, who had shed blood so freely, was now made accountable in a more stringent way for the shedding of blood (9:6).

God made a covenant with Noah and his descendants, an agreement between the two parties, which said that man would never again be destroyed by a flood. The rainbow was given as an everlasting symbol of an everlasting contract between Creator and creatures (9:8-17).

Ancient covenants or treaties were of two kinds: (1) The *suzerainty treaty*, which was a covenant or agreement between a superior party and an inferior party. As one might imagine, the superior party (in this case, God) dictated the terms of the agreement since he had the power to do so. His mercy only obliged him to observe the agreement. This is the type of covenant involved here. (2) The second kind was the *parity treaty*, which was an agreement between equals. In this type of treaty, both parties contributed to the agreement; and both bore equal obligations to see that it was preserved.

The Noah narratives end with a story involving a drunken Noah pronouncing a curse upon one of his sons who saw him naked. Somehow, the curse fell upon his grandson Canaan (9:20-27). Curses such as this were believed to have the power within them to carry out what was threatened. Likewise, blessings given in special times in life were believed to have this power.

[9]See Tikva Frymer-Kensky, "The Atrahasis Epic and Its Significance for our Understanding of Genesis 1–9," *The Biblical Archaeologist*, 40, 4 (December, 1977), 147–155.

Again, the narrator inserted a genealogy (Gen. 10) to introduce a new segment of his story. One purpose is to say something about the geography of the ancient Near East sometime in the period of the second millennium (2000–1000 B.C.). A second purpose is to express the author's conviction that the human race was a unity growing out of its descent from Noah. This serves us, then, as a background for what follows in Genesis 11.

THE TOWER OF BABEL (GEN. 11:1-9)

Humanity was united not only in language (11:1) but also in its determination to rebel against God. This rebellion took the form of building a tower to reach the heavens, where the challenge to God could be made (11:4). The rebellion was nipped in the bud, however. Men lost the ability to communicate with one another when their language, which had bound them together, now became a barrier—a babble which began with Babel. The ancient Israelites probably saw the great *ziggurats*, or pyramidlike towers, in Babylon built originally as a part of the worship of ancient Babylon deities. From them they concluded that this had caused God to confuse man by giving him many languages instead of one.

SUMMARY (GEN. 1–11)

Throughout these chapters, the narrator has been dealing with man on a universal scale. This has been the story of every man and his continuing fascination with sin. It is the story also of God's continuing efforts to deal with sin—both by means of judgment upon it and by his merciful guidance to those sinners who struggle to overcome it.

Again, a genealogy introduces a new phase of the story. The floodlights are darkened, and a lone spotlight focuses on a figure who now comes onto the stage to introduce the drama of a people chosen from the mass of humanity to be the bearers of the message of God to the mass of humanity. But before there was a people, there was a man—Abraham.

The Patriarchs

INTRODUCTION

With the story of Abraham, the Israelite storytellers move from the broad, sweeping view of history to concentrate on men of more vital interest to their own story. Left behind for a time are the genealogies designed to cover long spans of time. Genesis 12–50 is dominated by only four men—Abraham, Isaac, Jacob, and Joseph. The period is known as the period of the patriarchs, literally, the time of the "first fathers."

The time.   Dating the patriarchs is a problem with which scholars have wrestled for many years. The consensus is that the earliest Abraham could be dated would be 2000 B.C., some suggesting a much later date. At present, certain Israeli archaeologists are suggesting that the setting for the Abraham stories is no earlier than the period of the Judges (1200–1100 B.C.).[10] This does not mean, however, that Abraham came that late. In fact, other scholars suggest a date in the middle of the third millennium (around 2500 B.C.).[11] Abraham is usually associated with the movement of Semitic peoples from the Arabian Desert into the Mesopotamian region in the nineteenth to eighteenth centuries B.C.[12]

Joseph, the last of the four major figures in Genesis 12–50, is often associated with the Hyksos rule in Egypt. The Hyksos were foreign invaders of Egypt who conquered the country in the eighteenth century and established a dynasty that lasted from 1720 to 1570 B.C. Like the Hebrews (as the Israelites were first known), the Hyksos were Semitic peoples. They were the inventors of chariot warfare. They built cities noted for their distinctive fortifications, which consisted of a deep ditch or moat and a steep ramp leading up to the city walls, thus making direct attacks on the walls much more difficult. If Joseph did come in this period, then the patriarchs would be dated in the period from about 1900 to 1700 B.C.

Their life-style.   The picture given of Abraham, Isaac, and Jacob is that of people who habitually moved about; yet certain areas seem to have served as home base for them. As such, they were not true nomads like today's desert dwellers. Instead, they lived near the settled areas, moving as was necessary to find pastures for their flocks. Their chief beast of burden was the ass or donkey. Camels were not yet in general use.

In contrast to our limited families of today (which usually consist of parents and children, one or more grandparents sometimes included), the patriarchs were heads of extended families, consisting of wives, children, relatives of varying degrees, and servants—most of whom were undoubtedly slaves. A man's wealth was measured in terms of the number of wives, sons, and cattle he possessed (see Job 1). For all these persons, the

---

[10]For this view see Gaalyah Cornfeld, *Archaeology of the Bible: Book by Book* (New York: Harper & Row), p. 21ff.

[11]David N. Freedman, "The Real Story of the Ebla Tablets, Ebla and the Cities of the Plain," *The Biblical Archaeologist,* 41, 4 (December, 1978) 143–164.

[12]For a contrary view suggesting that Abraham came from Asia Minor, see Cyrus H. Gordon, "Where Is Abraham's Ur?" *The Biblical Archaeology Review,* III, 2 (June, 1977), 20–21, 52.

patriarch was the chief decision maker. He determined whom his sons married and which of his sons was to succeed him as patriarch. While it was customary for this latter honor to fall to the eldest son, it was not always so.

ABRAHAM, THE FIRST OF THE "FIRST" FATHERS

To discover what Abraham was like after some 4,000 years is no easy task. Although numerous stories gathered about him, they lacked many of the ingredients necessary for the writing of history. These narratives, called sagas, have a real person at the core, but what we can actually learn about the details of his life are quite limited. No dates are given, no events that can be confirmed in an independent study are mentioned, and many of the places named were not known by those names in Abraham's day so far as can be determined. No archaeologist has dug up a clay tablet saying "Abraham slept here." Nevertheless, we do have the biblical stories— stories that at least suggest that behind the stories was a great personality claimed by three great world religions—Judaism, Christianity, and Islam. Our purpose is to learn from the stories as they are.

From Ur to Egypt (Gen. 12). The stories of the patriarchs are religious history. Persons, places, and events are secondary to what the LORD is doing through those persons, places, and events. Abraham (called Abram until Gen. 17:5), a native of Ur of the Chaldees in southeastern Mesopotamia, moved to Haran in northwestern Mesopotamia while he was still in the clan of Terah, his father. There, Terah died and Abraham became patriarch (11:31-32).

In Haran, life took a new direction. Abraham was called by the LORD to leave the familiar faces of his kinsmen and the well-watered area of northwestern Mesopotamia to go to a new land the LORD would show him. It was a promise that carried with it universal meaning. Abraham would receive the blessing of a land, numerous descendants, and divine protection; and through him all nations were to be blessed (12:1-3). This promise was repeated with differing emphases a number of times in the Abraham stories (Gen. 12:7; 13:14-17; 15:17-21; 17:1-21).

While the biblical narratives picture Abraham as a man of God, he certainly is not presented as a plaster saint. Driven to Egypt by famine conditions in Palestine, he persuaded his wife to lie about her relationship to him, resulting in her being chosen for the Pharaoh's harem. When the truth was discovered, Abraham and his people were expelled from the land (12:10-20) to face the rigors of the famine.

Conflict and covenant (Gen. 13–16). Abraham settled in the Negev, the southern region of Judah, between the sown land and the desert region of Sinai. Here, possibly as a caravaneer—that is, a trader—he gained great wealth in the form of herds of animals. Conflict between his herdsmen and those of his nephew Lot arose, causing a parting of the ways. Lot chose the well-watered valley of the Jordan, while Abraham chose the hill country. Conflict and crisis brought a reaffirming of the promise from the LORD of numerous descendants and possession of the land (13:14-17).

Another kind of conflict is described in Genesis 14. Abraham appears as no ordinary desert chieftain but as one who was powerful enough to challenge the rulers of the area. Lot, captured in warfare between a group of kings, was carried off to northern Syria. Abraham, with his personal army of 318 men, rescued him. On his return Abraham paid tithes to Melchizedek, the king of Salem (later known as Jerusalem). The name used for God was *El Elyon*, "God Most High." His later descendants could point to Abraham's association with Jerusalem when it became David's capital city.[13]

Social and physical conflict is followed by mental conflict (15:1-21). No child had blessed the marriage of Abraham and Sarah. Their only heir was a foreign slave, Eliezer of Damascus, whom Abraham had adopted as his heir. Such a custom is known from the Nuzi tablets (about 1500 B.C.). Abraham agonized about his lack of a son by Sarah, and the LORD reassured him. Then followed a strange ceremony.

A sacrifice was made, but not on the usual altar. Instead, the larger animals were cut in half, one-half being laid on the ground opposite the other half. As the sun sank in the West, Abraham went to sleep. The vision came as a dream. The LORD spoke of the Egyptian sojourn. A smoking pot and flaming torch passed between the split animals, and the covenant was made. The boundaries of the land, essentially as they stood in the time of David, were described to Abraham.

Domestic conflict arose when, in keeping with custom, Sarah gave Abraham her maid Hagar as a secondary wife or concubine so that Hagar could have a child for her by proxy (16:1-15). Hagar's instant fertility gave her a feeling of superiority over her barren mistress (16:1-4). Hagar had to flee before the wrath of Sarah. Hagar's son, Ishmael, was said to have been the father of the Ishmaelites, who roamed the southern desert areas of Palestine (16:5-15).

The covenant and circumcision (Gen. 17). Here one finds a different view of the covenant. First, another name for God is used. He is *El Shaddai*, "God Almighty" (17:1). Then Abraham, called Abram to this point, is now called Abraham, "the father of a multitude" (17:5). In

[13]The first nonbiblical reference to the cities of the plain, mentioned in Genesis 14, may be found in the Ebla Tablets. See Paul C. Maloney, "Assessing Ebla," *The Biblical Archaeology Review*, IV, 1 (March, 1978), 4–10.

addition, circumcision (the cutting off of the male foreskin), is described as the symbol of the covenant with God. Furthermore, Sarah (formerly Sarai) also underwent a name change; and assurance was once more given that she would be the mother of Abraham's heir and successor as patriarch. All these suggest the emphases one might expect of the priests, causing this to be considered by many to be the priestly version of the covenant story.

The promise of new life and the forebodings of doom (Gen. 18–19).   The promise of a son and heir finally moved toward its fulfillment. The patriarch looked from his tent one day to see three strangers approaching. True to Oriental courtesy, he invited them in and gave them water to wash their dusty, tired feet. He spread before them "a morsel of bread," which in reality was bread, cheese, milk, and meat (18:1-8). In the story of the three strangers, the narrator described a theophany—an appearance of the divine to a human being.

The divine visitors had some good news and some bad news. First, they told Abraham that in the spring Sarah would bear a child. This struck Sarah, who was well past the age of childbearing, as somewhat ridiculous. Her giggles, as she hid behind the tent door, reached the ears of the divine messenger, who heard her and gave her a gentle rebuke (18:9-15).

Then came the bad news. Abraham was also told of the doom of Sodom and Gomorrah, the licentious cities in the Dead Sea area, where Lot lived. Despite Abraham's plea (18:16-33), judgment fell and only Lot and his family escaped (19:1-23).

The description of the destruction of these cities suggests that an earthquake occurred, which resulted in the sinking of the land. The fire and brimstone were burning gases and sulphur, both common in this region (19:24-29). There have been archaeological explorations in the shallow waters of the southern end of the Dead Sea to see if evidence can be found of long-lost cities.

The last picture of Lot is a sad one. Old and drunk, he was debauched by his own daughters (19:30-38).

Isaac and Ishmael (Gen. 21).   After another incident involving Sarah, which sounds much like Abraham's experience with the Pharaoh of Egypt (see Gen. 12:10-20 and 20:1-17), the long-expected child, Isaac, was born. Conflict again arose between Sarah (old enough to be her son's great-grandmother) and Hagar (the slave wife and mother of Ishmael). Jealousy forced Hagar to flee so that Isaac could have preeminence. Here again, the word used to refer to the divine being changes to *Elohim*, "God." Furthermore, in another narrative concerning conflict with a local chieftain Abimelech, the term *El Olam* ("the Everlasting God") is introduced. The shifting of terms may indicate that these are parallel traditions; that is, the same story coming from different tribes or clans. This could especially be true of the Sarah-Hagar conflict stories.

The test (Gen. 22).   The high point of the Abraham drama was played out on a high mountain, traditionally the site where Solomon's temple was to be built. Today the magnificent Muslim shrine, the Dome of the Rock, stands there. Child sacrifice was a common practice in Abraham's time. It was in this background that Abraham came to the conviction that Isaac was to be offered as a sacrifice to God. Following what he was convinced was God's command, he took his beloved son up the mountain to perform the fateful act. Poised to strike the fatal blow, his hand was stopped in midair. A ram, caught in the underbrush, became the victim. This priestly story (note the use of *God*) enshrined Abraham in the history of religion as the man of faith. Equally important, it sets out a distinctive mark of Israelite religion; namely, that human sacrifice never played the important role that it did in other religions.

Sarah's death and burial (Gen. 23).   When Sarah died, a burial place had to be bought. Having chosen the place he desired, Abraham went to the village elders and there engaged in a typical Oriental bargaining session, complete with flowery phrases and exaggerated gestures. Finally, a purchase price was named—after the owner had offered to "give" the land and the cave of Macpelah to Abraham. Today, the traditional site of the burial at Hebron is a sacred site for both Muslim and Jew.

A wife for Isaac (Gen. 24:1–25:18).   Before Abraham died, he had to see that Isaac was supplied with a wife. This custom of the parent's choosing a bride for his son is still practiced in parts of the modern world. Abraham sent his trusted servant back to Haran to find a wife for Isaac. Here we are introduced to the wily Laban, the brother of Rebekah, Isaac's future wife. While the storyteller credits the LORD with pointing out the right girl, Laban was quite willing to give up his sister when he saw the rich gifts Abraham had sent for the bride price (24:53-61).

As in Genesis 1–11, a genealogy is used to summarize and conclude the Abraham story (25:1-18).

ISAAC, THE HYPHEN BETWEEN ABRAHAM AND JACOB

Of the patriarchs, Isaac receives the least attention. He is pictured as an introvert—a shy, quiet, meditative person dominated by the stronger personalities around him. Such a person was Rebekah, his wife. The choosing of Rebekah as Isaac's wife, and her subsequent domination of her husband, receives more attention in the tradition than does Isaac himself (24:15-62; 25:20-24; 26:6-11; 27:5-17).

Even among the stories about Isaac, one of them is suspiciously like traditions about Abraham. He was said to have caused Rebekah to lie about her relationship to him to prevent trouble with a local chieftain, Abimelech (26:6-11; 12:10-20; 20:1-18). As in the past, the covenant was reaffirmed also with Isaac (26:1-5, 23-25). He did not have to wait as long for an heir as had Abraham, however.

JACOB, THE SUPPLANTER

Most of the stories about Jacob are the kinds of stories one prefers to tell about a relative who is long-since dead. If he were alive, one would only whisper about his escapades at family gatherings and hope that the neighbors had not found out about the wayward son's latest caper.

Jacob and Esau (Gen. 25:19-34; 27:1-45). Jacob was the twin of Esau. Esau was born first, but Jacob's later reputation as a schemer was such that the tradition arose that he had hold of Esau's heel when Esau was born, trying to pull him back so Jacob could come out of the womb first (25:19-26).

Esau was an outdoorsman and a man who lived by his emotions. Jacob, on the other hand, was more like his father but with the cunning of his strong-willed mother. Esau, as the elder of the two sons, was first in line to be the patriarch. In addition to the birthright, one had to secure the blessing of the patriarch as he came near death in order to have the right to succeed him (25:27-28).

The blessing was important because the spoken word, in primitive societies, was viewed as having much more power than it has today. The ancients believed that a blessing or a curse carried with it a sort of self-fulfilling power. Neither was given lightly, nor were they taken lightly. The blessing was greatly desired, and the curse was greatly feared.

It was for this reason, then, that Jacob—in trying to get the right to be patriarch himself over the firstborn Esau—had to secure both the birthright and the blessing. He had failed to get out ahead of Esau at birth, but that was not his last attempt to get ahead of him!

Buying the birthright (Gen. 25:29-34). The birthright was his first goal. Esau, slave to his appetites, fell into Jacob's trap like a hungry bird. Coming from an exhausting and probably futile hunt, Esau smelled the red bean soup Jacob was cooking. When he asked Jacob for food, Jacob set a high price—Esau's birthright. Esau, listening more to his hunger pangs than to his head, agreed. And so on a solemn oath, Esau sold Jacob his future for bean soup (25:33).

Stealing the blessing (Gen. 27:1-45). But the birthright was not enough; Jacob still had to have Isaac's blessing. On his side, he had a very powerful ally, his mother, Rebekah. Isaac favored Esau, perhaps because he saw those characteristics of strength and self-confidence he lacked and secretly longed to have. Isaac, as the saying goes, enjoyed poor health. Troubled by an eye disease (as was common in the Near East) and other ailments (either real or imagined), he feared that death might overtake him at any time. He decided, therefore, that the time had come to pass on to his older son the responsibility of being patriarch. Calling Esau in, he gave him instructions to prepare for him a dish of wild game and bring it to him. Then he would bless Esau (27:1-4).

As Esau left to hunt game, Rebekah (who had overheard the conversation), immediately gave Jacob instructions to kill a young goat and bring it to her. Taking the goat, she made stew, dressed Jacob in Esau's clothes, and put the fresh goat skins on Jacob's arms and neck so he would be hairy like Esau (27:5-17).

When Jacob went to Isaac, claiming to be Esau, Isaac was suspicious because the voice did not sound right. If it were Esau, he had returned rather quickly. Calling Jacob to him, he felt of his now-hairy arms and neck, and ate the savory stew. As he kissed Jacob, prior to the blessing, he smelled his clothes. The voice was Jacob's, but the body odor was Esau's! And so the blind Isaac—deceived by his sense of taste, feel, and smell— blessed the deceiver, Jacob, with a blessing he could not take back, even though Esau came in soon and Isaac learned the truth of what had been done (27:18-45).

Jacob on the run (Gen. 27:46–28:22). Rebekah, having overheard Esau's threats to kill Jacob, immediately persuaded Isaac to send Jacob to her brother Laban's home in Haran to escape the wrath of Esau. Taking the road northward through the central hill country, Jacob came to a place in the barren rocky hills north of present-day Jerusalem. Using one of the numerous limestone rocks for a pillow, he tried to get some sleep. In a dream the LORD appeared to him, saying:

> I am the LORD, the God of Abraham your father and the God of Isaac; the land on which you lie I will give to you and your descendants; and your descendants shall be like the dust of the earth . . . and by you and your descendants shall the families of the earth be blessed (28:13-15).

Jacob was awed by the experience. But even though he set up a memorial stone, he only committed himself to serve the LORD as his God if he returned to his father's house safely (28:18-22).

Jacob and Laban: an amateur versus a professional (Gen. 29:1-30).

On coming to the territory of Laban, Jacob met his cousin Rachel at a watering place for sheep. One look was all it took! He fell hopelessly in love with Rachel. Laban, shrewd man of the world, sized up the situation. Before Jacob knew it, Laban had him committed to work seven years for the privilege of marrying Rachel. The seven years passed swiftly; but when Jacob went forward to claim his prize, he received a shocking surprise. Custom decreed that the veiled bride be brought to the groom's tent under the cover of darkness. So it was that Jacob only saw his new bride after the honeymoon night. His bride was not Rachel—it was her unattractive older sister Leah.

Jacob, with murder in his eyes, was pacified by his new father-in-law with the promise that when the seven-day celebration for his marriage to Leah was over, he could marry Rachel. Of course, after the second wedding was over, he had to work an additional seven years to pay for her (29:27-30).

Jacob and Laban: the tables are turned (Gen. 30:1–31:55).

The years passed; and Jacob, the father of many children, had learned well his lessons from Laban. Getting Laban to agree to let him have any animal that was not white, Jacob used a mixture of folk medicine (30:37-39) and shrewd observation to cause more of the animals to be born spotted, speckled, or black. While Laban was away, Jacob gathered up his family and flocks and left the territory. Laban followed in angry pursuit when he found what had happened. Before he caught up with Jacob, God appeared to Laban in a dream and told him not to harm Jacob (30:40–31:24).

As a result, when he caught up with Jacob he could only bluster and accuse Jacob of stealing his household idols (31:30). Possession of the symbols gave the possessor claim to the family property.

For once Jacob was innocent. Rachel was the culprit. The idols were hidden in a camel saddle. As Laban came, with Jacob's permission, to search the tent, Rachel was sitting on the saddle. She excused herself from arising for, as she said, "The way of women is upon me" (31:35). In this way, the narrator ridicules the value of such idols. In this narrative, there are two new ways of referring to God. In 31:42, he is called the "*God of my father,* the God of Abraham, and the *Fear of Isaac.*"

In parting, a memorial stone was set up and a solemn oath calling on the "God of Abraham and the God of Nahor, the God of their father, [to] judge between us" (31:52-54) was taken. This ceremony, a kind of covenant, was sealed by the oath-taking and the sharing of a meal. It basically was a plea for the gods, as guarantors of the covenant, to keep an eye on both of them so they would not cheat each other again! (31:25-55).

Jacob and Esau: a man faces his past (Gen. 32:1–33:20).   The biblical narrator did not gloss over the weakness of his ancestors. It was not so with Abraham, nor was it so with Jacob, whose sons gave their names to the twelve tribes of Israel. The narrator believed in divine retribution; that is, that evil would be punished. Abraham's lies to the Egyptians concerning Sarah had resulted in expulsion from Egypt to face the risk of starvation in the famine conditions of Palestine. Likewise, Jacob's past came back to haunt him.

Traveling down the King's Highway, the major north-south route east of the Jordan, Jacob realized he would soon enter the territory of Esau. First, he sent messengers to Esau to tell him he was coming (32:2-5). When he received word that Esau, with an army of 400, was coming to meet him, he divided his forces and flocks, hoping an attack on the forward group would give the second group a chance to escape (32:6-8). The prayer of a man facing death and destruction was quite different from the prayer of the brash young man who had stolen his brother's blessing (28:20-22).

Another part of Jacob's strategy was to send an impressive gift to Esau. But even this was not enough to still his fears. We are told of a strange experience in the night where Jacob wrestled with a man (32:13-24). This, in part, suggests a theophany (the appearance of the divine); but it also suggests that Jacob's inner struggle was reaching a climax. From the experience Jacob derives a new name (Israel) symbolic of a changed man. To remember the experience, he received an injury that caused him to limp (32:25-32).

Jacob was the picture of abject humility when he met Esau. Surprisingly, Esau (now a prosperous desert chieftain) was generous to his brother who had cheated him. They parted, Esau going south to Seir, and Jacob going westward into the hill country near the ancient city of Shechem (33:1-20).

Trouble at Shechem (Gen. 34).   In a rare story about a woman, the narrator tells of the rape of Dinah (Jacob and Leah's daughter) and the subsequent vengeance taken by Simeon and Levi, two of Jacob's sons. This story is of interest for two reasons: (1) Levi is mentioned as a secular tribe, indicating that this story is quite old. (2) It is believed that this story is included here to indicate why Shechem did not have to be conquered by

Figure 3–1. "The same night he arose . . . and crossed the ford of the Jabbok" (Gen. 32:22). This site on the Jabbok River is the traditional site of Jacob's nighttime struggles prior to meeting his brother Esau.

Photograph by Ken Touchton.

the Israelites when they came out of Egypt. This would be because some of the Jacob tribes remained near Shechem and did not go to Egypt.

Back to Bethel and two genealogies (Gen. 35–36). The major stories in which Jacob plays a leading role end with a story of his return to Bethel, where he had experienced God's presence some twenty years or more before. His wives were instructed to put away foreign gods in preparation for worship (35:2), just as Joshua was to do to the tribes of Israel many years later (Josh. 24). Next, another story of Jacob's name change to Israel is associated with worship at Bethel (35:9-15). Finally, there is the account of Rachel's death. The cycle of stories, as is true throughout Genesis, is brought to a close by extended genealogies of Jacob (35:16-29 with the note that Isaac finally died!) and Esau (Gen. 36). Jacob's story is interrupted by the story of Joseph and the beginning of the Egyptian bondage.

JOSEPH, FROM PATRIARCH'S SON
TO PRIME MINISTER

The story of Joseph takes the form of a novella, or miniature novel. It is as if the storyteller has taken the Joseph traditions and sketched out a novel he is going to write. He introduces his hero, Joseph; the villains, his brothers. Then Joseph goes through a series of reverses and advances, climaxing with a suspense-filled scene where Joseph, the prime minister of Egypt, reveals his identity to his brothers who thought he was long-since dead.

The stories concerning Joseph differ in many ways from the stories of the patriarchs. First of all, they have about them certain characteristics of wisdom stories in the Near East: (1) The theme of the stories is that goodness is always rewarded and evil is always punished, which is a major theme of the book of Proverbs. (2) The theme of the oppressed, righteous man who overcomes all obstacles and comes out on top, particularly because he possesses the wisdom to interpret dreams, is like that found in the stories concerning Daniel.

A second difference in these stories is in how God communicates with Joseph. Here there are no divine messengers—no theophanies. Instead, God himself guides Joseph through the events and circumstances of life.

A third major difference is in the background reflected by the Joseph stories. It is an Egyptian background. The names of the characters, the bestowing of the signet ring and the gold chain as symbols of office to Joseph, and the emphasis on dreams—these and other matters are known from Egyptian records to be characteristic of that civilization.

Finally, these stories differ in that they are more than a collection of stories. Here, there is more of a unified single story, without the repeating of similar stories as was true in the Abraham-Isaac-Jacob cycles of stories. The only interruption is for the Judah-Tamar story (Gen. 38), which seems to have been inserted there to indicate the passing of time, especially since Joseph ages considerably between Genesis 37 and 39.

A fancy coat and angry brothers (Gen. 37:1-36). Joseph, the eleventh of Jacob's twelve sons, was his father's favorite. He relished the position, lording it over his older brothers by showing off his fancy clothes and telling them of dreams in which he came out superior to them.

Rough shepherds that they were, they decided to take drastic action to squelch their obnoxious younger brother. Some wanted to kill him, but Reuben prevailed upon them to put him into a pit in the dry country, hoping later to rescue him. Instead, he was sold to a caravan, either of Ishmaelites (37:25,27) or Midianites (37:28,36). (Here is one of the few places that the text shows a blending of traditions.) Eventually, he was sold in Egypt to Potiphar, an officer of the Pharaoh.

Judah and Tamar (Gen. 38).   A rather uncomplimentary story about Joseph's brother Judah interrupts the Joseph narrative. Judah failed to observe the customary law regarding the obligation to give his widowed daughter-in-law another of his sons as her husband. The purpose was so that the name of the first husband could be preserved when a male child was born to the second marriage. Since there was no belief in life after death in that time, the only hope one had for a continued existence was through one's sons. Tamar, the widow, tricked her father-in-law into having a child by her. When Judah found out she was pregnant, he accused her of prostitution, only to find that he was the one who was responsible. This story may have been inserted to indicate the passage of time. Its purpose most certainly was not to compliment Judah for admitting his guilt.

Joseph loses another cloak and lands in jail (Gen. 39:1-20).   Years passed, and Joseph was put in charge of Potiphar's business. Mrs. Potiphar tried to seduce the handsome young servant. When he refused her advances, she seized his cloak. He ran off without it to get away. She accused him of rape, and he landed in jail.

Joseph, the prisoner and interpreter of dreams (Gen. 39:21–41:36).   Joseph, ever the man of responsibility, soon became a trusted prison aide (39:22). When the king's butler and baker, imprisoned because they were in disfavor, had strange dreams, Joseph interpreted them correctly. As he predicted, the butler was restored and the baker was hanged. The butler forgot Joseph after promising to reward him (40:1-23).

Then the pharaoh began to have dreams. When all his wise men failed to interpret them, the butler finally remembered Joseph. Joseph was summoned before the pharaoh, where he interpreted the dreams as predicting seven years of prosperity to be followed by seven years of famine. The pharaoh was so impressed by Joseph that he elevated him from chief trusty in his prison to prime minister in the kingdom in charge of preparations for the great famine (41:1-36).

Joseph and his brothers again (Gen. 42–45).   The famine came. Joseph's brothers came to Egypt to buy grain, little realizing that their obnoxious younger brother was now Egypt's chief grain salesman. They did not recognize him (42:8), but Joseph knew them and began a series of tests to find out what sort of characters they now were. First, he accused them of being spies (42:9). Vowing their innocence, they agreed to leave one of their number in prison as a surety until they could return home and bring Benjamin, their younger brother with them, as Joseph had demanded. On the way home, they found all their money was in their grain sacks (42:1-38).

Returning to Egypt, they took Benjamin over Jacob's strong objections. Judah vowed to his father that Benjamin would be kept safe at the cost of his own life (43:9). When Benjamin arrived, Simeon was released; and the brothers ate in Joseph's house with Benjamin receiving special treatment (43:34). When they left, however, Joseph's cup was hidden in Benjamin's sack. Joseph's soldiers pursued them, brought them back, and the cup was discovered. Judah made a stirring plea for his younger brother, citing the drastic effect the failure of Benjamin's return with them would have on their father (44:18-34). Joseph, convinced that his brothers had suffered enough, revealed himself to them (45:1-4). Rather than blaming them for their mistreatment of him, he interpreted it as the providential work of God, sending him to Egypt to preserve them (45:7).

The family in Egypt (Gen. 46–50).   The brothers returned to Palestine and brought their father to Egypt. His meeting with the pharaoh involved some verbal sparring to determine who was the older of the two. Jacob was and, therefore, had to pronounce a blessing on the pharaoh (47:7-12). Some see this as evidence that the Egyptian ruler was a Semite, as was Jacob, since a native Egyptian would not seek blessing from a Semite, whom he would hold in contempt. This would have taken place, then, during the Hyksos rule (1720–1570 B.C.) since they were Semites.

Genesis ends with the blessing of Jacob's sons (Gen. 49), the story of Jacob's death and burial, and finally Joseph's death, preceded by his request not to be buried in Egypt (Gen. 50).

Summary on the patriarchs.   The patriarchal history was composed by later historians from traditions from different times and different places. The many names for God that have been noted, the different versions of the same story, the different emphases in the accounts of the covenant, and the shifting back and forth of certain personal names (Jacob-Israel)—all of these indicate something of the variety of the sources that were used. But to concentrate on these differences would be to miss the main purpose the writers had in mind. As in Genesis 1–11, Genesis 12–50 has much to say about God and his relationship to the world, but more particularly to a people—Israel.

The later Israelites were convinced that they were a people, chosen by God to fulfill his purpose in the world. That choice was embodied in a particular man, Abraham, and was symbolized by the covenant, a binding contract between God and Abraham that involved Abraham's loyalty to God and God's blessing of Abraham through his descendants. The covenant was reaffirmed to each succeeding patriarch, but it also demanded their commitment to it. Thus, Jacob had to be purified through long years of subjection to the wiles of Laban and the frightening confrontation with Esau before he could be called Israel, "prince of God." The writers knew that God had to work through imperfect men because those were the only kind of men available. Through the long years God was preparing, first, a man; then, a family; and, finally, a people to be his.

STUDY QUESTIONS

1. Point out the similarities and the differences between *enuma elish* and the biblical story of creation.
2. What do Genesis 1:1–2:4a and 2:4b–25 tell us about the Israelite understanding of God?
3. What does the story of the Fall (Gen. 3) tell us about the Israelite understanding of sin?
4. Identify:
   a. *enuma elish*
   b. Atrahasis
   c. Covenant
   d. Ziggurat
5. What was the theological importance of the biblical flood story?
6. Why was the Tower of Babel story used to climax the primeval history (Genesis 1–11)?
7. What factors contribute to a dating of the patriarchs in the period of 2000 to 1500 B.C.?
8. The patriarchs were heads of extended families or clans. What does this mean?
9. Compare the covenant accounts in Genesis 13:14-17, 15:17-21, and 17:1-21. How are they alike and how do they differ?
10. Genesis 14 is often said to be different from the other Abraham narratives. Read it carefully and see if you can understand why such a statement would be made.
11. Trace the theme of conflict between Sarah and Hagar in the Abraham stories.
12. If Abraham were living today and attempted to sacrifice his son, how would you view it? Why should your view of what he did be any different in the light of his times?
13. Define theophany.
14. How did Abraham try to fulfill the promise of an heir on his own?

15. How do you account for the similarities between the stories about Sarah and Abimelech (Gen. 20:10-20) and Rebekah and Abimelech (Gen. 26:6-11)?

16. In a good Bible dictionary read about "Blessing." See how it relates in the Jacob-Esau stories.

17. What do the Jacob stories say about the belief among ancient people about the spoken word?

18. Why do you suppose the biblical story teller glorifies Jacob's deceptive ways?

19. What effect, other than change of name, did Jacob's experience at the Jabbok River have upon him?

20. How do the stories about Joseph differ from other patriarchal stories?

21. What period in Egypt's history is the most likely time for the Joseph stories?

22. After reading Genesis 45, how does the narrator interpret the purpose of Joseph's experiences?

23. Briefly trace the covenant theme as it appears in the patriarchal narratives.

FOR FURTHER STUDY

Genesis

FINEGAN, JACK. *In the Beginning*. New York: Harper & Row, 1962.

SPEISER, E. A. *Genesis*. Vol. 1 in *Anchor Bible*. Garden City, N.Y.: Doubleday, 1964. One of the best volumes in this series.

VAWTER, BRUCE. *On Genesis: A New Reading*. Garden City, N.Y.: Doubleday, 1977. A fine commentary by a leading Roman Catholic scholar.

VON RAD, GERHARD. *Genesis*. Philadelphia: Westminster, 1962. A superb theological commentary.

The Patriarchal Period

See *Biblical Archaeologist* and *Biblical Archaeology Review* for articles on the continuing discussions concerning background and dating of the patriarchal narratives, especially in the light of the Ebla discoveries.

ALBRIGHT, W. F. *From Stone Age to Christianity*, 2nd ed. Baltimore: Johns Hopkins University, 1946. Still important despite its age.

ALT, ABBRECHT. "The God of the Fathers" in *Essays on the Old Testament.* Trans. by R. A. Wilson. Garden City, N.Y.: Doubleday, 1967. A paperback in Doubleday's Anchor series. See especially pp. 10–100.

BRIGHT, JOHN. *A History of Israel,* 2nd ed. Philadelphia: Westminster, 1976. Bright argues for the historicity of the patriarchs. See pp. 45-102.

FREEDMAN, DAVID NOEL, and CAMPBELL, EDWARD F., eds. *The Biblical Archaeologist Reader,* II and III. Garden City, N.Y.: Doubleday 1964, 1970. Contains a number of articles relating to this period.

HOLT, JOHN M. *The Patriarchs of Israel.* Nashville: Vanderbilt University Press, 1964.

CHAPTER FOUR

Israel Becomes a People: Exodus and Wilderness

What July 4 is to citizens of the United States, Bastille Day is to the French, and the Bolshevik Revolution is to the Russians, the Exodus was to the Israelites. The Israelite writers have mentioned the Exodus more than any other event in their history. In the book of Psalms, for instance, the Exodus theme is sounded time and again. A good example is in Psalm 105. After recounting the plagues, the psalmist says:

> Then he led forth Israel with silver and gold,
>   and there was none among his tribes who stumbled.
> Egypt was glad when they departed,
>   for dread of them had fallen upon it.
> He spread a cloud for a covering,
>   and fire to give light at night.
> They asked, and he brought quails,
>   and gave them bread from heaven in abundance.
> He opened the rocks, and water gushed forth:
>   it flowed through the desert like a river.
> For he remembered his holy promise,
>   and Abraham his servant.   (Psalm 105:37-42)

The Nature of the Exodus and the Exodus Materials

The picture that emerges from a superficial reading of the narrative portions of the books of Exodus and Numbers gives the familiar outline of the Exodus as most people know it—the sojourn of Israel in Egypt; the

(50)

birth and preparation of Moses; the Exodus with its dramatic delivery of the Israelites at the Sea; the wilderness wanderings and the rebellious murmurings of the people; the giving of the Law at Sinai; and the subsequent experiences of the people in the years before the invasion of Palestine.

The picture given is, however, the simplified version of a more complicated process. Just as the citizens of our country, whether their ancestors came to the United States two generations ago or were among those who founded the colony of Jamestown in 1608, speak with pride of "our" founding fathers, so the later Israelites spoke as though all of them were direct descendants of those whom Moses led out of Egypt.[1] The Exodus was part of a larger movement of Amorite peoples into the Palestinian region between 1400 and 1200 B.C., at a time when Egyptian control over the area weakened considerably. A careful reading of the book of Exodus reveals how traditions from various sources have been brought together to tell the story of what the LORD had done for Israel. While Moses is the major human character in the Exodus narratives, they are designed, however, not to glorify Moses but to glorify the LORD, the God of Israel. It was the LORD of history and the master of the created order who brought Israel out of Egypt. The narration of the Exodus events was a central theme in the worship of Israel, and no word of praise was too elaborate to describe what the LORD did in bringing his people from Egyptian slavery.

Moses: Birth and Wilderness Years

CHANGED TIMES AND CHANGED CIRCUMSTANCES (EX. 1)

Joseph could not live forever, nor could one expect the Hyksos rulers to dominate Egypt forever. Joseph died and the Hyksos were overthrown. As native Egyptians regained the government, the circumstances of the Hebrews changed. The Hebrews had been settled in northeastern Egypt east of the delta, where the Nile broke up into a number of branches like the fingers on a hand. The area known as Goshen was suitable for the grazing of sheep and cattle of the tent-dwelling Hebrews.

Since such a thing as birth control was unknown to the Israelites, and since the mention of such an idea would have been an insult, the

---

[1]This viewpoint is elaborated on by Martin Noth, *The History of Israel*, 2nd ed., (New York: Harper and Brothers, 1960), pp. 110–120.

original seventy people who came with Jacob enthusiastically followed the command to "multiply and replenish the earth." This alarmed the rulers of Egypt, who, in typical political exaggeration, said that the people of Israel were "too many and too mighty for us" (1:9). This was their justification for enslaving the Hebrews for building projects at the cities of Pithom and Raamses (1:11).

DATING THE EXODUS

It is the mention of these two cities that gives a valuable clue to the dating of the Exodus. While the evidence is not beyond dispute, indications are that these cities were built during the reigns of Seti I (1308–1290 B.C.) and Rameses II (1290–1224 B.C.). This has led to the conclusion that Seti I was the pharaoh of the oppression and that Rameses II was the pharaoh of the Exodus. Other items of evidence seem to support this conclusion. These include: (1) The Edomites, living in the area south and east of the Dead Sea, are said to have opposed Israel's attempts to travel northward on the King's Highway. There are evidences which suggest that this territory had no permanent cities until about 1300 B.C. (2) A number of cities in Palestine show evidence of being destroyed in a violent manner in the thirteenth century (1300–1200 B.C.). While we now know that the Exodus was not just one massive surge of people entering the land but may have involved a number of smaller invasions, the main group under Joshua's leadership seems to have invaded the land in that period. (3) The Stele of Merneptah, a stone monument set up by Pharaoh Merneptah in 1220 B.C. to boast of his exploits, tells of defeating the Israelites in Canaan. This is the first-known historical reference (outside the Bible) to Israel as a people. If they, therefore, were in Egypt in the time of Seti I (1308–1290 B.C.) and in Canaan by 1224 B.C., one could assume that the Exodus would be dated around 1280 B.C., or shortly thereafter, and that Joshua led his group into Canaan around 1250 B.C.

How many people were involved in the Exodus from Egypt? In Exodus 1 is information which may shed some light on that question. The pharaoh called in the two Hebrew midwives whose job it was to assist the Hebrew women at birth. The women were instructed to kill all male children at birth to reduce the surplus population (1:16). The midwives, however, failed to carry out the instructions. They claimed that the Hebrew women had their children so quickly that the children arrived before they could.

The importance of this information for determining the number of people involved in the Exodus is that two midwives could not have served an overwhelmingly large population. More will be said about this question later.

MOSES' BIRTH AND EARLY MANHOOD (EX. 2)[2]

If the Exodus was Israel's Declaration of Independence, then Moses was Israel's George Washington, Thomas Jefferson, and Continental Congress all rolled into one. While there are no records of the man Moses outside of the Bible, the marks he left on the nation and the traditions that grew up around his name are proof enough of the reality and the greatness of the man. True to an honest portrayal of its characters, the Bible lays out Moses' strengths and weaknesses with equal frankness. The story of Moses is the story of the people; without him, the people would not have been.

The story of Moses' birth, his mother's attempt to save him by putting him in the Nile in a small boat made of bulrushes, and his subsequent discovery by the daughter of the pharaoh is a familiar theme in ancient literature—famous men have humble beginnings. Another, more ancient, story about Sargon, the king of Akkad, is similar to the story of Moses. Sargon's mother also hid him in the river in a basket. A major difference was that Sargon was a royal son whose mother had somehow fallen into disfavor in the court. He was found and reared as a gardener, while Moses, a slave, was found and reared in the royal court.[3]

For Israel, this was the providence of God. Growing up in the pharaoh's household, yet with his own mother as his nursemaid, Moses had a feeling for the problems of his people. His feelings came out in a violent manner one day when he saw an Egyptian beating a Hebrew. Thinking no one was looking, he killed the Egyptian and buried his body in the sand (2:11-12). But his secret got out. Trying to break up a fight between two Hebrews, he was taunted by one of the men about killing the Egyptian (2:13-15).

Realizing he was in difficulty, Moses fled across the Sinai Peninsula to Midian, located to the east of the Sinai Peninsula, although the name Midian also may have been applied to parts of the Sinai region in Moses' day. There, in a manner strangely like Jacob's encounter with Rachel, Moses met Zipporah, the daughter of a Midianite priest, who is called Ruel in one story (2:18) but Jethro in another (3:1). He married into the Midianite clan and began the life of a family man (2:15b-22). Meanwhile, back in Egypt things were going from bad to worse (2:23-25).

---

[2]For an excellent work on the life of Moses from a responsible conservative scholar, see Dewey Beegle, *Moses: The Servant of Yahweh* (Grand Rapids: Wm. B. Eerdmans), 1972.

[3]For the story of Sargon, see Pritchard, *The Ancient Near East*, p. 85.

THE CALL OF MOSES (EX. 3:1–4:17)

Moses was not destined to be a sheepherder all his life. His solitary job through the years had given him a knowledge of the desert that was to be invaluable in the work of leading the people from Egypt. It was not conscious preparation on Moses' part. Rather, for the biblical writer, it was the providence of God working to prepare the man for the work he was to do.

Those years of preparation came to an end on a mountain called Horeb in one tradition (3:1) and Sinai in another (19:11). While pasturing his flocks, Moses suddenly became aware of a bush that was aflame, seemingly without burning up. As he went near to get a closer look, he became aware of a Presence. Out of this experience came Moses' call to lead the people out of Egypt. This call experience was significant because it was said to be the time when God revealed his personal name to Moses. Of the two major terms used by Israel to speak of God, *Elohim* was what one might call the general, or, to use a common analogy, the "family" name for God. It was not only used to refer to the one God but also might be used to refer to any god, or gods (3:1–5).

The name *YHWH* (translated I AM WHO I AM by the RSV in Ex. 3:14 but elsewhere as the LORD), which was revealed first to Moses on the mountain, was the personal name of God. For example, there might be a large family of Fafoofniks, but only one Fafoofnik with the personal name Abercrombie. Thus, there were many *elohims* but only one *YHWH*.

The proper pronunciation and meaning of the four letters that represent the personal name of God are subject to much debate since it ceased to be pronounced sometime after the Babylonian Exile. It is believed, however, that it was pronounced as *Yahweh*. In Jewish religious services today, the Tetragrammaton, *YHWH*, is not pronounced since to pronounce it wrongly would defile the holiness of God. A substitute word *Adonai* (translated LORD) is used. This practice of using LORD for *YHWH* is followed in this textbook. Its meaning is variously interpreted: I AM WHO I AM, I WILL BE WHO I WILL BE, I CAUSE TO BE WHAT IS. Each translation has strong arguments in its favor.

MOSES' EXCUSES

When he called Moses, God identified himself as the God of the patriarchs (3:6). While Moses was awestruck, he was not so awed that he could not argue, especially when the LORD said, "I will send you to Pharaoh that you may bring my people, the sons of Israel, out of Egypt." Moses immediately began to make excuses: (1) The excuse: "Who am I that I should go?" (3:11); the answer: "You will have the LORD'S presence with you, and he will bring the people to this mountain" (3:12). (2) The excuse: "Who are you that you are sending me?" (3:13); the answer: "You shall say, 'YHWH [the LORD], the God of the Fathers, the God of Abraham, of Isaac and of Jacob has sent me' " (3:14-22). (3) The excuse: "But they will not believe me" (4:1); the answer: "I will give you signs—a rod changed into a snake, a leprous hand healed" (4:2-10). (4) The final excuse: "LORD, I cannot talk!" (4:10); the answer: "I will give you your eloquent brother Aaron to be your spokesman" (4:14-17).

ON THE ROAD TO EGYPT (EX. 4:18-31)

His excuses left in tatters by the Divine answers, Moses set out for Egypt, with the blessing of Jethro. The story of the return to Egypt contains a strange incident (Ex. 4:24-26). At a lodging place in the wilderness, it is said that the LORD attempted to kill Moses. He was saved when Zipporah, his wife, circumcised their son and touched Moses with the bloody foreskin, saying, "Surely you are a bridegroom of blood to me!" While the meaning of this ancient story is not at all clear, it probably indicated that Moses was not circumcised. Furthermore, in much of the Old Testament the LORD is looked upon as the cause of everything. This is reflected in the saying of the prophet Amos: "Can evil befall a city, unless the LORD has done it? (Amos 3:8). The idea of an evil force in the world outside God's control that caused bad things to happen did not come into prominence until the postexilic period of Israel's history. They did believe in demons, but the demons were under divine control. For this reason, this may reflect the idea of a demonic attack on Moses. Why it is included here no one knows.

Aaron, hearing that Moses was returning to Egypt, met him on the way. Moses briefed him on what they were to do. As soon as the brothers got to Egypt, Aaron, in turn, told the Hebrews what was to happen.

Moses: The Struggle with Pharaoh

THE STRUGGLE BEGINS: MOSES AND AARON
BEFORE PHARAOH (EX. 5:1–6:1)

The task before Moses and Aaron was not an easy one. As an excuse to get the people out of Egypt, they asked the pharaoh to let the people take a three-day journey in the wilderness to worship. Pharaoh's reaction was an outright rejection of the request and an increase in the workload on the Hebrews (5:1-19), who vented their anger on Moses and Aaron, calling down the LORD's judgment upon them (5:20-21). Moses, in turn, complained to the LORD, who assured him that there would soon be action (5:22–6:1).

MOSES' CALL, THE COVENANT AND A GENEALOGY
(EX. 6:2–7:7)

In an account of Moses' call told from a different perspective, there is a strong emphasis on the covenant made with the patriarchs. They (Abraham, Isaac, and Jacob) knew God as *El Shaddai* (God Almighty) and not as *YHWH*) (the LORD) (6:2-3). Moses was to remind the Hebrews of the covenant made with the patriarchs as an assurance that he would (1) deliver them from Egypt, (2) make them his people, (3) be their God, and (4) give them their own land (6:4-8). Moses told the people, but they would not listen to him. When he told the LORD, all he got was a repetition of his responsibilities to keep on telling them (6:9-13).

In this version of the call of Moses and Aaron, the priestly authors felt it necessary to point out that Moses and Aaron had the proper pedigree, so they included their genealogy. While the genealogy is rather dull reading, there follows a statement in Ex. 7:1 that says something about Aaron's role in relation to Moses. In the earlier account of Moses' call (3:1–4:17), Moses had complained about his speech problems. The complaint was repeated (6:30), and the answer was, "See, I make you as God to Pharaoh; and Aaron your brother shall be your prophet." This word "prophet" was the same term used to describe the great prophets of Israel. Just as Aaron was spokesman for Moses, so the prophets were spokesmen for God.

THE GOING GETS ROUGH: THE PLAGUES
(EX. 7:8–11:10)

The stage was set for the struggle to free the people. It was not just a struggle between human powers; rather it was a struggle between the LORD and the gods of Egypt, in the person of their earthly representative, the divine pharaoh. Since the gods of Egypt were associated with the Nile, Moses chose to challenge them on their home court, so to speak.

After an opening round where the Egyptian magicians duplicated the actions of Moses and Aaron (the use of serpent magic, the reddening of the Nile, and the plague of frogs), the Egyptian magicians surrendered, saying, "This is the finger of God" (8:19). From that point on, the plagues increased in intensity until the climax was reached with the death of the first-born and the escape from Egypt.

The number of plagues varies according to the source. Psalms 78:43-

51 lists eight plagues. It is believed to be based on an old epic source (or J according to the Documentary Hypothesis) and emphasizes the role of Moses in Exodus. Psalm 105:27-36 seemingly is based on the Priestly tradition that magnifies Aaron's role. Exodus shows evidence of both traditions.[4]

The plagues were evidence for later Israel that the LORD had been at work on their behalf, using his power over nature to convince the pharaoh that he must free them from bondage. Israel's later retelling of the events did not have as its primary purpose the recording of history for twentieth-century readers, but "as a celebration of God's great victory whereby he is glorified and acknowledged as sole sovereign and savior."[5] This is not to deny that the accounts of the plague did not grow out of actual events but rather to say that Israel was more concerned about praising God than it was about writing history.

The plagues as miracle.   "Miracle" is a term often used in religious circles. A rather common element in many definitions of miracle is that it is something that happens which cannot be explained by ordinary means. A believer in God would say it was evidence of God's power. But any definition of the miraculous which requires that the happening must not be explainable in human terms means that once it can be explained, it will no longer be a miracle. Our great-great-grandfathers would say that television is a miracle, but to us it is a common, everyday fact of life. We do not look at it as a miracle. This lack of one's ability to explain an event, therefore, is not a reliable standard for judging what is miraculous.

All definitions of miracle start with the basic idea that it is a religious interpretation of an event. If this be true, then, whether an event is miraculous or not depends, to a certain extent, on the one who views that event. It might be illustrated in this fashion: A bear was chasing an Indian through Yellowstone Park. The Indian ran across the site of the Old Faithful Geyser, which erupts every hour. The bear, close behind, crossed the geyser the split second it erupted, throwing him high in the air and scalding him to death. To the onlookers, it was a spectacular event; to the Indian, it was a miracle; but to the bear, it was a catastrophe![6]

To develop a workable definition of miracle, it is necessary to examine the Israelite view of God's relationship to the world. According to the creation story in Genesis 1–2, the world was created through God's power.

[4]For a more detailed discussion with a chart comparing the different traditions, see Bernhard W. Anderson, *Understanding the Old Testament*, 3rd ed., (Englewood Cliffs: Prentice-Hall, 1975), pp. 60–62.

[5]J. L. Mihelic and G. E. Wright, "Plagues in Exodus," *Interpreter's Dictionary*, III, 822.

[6]From Chester Warren Quimby, "Straight from the Classroom," *Journal of Bible and Religion*, XXI, 1 (1953), 62.

It is his world, and he is active in it, bringing both judgment (as in the case of Sodom and Gomorrah) and blessing (the promise to Abraham). Nothing happens in the world except as God wills it to happen. To the Israelite, there was no such thing as a natural event. God was in everything—whether it was a storm, a drought, or a baby's birth. In short, the biblical writer—especially the Old Testament writers—did not make the distinctions between natural and supernatural that we make.

In this light, the plagues were viewed by the Israelites as the activity of God because he was active in everything. Two things characterized them as miraculous for Israel: (1) Moses predicted them, and (2) their timing was right for Israel's needs. Had these same events happened at a different time or under different circumstances, Israel may well have interpreted them in an entirely different light. A miracle, then, could be defined as follows: any event, which, when seen through the eyes of faith strengthens the faith of the believer.

The plagues as natural events.[7]   While being aware that the plague narratives were primarily developed to be used in worship, the first nine plagues can be understood also in terms of unusual natural occurrences, associated with the annual flooding of the Nile River, during a period from August to March. The first plague, the reddening of the Nile, has been interpreted in two ways: (1) a literal view that the water was actually changed to blood, or (2) that the condition might have arisen from two different causes—red soil washed down from the Ethiopian highlands, and a blood-red algae, similar to the one which causes the so-called red tide that sometimes occurs in the coastal waters off Florida. Regardless of the cause, for Israel it was the LORD who changed the life-giving waters of the Nile into a stinking river of death (7:14-24).

Frogs, the second plague (7:25–8:15), were common when the Nile flooded, leaving stagnant pools where their long strings of eggs could hatch into tadpoles and then change into young frogs. The unusual flooding conditions brought enormous numbers of frogs, far more than the ibis, an Egyptian bird that lived on frogs, could eat. The frogs, forced from the polluted water, carried with them germs that killed them. Although the stench of their rotting carcasses polluted the air,

---

[7]Among the first who emphasized the plagues as natural events were W. O. E. Oesterley and T. H. Robinson, *History of Israel*, I (Oxford: Clarendon Press, 1932), p. 85. J. L. Mihelic and G. E. Wright, "Plagues in Exodus," *Interpreter's Dictionary*, III, pp. 822–24 see a natural basis for all the plagues except the death of the first-born but emphasize their use in liturgy. Greta Hort, "The Plagues in Egypt," *Zeitschrift für die alttestamentliche Wissenschaft*, 69 (1956), 84–103; 70 (1958), 48–59, expands on Oesterley and Robinson's suggestion that the plagues were associated with the rise of the Nile and proposes that they represent a chain of events occurring from August to March. This is also the position of Beegle, *Moses*, pp. 97–118.

"Pharaoh . . . hardened his heart" and would not let the people go (8:14).

The third plague, called gnats by the Revised Standard Version (8:16-19), more likely was mosquitos,[8] bred in the standing and stagnant pools of water. This was too much for the Egyptian magicians, who acknowledged that Israel's God was more powerful than theirs (8:19). The fourth plague, flies (8:20-24), bred in the filth of the primitive living conditions of ancient villages, were naturally attracted to the piles of dead and decaying frogs.

When this plague hit Egypt, the pharaoh began to yield a bit. Calling Moses in, he told him he would release the people from work long enough to have their worship services, but only on the condition that they remain within Egypt. Moses refused to compromise. Pharaoh then agreed that the people could leave the country to sacrifice if Moses would pray for an end to the plagues. Moses agreed to pray; but when the flies disappeared, Pharaoh changed his mind (8:25-32).

The time now was late December or early January, when flies disappear in Egypt because of changes in weather conditions. Goshen, where the Hebrews lived, was much cooler because of the sea breezes. For this reason, it would not have had the flies, which are common in the rest of the country.

The fifth plague, a disease of cattle (9:1-7), came in January when the cattle were turned out to graze in the fields after the flood waters receded. The disease that killed the frogs was probably anthrax, which also is fatal to cattle. Grazing where the dead frogs had been, the cattle became diseased and died. The Hebrews' cattle were spared because the land of Goshen was the last place to dry out after the flood, so the Hebrews' cattle were still in their stalls. But the pharaoh was unmoved (9:7).

The flies of the fourth plague probably contributed to the sixth plague, which consisted of painful boils on both men and animals. The flies were not the common housefly so familiar to Americans but a tropical fly which bit the legs of men and animals. It would have served as a carrier for the virus that caused the boils. The fact that the magicians "could not stand before Moses" (9:11) could quite literally mean that the feet and legs were most affected by the boils.[9]

After a speech in which Moses told the pharaoh of the LORD's patience with him (9:13-21), Moses then warned the pharaoh that since he had not released the Hebrews, a devastating hailstorm would come. This seventh plague came in a violent thunderstorm accompanied by both hail

[8]Beegle, *Moses*, p. 106.
[9]*Ibid.*, p. 111.

and lightning (9:13-26). A heavy hailstorm can be devastating to plant life and even to animals, especially younger animals. Moses had warned the pharaoh to keep his people and their remaining animals inside because of the danger (9:19). Hailstorms are usually limited in scope, so Goshen was once again spared.

The ruined crops brought the specter of famine and softened the pharaoh's resolution not to let the Hebrews leave. It hardened again rather quickly when the storm ended (9:27-35).

Pharaoh's compromise offer and the eighth and ninth plagues (Ex. 10:1–11:10).   Pharaoh's advisers urged him to give in to the demands of Moses and Aaron, but the proud ruler did not want to admit complete defeat. Calling the Hebrew leaders in, he offered a series of compromises. He asked Moses who was to go. Moses replied that all their families and flocks had to go. The pharaoh offered his first compromise: "Go, but take only the men."

The LORD's reply through Moses was a plague of locusts. These insects, a variety of grasshopper, have been a plague of Africa and the Eastern countries throughout recorded history. Their devastation was chillingly described in the words of the prophet Joel:

> What the cutting locust left,
>   the swarming locust has eaten.
> What the swarming locust left,
>   the hopping locust has eaten.
> What the hopping locust has left,
>   the destroying locust has eaten.
>
> . . .
>
> It (the plague) has laid waste my vines
>   and splintered my fig trees:
> It has stripped off their bark and
>   thrown it down;
> Their branches are white.
>
> . . .
>
> The fields are laid waste,
>   the ground mourns
> Because the grain is destroyed.   (Joel 1:4,7,10)

The locusts were blown into the land by a strong east wind, the dread sirocco, which blew in from the Sinai Desert. Another wind, called a "strong sea breeze" by the Hebrew text and thus a north wind in Egypt, caused the plague to be lifted when Moses prayed (10:18-20). But when the pressure let up, the pharaoh went back to his old ways.

The ninth plague (10:21-29) was "a darkness to be felt" (10:21). This would be the blinding sandstorms that come with the west winds from the Sahara Desert in March. This wind today is called the "Khamsin," known by the Arabs as the "fifty-day wind." In this case it lasted for three days,

Figure 4–1. "Then Pharaoh said to [Moses], 'Get away from me . . . never see my face again' " (Exod. 10:28). This statue is a representation of Rameses II, believed to be the pharaoh of the Exodus.

Courtesy of Alinari/Editorial Photocolor Archives.

not fifty; but three days were enough to get the pharaoh in a compromising mood.

He called Moses and Aaron in and tried to deal with them again. This time he offered to let them take their families, but they had to leave their herds (10:24). Moses quickly rejected any compromise: "Not a hoof shall be left behind," he declared. After all, one could not have a sacrifice without a victim. With that rejection, Moses was ordered from the presence of the pharaoh.

The final plague: the death of the first-born (Ex. 11:1-10; 12:29-32). While timing was the significant factor in the first nine plagues, causing them to be "wonders" in the eyes of the Hebrews, both the timing and the selective nature of the tenth plague made it the climactic event for Israel. The first-born was the most important child in the family, especially from the practical standpoint. This was illustrated by Jacob's devious actions designed to secure the rights of the first-born for himself. To lose a first-born child was (and still is) a devastating psychological blow to a family, and more especially so in ancient days if the first-born were a son. For the first-born son of the pharaoh, who considered himself to be divine, to die would be the crowning blow in the struggle between the LORD and the gods of Egypt.

Some people might question whether every first-born child and animal actually died (11:5). It must be remembered that these traditions passed through many generations before they were written down. Their use of "all" and "every" was much like our own; that is, to indicate that a large number of people, especially children, died. The death rate among children in parts of Africa today still runs 60 to 75 percent for children under ten years of age. There are unexplainable elements in this plague but, like all the others, it was a "wonder" to the Israelites (11:10).

The Exodus

PREPARATION FOR THE PASSOVER (EX. 12:1-28)

The Passover, which was later combined with the Feast of Unleavened Bread, became the festival for celebrating the Exodus. In reality, the festival itself probably was older than the Exodus, having been a spring festival of shepherds among Israel's ancestors. As the result of the Exodus, it was taken over the celebrate that momentous event and was given a new interpretation. The Feast of Unleavened Bread, a celebration of the barley harvest, was joined with Passover to make an eight-day festival.

69

Such festivals became a vital part of the Israelite religious tradition, which continues to this day in Judaism. In the celebration of Passover–Unleavened Bread, the worshiper relived the events of the Exodus. The aim was to make the Exodus experience the experience of each new generation, and the ritual even today is so designed to help the worshiper to identify with the Exodus generation.

Passover was a family festival, a meal that consisted of roast lamb which had been killed with the proper ritual. It was eaten at night with unleavened bread and bitter herbs (12:3-12). The blood of the lamb was to be sprinkled on the doorposts and lintel to signify that an Israelite lived there (12:13). The instructions for the Feast of Unleavened Bread reflect a later time since it involved eating unleavened bread over a seven-day period to remind the people that since they left Egypt in a hurry, they had no time to let the bread dough rise (12:14-20).

FORWARD! MARCH! (EX. 12:29-42)

The last blow was struck! Pharaoh had had enough! Summoning Moses and Aaron, he told them to take their families and animals and leave. Their Egyptian neighbors also were anxious for the Israelites to leave, even giving the Israelites jewelry and clothing. From Raamses they set out to Succoth, a company of Israelites accompanied by "a mixed multitude" (12:38), who presumably were non-Israelite.

HOW MANY WENT?

How big was the group that left Egypt? English translations say, "Six hundred thousand men . . . besides women and children." If the average family were only five persons, this would mean more than three million persons. This figure is too high for a number of reasons: (1) Not discounting God's power to sustain them in the desert, nevertheless, under ordinary circumstances, the Sinai could never sustain life for that many people. (2) Three million persons is more people than have lived in Palestine at most any time in its history. (3) The word translated "thousands" does not necessarily mean that. It has a number of meanings. The most likely meaning is a village or district which provides soldiers. A more likely figure is 6000 men and a total not exceeding 25,000 to 30,000 people. Some would explain the figure as a census figure from Davidic times.[10]

This smaller number was more in keeping with the fact that only two

---

[10]G. Ernest Wright, *Biblical Archaeology*, rev. ed. (Philadelphia: The Westminster Press), pp. 66–67, discusses this problem. See also Cornfeld, *Archaeology*, p. 39ff.

Figure 4–2. The Exodus and Sinai.

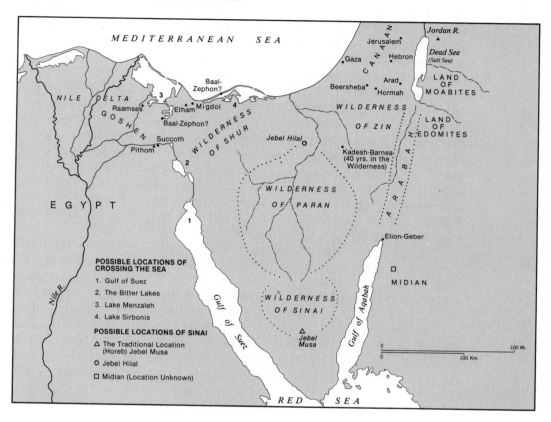

midwives were needed by the Hebrews (1:15-22). They really would have had difficulty delivering babies in a population of three million. Even 6000 families would keep them quite busy in a time of unlimited pregnancy.

WHICH WAY DID THEY GO?

The route of the Exodus would be simple to trace if all the places mentioned could be identified. They did not travel the easiest route, designated in Exodus 13:17 by a later name, "the way of the Land of the Philistines." This was the international road from Egypt up the Palestinian coast to all points north and east. This route, lined with Egyptian fortresses, was too risky. Instead, they went "round by the way of the wilderness toward the Red Sea" (13:18, RSV). This translation, "Red Sea," is based on the Greek version of the Old Testament. The Hebrew text says, *"Yam Suph,* 'Sea of Reeds.' " The possibilities for the body of water actually crossed are these: (1) what we know as the Gulf of Suez, which is an extension of the Red Sea; (2) the Bitter Lakes, a shallow, marshy area north of the Gulf of Suez along what is now the route of the Suez Canal; (3) Lake Menzaleh, an arm of the Mediterranean into which today the Suez Canal empties; (4) Lake Sirbonis, cut off from the Mediterranean Sea by a narrow sandy strip of land and located on the northern Sinai Coast. Each of these is difficult to explain. The first is too far south of the identifiable sites mentioned in Northern Egypt. The second has somewhat the same problem. The third possibility is shown as the crossing place on many modern maps because of tentative identification of two or three key sites. If present-day archaeological site identifications are correct, the fourth possibility has strong arguments in its favor. Pithom, Raamses, Succoth, Etham. Migdol, and Baal-Zephon all have been identified and lead directly to the strip of land surrounding Lake Sirbonis.[11]

If this is true, when the forces of the pharaoh overtook the Israelites, they had their backs to the Mediterranean Sea. He pursued them out on the narrow strip of land along the lagoon. Finally, they came to the inlet separating them from the land again. Night came and with it a strong east wind (14:21) that blew throughout the night. When the morning came, the east wind, which perhaps contributed to an unusually low tide, had left the land so dry that the frightened Israelites could pass over to the mainland once again. By the time they had crossed, the wind ceased; and the returning water bogged down the heavy Egyptian chariots in the sea (14:1-31).

Regardless of where the crossing took place, the important point for Israel is found in the words of the biblical writer, who says:

> Thus the LORD saved Israel that day from the hand of the Egyptians . . . and Israel saw the great work which the LORD did against the Egyptians, and the people feared the LORD; and they believed in the LORD and in his servant Moses (14:30-31).

SING PRAISES TO THE LORD (EX. 15:1-21)

The importance of the Exodus to the Israelites is shown by the many songs that commemorate the event. One such song is found in Exodus 15:1-18. This was a later song, probably used in festivals celebrating the Exodus. It was based, however, on the song of Miriam, Moses' sister (Ex. 15:21):

[11]This view is suggested by Noth, *The History of Israel*, p. 115ff. See also Cornfeld, *Archaeology*, pp. 38ff.

Sing to the LORD, for he has triumphed gloriously;
the horse and his rider he has thrown into the sea.

This short poem, celebrating the LORD's victory through the forces
of nature over the pharaoh, comes from a time very near the actual event.

Troubles in the Wilderness

WHICH WAY TO SINAI?

The destination of the Israelites was Mt. Sinai (Horeb), where the
LORD had appeared to Moses. Unfortunately, there have never been any
long-term settlements in the Sinai region except for a few military outposts
guarding mining operations of the Egyptians and at one or two major
oases. For this reason, there can be little or no archaeological verification
of sites mentioned in the biblical record. The traditional location is Jebel
Musa (Mt. Moses) in the southern end of the Sinai Peninsula. On this
mountain is St. Catherine's Monastery, founded in A.D. 527, to mark the
traditional site. A second possibility is Jebel Hilal, 30 miles west of Kadesh
Barnea, the large oasis in the northeastern Sinai region, which served as
a base for the wilderness wanderings. A third possibility is the region of
Midian, east of the Sinai Peninsula near the Gulf of Aqabah. This was a
volcanic region, and the "pillar of fire and of cloud" (14:24) may refer to
an active volcano.[12]

The traditional location would require a route on the west side of
the Sinai Desert along the Gulf of Suez. It would also seem to presuppose
the location of the Red Sea (Sea of Reeds) as either the Bitter Lakes or the
Gulf of Suez. However, the third and fourth theories lend support to a
northern route. The evidence for neither location is decisive.

TROUBLES ON THE WAY (EX. 15:22–17:7)

The Sinai Desert very quickly put to the test the leadership skills of
Moses. Egypt, even with its slavery, did provide at least a minimum of
food and plenty of water to drink. In contrast, the Sinai made Egypt look
like the Garden of Eden. First, the stagnant pools of water they found at
Marah caused complaint. Moses threw the bark or leaves of a desert shrub

---

[12]This theory on the location of Sinai was brought to the author's attention first by the
late J. Philip Hyatt of Vanderbilt University. On the other alternatives, see Cornfeld,
Archaeology, p. 40.

into the water to make it drinkable (15:22-25). Soon, they found an oasis at Elim which had plenty of fresh water (15:27).

The next complaint was food. The supplies they brought from Egypt began to run low, and the complaints increased (16:1-3). Again, the LORD through nature met the needs of the people through (1) manna and (2) quail. Manna was the secretion of a tiny scale insect, still eaten today by the Bedouin. Quail, similar to the American bird of the same name, often fall exhausted in the northern Sinai after migratory flights over the Mediterranean. They can be captured easily by hand during this time (16:4-36).

Water again became a problem. Moses' experience as a desert sheepherder again stood him in good stead for he found a water-bearing rock that satisfied the thirst of the people (17:1-7).

THE AMALEKITE RAID (EX. 17:8-16)

An even greater danger was ahead. At Rephidim the people were attacked by the Amalekites, a fierce tribe of desert dwellers. The task of leading the people to battle was given to Joshua, the son of Nun, who one day would become the leader. While Moses held up his rod, the battle favored the Israelites; but when his arms fell down, the tide of the battle changed. The effect of the rod was psychological since it reminded the people how the LORD had defeated the pharaoh who was much more powerful than the Amalekites (17:8-16). The Israelites won the battle, and Moses found a general.

A FATHER-IN-LAW'S ADVICE (EX. 18:1-27)

The people came at last to Sinai. Soon afterward, Moses' family—accompanied by his father-in-law, Jethro—joined him there. It did not take the older man long to see that Moses was overworking himself, trying to do everything for the people. Calling Moses aside, he advised him to set up a system whereby the people would be divided into groups of 10, 50, 100, and 1000. A leader would be responsible for handling all problems that arose in his group. If he could not handle them, he would consult the leader of the larger unit of which his smaller group was a part. That way, only the most pressing problems reached Moses. This allowed him to devote his time to the more important work of interceding with God for the people and in teaching them God's laws (18:17-27).

This tradition of the influence of Jethro on Moses may be evidence of other influences. Some people have suggested that even the personal name for God *(YHWH)* may have originated with Jethro's clan. At present, however, there is no conclusive proof for it.

Sinai and the Giving of the Law

ISRAEL'S CONSTITUTIONAL CONVENTION (EX. 19–24)

Moses finally reached one of his major goals: he brought the people to Sinai. It was there that the constitution of the Israelite people was made and ratified. The LORD told Moses on the mountain that the people had to make a choice. That there was a choice they had to make is to be seen in the phrase, "If you [the people] will obey my voice and keep my covenant, you shall be my own possession among all the peoples" (19:5). If the conditions were met, the people were to be "a kingdom of priests

Figure 4–3. "On the third new moon after the people of Israel had gone forth out . . . of Egypt . . . they came into the wilderness of Sinai" (Exod. 19:1). Jebel Musa, the traditional site of Mt. Sinai, is located in this range of mountains.

Photograph © Broadman Films. Used by permission.

and a holy nation" (19:6). To be a holy people meant to be a people set apart for special service for the LORD, since holiness carried with it the idea of separation.

When he came down from the mountain, Moses called the leaders of the people and told them the conditions of the convenant. They agreed to do as the LORD commanded (19:7-8). Then, instructions were given for the all-important covenant-making ceremony. Elaborate preparations relating to cleanliness and sexual abstinence (19:10,14-15) had to be made. Boundaries were established around the holy mountain so the people would not come too close. The ancient belief in the power and awesomeness of the Holy was evidenced by the threats of death by stoning to any who violated the boundaries around the sacred mountain (19:12-13).

On the great day came thunder and lightning from the cloud-shrouded mountain, accompanied by the loud blast on the ram's horn trumpet known as the *shophar*. Descriptions of the appearance of God (theophany) in the setting of the thunderstorm are common in the Old Testament (Judg. 5:4-5; Psa. 18:8-16; 29:4-9). The summons came for Moses to go up on the mountain. At the LORD's command he went back down and took Aaron with him (19:16-25).

THE TEN WORDS (EX. 20:1-17)

As they now stand, the Ten Commandments (known as the Ten Words in Judaism) are expanded from the earliest form, which is believed to have consisted of ten concise statements:

1. You shall have no other gods *(elohim)* before me.
2. You shall not make for yourself a graven image.
3. You shall not take the name of the LORD your God in vain.
4. Remember the Sabbath day and keep it holy.
5. Honor your father and your mother.
6. You shall not murder.
7. You shall not commit adultery.
8. You shall not steal.
9. You shall not bear false witness against your neighbor.
10. You shall not covet.

As evidence that the Commandments in their longer form represent an expansion, one needs to compare the version found in Deuteronomy 5:6-21 and, more particularly, the Fourth, Fifth, and Tenth Commandments. The Fifth Commandment says:

Exodus 20:12. Honor your father and your mother that your days may be long in the land that the LORD your God gives you.

Deuteronomy 5:16. Honor your father and your mother, *as the LORD your God commanded you*; that your days may be prolonged, *and that it may go well with you*, in the land which the LORD your God gives you..

A more important difference is to be found in the Tenth Commandment:

Exodus 20:17. You shall not covet your neighbor's *house*; you shall not covet your neighbor's *wife*, or his manservant, or his maidservant, or his ox, or his ass, or anything that is your neighbor's.

Deuteronomy 5:21. Neither shall you covet your neighbor's *wife*; and you shall not desire your neighbor's house, his *field*, or his manservant, or his maidservant, his ox, his ass, or anything that is your neighbor's.

These differences are such that they suggest a changing view of the Commandments in their applications to specific situations. The Tenth Commandment, in particular, reflects either a change in the status of women, or possibly, a difference in their status (in a later time) from one section of the country to another.

For Israel, the Ten Commandments were the constitution, the laying down of the basic principles from which a legal system would develop. There are two basic divisions in the Commandments, reflecting the two poles of Israel's existence as a people. (1) Commandments 1 to 4 are concerned with Israel's relationship to God: absolute loyalty, imageless worship, reverence for the Name (*YHWH*), and regular worship. (2) Commandments 5 to 10 deal with the Israelites' relations to the social order: family solidarity, reverence for life, respect for marriage vows, respect for property, truthfulness in speech, and proper attitudes toward others and their property. No other set of moral principles have been so influential in Western legal systems.

ABSOLUTE LAW AND CASE LAW

The Ten Commandments were also unique in their form. They are stated as absolutes; that is, they allow for no contradictions. This kind of law is known as *apodictic* law and was rarely found in the ancient Near East outside the Israelite law codes. A second type of law is *casuistic* or case law. It, too, was found in Israel but also was common in other law codes. Case law stated a condition and then told what the penalty was if the condition existed.

THE TEN COMMANDMENTS AND COVENANT CEREMONIES

When the covenant ceremony in which Israel accepted the obligations of the Ten Commandments as the basic law of their existence is compared with covenant ceremonies among other peoples, some interesting parallels appear. Among the Hittites, a fourteenth-century B.C. people from Asia Minor, there were suzerainty treaties or covenants (those involving a stronger and weaker party) that had six major elements: (1) a prologue identifying the maker of the covenant; (2) a historical record stating why the suzerain or lord had a right to make the covenant; (3) the conditions of the covenant; (4) the requirement for preservation and the periodic public reading of the text; (5) a list of the gods who were witnesses to the covenant; and (6) curses and blessings directed toward those who kept and those who neglected the covenant.[13]

These elements, with one or two exceptions, can be seen in Exodus 20:2-17 and 24:3-8:

Exodus 20:2

Prologue:	"I am the LORD your God,"
Historical record:	"who brought you up out of the land of Egypt, out of the house of bondage."

Exodus 20:3-17

Stipulations:	The Ten Commandments.

Exodus 24:4,7

Preservation and public readings:	"And Moses wrote all the words of the LORD . . . Then he took the book of the covenant, and read it in the hearing of the people; and they said, 'All that the LORD has spoken, we will do, and we will be obedient.' "

List of the gods as witnesses:	These obviously would not appear in light of the First Commandment.
Blessings and curses:	These do not appear in connection with the Ten Commandments, but Deuteronomy 27:11-26 preserves a cursing ceremony which may have originally been used in a covenant-renewal festival where each generation accepted the obligations of the Commandments and subsequent laws which grew out of them.

[13]George E. Mendenhall, *Law and Covenant in Israel and the Ancient Near East* (Pittsburgh: Biblical Colloquium, 1955), is the primary study in this area.

The Principles Made Practical: The Law Codes

Just as the American Constitution was the beginning of the American legal system, so the Ten Commandments were the beginning of law for Israel, not the finished product. The working out of the principles took the form of laws. These laws are found in three major codes, or groups, in the Old Testament: The Covenant Code (Ex. 20:33–23:33); the Deuteronomic Code (Deut. 5:1–28:68); and the Priestly Code (principally in the book of Leviticus, but with some laws found in Exodus and Numbers). The narratives present the laws as if all of them were given directly to Moses, but closer examination reveals that they developed over a long period of time. Moses was the law-giver in the sense that the basic principles from which all the laws for Israel were to come were given through him.

THE COVENANT CODE (EX. 20:22–23:33)

This probably was the oldest Israelite Code but not the oldest Near Eastern Code. There were a number of older Near Eastern law codes, the best known being the Code of Hammurabi, which dates from the nineteenth century B.C. There are laws from Hammurabi's Code which are very similar to laws in the Israelite codes. Compare, for example, the laws concerning oxen, which were known by their owners to be dangerous:

Hammurabi's Code

If a seignior's ox was a gorer and . . . [it was] . . . made . . . known to him that it was a gorer, but he did not pad its horns (or) tie up his ox, and that ox gored to death a member of the aristocracy, he shall give one-half mina of silver.[14]

Covenant Code

If the ox has been accustomed to gore in the past, and its owner has been warned, but has not kept it in, and it kills a man or a woman, the ox shall be stoned and the owner shall be put to death. If a ransom is laid on him, then he shall give for the redemption of his life whatever is laid on him (Ex. 21:29-30).

The Covenant Code contains laws designed for a society in which agriculture was the major means of earning a living—a condition that did not exist for Israel until it entered the land of Canaan. It contained laws that are classed as civil or criminal laws, but religion was such a basic part

[14]James B. Pritchard, *The Ancient Near East*, p. 165.

of its life-style that religious offenses were subject to criminal penalties. A brief summary of its contents is as follows:

20:22-23	A repetition of the commandment against idols.
20:24-26	A demand for only earthen altars or altars of uncut stones in opposition to the elaborate high alters of the Canaanites.
21:1-11	Regulations concerning slaves, male and female.
21:12-32	Crimes against fellow Israelites and their penalties.
21:33–22:17	Laws governing property.
22:18–23:9	Miscellaneous laws, many of which relate to the treatment of the weak and defenseless, i.e., (1) the treatment of strangers, widows, and orphans (22:21-24); (2) the lending of money to the poor (22:25-27); (3) another warning against oppressing the stranger (23:9).
23:10-19	The sabbatical year, the sabbath, and the three major feasts.
23:20-33	A promise of success in the conquest if the law was faithfully kept.

THE PRIESTLY CODE

Unlike the Covenant Code and the Deuteronomic Code, the Priestly Code is much more complex and widely scattered. For this reason only some outstanding sections of this code will be mentioned. While it follows the Covenant Code in the biblical order, it actually came later than either of the other codes, probably reaching its final form sometime during, or immediately after, the Babylonian Exile. Like the other two codes, it is comprised of a mixture of earlier and later laws. A major difference was that the Priestly Code was primarily concerned with proper worship. For example, in Exodus 25–31 a detailed description of (1) the ark and (2) the tabernacle is given. The ark (described in Exodus 25) was a rather elaborate wooden box, carried by two long staves or poles that passed through rings on the corners of the box. It was approximately 45 inches long, 27 inches wide, and 27 inches high, overlaid with gold with a mercy seat on top, with winged figures on either end. This seat represented the throne of God. The ark symbolized the presence of God among the people. It was thought to be especially effective when carried with the people as they fought their enemies.

The tabernacle (Ex. 26–27) was a tent of skins in which the ark was kept. It was surrounded by a fence of skins that formed a sort of courtyard. Inside the tent there were two rooms, made by a curtain across one end. The larger room was the Holy Place. Its furnishings were (1) a table for the "bread of the Presence" (25:23-30), which was one of the sacrificial offerings; (2) a seven-branched lamp called the *menorah* (25:31-40); and (3) the altar for burning incense (30:1-10). The priests entered the Holy Place daily in carrying out their duties.

The smaller room, separated from the Holy Place by a curtain, was the Most Holy Place or Holy of Holies. Here the Ark of the Covenant was kept. Only the High Priest could enter the Holy of Holies one day in the year on *Yom Kippur*, the Day of Atonement. His activity on that day was for the purpose of securing forgiveness of the people's sins.

Much attention is devoted in the Priestly Code to the priests and their activities. An example of this is Exodus 28:1–29:46, which is devoted to a description of the priestly garments and to the ordination of Aaron and his sons. Leviticus 6:1–9:24 discusses the function of the priests in sacrifices and then turns again to the dedication of Aaron and his sons to the priesthood.

These examples should serve to emphasize the important role the priest played in ancient Israel. In the patriarchal days, the patriarch himself functioned as the priest. When Israel became a nation, the priesthood became a separate group of men whose sole job was to function as priests. While the descriptions found in the law codes may well reflect a later, more developed priestly establishment, there can be no doubt that the priesthood played a role in Israelite life in the wilderness.

The power of the priest lay in the belief that he controlled the access to God. He was the expert in communicating with the awesome Deity, who was responsible for bringing Israel out of Egypt. The power controlled by the priest carried with it the temptation to corruption; but the continued existence and positive influence of Israelite religion over many centuries must be credited, in part, to the integrity of many of the priests.

Sacrifice and sacrifices.   One of the main functions of the priests was to carry out the sacrifices prescribed in the laws. Since most of the people were illiterate, sacrifice was a visual aid to worship. Its effectiveness as an aid to worship depended, in large measure, upon how it was viewed. Three basic views of sacrifice prevailed in ancient societies: (1) that sacrifice was made to appease an angry deity—in short, to bribe him; (2) that sacrifice was an act of communion whereby the worshiper had fellowship with the deity; (3) that the sacrifice was a gift to the deity, designed to praise him. The sacrifice of an animal was regarded as substituting for the life of a man, but it had a deeper meaning than mere substitution.

What then, did it mean when an Israelite had sinned and brought a sacrifice to be offered at the altar? Basic to any understanding of this question is the conception of one's relatedness to all that he had including family and possessions. One's land and possessions were bound up with his life because they were the means of sustaining life. Naboth's reluctance to surrender his land to Ahab, even for a fair price, is a vivid illustration of this feeling of oneness which the Israelite had for land and possessions (I Kings 21:3). It is also illustrated by the destruction of Aachan, his family and all his possessions, because he had sinned (Joshua 7:24). All he had was contaminated by his sin because it was thought of as being a part of him. When one brought an animal to sacrifice it, it was his possession and therefore was a part of himself. He laid his hands on its head to symbolize his identity (oneness) with it (Leviticus 1:4). When its blood was shed in the ritual, the life that was given was his life given symbolically. It was not a substitute; it was the offerer giving of himself.[15]

The major kinds of sacrifice are described in Leviticus 1:1–6:7. (1) The whole burnt offering was the major daily sacrifice and had as its purpose making the people right with God; that is, atoning for sin (1:1-17). (2) Cereal offerings were peace offerings, expressing thanks for the produce of the land (2:1-16). (3) In contrast to the whole burnt offering was the peace offering. The animal was slain, its blood was thrown against the altar, the fat and internal organs were burned, and the meat was eaten by the priests and worshipers in an act of communion (3:1-17). (4) The sin offering for "any one [who] sins unwittingly," was also a whole burnt offering (4:1–5:13). (5) The guilt offering involved not only a sacrifice but an act of restoring any loss that had resulted from his sin (5:14–6:7).

Holidays and holy days (Lev. 23:1-44). (1) Passover–Unleavened Bread, which came in March or April, was to celebrate the Exodus events. (2) The Feast of Weeks, which celebrated the wheat harvest, came fifty days after Passover, which was why it was called Pentecost in the New Testament (Acts 2:1). (3) The Feast of Booths (Tabernacles) came in the early fall and celebrated the fruit harvest. (4) The most solemn holy day of the year was the Day of Atonement, when the High Priest entered the Holy of Holies in the Tabernacle to make atonement for the sins of the people (Lev. 16:1-34).

The Holiness Code (Lev. 17–26). Mention needs to be made of one other major section of the Priestly Code. Chapters 17–26 constitute a major section containing many ancient traditions grouped around the theme of Israel's need to be a holy people, set apart and dedicated to the

---

[15]John H. Tullock, *Blood Vengeance Among the Israelites in the Light of Its Near Eastern Background.* (Ann Arbor: University Microfilms, 1966), p. 255 ff.

service of God. Chapter 19, in particular, highlights the idea of holiness as embodied in its most famous line, "You shall love your neighbor as yourself" (19:18).

THE DEUTERONOMIC CODE

The Deuteronomic Code, found in the book of Deuteronomy, was first discovered during the reign of Josiah of Judah in 621 B.C., many centuries after the Exodus. But, like the Covenant Code and the Priestly Code which came after it, it contained many ancient laws as well as laws that were brought into being much nearer the time of its discovery. It, too, had a version of the Ten Commandments (5:6-27). As its Greek title Deuteronomy ("second law") suggests, it was a restatement of the law; in short a sort of updating, or modernizing, of the law to fit a changed situation. For this reason, old laws still usable were kept while new laws, suitable for new conditions that had arisen, were added. It may be summarized as follows:

5:1–11:32	The Ten Commandments and exhortations to keep them.
12:1-31	The command to have all worship in one central sanctuary.
13:1-18	The awfulness of idolatry.
14:1–15:23	Regulations for a holy people. Warnings against pagan customs, regulations about clean and unclean animals, the law of the tithe, the sabbatical year as related to debts and slavery of Hebrews, offering of first-born animals.
16:1-17	The major festivals: Passover–Unleavened Bread; Festival of Weeks (Pentecost in the New Testament) or wheat harvest festival; and Festival of Booths or Tabernacles, which celebrated the fruit harvest.
16:18–17:20	Rules for the administration of justice.
18:1-22	How to worship God in a proper manner.
19:1-21	Legal problems: the problems of manslaughter, property fraud, proper evidence for determining guilt in a crime.
20:1-20	How to conduct a holy war.

21:1–23:14	Various laws concerning unsolved murder, treatment of captive women, disrespect for parental authority, rules for hanging a man, responsibility for a man's lost property, a woman's use of man's clothes, protection of bird life, building codes, the mixing of unlike things, relations between the sexes, relations to outcasts and other peoples, proper sanitary procedures.
23:15–25:19	Humanitarian and religious laws: runaway slaves, cult prostitution, taking of interest on loans, making vows to God, respect for property, divorce procedures, the newly married, taking security for debts, stealing, rules for the leper, extending credit, relation to poor and needy, individual responsibility, the sojourner and widow, law of punishment, just payment for services, law of the levirate marriage, dirty fighting, false weights and measures, relations to the Amalekites.
26:1-19; 28:1-68	Rules for worship: the service of first fruits, the tithing ceremony. A plea to observe the law and the consequences of failing to do so.

The Ten Commandments and the Codes

By taking one of the Commandments and showing how it was used in the codes, one perhaps can see the differences which the passage of time brought in the interpretation of the Commandments. The Sixth Commandment is "You shall not kill." See how the three codes developed this command on page 91.

After the Covention Was Over

THE COVENANT BROKEN (EX. 32)

The people's commitment to the covenant did not erase their proneness to rebellion. When Moses delayed coming down from the mountain, they assumed the worst had happened and demanded of Aaron that he make images for them to serve as gods. Aaron did as they requested, trying still to point them to the LORD (32:1-6). This incident reflects a theme common throughout Israel's history; that is, the temptation to dilute the religion of the God of Sinai with the popular religions of the

Covenant Code
Ex. 21:12-14

Whoever strikes a man so that he dies shall be put to death. But if he did not lie in wait for him, but God let him fall into his hand, then I will appoint for you a place to which he may flee. But if a man willfully attacks another to kill him treacherously, you shall take him from my altar, that he may die.

Deuteronomic Code
Deut. 19:4-6; 11-13

This is the provision for the manslayer, who by fleeing there may save his life. If any one kills his neighbor unintentionally without having been at enmity with him in time past—as when a man goes into the forest with his neighbor to cut wood, and his hand swings the axe to cut down a tree, and the head slips from the handle and strikes his neighbor so that he dies—he may flee to one of these cities and save his life; lest the avenger of blood in hot anger pursue the manslayer and overtake him, because the way is long, and wound him mortally, though the man did not deserve to die, since he was not at enmity with his neighbor in time past.

But if any man hates his neighbor, and lies in wait for him, and attacks him, and wounds him mortally so that he dies, and the man flees into one of these cities, then the elders of his city shall send and fetch him from there and hand him over to the avenger of blood, so that he may die. Your eye shall not pity him, but you shall purge the guilt of innocent blood from Israel, so that it may be well with you.

Priestly Code
Num. 35:11-12; 16-24

Then you shall select cities of refuge for you, that the manslayer who kills any person without intent may flee there. The cities shall be for you a refuge from the avenger, that the manslayer may not die until he stands before the congregation for judgment.

But if he struck him down with an instrument of iron, so that he died, he is a murderer; the murderer shall be put to death. And if he struck him down with a stone in the hand, by which a man may die, and he died, he is a murderer; the murderer shall be put to death. Or if he struck him down with a weapon of wood in the hand, by which a man may die, and he died, he is a murderer; the murderer shall be put to death. The avenger of blood shall himself put the murderer to death; when he meets him, he shall put him to death. And if he stabbed him from hatred, or hurled at him, lying in wait so that he died, or in enmity struck him down with his hand, so that he died, then he who struck the blow shall be put to death; he is a murderer; the avenger of blood shall put the murderer to death, when he meets him.

But if he stabbed him suddenly without enmity, or hurled anything on him without lying in wait, or used a stone, by which a man may die, and without seeing him cast it upon him, so that he died, though he was not his enemy, and did not seek his harm; then the congregation shall judge between the manslayer and the avenger of blood, in accordance with these ordinances.

time. Moses' magnificent prayer of intercession following the LORD's threat to destroy the rebels revealed the depth of the man's commitment to his people (32:7-14). That love for the people did not keep him from a wrathful explosion when he came down from the mountain and found the people dancing around a golden calf. In a fit of temper, he threw down the tablets on which the Commandments were written, literally breaking the Ten Commandments! The calf, probably a gold-covered wooden frame, was destroyed (32:15-20).

Moses then turned on Aaron, whose excuse sounded as pathetic as a small boy caught in the act of stealing cookies. There followed a violent purge of the rebels, led by the Levites. Moses again made intercession for the people and received the command to be on the road toward the Promised Land again (32:21-35). Before the march began, however, Moses sought the LORD's leadership (33:1-23), the covenant was renewed, and the promise was repeated (34:1-16).

ON THE ROAD TO KADESH-BARNEA
(NUM. 10:11–12:16)

Following a report of a census (Num. 1:1–4:49), another section of the Priestly Code (5:1–6:26) and narratives concerning the tabernacle, the account of the journey resumes. A song that was sung on the march is preserved in 10:35-36:

> Arise, O LORD, and let thy enemies be scattered;
> and let them that hate thee flee before thee . . .
> Return, O LORD, to the ten thousand thousands of Israel.

But the songs did not muffle the complaints, whether it was food (11:4-35), or Aaron and Miriam's complaint about Moses' Cushite wife (12:1-16), which is an early example of racial prejudice.

SPYING OUT THE LAND (NUM. 13:1–33)

A second major time of decision had arrived. The march had brought the people to the southern reaches of the Negev, Palestine's southernmost habitable region. This was the most logical place from which to launch an invasion of the land.

Choosing twelve men (a representative from each tribe), Moses sent them northward into the hill country to estimate the chances of a successful invasion (13:1-24). The returning spies gave a glowing report of the richness of the land, especially when compared with the barren territory through which they had come. But for ten of the men, the minuses in the form of walled cities, far outweighed the pluses. In view of the disadvantages, they gave a majority report which counseled against an invasion (13:28-29, 32-33). Caleb and Joshua gave a strong minority report, recommending an invasion (13:30-31).

THE INVASION NOBODY BELIEVED WOULD SUCCEED—AND IT DIDN'T (NUM. 14:1-45)

Rebellion flared once again, coming almost to the point of the people's stoning Moses and Aaron (14:1-10a). Moses had to intercede to prevent the people's destruction, pleading that such an action would reflect on both the honor and the ability of the LORD to do what he had promised to do (14:10b-19). The rebellion condemned that generation to the wilderness, except for Caleb and Joshua (14:20-35). A plague convinced the people that an invasion was imperative, although Moses warned that it was doomed to failure. He was right, for the Israelites suffered defeat at the hands of the Amalekites and Canaanites (14:36-45). Some Israelites probably stayed in the northern Negev, however, joining forces with the Joshua-led group some forty years later when it invaded from east of the Jordan. After this failure, Kadesh-Barnea became the base of operations for the main body of Israelites for the next generation.

THE KADESH YEARS AND MORE PRIESTLY LAWS (NUM. 15:1–19:22)

The Israelite storyteller gave little attention to what happened in the years at Kadesh-Barnea. Chapter 15 contains laws concerning offerings and an incident about a man who violated the Sabbath law on work (15:1-41). The major headline was the rebellion led by a trio named Korah, Dathan, and Abiram (16:1-19). Their subsequent punishment, as well as that of their whole families, illustrates the concept of corporate responsibility that was a commonly held view in biblical times. The idea was that a man's actions affected his whole family, either for good or ill. They shared in his guilt or his glory (16:20-50).

The passing of time is indicated by the insertion of more of the Priestly Code dealing with priestly stories and duties, as well as the ritual for purifying a person made unclean by contact with a corpse (17:1-20).

Figure 4–4. "And the people of Israel . . . came into the wilderness of Zin . . . and the People stayed in Kadesh" (Exod. 20:1). Kadesh–Barnea, the largest oasis in the Sinai peninsula, was headquarters for the Israelites during much of the wilderness period.

Courtesy of George L. Kelm.

On the March Again

BOUND FOR THE PROMISED LAND (NUM. 20:1-13)

Time passed and the older generation passed on with it, including Miriam and Aaron. Miriam died before Israel left Kadesh-Barnea (20:1). Time did not get rid of the rebelliousness of the people, however. As they moved away from the oasis at Kadesh to continue their movement toward the land promised to them, lack of water—an ever-present problem when the people were on the move—once again brought still another crisis. Moses, commanded by the LORD to strike a rock to find water, seems to have struck it in anger, bringing the LORD's judgment that Moses, too, would die on the trail and would never enter Canaan (20:2-13).

Trouble not only came from within but also from external forces. Failing in attempts to invade Canaan from the south, Moses then proposed to cross the Arabah, the continuation of the great Rift valley south of the Dead Sea, and to follow the King's Highway northward through the territories of Edom and Moab. Contacting the king of Edom, Moses promised to pass through the land peaceably, paying for any water used. The Edomites refused passage, however, and threatened to attack Israel (20:14-21).

Aaron died and was buried on Mt. Hor. This left only Moses of the first-generation leaders (20:22-29). Eventually, the people set out in the direction of the Gulf of Aqabah (called the Red Sea) in an attempt to go around Edom. They encountered numerous poisonous snakes on the way. Moses was instructed to make a fiery serpent and to make the people look at it and be healed when they were bitten. Recently, in this same general area in a Midianite archaeological site, such a bronze serpent was found. This suggests that such a technique was used among the Midianites in the case of snakebite. Furthermore, it is another evidence of an ancient relationship between Israel and the Midianites.[16]

THE MOABITES AND BALAAM (NUM. 21:10–24:25)

Unable to go around Edom, the Israelites turned northward along the Arabah, coming at last to the southern end of the Dead Sea. Passing along through the valley of the Brook Zered, which served as the border between Edom and Moab, they finally were able to get to the major caravan road, the King's Highway (21:10-21). Not wanting trouble with the Moabites, Moses asked permission to pass through the territory peaceably. When the king refused, Israel attacked, took control of much of the Moabite kingdom, and even took some of the Amorite territory to the north of Moab (21:21-35).

At this point entered Balaam, one of those characters about whom the Israelites were to talk for many generations. As a matter of fact, not only did the Israelites talk about the famous prophet Balaam, but others did also. A recent archaeological discovery of an inscription in Jordan has shown this. In the inscription, Balaam is called "seer of the gods," indicating that he was by no means an Israelite prophet nor a follower of *YHWH* (the LORD). There is mention also of goddesses, another idea foreign to Israelite religion. As in the biblical account, he is pictured as one who pronounced curses.[17] It is in light of this discovery, then, that the Balaam stories in Numbers are to be examined.

Desperate for a way to stop the marauding Israelites, Balak the king of Moab sent for the famous Balaam, a holy man who lived in Mesopo-

[16]See Suzanne Singer, "From these Hills," *The Biblical Archaeology Review*, IV (June, 1978), 16–27.

[17]Jacob Hoftijzer, "The Prophet Balaam in a 6th Century Aramaic Inscription," *Biblical Archaeologist*, 39, 1 (March, 1976), 11–17.

tamia. Balak wanted Balaam to curse the Israelites so that they could not defeat his armies (22:1-6). Taking money with them, the messengers came to Balaam, who told them he would give an answer in the morning. In the morning, he told them that the LORD would not let him go (22:7-14). After reporting to Balak, the messengers came back with a much larger sum of money. That time Balaam agreed to go under instructions to do as God told him (22:8-21).

At this point the text seems to contradict itself. After saying that Balaam went on God's command (22:20), it says that God was angry with him for going (22:22). It must be remembered, however, that God was believed to cause everything. Thus, for him to cause a person to commit an action and then be angry at him for doing it was not viewed as an inconsistency on God's part. If we were telling the story today, we would probably say that the large sum of money Balaam was offered was what changed his mind, with the result that God was angry with him because he went with the Moabites.

Then follows the most famous part of the Balaam story. Saddling his donkey, Balaam set out to go to Moab. On the way, strange things began to happen. Donkeys are noted for their stubbornness. The donkey, seeing things that Balaam did not see, ran off the road and then crushed Balaam's foot against a stone wall. Finally, the donkey lay down in the road. Balaam, who had been beating the donkey for its seeming stubbornness, suddenly heard the donkey begin to speak up in its own defense (22:22-30)! To top it off, the LORD spoke out in defense of the donkey, telling Balaam that he had been trying to get his attention through the donkey. Balaam was told he was to go on with the Moabites (22:31-35). Did anyone else hear what the donkey and God said to Balaam? The text is silent on this point.

When Balaam came to the Moabites, he made preparations to carry out the request of Balak. But, try as he might, each time he started to pronounce a curse, a blessing was pronounced upon Israel. Needless to say, Balak was most unhappy. He soon sent Balaam back the way he came (22:36–24:25).

TROUBLE AT PEOR (NUM. 25:1-17)

While the Israelites were in Moabite territory, they encountered the worship of fertility gods. These were nature deities believed to have the power to make crops grow. This type of worship, which was to be such a problem for Israel in later years, involved the so-called holy women, who played the role of the goddesses in sacred prostitution. The Israelite men were attracted to the worship, so much so that one brought a Moabite prostitute into camp. An epidemic, probably a venereal disease, broke out in the camp. Again, radical action was taken, Moses ordering the killing of anyone who had patronized the fertility cult. In this way the disease was checked.

MISCELLANEOUS MATERIALS (NUM. 26–35)

The latter part of the book of Numbers contains a variety of materials: a census (26:1-65); an incident concerning the property of a man who had no sons to receive his inheritance (27:1-11); the appointment of Joshua as Moses' successor (27:12-23); a series of regulations concerning offerings for the major holidays—the Sabbath, the New Moon, Passover–Unleavened Bread, Feast of Weeks or Wheat Harvest, the New Year's Festival, the Day of Atonement, and the Feast of Booths or Fruit Harvest (28:1–29-40); the law of vows (30:1-16); holy war against Midian (31:1-54); the story of assigning the territory east of the Jordan to the tribes of Reuben, Gad, and Manasseh (32:1-42); a summary of the journey from Egypt to Moab (33:1-56); a discussion of the territorial boundaries of the people in Canaan (34:1-29); a discussion of the Levitical cities and the cities of refuge (35:1-34); and finally a discussion of a married woman's inheritance (36:1-13).

The most important matter in this section of Numbers is the holy war against Midian. The holy war concept will be discussed at some length in the discussion of the Conquest.

DEUTERONOMY'S CONTRIBUTION TO THE WILDERNESS STORY (DEUT.)

The name "Deuteronomy" comes from the Greek name for this book and means "the second law." The Hebrew title is "These are the words," based on the first verse in the book. The word "Deuteronomy" is very descriptive of the contents of this book because 1:1–4:49 is a summary statement of the wilderness wanderings of the Israelites, presented in the form of an address to the people in the plains of Moab.

The second major section (5:1–26:19; 28:1-68) has already been discussed under the section on the law codes. Two major themes in this section deserve more lengthy comment: (1) the command for a single place of worship, and (2) the concept of the holy war.

The command to have a single place of worship is found in 12:5,11,18,26. In its original time and context, it probably referred to either Shiloh or Shechem. Both seemed to have served as the major worship center at one time or another. When the essentials of what is known today as Deuteronomy was discovered, or rediscovered, in the time of King Josiah (621 B.C.), the references to a single place of worship were taken to mean Jerusalem. By that time, Jerusalem was the capital of all that remained of the Israelite kingdoms. Even more important was the fact that the Temple was located there and was controlled by a powerful and influential priesthood.

The second important theme was the holy-war concept. The transliterated Hebrew word for it is *cherem*, sometimes translated as "the ban." The key passage is Deuteronomy 20:16-18:

> But in the cities of these peoples that the LORD your God gives you for an inheritance, you shall save alive nothing that breathes, but you shall utterly destroy them, the Hittites and the Amorites, the Canaanites and the Perizzites, the Hivites and the Jebusites, as the LORD your God has commanded; that they may not teach you to do according to all their abominable practices which they have done in the service of their gods, and so to sin against the LORD your God.

The justification for such an action is found in 20:18, which says, in effect, that the people of the land were like an infection in the body. It must be gotten rid of, even though the solution was a radical one. Similarly, today the amputation of a limb is viewed as a radical solution to a physical ailment. Yet, at times it is the only available solution to the problem.

But the question may come to mind, "How does one justify such actions?" The simple answer is that there is no way it can be justified. The best one can do is to understand that the Israelites practiced holy war in a time when many nations practiced holy war. They justified their actions in much the same way people have justified war down through the ages. The best that can be done is to try to understand why it was the way it was.

THE OLD PASSES—THE NEW COMES
(DEUT. 29:1–34:12)

As in other Pentateuchal materials, Deuteronomy has a strong emphasis on the covenant. The description of a covenant ceremony in Moab is found in 29:1-29. This was a part of the third major section of Deuteronomy and is followed by an exhortation which could be titled "The Two Ways" (30:1-20). In it the people were given the choice of the blessing or the curse, depending on whether they chose the good way of obedience to the LORD or the way of disobedience.

After Deuteronomy's version of the choosing of Joshua as Moses' successor (31:1-8), there is a command to have a ceremony of covenant renewal every seven years at the time of the Feast of Booths (31:9-29). Much debate was taken place among Old Testament scholars about whether in early Israel this ceremony was like a New Year's festival celebrated by the Babylonians. There is little direct biblical evidence for such a festival; therefore, drawing a certain conclusion from parallels is not possible. The important point is that such a ceremony of covenant renewal was designed to make the covenant meaningful for each generation.

Deuteronomy concludes with two songs (32:1-43 and 33:1-29), the first of which is probably designed for use in ceremonies celebrating the Exodus events. It is quite similar to songs in the book of Psalms. The second is in the form of a deathbed blessing comparable to the blessing of Jacob in Genesis 49.

Moses, the servant of the LORD, saw the land of promise; but he died on Mount Pisgah (34:1-8). His epitaph could well be the final words of the book of Deuteronomy:

> And there has not arisen a prophet since in Israel like Moses, whom the LORD knew face to face, none like him for all the signs and the wonders which the LORD sent him to do in the land of Egypt, to Pharaoh and to all his servants and to all his land, and for all the mighty power and all the great and terrible deeds which Moses wrought in the sight of all Israel (34:10-12).

STUDY QUESTIONS

1. Evaluate the role that Moses played in the events of the Exodus.
2. What are the evidences for dating the Exodus in the period from 1300 to 1200 B.C.?
3. For Israel, what role did the LORD play in the events of the Exodus?
4. How does the biblical narrator interpret the meaning of the events in Moses' life leading up to the Exodus?
5. Of what importance was the experience of Moses on Horeb (Exodus 3–4) to his later work?
6. What is the importance of Aaron in Exodus 6:2 to 7:7 as compared with his place in the call of Moses in Exodus 3 and 4? How do you account for the differences?
7. If the plagues were largely natural events, how could they be called miraculous?
8. Of what importance were the plagues for the Exodus?
9. Although they are now associated with the Exodus events, what were the probable origins of the Jewish festivals of Passover and Unleavened Bread?

10. What evidences suggest that a much smaller number than 600,000 men went out of Egypt in the Exodus?

11. What were the four possible places for crossing the Sea?

12. Where was Sinai?

13. How did Jethro help Moses solve the problem of overwork?

14. What are two major kinds of ancient covenants and how did the covenant between the LORD and Israel relate to them?

15. How are the Ten Commandments related to the various codes of law in the Old Testament?

16. Why is Moses called the "lawgiver"?

17. What are the characteristics of the three major Israelite law codes?

18. Put in your own words the basic intent of sacrifice as practiced in early Israel.

19. Why did Israel fail in its attempt to invade Canaan from the South (Numbers 13 and 14)?

20. Look up "Curse" in a Bible dictionary and see how it relates to the Balaam stories.

21. What two important ideas were stressed in Deuteronomy as related to the conquest of the land of Canaan?

FOR FURTHER STUDY

The Exodus

ANDERSON, BERNHARD. "Liberation from Bondage" and "Covenant in the Wilderness," chaps. 2 and 3 in *Understanding the Old Testament*, 3rd ed. Englewood Cliffs, N.J.: Prentice-Hall, 1975. A good discussion of the Exodus in the light of modern scholarship.

BEEGLE, DEWEY M. *Moses: The Servant of Yahweh.* Grand Rapids: Wm. B. Eerdmans, 1972. A thorough discussion of Moses by a responsible conservative scholar.

BUBER, MARTIN. *Moses: The Revelation and the Covenant.* New York: Harper & Row, 1958. A Jewish view of Moses' life.

CHILDS, BREVARD S. *The Book of Exodus. The Old Testament Library.* Philadelphia: Westminster, 1974. A comprehensive commentary on Exodus emphasizing its relevance for Christians.

CRAIGIE, P. C. *The Book of Deuteronomy. The New International Commentary on the Old Testament.* Grand Rapids: Wm. B. Eerdmans, 1976.

MARSH, JOHN. "The Book of Numbers: Introduction and Exegesis" in *Interpreter's Bible,* II. New York: Abingdon, 1953.

MEEK, THEOPHILE J. *Hebrew Origins*, rev. ed. New York: Harper & Row, 1950.

MICKLEM, NATHANIEL. "The Book of Leviticus: Introduction, Exegesis and Exposition" in *Interpreter's Bible*, II. New York: Abingdon, 1953.

NOTH, MARTIN. *Numbers: A Commentary.* Trans. by James D. Martin. *The Old Testament Library.* London: SCM Press, 1966.

RAD, GERHARD VON. *Deuteronomy.* Trans. by Dorthea Barton. *The Old Testament Library.* Philadelphia: Westminster, 1966. One of the best commentaries on Deuteronomy.

———. *Moses.* London: Lutterworth, 1960. A brief but valuable book on Moses.

ROWLEY, H. H. *From Joseph to Joshua.* The British Academy, 1960. A series of studies on subjects relating to the Exodus.

WRIGHT, G. ERNEST. "The Book of Deuteronomy: Introduction and Exegesis" in *Interpreter's Bible*, II. New York: Abingdon, 1953. A fine commentary on Deuteronomy.

Law, Covenant, and Worship

ALT, ALBRECHT. "The Origins of Hebrew Law." *Essays on Old Testament History and Religion.* Trans. by R. A. Wilson. Garden City: Doubleday, 1967.

BEYERLIN, WALTER. *Origins and History of the Oldest Sinaitic Traditions.* Trans. by Stanley Rudman. Oxford: Blackwell, 1965.

DE VAUX, ROLAND. *Studies in Old Testament Sacrifice.* Cardiff: University of Wales Press, 1964.

HILLERS, DELBERT. *Covenant: The History of a Biblical Idea.* Baltimore: John Hopkins, 1969.

KRAUS, HANS-JOACHIM. *Worship in Israel.* Richmond: John Knox, 1966.

MCCARTHY, DENNIS J. *Old Testament Covenant.* Richmond: John Knox, 1972. McCarthy gives a good summary of discussions on the covenant.

MENDENHALL, GEORGE. *Law and Covenant in Israel and the Ancient Near East.* Pittsburgh: Biblical Colloquium, 1955. This is a combination of his articles in *The Biblical Archaeologist*, XVII, 2 (May, 1954), 26–46 and XVII, 3 (September, 1954), 49–76. Mendenhall shows how biblical covenants are illustrated by Hittite parallels.

NEWMAN, MURRAY LEE, JR. *The People of the Covenant: A Study from Moses to the Monarchy.* New York: Abingdon, 1962.

ROWLEY, H. H. *Worship in Ancient Israel: Its Form and Meaning.* Philadelphia: Fortress, 1967.

————. *The Biblical Doctrine of Election.* London: Lutterworth, 1950.

STAMM, J. J., AND M. E. ANDREW. *The Ten Commandments in Recent Research.* Studies in Biblical Theology, 2nd ser., no. 2. Naperville, Ill. Alic R. Allenson, 1967.

TRUEBLOOD, ELTON. *Foundations for Reconstruction.* New York: Harper & Row, 1946. A good sound discussion of the meaning of the Ten Commandments.

CHAPTER FIVE

Israel Gains a Home: The Conquest

"Time stands still for no man," nor did it stand still for Israel. The older generation had passed away. A new generation, with new leadership, had arisen—and to them came a new challenge. They had come to the east bank of the Jordan River. On the other side of the narrow stream stood Canaan, occupied by talented and highly civilized groups of people. Israel was still a small group of desert wanderers, ill prepared and ill equipped by any rational standard. The odds against them were great, but the war had to be fought.

The Invasion of Canaan

PREPARATIONS FOR THE INVASION (JOSH. 1:1–2:24)

Israel's new leader was no newcomer to responsibility. As a soldier, he had proved his ability as a leader in the battle against the Amalekites (Ex. 17:8-16). As one of the twelve spies, he had already got a first-hand look at the territory to be invaded. He had come away firmly convinced that it could be conquered despite the fact that only one other of the twelve (Caleb) agreed with him (Num. 13:1-33). Assured of the LORD's presence and leadership (1:1-9), he began the preparations for the invasion.

First of all, he ordered the people who were to cross the Jordan to prepare themselves. Then, he placed them under strict orders of obedience to his authority (1:10-18). Next, he sent out two spies to Jericho to bring back information about the enemy. As a natural cover-up, they went to the house of a prostitute named Rahab. The ruse did not work because the king of Jericho sent men to Rahab's house to try to find them. She had hidden them, however, and was able to convince the king's men that they were not in her house. Since her house was built on the wall of the city, she was able to let them down by a rope on the outside of the wall. Returning to Joshua, they gave their report (2:1-24).

THE WATERS PART AGAIN (JOSH. 3:1–5:1)

There followed another of the remarkable series of timely events that Israel saw as the "wonders" of God. Several miles above Jericho stood the city of Adam, or Adamah. At this site the Jordan follows its twisting path between high clay banks. At times, the river undercuts the banks so that they fall into the river, forming a natural dam that holds it in check for several hours. When Israel needed it to happen, it did. As the biblical writer describes it:

> So, when the people set out from their tents, to pass over the Jordan with the priests bearing the ark of the covenant before the people, and when those who bore the ark had come to the Jordan, and the feet of the priests bearing the ark were dipped in the brink of the water (the Jordan overflows all its banks throughout the time of harvest), the waters coming down from above stood and rose up in a heap far off, at Adam, the city that is beside Zarethan, and those flowing down toward the sea of the Arabah, the Salt Sea, were wholly cut off; and the people passed over opposite Jericho (3:14-16).

The ark of the covenant, symbol of the LORD's presence with the Israelites, was carried to the midst of the riverbed to remind them that it was the LORD's doings that were enabling them to cross the flooded river (3:17).

The passage through the Jordan was commemorated by a pile of stones set up as a memorial to the event. They were to serve as a teaching aid so that when the children of future generations asked, "What do these stones mean?" the elders would tell them of the LORD God's deliverance of the people (4:1–5:1).

AND THE WALLS CAME TUMBLING DOWN
(JOSH. 5:13–6:27)

After crossing the Jordan, all the men and boys underwent circumcision as an act of consecration to the LORD (5:2-12). When they had recovered, preparations got underway for the attack on Jericho. In a vision Joshua saw the leader, or the commander, of the LORD's army. The purpose seems to have been to assure Joshua of divine leadership in the days ahead (5:13-15).

Jericho, the first major target of the Israelites after they crossed the Jordan, is one of the world's oldest continuously existing cities. Located just north of the Dead Sea, this well-watered oasis was settled at least as early as 7000 B.C. Much archaeological effort has been spent in excavating at Jericho, and interpretations about what has been found have changed with each new effort. As the situation now stands, there are no archaeological data to confirm or deny the fall of the city to Joshua's army. All we have to go on is the biblical material itself.

In the description of the fall of the city, there are some significant features. For one thing, the religious nature of Israelite warfare can be seen in the act of carrying the ark around the walls of the besieged city, accompanied by the raucous blaring of the ram's horn trumpets (6:1-11). In the second place, the prominent role the number 7 plays in the story indicates an important feature in Hebrew thought concerning the signifi-

Figure 5–1. "And the LORD said to Joshua, 'See, I have given into your hand Jericho'" (Joshua 6:2). Jericho, "the city of palms," as seen from the *tell* of ancient Jericho. Any evidence of Joshua's conquest has long since been destroyed.

Photograph by John H. Tullock.

cance of certain numbers, particularly 1, 3, 4, 7, 10, and 12. These numbers and their multiples by 10 and 12 had meanings other than their numerical value. Seven symbolized completeness, 10 perfection, and 12 completeness (6:12-16).

Of great significance is the fact that this was a holy war. Everything was to be destroyed as an act of dedication to God. Only the prostitute Rahab, who had helped the spies, was to be spared (6:17-25). Finally, when the city was conquered, a curse was pronounced upon it to prevent its rebuilding (6:26-27).

TROUBLE IN THE CAMP (JOSH. 7:1-26)

As harsh as the requirements of the holy war might seem, an incident involving an Israelite named Aachan would make it seem even more harsh. Strict regulations governed the disposal of the goods that were captured in the holy war. A violation of the ban on the taking of any spoils of war for personal use was punishable by the death of the offender. In the battle for Ai, a stronghold in the hill country west of Jericho, the Israelites were driven back. Unknown to Joshua, Aachan (one of his warriors) had taken certain banned objects at Jericho (7:1): a beautiful robe, a large number of silver coins, and a bar of gold. Undoubtedly, like Moses' killing of the Egyptian, the word got out that Aachan had taken the things. Such knowledge would have had a divisive effect on the army if it were known, since others probably had been tempted to take the spoils of war but had resisted the temptation. In any case, when the battle for Ai—or perhaps for Bethel as the archaeological evidence seems to suggest—was begun, Israel suffered a stinging defeat (7:2-5).

Joshua was perplexed, feeling that the LORD had let him down (7:6-9). But Joshua was made to realize that such was not the case. Instead, the word came from the LORD that someone had violated the ban against taking spoils of war (7:10-15). An investigation revealed Aachan as the culprit and, in due course, he confessed his sin (7:16-26).

What followed would seem to be unjust by our standards of justice, for the text says:

> And Joshua and all Israel took Aachan . . . and the silver and the mantle and the bar of gold, and his sons and daughters, and his oxen and asses and sheep, and his tent, and all that he had; . . . and all Israel stoned him with stones; they burned them with fire, and stoned them with stones (7:24-25).

Why did his family suffer the consequences of his sin? Because of a view that is best described by the term "corporate personality." This was the view that a person was thought of not as an individual but as part of the larger unit—the family, the tribe, or the clan. Our society emphasizes the importance of the individual. Israelite society emphasized the importance of the group. Because of this, whatever action a person took was thought to affect not only himself but the group as a whole, either positively or negatively. For this reason, his guilt had to be shared by the group of which he was a part. Furthermore, it affected not only those related to him but also whatever he possessed. The destruction of Aachan, his family, and his possessions was looked upon as the only way to clear the larger group, the people as a whole, of Aachan's sin. When the punishment was carried out, the battle was renewed and was won (8:1-29). There follows an account of building an altar on Mount Ebal in the Shechem area. It may possibly belong with Joshua 23–24, where an account of a covenant ceremony is given. It will be discussed there (8:30-35).

THOSE TRICKY GIBEONITES (JOSH. 9:1-27)

Gibeon, some 6 to 7 miles northeast of the present city of Jerusalem, was typical of the small Canaanite villages of the time. Having heard of the brutal Israelite conquest of the nearby towns, the Gibeonites decided that they would rather not have to face such a fate. They put on their most ragged clothes and worn-out sandals, took stale bread and wineskins that were brittle with age, and set out for the Israelite camp. When they arrived, they told the Israelite leaders a fanciful tale, designed to appeal to the Israelite ego, about how they had heard of the greatness of the Israelites, but more especially of the greatness of the LORD their God (9:3-10). As a result, they said they had set out to find these people who worshiped the LORD in order to make a covenant with them.

The Israelites were completely taken in by the story. Without any investigation, they made a covenant with the Gibeonites. They confirmed the covenant by a covenant meal and by taking a solemn oath. Under the terms of the covenant, the Gibeonites were to be spared and thus would become a part of Israel (9:11-15).

After the covenant was made, the truth came out. Their word having been given, the Israelites could not change the terms except to make the Gibeonites "hewers of wood and drawers of water for the congregation" in the central religious shrine (9:27). This is one of the few breaks in the idealized picture of the conquest, and it reveals an important fact—namely, that many of the people who were later counted in Israel never came from Egypt and were joined to Israel by covenant in the worship of the LORD.

THE FIVE KINGS OF THE SOUTH (JOSH. 10:1-27)

The local kings, who really were kings over small cities of a few hundred people, became alarmed over the Israelite successes. Five of them joined forces, including the kings of Jerusalem, Hebron, Eglon, Lachish, and Jarmuth (10:3). The battle took place in the valley of Aijalon. This valley was one of the few routes from the coastal plain up into the southern section of the central hill country. The attack, which probably came at dawn, was aided by a violent hailstorm that lasted up into the day. The great hailstones killed many of the enemy and caused the Israelite minstrels to sing a song about the sun standing still at Gibeon (10:1-14).

The kings were captured, and a symbolic ceremony was conducted in which the Israelite leaders placed their feet on the kings' necks. As they did, Joshua charged them to be strong. He promised that the LORD would lead them to be just as successful against all Israel's enemies if they remained faithful to him (10:15-27).

JOSHUA'S CONQUESTS (JOSH. 10:28–12:24)

The view of the conquest presented by the book of Joshua is an idealized version. As will be seen later in the book of Judges, Joshua's campaigns were not quite the smashing successes they appear to be in the Joshua accounts. In the main, success was confined to the hill country, most of the plains and coastal cities still under the control of the Canaanites. Summary statements of Joshua's accomplishments are found in 10:28-43 and 11:16–12:24. It was a war of extermination with the LORD's assistance, as explained by Joshua 11:20:

> For it was the LORD's doing to harden their hearts that they should come against Israel in battle, in order that they should be utterly destroyed, and should receive no mercy but be exterminated, as the LORD commanded Moses.

The battle against one city in particular is singled out—the battle against Hazor, the New York City of early Palestine, located some 10 miles north of the Sea of Galilee. The great mound of Hazor is the largest archaeological site in Palestine today, covering more than 200 acres. By comparison, the average size of a city mound or *tell* is 5 to 10 acres, a *tell* of 30 acres considered to be large. Archaeological work at Hazor has tended to confirm the destructive attack of the Israelites under Joshua in keeping with the biblical account.[1]

Dividing the Land and Renewing a Covenant

THE DIVIDING OF THE LAND (JOSH. 13:1–21:45)

A part of the idealized view of Joshua is a description of the tribal boundaries found in Joshua 13–21. While Joshua speaks as though the land were already conquered, these boundaries were actually as they existed much later. In effect, they represented the territory each tribe was responsible to conquer, not what they had conquered.

Of special interest are the cities assigned to the Levites (21:1-42). They had no territorial boundaries, but they were to receive cities within each of the territories, centrally located to provide (1) accessible worship centers, and (2) centers for the administration of justice, including refuge centers where an accused criminal could come until some disposition was made of his case. Otherwise, he would be at the mercy of the "avenger of blood," a member of the family against whom he had committed a crime. The avenger felt a moral obligation to punish the criminal for his crime since there was no state to carry out punishment.

THE ALTAR THAT WAS NOT AN ALTAR
(JOSH. 22:1-34)

An insight into how the early Israelites dealt with problems that arose between tribes can be seen in the story of the building of an altar by the tribes east of the Jordan. When word came back to the tribes in the west, an alarm was raised. Such an altar would seem to violate a ban on worshiping anywhere except at one central shrine, which in those days probably was Shechem or possibly Shiloh (22:12). In a tribal assembly it was decided to send Phineas, a priest, accompanied by ten tribal representatives, to investigate the situation. When they inquired of the Reubenites, Gadites, and the half tribe of Manasseh, they were told that the altar was a memorial, "a witness between us and you . . . that we do perform the service of the LORD in his presence with our burnt offerings and

---

[1]Yigael Yadin, *Hazor: The Rediscovery of a Great Citadel of the Bible* (London: Weidenfeld and Nicholson, 1975) is a fascinating study of this famous site from an archaeological standpoint.

Figure 5–2. The Division of the Land (Joshua 13:1–19:51).

sacrifices" (22:27). Satisifed about the purpose of the altar, the tribal representatives returned and the planned attack was averted (22:30-34).

JOSHUA'S FAREWELL AND A COVENANT-RENEWAL CEREMONY (JOSH. 23:1–24:28. SEE ALSO JOSH. 8:30-35 AND DEUT. 27:1-26)

A recognition that Joshua's conquest was not complete appears in Joshua's farewell address to the Israelite leaders. The LORD God had given them the land from the Jordan to the "Great Sea in the west," and he would "enable them to conquer the people who still occupied the land provided." Israel was faithful to his law as given to Moses (23:1-13). Unfaithfulness would lead to loss of life and land (23:14-16).

The climax of the book of Joshua is the covenant-renewal ceremony described in Josh. 24:1-28. The site of the ceremony was Shechem, an ancient religious center (Gen. 34) located at the head of a pass between Mount Gerizim and Mount Ebal in the central section of the hill country. Shechem is not mentioned among the cities conquered by Joshua, leading to the probability that the natives of the area were somehow related to the Israelites and that they joined Israel by a covenant in which they agreed to worship the LORD.

Deuteronomy 27:1-8 contains a command for the people to set up a memorial on Mount Ebal when they entered the land. Joshua 8:30-35 describes the fulfillment of this command and goes on to describe briefly a covenant-renewal ceremony. An altar was built, sacrifices were offered, a copy of the law was written and read to the people, and a ceremony of blessing and cursing was carried out, half of the Levites standing on Mount Gerizim and the other half standing on Mount Ebal (Josh. 8:33; but see Deut. 27:12-13 where all the tribes are mentioned with Levi counted as a secular tribe).

Shechem, then, obviously had strong traditions connecting it to the early days of Israel's history. The covenant-renewal ceremony at Shechem described in Joshua 24 has about it many of the same elements of the suzerainty (superior-inferior) treaty. The important men of Israel gathered at the sanctuary (24:1). Joshua recounted the LORD's call of the patriarchs—how he brought the people out of Egypt through the leadership of Moses and Aaron and how he brought them into the land of Canaan (24:2-13). After reminding them of the LORD's blessing, he called on them to take the obligations of the covenant. Joshua 24:14 indicates that not all the people present were descendants of those who came out of Egypt, for he spoke of those who were worshiping "the gods which your fathers served . . . beyond the river or the gods of the Amorites in whose land you dwell." This seems to be a clear reference to people of the land since those whose ancestors had been at Sinai would not be worshiping Mesopotamian deities. Furthermore, the Gibeonites were non-Israelite people who had earlier tricked Israel into making a covenant with them (9:1-27). It would seem, then, that at least four different groups of people were present: (1) the Israelites led by Joshua; (2) Israelites who had filtered into the land from Egypt separate from the Joshua-led group; (3) Semitic peoples who had never been in Egypt but who shared in the patriarchal traditions with Israel, and (4) non-Semitic peoples who joined Israel by covenant.

SUMMARY ON JOSHUA'S VERSION OF THE CONQUEST

In the strict sense, the complete story of the conquest is not told in the book of Joshua. That is not the purpose of the book. Instead, the purpose is to glorify the LORD by giving examples of the marvelous way he led the people to the land he had promised to the patriarchs. Further, the book says that any failure was a failure on the part of Israel to walk in faith with God. This is part of a theme spoken of first in Deuteronomy and which is given its clearest expression in the Book of Judges. Because of its origin in Deuteronomy it has been designated as the Deuteronomic theme.

STUDY QUESTIONS

1. How does the description of the fall of Jericho indicate the religious nature of the event?
2. How does the story of Aachan illustrate the principles of Holy War?
3. Why did the Israelites not attack the Gibeonites?
4. What does the account of a covenant renewal ceremony in Joshua 23 and 24 tell us about the makeup of the people of Israel?
5. What was the purpose of the covenant renewal ceremonies?

FOR FURTHER STUDY

BRIGHT, JOHN. "The Book of Joshua: Introduction and Exegesis" in *Interpreter's Bible,* II. New York: Abingdon, 1953.
KAUFMANN, YEHEZKEL. *The Biblical Account of the Conquest of Palestine.* Trans. by M. Dagut. Jerusalem: Magness, 1953.

Soggin, J.A. *Joshua*. Trans. by R. A. Wilson. Old Testament Library. Philadelphia: Westminster, 1972.

Wright, G. Ernest. "Fresh Evidence for the Philistine Story" in *The Biblical Archaeologist*, XXIX, 2 (May, 1966), 70–86. See also *Biblical Archaeology*, 2nd ed. Philadelphia: Westminster, 1960, pp. 69–85.

CHAPTER SIX

Israel Confused:
The Period of the Judges

"They came, they saw, they conquered" is the English translation of a famous Latin phrase. When one reads the book of Joshua, that saying would seem quite appropriate until one reads the opening verses of the book of Judges. Then the saying would have to read, "They came, they saw, and sometimes they conquered."

The International Scene

That the Israelites were able to do as well as they did was due again, in large measure, to the timing of their entry into Canaan. Canaan, later known as Palestine, had been dominated by the Egyptians for a long time, but by the time of Joshua's entry into the land, Egypt was exhausted from a war with the Hittites of Asia Minor. Like two boxers of equal strength and ability, the two contenders for control of the vital land bridge between Africa and the Asian countries fought an exhausting war. Egypt probably was the winner, but it left her weakened. This war was during the reign of Ramses II around 1285 B.C. It was about that time that the Exodus took place.

Another problem for Egypt arose in the form of an invasion by the "Sea Peoples," a people who seem to have come from the area of modern Greece. Merneptah (1224–1216 B.C.), the son of Ramses II, succeeded in driving the invaders off, but after his death the Egyptian Empire went into rapid decline. As was pointed out earlier, Merneptah mentions the Israelites in a monument for a battle fought in 1220 B.C.

The "Sea Peoples," driven out of Egypt, settled on the southern coast of Canaan and became known as the Philistines. It was from them that Canaan got the name Palestine. Israel's major problem was to fight the people of the land, since the Egyptians, the Hittites of Asia Minor, and Assyrians of the Mesopotamian region were too weak to interfere in Canaan in the twelfth century B.C.

Another Look at the Conquest

ON WITH THE CONQUEST (JUDG. 1:1–2:5)

Once the territory had been assigned to the tribes, the hard part began. The warfare was extended over many years. The boundaries described in Joshua were actually never achieved until the time of David. Judah asked the tribe of Simeon to join with it in the conquest of southern Palestine. The impression is given (1:8) that they conquered Jerusalem, but in a later account David is named as the conqueror of Jerusalem. There is also the mention of the capture of three cities of the Philistines: Gaza, Ashkelon, and Ekron. The Greek Old Testament, however, specifically says that these cities were not captured. As a whole, this section is a record of failure—the failure of the majority of the tribes to conquer the territory assigned to them. For the historian it was a failure to keep the LORD's covenant that had brought the military failure, and it would continue to haunt them as long as they were unfaithful to the covenant.

A PREVIEW OF THE BOOK (JUDG. 2:6–3:6)

After a description of the death and burial of Joshua comes a verse reminiscent of Exodus 1:8: "There arose a new king . . . who did not know Joseph." Judges 2:10 says in part, "There arose another [new] generation . . . who did not know the LORD or the work which he had done for Israel."

Following these words is a sermon: (1) "The people of Israel did what was evil in the sight of the LORD" (2:11). (2) "So the anger of the LORD was kindled against Israel, and he gave them over to plunderers, who plundered them" (2:14). (3) "The LORD was moved to pity by their groaning because of those who afflicted and oppressed them" (2:18). (4) "The LORD raised up judges, who saved them out of the power of those who plundered them" (2:16). A more concise statement of this four-point sermon can be found in Judges 3:7-11, where the story of the judge, Othniel, is given.

Two matters of major interest come from this passage. First, biblical scholars call this theme of sin-punishment-repentance-deliverance the Deuteronomic theme. It is so named because scholars believe the books beginning with Joshua and extending through 2 Kings (with the exception of Ruth) were put in their present form by Jewish historians who had been influenced by the book of Deuteronomy during the Bablylonian Exile. A major portion of Deuteronomy, with its strong emphasis upon the necessity of Israel's faithfulness to the covenant, had been found in 621 B.C. during a major repair job on the Jerusalem Temple when Josiah reigned. Its discovery had led to a strong religious revival for a time; but after Josiah's death the revival quickly died. In just a few more years, the Babylonians invaded and carried the Israelites into captivity. The historians of Israel came to the conclusion that their troubles had been caused by the failure to be faithful to the covenant; and that the whole history of the people, from the time of the entry into the land, had been marred by this same unfaithfulness to the covenant. Thus, their version of the history of Israel was interpreted in the light of their conviction that all Israel's troubles stemmed from the failure to keep the covenant.

In the second place, it is in this section of the book that the judges are first mentioned. From the description given in 2:16: "And the LORD raised up judges who saved them out of the power of those who plundered them," one can discover the major function of the judges of the book of Judges; namely, they were military leaders. They have been described as "charismatic military leaders." By this it is meant that they were persons who had about them those qualities that inspired others to follow wherever they led.

No one of them, however, was able to get all the people of Israel to follow his or her leadership. Israel was composed of twelve tribes. In the period of the judges, the tribe was more important than the nation. There was little, if any, national unity. It was not to be until the monarchy of David that tribal feelings took second place to national feeling.

Here Come the Judges

OTHNIEL (JUDG. 3:7-11)

He was a minor judge who was said to have delivered Israel from Cushan-rishathaim "the king of Mesopotamia." This king is not known from any historical record, so he must have been a minor king.

EHUD, THE LEFT-HANDED BENJAMINITE
(JUDG. 3:12-30)

The oppressor was Eglon, king of Moab. Ehud, of the tribe of Benjamin, was chosen to take the annual payment to Eglon, which kept him from attacking the Israelites. Strapping a short sword to the inside of his right thigh, Ehud sought a private conference with the king after the money had been paid. Eglon granted his wish. When they were alone, Ehud drew his sword and stabbed Eglon in the belly:

> And the hilt also went in after the blade, and the fat closed over the blade, for he did not draw the sword out of his belly; and the dirt came out (3:22).

Ehud's bold assassination of Eglon rallied the Ephraimites around him so that the Moabite oppression was ended (3:26-30).

SHAMGAR: THE MAN WITH THE GOAD (JUDG. 3:31)

The oppressors were the Philistines. Shamgar is said to have used an ox-goad, a sharpened stick used to prod the oxen as they plowed the fields, as his weapon to kill 600 Philistines.

DEBORAH AND BARAK: WOMEN'S LIBERATION IN THE TWELFTH CENTURY B.C. (JUDG. 4:1–5:31)

Many pages have been written about the low status of women in ancient times, but the story of Deborah is an indication that outstanding women had a way of making their mark. Two versions are given of Deborah's story—a later prose version that appears in Judges 4:1-24 and the original poetic version that is found in Judges 5:1-31.

The two accounts differ somewhat. The prose story speaks of Jabin, the king of Hazor, as being Israel's oppressor (4:2). According to Joshua 11, Joshua defeated a king Jabin and destroyed Hazor some years earlier. The poetic account does not name Jabin, nor does it mention Hazor. Only a Sisera, a general, is mentioned.

Deborah, described as a prophetess (4:4), was judging Israel near Bethel in the hill country of the tribe of Ephraim (4:5). She seems to have functioned as an adviser on personal matters and in settling disputes between contending parties. The oppression got so bad that

> In the days of Shamgar, son of Anath,
>   in the days of Jael, caravans ceased
>   and travelers kept to the byways.
> The peasantry ceased in Israel, they ceased
>   until you arose, Deborah,
>   arose as a mother in Israel (5:6-7).

Deborah's role was to rally the people to fight against the enemy. Barak served as her general, but he refused to go unless she went with him. She agreed, but she told him that a woman could get the glory for winning the battle (4:6-10).

The poetic version calls the roll of the tribes who joined in the battle that took place near Mount Tabor, which is located at the apex of the triangular plain of Megiddo or Esdralon. After speaking of Ephraim, Benjamin, Machir, Zebulun, and Issachar as tribes who contributed soldiers to the cause, the poet speaks of those who refused:

> Among the clans of Reuben
>   there were great searchings of heart.
> Why did you tarry by the sheepfold,
>   to hear the pipings of the flocks?
>
>   . . .
>
> Gilead stayed beyond the Jordan;
>   And Dan, why did he abide with the ships?
> Asher sat still at the coast of the sea,
>   settling down by his landings (5:15d-17).

The Canaanites, equipped with the heavy war chariots (4:3), were drawn up on the level plain, while the ill-equipped Israelites were on the slopes of Mount Tabor. A heavy storm broke! The Kishon River, usually having no more than a trickle of water, became a raging torrent. It flooded the plain and turned it into a miry swamp. The heavy iron chariots, so fearsome on solid ground, became liabilities instead of assets. The Israelites rushed down from the mountain to cut the enemy to pieces (4:13-16; 5:19-21).

When he saw how the battle tide had turned, Sisera decided to take care of the most important person he knew—himself. He fled on foot from the battlefield. After some time, he came to the tent of a Kenite named Heber. Jael, Heber's wife, was at home. When Sisera asked for refuge in her tent, Jael, true to the law of custom, invited him in and gave him refreshment. While he was eating and drinking, she killed him by

Figure 6–1. "[Deborah] summoned Barak . . . and said to him, 'The LORD . . . commands you, Go, gather your men at Mt. Tabor'" (Judges 4:6). Barak and his men rushed down from the slopes of Mt. Tabor to destroy the forces of Sisera, whose iron chariots were bogged down on the muddy plain.

Courtesy of George L. Kelm.

driving a tent peg through his skull. Like the gunfighter in a Western movie,

> He sank, he fell,
>   he lay still at her feet;
> at her feet he sank, he fell;
>   where he sank, there he fell dead (5:27).

The poetic version ends with a picture of Sisera's mother looking for him, not knowing that he was dead. The closing line is:

> So perish all thine enemies, O LORD!

GIDEON: THE MASTER OF PSYCHOLOGICAL WARFARE (JUDG. 6:1–8:35)

More stories are told about Gideon than any other judge except Samson. The oppressors were the Midianites, who were aided by the hated Amalekites and "the people of the East" (6:3). In their raids, they (like the locusts) destroyed crops, bringing famine on the land (6:1-6).

The people cried to the LORD, who reminded them through a prophet that they had been unfaithful to him (6:7-10).

Deliverance began when Gideon, a member of the tribe of Manasseh, received a divine visitor, who told him he was chosen to lead the war against the Midianites (6:11-24).

The first thing he did was to destroy his own father's altar to Baal, the chief diety of the Canaanite fertility cult. In its place, he built an altar to the LORD and made a sacrifice on it (6:25-32).

Next, he prepared to attack the Midianites. First, he sent messengers through the country, calling for volunteers to fight. Then, he asked God for a sign to show that he approved of what Gideon was doing. When the sign was positive, Gideon prepared his forces for battle (6:33-40).

Having too many volunteers, a series of tests was given by Gideon to reduce the number. Only 300 were left when the testing was over (7:1-8). These 300 men gathered in the hills surrounding the main Midianite camp, located in a valley. Gideon divided his small army into three parts, giving each soldier a torch, a pitcher to cover it with, and a ram's horn trumpet (7:9-18).

He stationed his men at strategic places, where they waited until the Midianites were asleep. When the signal was given, they raced down from the hills, waving their torches, blowing their trumpets, and yelling, "A sword for the LORD and for Gideon" (7:20). The Midianites, who were awakened from their sleep and probably thought all the Israelites in the world were attacking them, fled in terror and confusion. Gideon's men were then joined by others in pursuit of the disorganized Midianites (7:19–8:3).

As the battle ended, Gideon captured two Midianite chieftains (Zebah and Zalmunna), who had killed two of his brothers. Gideon tried to disgrace them by telling his teen-age son to kill them. This deeply offended Zebah and Zalmunna. They said to Gideon, "Rise yourself, and fall upon us, for as a man is, so is his strength." What this meant was, "Kill us yourself. A man has a right to be killed by one who is his equal." This sense of rank and honor was common in ancient societies and it is still strong in many Eastern societies today. A person feared disgrace more than he feared death (8:4-21).

Returning from the defeat of the Midianites, Gideon was so popular that the people tried to make him king. He refused; but he made a religious image, possibly to commemorate the victory, and urged the people to follow the LORD. Instead, the image he made became an idol the people worshiped. He died, shunned by the people whom he had rescued (8:22-35).

ABIMELECH: A NOBODY WHO THOUGHT HE WAS SOMEBODY (JUDG. 9:1-25)

Abimelech, Gideon's son by a slave wife from Shechem, saw an opportunity to capitalize on his father's popularity. Going to the leading men of Shechem, he proposed that they choose him from Gideon's seventy sons to be their king. Since his mother was a Shechemite, they gave him their financial support, with which he hired a group of thugs to be his personal army. The first thing he did was to have his own brothers murdered. Then he had himself proclaimed king at Shechem (9:1-6).

One brother, Jotham (who was Gideon's youngest son) escaped his murderous brother's slaughter. Climbing to the top of Mount Ebal, he shouted to the Shechemites and told them a fable, the moral of which was this: When good men fail to act, evil men will act for them with evil results. Their response to his father's leadership had been to choose the worst of his sons to rule them. The results of their foolishness would soon be known (9:7-21).

Rebellion, led by Gaal the son of Ebed, was not long in coming. He stirred up the Shechemites against Abimelech; but Abimelech's supporters in the city betrayed Ebed, causing his defeat (9:22-41). Abimelech then burned the city of Shechem, including a large number of people who had taken refuge in the Tower of Shechem (9:42-49). Abimelech's victory was short-lived, however. In his attempt to capture a tower at Thebez, a woman dropped a millstone on his head. Not wanting the disgrace of having been killed by a woman, he asked his armor bearer to kill him, which he did (9:50-57).[1]

JEPHTHAH: A MAN WHO MADE A FOOLISH VOW AND KEPT IT (JUDG. 10:6–12:7)

Two minor judges, Tola (10:1-2) and Jair (10:3-5), are mentioned before Jephthah is introduced. Israel had been unfaithful again. Gilead, a Transjordan tribe, had fallen under the heel of the Ammonites, who also crossed the Jordan to raid southern Palestine (10:6-9).

Repenting of their unfaithfulness, the people pleaded for deliverance (10:10-16), promising their support to anyone who would lead them (10:17-18). For a leader, they chose an unlikely prospect. Jephthah was the son of a harlot, cast out by his half-brothers because of his illegitimate

---

[1]For a discussion of the archaeological findings at Shechem during this period, see Cornfeld, *Archaeology*, pp. 77–79.

birth. He became an outlaw, probably raiding caravans on the King's Highway (11:1-3).

The Gileadite leaders, desperate for someone to lead them, went to Jephthah and pleaded with him to lead them. He agreed, on the condition that, if he were successful, he would be the permanent head of the tribe. In desperation, the elders agreed (11:4-11).

Jephthah began by sending a message to the king of Ammon proposing peaceful relations, which was promptly refused (11:12-28). This done, Jephthah rallied the people around him and prepared for war. Before he began the battle, he vowed that if he were successful, he would sacrifice to the LORD the first thing he saw when he returned from the battle.

He was successful. When he returned, the first thing he saw was his daughter. He kept his vow, thus giving perhaps the only clear example of a human sacrifice to the LORD found in the Old Testament (11:29-40). Such a practice was strongly denounced by the great prophets of Israel.

Not all battles were fought against non-Israelites. The Ephraimites again became jealous (as they did in the case of Gideon) because they had not shared in the glory of Jephthah's victory. They decided, therefore, to attack Jephthah and the Gileadites, but got the worst of the battle. As the fugitives from the battle tried to slip back across the Jordan, the Gileadites, who controlled the crossing places, made each person prove where he was from by giving a password. If he said "Shibboleth," he was released, for he was not an Ephraimite. If, however, he said "Sibboleth," he was seized and killed, for only those who spoke the Ephraimite dialect pronounced the Hebrew *sh* sound as an *s* (12:1-7).

SAMSON: A BRILLIANT FAILURE (JUDG. 13:1–16:31)

Three other minor judges—Ibyan (12:8-10), Ebon (12:11-12), and Hillel (12:13-15)—are mentioned before Samson is introduced. The most important thing said about any of them was the large size of their families.

The Samson stories are introduced by a familiar theme: "And the people of Israel again did what was evil in the sight of the LORD." Oppression came from the Philistines, who would be Israel's mortal enemies until David would conquer them.

The Philistines controlled the southern Palestinian coast from five strong cities: Gaza, Ashdod, Ashkelon, Ekron, and Gath. Having come to Palestine about the time of Joshua's invasion from east of the Jordan, religion aside, theirs was a much more highly developed civilization than that of the Israelites. Their pottery was a distinctive blue and white decorated ware that has been found in a number of Palestinian archaeological sites. In contrast, Israelite pottery from the same period (the early

Iron Age) was very crude and rough. More important, the Philistines possessed the secret of smelting iron, giving them weapons for war far superior to the stone and bronze weapons of the Israelites. Israel would not possess such weapons until David's time.

The pressure begun in Samson's time would mount until it would do what none of the judges had been able to do—that is, it would finally drive the stubbornly independent Israelite tribes into uniting under a single leader. Samson had the flair for the dramatic. This trait might have made him that leader; but, unfortunately, he did not possess either the will or the character to be such a leader.

The story of Samson's birth has the familiar theme of the barren wife, who, after many years, bears a son. Because of a pledge made by his mother before his birth, Samson was to be a Nazirite. The Nazirite vow required that a person (1) not cut his hair, (2) not drink wine, and (3) not touch a dead body (13:1-25).

Samson's home was in the foothill country, bordering on the Philistine territory. His mother's pledge that he would be a Nazirite did not keep him from growing up as a domineering and arrogant young man, one who was accustomed to having what he wanted. The first thing he wanted was to marry a Philistine woman, an unthinkable thing for a well-brought-up young Israelite man. But Samson knew what he wanted, and so his browbeaten parents gave in. The Israelite storyteller interpreted it as the LORD's way of getting an excuse for Samson to strike a blow at the Philistines (14:1-4).

On his way to see the girl, a young lion attacked Samson. Samson killed the lion and left the carcass by the roadside. Later, as he came back, he found a swarm of bees in the body of the lion. When the wedding festivities were taking place, Samson made a bet with the Philistine men that he could give them a riddle they could not solve. If they did within the seven-day period of the feast, he would give them thirty linen garments and thirty festal garments. The riddle was:

> Out of the eater came something to eat,
> Out of the strong came something sweet (14:14).

Unsuccessful at first, they finally threatened Samson's bride, telling her they would kill her if she did not get the answer from Samson and tell them. She tried a number of ways to get the answer. Finally, she used the ultimate weapon—tears—and Samson told her.

When the Philistines gave him the correct answer, he immediately knew that his wife had told them.

> And the Spirit of the LORD came mightily upon him, and he went down to Ashkelon and killed thirty men . . . and took their spoil and gave the festal garments to those who had told the riddle (14:19).

Note that Samson's great strength is said to be because the "Spirit of the LORD came . . . upon him," in keeping with the idea that all things were from the LORD (14:5-20).

Thus began a series of conflicts between Samson and the Philistines. His wife was given to another man, causing Samson to get his vengeance by setting the grain fields on fire by tying torches to foxes' tails and loosing them in the fields. (Today, a fox with a burning tail is the Israeli equivalent of Smokey the Bear.) Instead, the Philistines burned his ex-wife and her father to death (15:1-8).

Next, they put pressure on the men of Judah to capture Samson for them; else they would make war against Judah. Samson allowed himself to be captured, only to break the ropes that bound him once he was in the hands of the Philistines. Seizing the jawbone of an ass, he cut a deadly swath with it, leaving dead Philistines in his path (15:9-20).

Pretty women kept getting Samson in trouble. A harlot in Gaza almost caused him to be captured (16:1-3). Then came the *femme fatale* who would finally lay Samson low. Delilah was her name, a temptress from the Vale of Sorek. Completely controlled by the Philistines, she set out to lead Samson to his downfall. Some lines from the book of Proverbs describe his response:

> With much seductive speech she persuades him;
> With her smooth talk she compels him.
> All at once he follows her,
> as an ox goes to the slaughter,
> or as a stag is caught fast
> till an arrow pierces his entrails;
>
> . . .
>
> he does not know that it will cost him his life (Prov. 7:21-23).

She began a campaign to find the secret of his strength. He played along with her, giving her different, but wrong, answers each time. Each failure on her part frustrated her even more. Finally, her tears flowed and the secret was told—his strength lay in his hair (16:4-17).

All that was left was to tell the Philistines and then lull Samson to sleep so she could cut his hair (16:18-19).

The magic was gone for Samson. When he awoke, the Spirit of the LORD was no longer with him. He had abused the power, and he had lost it. He was blinded and put to doing menial work in a prison (16:20-22).

Finally, Samson died. When he was brought out to entertain Philistine notables in the shrine of the Philistine god Dagon, his strength returned long enough for him to pull down the temple on himself and the worshipers (15:23-31).

There Was No King in Israel: Three Stories

MICAH AND THE LEVITE (JUDG. 17:1-13)

The final chapters of Judges illustrate the troubled and confused times preceding the establishment of the monarchy. Religious confusion is illustrated in the story of a man named Micah, who confessed to his mother that he had stolen 1100 silver coins from her. When he confessed to her, she gave the coins to him. He, in turn, made an idol to worship (17:1-6). A traveling Levite passed through and Micah hired him to be his priest, on the assumption that a Levite could make his worship of the LORD legitimate (17:7-13).

THE MOVE OF THE TRIBE OF DAN (JUDG. 18:1-31)

The pressure exerted by the Philistines is illustrated by Judges 18. The tribe of Dan had been assigned a territory lying between Judah and the coast of central Palestine. This put them in a nutcracker between Judah and Ephraim, Israel's two most powerful tribes, and the dreaded Philistines. They sent out spies to locate a new place to settle. Eventually, they came to a place in northern Palestine, where the sources of the Jordan River arose at the base of Mount Hermon. On their return, they also discovered Micah, his Levite, and his idol. When the tribe moved northward, they took Micah's idol and his priest and set up a shrine in their new territory that they captured (18:1-31).

THE LEVITE AND THE SIN OF BENJAMIN
(JUDG. 19:1–21:25)

A strange but fascinating story closes the book of Judges. A Levite living in Ephraim had to go to Bethlehem in Judah to bring his slave wife back after she ran away to her father's home (19:1-9). On the way back, they thought of stopping at Jebus (Jerusalem) for the night, but decided against it since it was not an Israelite city. Instead, they went on to Gibeah, a Benjaminite city near Jerusalem. They were invited into the home of an elderly Ephraimite who lived in Gibeah after no Benjaminite had extended hospitality to them (19:10-21).

During the night, some local men demanded that their host give up the Levite so they could make a homosexual attack upon him. This was a *nabalah*, the most vile crime imaginable (19:23). When they threatened violence, the Levite finally gave them his slave wife, whom they raped repeatedly. The next morning her dead body was found at the door (19:22-26).

Taking her body home, he cut it into twelve pieces and sent one to each tribe (19:27-30). This seems to have been a signal whereby an emergency meeting of all the tribes was called. Saul, in later years, cut up a team of oxen to call the people to war against the Ammonites (1 Sam. 11:7).

The tribal leaders, along with their soldiers, assembled at Mizpah. The Levite told what had happened. A decision was made to attack Gibeah to punish its people for allowing such a crime to happen there (20:1-11). First, however, they gave the tribe of Benjamin (in whose territory Gibeah was located) a chance to surrender the men who had committed the crime. Instead, the Benjaminites took up arms against the other tribes in defense of Gibeah (20:12-17).

At first, the tide of battle favored Benjamin (20:18-28). Finally, however, they were soundly defeated and their towns were burned to the ground (20:29-48).

The victory turned to ashes when the other tribes realized that they had practically wiped out one of the twelve tribes. Another meeting was called to assemble at Bethel to deal with the situation. What was needed was wives for the surviving Benjaminite men so they could raise families. Yet, a vow had been taken that none of the other tribes would permit their women to marry a Benjaminite.

What could be done? Two solutions were proposed and carried out. First, the city of Jabesh-Gilead in Transjordan had not supported the war against Benjamin. Because of this, the city was attacked and 400 young girls were taken and given to the Benjaminites for wives (21:1-15).

But that was still not enough. Another solution was proposed. Each year at Shiloh there was a dance for the grape harvest. The men who needed wives were told to go hide in the vineyards, so that when the young girls came dancing through the vineyard, each man could grab a girl and run. This solved the problem, and Benjamin survived as a tribe in Israel (21:16-24).

SUMMARY OF THE BOOK OF JUDGES

The book of Judges is summarized quite well by its final verse:

In those days there was no king in Israel; every man did what was right in his own eyes (21:25).

The final chapters illustrate that theme, but they also say some important things about the times and the ways by which the tribes functioned in emergencies. It was a time of developing crisis as the Philistines began to exert more pressure on the Israelite territories. The Israelites were poorly organized and really were not prepared to respond to the Philistine threat.

Yet, as the story of the Levite and his concubine show, there was a kind of organization among the tribes. Scholars have used the term "amphictyony," a term used to describe a league of tribes in ancient Greece, to describe it. This tribal league seems to have been presided over by a priest who served at a central religious shrine and who called the tribes together for two purposes: (1) for major religious ceremonies, such as the covenant renewal ceremony (Josh. 24); and (2) when a situation arose that demanded the military power of all the tribes. In this latter sense, the chief official at the shrine functioned like one of the judges, because war was a matter for religion also. The opening chapters of 1 Samuel show two such priest-judges in action—Eli and Samuel.

STUDY QUESTIONS

1. Who were the "Sea Peoples" and how were they to affect the history of Israel?
2. Why does Judges 1 give us a different view of how extensive the conquest was from that of the book of Joshua?
3. What is the Deuteronomic theme and why is it so named?
4. What is meant when one says the judges were "charismatic leaders"?
5. What role did women play in the defeat of the army of Sisera?
6. How did Gideon use psychology to defeat the Midianites?
7. What was the meaning of Jotham's fable (Judges 9:7-15)?
8. How do you interpret Jephthah's vow that resulted in his sacrifice of his daughter in light of Genesis 22?
9. How was Samson an example of talent wasted?
10. What was the amphictyony and what sort of event could call it into action?
11. What could cause the twelve tribes to be called together by the priest-judge who presided over Israel's central religious shrine?

FOR FURTHER STUDY

ALBRIGHT, W. F. *Yahweh and the Gods of Canaan.* Garden City, N.Y.: Doubleday, 1969. This is in the Anchor paperback series.
———. *Archaeology and the Religion of Israel,* 2nd ed. Baltimore: Johns

Hopkins, 1946. Also in a Doubleday Anchor paperback, 1969. See chapter 4.

DAGLISH, EDWARD R. "Judges" in *Broadman Bible Commentary,* II. Nashville: Broadman, 1970.

MCKENZIE, JOHN L. *The World of the Judges.* Englewood Cliffs, N.J.: Prentice-Hall, 1966.

RUST, ERIC C. *Judges, Ruth, and Samuel.* Richmond: John Knox, 1961.

WRIGHT, G. ERNEST. *The Old Testament Against Its Environment.* Studies in Biblical Theology, no. 2. Naperville, Ill.: Alic R. Allenson, 1950.

In addition to the above, see the *Macmillan Bible Atlas,* pp. 46–57 on the military aspects of this period.

CHAPTER SEVEN

Israel Gains a King:
The United Monarchy

CH. 6

Samuel: The Judge Who Appointed Kings

Things looked dark for Israel. Although there was no threat from Egypt, Mesopotamia, or Asia Minor, there was a more immediate threat right on her doorstep. The Philistines were increasingly warlike and in a mood to expand their holdings in Palestine. The Israelites controlled all the land near them, and they could only increase their territory at the expense of Israel. Since the Israelites had to fight the Philistines, they did not have time either to ignore each other or to fight each other. To survive, they had to unite. To unite, there had to be leadership. That leadership came from a man who was to dominate Israelite life for many years—as a priest and as a chief judge of Israel, as a prophet and as a wise counselor, as a maker of kings and as a breaker of kings. His name was Samuel.

A WORD ABOUT THE SOURCES

Like all writers, the Deuteronomic historians had sources (1 and 2 Samuel and 1 and 2 Kings were the final product of a long process of history writing). This can be seen by the fact that 2 Kings 25:27-30 tells of the release of King Jehoiachin from a Babylonian prison in 560 B.C. Since Samuel lived in the mid–eleventh century B.C. (1050 B.C.), this must mean that the history went through a long process of writing before the final version was finished sometime after 560 B.C.

Some of the sources used can be determined by reading the materials. One such source has been called the Court History of David, found in 2 Samuel 9–20 and 1 Kings 1 and 2. It obviously was written by someone close to David's court. As such, it gives us a picture of David unique among descriptions of the reigns of ancient kings. It is part of a larger block of material referred to by scholars as the Early Source—a source that believed the kingship was good for Israel. Another, or Late Source, that came from a time after David and Solomon when the kings had become Oriental despots, gives a negative view of the monarchy. Including conflicting viewpoints like this undoubtedly reflects the true state of affairs concerning the monarchy—that is, from the very beginning there were those individuals who saw the monarchy as the means of salvation for Israel, while others had the equally strong view that it could only lead to ruin for the people.

There is another version of the history found in 1 and 2 Samuel and 1 and 2 Kings. This version is found in 1 and 2 Chronicles, a history of Israel written some time after the Babylonian Exile. Many passages in Chronicles are lifted word for word from the Samuel-Kings history; yet, there are important differences. David's weaknesses are glossed over in the Chronicles, as are the weaknesses of other Judean kings such as Manasseh. Much attention is given to genealogies and to the activities of the priests and of other Temple officials. There is also a difference in theological viewpoint. Whereas 2 Samuel 24:1 says the LORD moved David to number the people, 1 Chronicles 21:1 says "Satan" caused David to number them. Even with these differences, 1 and 2 Chronicles preserves valuable supplemental information about Israel's history.

SAMUEL: HIS BIRTH AND DEDICATION
(1 SAM. 1:1–2:10)

Hannah, the favorite wife of Elkanah (an Ephraimite), bore one of the heaviest burdens an Israelite woman could bear—she was childless. Peninah, the other wife, was fruitful and lorded her success in childbearing over Hannah. It was a bitter pill for Hannah to swallow (1:1-8).

On an annual trip to Shiloh for one of the major festivals, Hannah was so distressed and earnest in prayer to the LORD that Eli, the head of the shrine, thought that she was drunk and started to scold her for her supposed drunkenness. Hannah explained the cause of her distress and left with the assurance from Eli that her prayer would be answered (1:9-18).

Eli must have known something, because soon Hannah was pregnant.

In due time, the promised son was born. Hannah did not go to the festival again until Samuel was able to eat solid foods. Then, she took him, offered a sacrifice, and dedicated him to serve the LORD at the Shiloh shrine (1:19-28). As a part of the description of that service, there is a beautiful psalm of thanksgiving called the Song of Hannah. Later, parts of this poem were quoted in the Song of Mary in Luke 1:46-55 (2:1-10), in which Mary expresses her joy at the promise of the birth of Jesus.

SAMUEL: HIS TRAINING AND CALL TO SERVICE (1 SAM. 2:11–4:1)

Samuel was left with Eli, who was to train him for the priesthood (2:11). Unfortunately, Eli's sons, who served as priests at the shrine, were poor examples. The Hebrew text calls them "sons of Belial," which was a term of cursing and condemnation (2:12). They were greedy and irreverent (2:13-17). They used the women who served at the shrine for their own sexual pleasure (2:22). Because of this situation, a prophet (a man of God) came to Eli and told him that his family would lose the privilege of serving at the shrine because his sons had abused their office as priests and leaders (2:22-36). Despite the bad examples before him, Samuel grew "both in stature and in favor with God and man" (2:26).

The corruption at the Shiloh shrine was a symptom of the times. "The word of the LORD was rare in those days; there was no frequent vision" (3:1). The Deuteronomic historian sees the lack of moral integrity in the family of the Israelites' most important leader as contributing to a state of religious apathy throughout the country so that few were in spiritual condition to receive a revelation from God.

Then came Samuel's call from the LORD. He was still a young boy when he heard the LORD speak to him in the night. Thinking Eli was calling him, Samuel awakened the old man to ask what he wanted. Eli told him that he had not called. Samuel heard the voice once again, and once more went to Eli with the same result. The third time, Eli told him that the LORD must have been calling. Then Samuel answered and was told that he would replace Eli. Furthermore, Eli's family would meet with disaster (3:2-14).

When Samuel arose in the morning, he tried to avoid telling Eli what had happened. When Eli insisted on being told, however, Samuel related his vision to Eli. Gradually, the word spread that Samuel was a prophet in Israel (3:15–4:1a). As a prophet, he was looked upon as one who had direct access to God and who acted as his earthly spokesman. For this reason, the prophets introduced their messages, not with "I say," but, "Thus says the LORD." A fuller discussion of prophets and prophecy will come later.

The Beginning of the Philistine Wars

THE BATTLE FOR EBENEZER (1 SAM. 4:1-22)

Israel's internal confusion, coupled with the increasing Philistine strength, finally led to a full-scale attack by the Philistines. The Philistine army massed at Aphek, where the great international trade road was forced inland by the swamps caused by the slow-flowing Yarkon River. At Aphek, the hill country was only a short distance away. The Israelites were camped at Ebenezer in the edge of the hills.

Figure 7–1. "[The Israelites] encamped at Ebenezer, and the Philistines encamped at Aphek" (1 Sam. 4:1). Aphek was a strategic point on the great coastal highway. The remains of a sixteenth century Turkish fort now occupy much of the site.

Courtesy of George L. Kelm.

The Philistine war plan obviously was to cut the country in half by driving through the mountains to the Jordan. The prospects looked bleak for Israel, because the Philistines had iron weapons that were far superior to anything the Israelites had.

The first day's battle ended with heavy losses for Israel. In desperation they decided to invoke the memories of the holy war by carrying the ark of the covenant before them into battle the next day. But even the ark of the covenant could not save them since the holy object was carried by Eli's two unholy sons, Hophni and Phineas (4:1-5).

The result was a disaster for Israel. The Philistines were inspired to fight harder. Not only did they defeat the Israelites, but they killed Hophni and Phineas and captured the ark (4:6-11). Furthermore, when a messenger took the word to Eli, the shock was so great that it killed him (4:12-18). Last of all, the wife of Phineas died as she gave birth to a son. Before she died, she gave him the name "Ichabod," symbolic of the disastrous day. The child's name meant, "The glory (presence of God) has departed" (4:19-22).

THAT TROUBLESOME ARK (1 SAM. 5:1–6:21)

The Philistines carried the ark, symbol of the presence of Israel's God, home in triumph. Before long, however, they wished they had never seen it. First, they put it in the temple of their chief deity, Dagon, as a symbol of Dagon's superiority to the Israelite God. The next morning Dagon's image was lying on the floor, face downward (5:1-5).

Next, a plague struck Ashdod. People began to have skin tumors. The people at Ashdod decided the people at Gath had a right to keep the battle prize for a while, so they sent the ark there. They, too, broke out in sores. They decided that the people at Ekron surely would want to see the famous ark. The disaster was repeated (5:6-12). Panic mounted in the Philistine towns.

The result was a decision that the ark was bad luck and that the only thing to do was to send it back home where it belonged. Since no one volunteered to carry it back home, they decided upon a plan. They hitched two cows to a cart, placed the ark on the cart, put an offering of gold with the ark to appease the Israelite God, and turned the cows loose, heading them toward Beth-Shemesh in Israelite territory (6:1-13).

When the ark was found by the Israelites, the cart was broken up and the cattle were sacrificed. However, a number of Israelites died, perhaps because the holy ark was not handled properly. Ancient peoples feared holy things so much so that such a fear could actually cause death.

A similar thing happens today among those people who believe in voodoo, macumba, or similar rites of black magic (6:14-20).

While the text is silent about the matter, Shiloh must have fallen while the ark was held by the Philistines. It was taken to a private home in Kiriath-jearim after being returned to the Israelites (6:21–7:2). It was to remain there until David became king and had it moved to Jerusalem (2 Sam. 6:2; see also 1 Chron. 15:1-29).

The Roles Samuel Played

It is difficult to realize the importance of Samuel for the history of Israel. Just as the plagues, the crossing of the sea, the stopping of the Jordan, and the great storm that brought victory to the forces of Deborah and Barak were evidence of the LORD's action in natural events which convinced Israel of his providential care for them, so Samuel must rank with Abraham, Moses, and David as a leader who was provided at a time when Israel was in great need. He was a man who played many roles on the stage of Israel's history.

SAMUEL, THE JUDGE (1 SAM. 7:3-17)

Samuel was a judge with a difference. He was, first of all, a spiritual leader who reminded the people of their obligation to live by the covenant (7:3-4). Furthermore, he did not lack leadership ability in military matters since he was able to hold the Philistines in check much of his career (7:5-14). But, he was more than a military man. He was a judge in the present sense of that term—one who administered justice. He single-handedly functioned as Israel's supreme court, going on a circuit in four major cities in the hill country—Bethel, Gilgal, Mizpah, and Ramah (7:15-17).

SAMUEL, THE PROPHET (1 SAM. 8:1–9:14)

The picture of Samuel given in 8:1-22 is in keeping with the sense of responsibility of Israel's great prophets. Theirs was the job of speaking God's message to the people, warning them of the consequences of their decisions and of the responsibilities that came when decisions were made. Chapter 8 also reflects the strong resistance that existed in Israel to the idea of having a king to rule the people. Such a feeling continued long after the monarchy was established. In some ways, certain of the great prophets reflected the anti-kingship feeling with their condemnation of the ruling monarch.[1] Thus, 1 Samuel 8:4-22 has Samuel telling the people of the dangers they would face if they had a king. The people did not listen, but they insisted that a king be chosen for them. Finally, the LORD and Samuel gave in (8:22).

It was in his role as prophet that Samuel first met Saul, the son of Kish. Like the hero in a romantic movie, Saul was tall, dark, and handsome:

> There was not a man among the people of Israel more handsome than he; from his shoulders upward he was taller than any of the people (9:2).

Saul was sent out by his father to find some donkeys that had strayed away. After searching for some time without success, Saul (at his servant's suggestion) went to consult the famous prophet Samuel at his home in Ramah.

Samuel seemingly had what is called "second sight" or powers of clairvoyance. As such, he was called "the seer" (9:9), a term used to describe many of the early prophets who functioned more as fortune-tellers than they did as spokesmen on the moral issues of the time. As a prophet, Samuel seemed to function in both roles: (1) as a moral spokes-man, and (2) as a clairvoyant who could help find lost objects. It was, then, as a clairvoyant that Samuel first met Saul (9:3-14).

SAMUEL, THE KING-MAKER (1 SAM. 9:15–10:27)

Saul was so impressive on first sight that Samuel was convinced that he was the LORD's choice to be the king. Saul's journey to find his father's donkeys, then, brought a rather shocking result. Samuel told him that the donkeys were already at home. Then, he invited Saul to a banquet at the shrine. When Saul arrived, thirty persons were present. He, an obscure young man from one of Israel's smallest and weakest tribes, was given the seat of honor and was served the choicest portion of the meat (9:15-24).

Undoubtedly, Saul was mystified by all this. But the greatest surprise was yet to come. After spending the night in Ramah as Samuel's guest, Saul prepared to return home. Samuel, going with him to the outskirts of the city, asked Saul to send his servant on ahead so the two of them could be alone. When the servant had gone, Samuel took a vial of olive oil, poured it on Saul's head, and told him he was to be Israel's first king (9:25–10:1).

---

[1]See Jeremiah 22:10-30, also Amos 6:1-14, where criticism is directed to all the ruling class.

THE MEANING OF ANOINTING

Samuel's act of anointing Saul marked the king as God's man. It was an act separate and apart from the actual installation of the king, especially in the early monarchy. Saul was not crowned as king for a week after he was anointed (10:8). David, who succeeded Saul, was anointed by Samuel several years before he actually became king. In later times, anointing was probably a part of the coronation of the king; or, at most, it came only a short time before.

Later, when Israel had no king, the terms "to anoint" and "the anointed one" took on new meaning. Israel looked back at its days of glory. David, her greatest king, became the example for the kind of king Israel wanted in a future time of glory, which she believed the LORD would bring. Because of that hope the term *meshiach,* "the anointed one," was chosen to speak of the hoped-for king. When *meshiach* was put into Greek letters, it became *Messias,* which, in turn, became "Messiah" in English. Furthermore, when *meshiach* was translated into Greek by Christian writers, it became *Christos,* which becomes "Christ" in English. Thus, the title "the Christ," which was applied to Jesus of Nazareth by early Christians, means "God's Chosen One," or "God's Anointed One."[2]

After Samuel had anointed Saul, he told him to return home for seven days. On the way, certain signs would be given to him that he was the LORD's choice as king. One of them was that he would meet a group of ecstatic prophets. When he did, he would be overwhelmed by the "Spirit of the LORD," which would cause him to prophesy with them. These prophets represented another kind of prophet—those who went about in groups and whose prophesying was accompanied by various expressions of extreme emotionalism, such as trances, mass hysteria, and emotional frenzy (10:2-8).

When things came to pass as Samuel had said, it resulted in some people ridiculing Saul. The question, "Is Saul also among the prophets?" (10:11) was asked in a mocking tone rather than a tone of approval (10:9-13). When his uncle asked him where he had been, Saul told about the visit to Samuel; but he said nothing about being anointed as king (10:14-16). This basic shyness would be a major problem for Saul throughout his life.

Even when Samuel called the tribal league together at Mizpah to select a king, Saul showed the same kind of shyness. When he was finally chosen and certified by Samuel as the LORD's choice, the people had to search for him because he was hiding among the baggage. This shyness

[2]One of the earliest uses of this title was to refer to King Cyrus of Persia. Isa. 45:1 (LXX).

almost certainly caused many to be slow to follow Saul. Others, however, gave their wholehearted support to him (10:17-27).

Saul: The Last Judge and the First King, 1020–1000 B.C.(?)[3]

SAUL BECOMES A HERO (1 SAM. 11:1-15)

Saul made no move to exert his authority as king, even though he had been crowned in a public ceremony. Instead, he went on leading the life of an Israelite farmer until circumstances forced him to take action. Jabesh-gilead, a town located just east of the Jordan River and about 25 miles south of the Lake of Chinnereth (Sea of Galilee), came under attack by the Ammonites. To avoid wholesale slaughter by the superior Ammonite forces, the men of Jabesh-gilead asked for peace. The Ammonites agreed, but only on the condition that they could gouge out the right eyes of all the men of the town. After asking for seven days to consider the proposition, the elders managed to get the men out of the city, who went to Gibeah where Saul lived to ask for his help (11:1-4).

On hearing the request, Saul reacted strongly for "the spirit of God came mightily upon Saul" (11:6). Taking the team of oxen with which he had been plowing, he killed them and cut them into twelve parts and sent one piece to the leaders of each of the twelve tribes. That, of course, was the signal to mobilize for war. Men responded quickly to his call, especially from the tribe of Judah (11:8). Dividing his forces into three groups, he attacked the Ammonites early in the morning and routed them. Saul's successful troops, inspired by his leadership, were ready to turn their wrath upon those Israelites who had refused to support Saul, but he would not let them do so. Saul was confirmed as king in a service of celebration at Gilgal (11:5-15).

SAMUEL ACCOUNTS FOR HIS MINISTRY (1 SAM. 12:1-25)

This version of Samuel's farewell address contains familiar themes. First, the sense of honor and honesty characteristic of the themes of Israel's great prophets can be seen in Samuel's demand for the people to

---

[3]This date, as well as the dates of David and Solomon, is approximate and may vary as much as ten years in the different chronologies. Later dates are more accurate. The chronology followed in this text is that followed by Bernhard W. Anderson, *Understanding the Old Testament*, (Englewood Cliffs: Prentice Hall, Inc., 1975), pp. 601–606.

testify against him if they knew of any act of fraud or dishonesty he had committed (12:1-5).

A second theme that appears throughout the Old Testament is a recounting of the wonderful works the LORD had done on Israel's behalf in the Exodus and Conquest; in the exploits of the judges (note that Samuel is mentioned and in the past tense [12:11], which suggests the influence of a later hand); and Saul's victory over the Ammonites (12:6-12). The later qualms about the kingship are reflected in the warning that no king could lead them to be successful if they were not faithful to the LORD (12:13-17).

A thunderstorm added emphasis to Samuel's warning and gave occasion to repeat the warning that "righteousness brings blessing—sin brings punishment" (12:18-25).

THE NATURE OF SAUL'S KINGSHIP

Saul was not a king in the usual sense of the word. He might best be described as a charismatic judge, who, because of circumstances, was able to gain the majority support of the people. Part of that support grew out of the fact that Saul was an impressive man physically; and obviously he had certain personality traits, which, on first impression, caused people to follow him. He remained a man of the people who never "got the big head." His residence, the remains of which has been uncovered at Gibeah (Tell en-Nashbeh), was not elaborate. Instead, it was a rough stone fortress designed not for luxury but as a stronghold for defense against an enemy attack.

The fear of an enemy attack, coming from the Philistines, was the second major element in Saul's support. Israel faced the real possibility of being destroyed by the Philistines unless they united and, at that moment, Saul offered the best hope for rescue from the Philistine danger.

But even more important than Saul's own abilities and the Philistine threat was the influence of Samuel. He was old, but he was still a powerful man. His influence had been enough to put an obscure Benjaminite on the throne of Israel. As time would show, the withdrawal of his support would be a devastating blow to Saul, virtually destroying him as a leader.

THE LENGTH OF SAUL'S REIGN (1 SAM. 13:1)

The length of Saul's reign is uncertain since a number is missing in the Hebrew text, which simply says, "he reigned . . . and two years" (13:1). Most scholars would say he ruled about 22 years.[4] If one takes the biblical

---

[4]See the chronological chart in this text, pp. 422–426.

evidence, 12 years might be more logical. The ark was captured by the Philistines some time before Saul began to reign. According to 1 Samuel 7:2, it was kept in Kiriath-jearim "some twenty years." It was taken to Jerusalem in the early part of David's reign (2 Sam. 6:1-15), but David reigned for over 7 years at Hebron before Jerusalem was captured (2 Sam. 5:5). If this 20 years is to be taken literally or even as meaning around 20 years, it would seem to limit Saul's reign to no more than 12 years.

SAUL'S EARLY SUCCESSES AGAINST THE PHILISTINES (1 SAM. 13:2-4)

Saul gained more support through some early victories over the Philistines. Much of his success came from the courage and skilled leadership of his son Jonathan, who led the army to victory at Geba (located about 5 miles northeast of Gibeah). The reference to the battle for Geba shows how the Philistines had penetrated the central hill country as part of their strategy to cut the country in two (13:2-4).

SAUL'S MISTAKE AT GILGAL (1 SAM. 13:5-15a)

Samuel's support of Saul began to change rather quickly. Like the elderly person who insists that someone should take his place and then resents it when someone does, Samuel had made his farewell speech; but he was not about to give up all his power. He insisted, as chief religious official of the kingdom, that no battle should take place without the proper religious ceremonies.

Things came to a head when Saul gathered his army at Gilgal for an attack on the Philistines. He was impatient to get started. But, although he waited seven days for Samuel to come, Samuel did not appear. Saul decided to take matters into his own hands. He offered the burnt offering himself only to have Samuel appear just as he finished (13:5-10).

When Samuel asked Saul why he had not waited, Saul said that the people were getting impatient. Samuel rebuked him and told him that he had disobeyed God. As a result, his kingdom would not continue (13:11-15a).

JONATHAN'S HEROICS AT MICHMASH (1 SAM. 13:15b-14:15)

Saul had only 600 soldiers at Gilgal (near Jericho) to face the large Philistine force encamped at Michmash, which was about 10 to 12 miles west. The problem was compounded by the fact that there were only two iron swords in the Israelite army, and they belonged to Saul and Jonathan (13:22). The narrator makes the problem more vivid by telling how any Israelite who had an iron tool or weapon had to take it to the Philistines to have it sharpened. Imagine what would happen if an Israelite went to the Philistines and said, "I want to start a war with you tomorrow. Would you sharpen my sword?" (13:15*b*-23).

Courage and ingenuity saved the day for Israel. Jonathan and his armor-bearer crept up to the Philistine camp and then stood up and called to the Philistines to get their attention. They had already agreed that if the Philistines challenged them to come up to fight it would be a sign that the LORD would give them victory. Seemingly, they fought the Philistines in a narrow pass so that they would only have to fight a few at a time. Jonathan would knock them down, and his servant would finish them off. The Philistines were so demoralized by Jonathan's success that they fled in fear. An earth tremor added to the Philistine panic (14:1-15).

SAUL BLUNDERS AGAIN (1 SAM. 14:16-46)

Word got back to the camp about the uproar Jonathan was causing among the Philistines. Saul started to consult the priest, but so many of his men were rushing to join the battle that he went on without the religious service. Before he did, however, he gave an order that no one was to eat anything until the Philistines were defeated. To do so would bring death by execution (14:16-24).

Jonathan, unaware of the order, came upon some honey in a forest. After he had eaten some of it, one of the men following him told him what Saul had sworn. Jonathan openly criticized his father for taking a foolish oath since the people were weak with exhaustion. As a result of their hunger, when the battle was over they seized cattle and killed them, eating blood with the meat (14:25-32). This was a violation of an ancient prohibition among the Israelites. Leviticus 17:14 clearly expresses this prohibition:

> For the life of every creature is the blood of it; therefore I have said to the people of Israel, You shall not eat the blood of any creature, for the life of every creature is its blood; whoever eats it shall be cut off.

This principle led to the development in Israel, and later Judaism, of strict rules about how animals were to be killed. Such rules are still observed by Orthodox Jews today.

Saul ordered the people to stop what they were doing. He took it upon himself to make an altar to offer a sacrifice for them. He also saw that they were properly fed (14:33-35).

Afterward, Saul wanted to continue the battle on into the night, but the priest suggested that he ask for a sign from God. When no sign was forthcoming, Saul took it to mean that someone had violated the oath. To find the culprit, he consulted the Urim and Thummin, which were probably two marked stones thrown to get yes and no answers to questions. In our day, this would be considered a game of chance; but it was not thought to be such in Saul's time. The LORD controlled how the holy stones fell, and in this manner, his will was revealed. The first question was, "Did some of the people violate the oath?" The Urim and Thummin said no. When the question related to Saul and Jonathan, the answer pointed to Jonathan (14:36-42).

Saul, determined to kill Jonathan, was overruled by the people. Jonathan was a hero to them, and it was unthinkable that he should be killed. Either an animal was sacrificed in his place, or perhaps someone volunteered to die in his place. Either way, Saul lost the people's confidence by his bad judgment (14:43-46).

SAUL DISOBEYS SAMUEL AGAIN (1 SAM. 15:1-35)

After a summary statement about Saul's military activities (14:47-52), the story of Saul's final break with Samuel is told. Samuel brought an oracle from the LORD telling Saul to wage a holy war against the Amalekites. He was to:

> utterly destroy all that they have; do not spare them, but kill both man and woman, infant and suckling, ox and sheep, camel and ass (15:3).

The Amalekites (who lived in the Negev and the upper Sinai) had attacked the Israelites when they came out of Egypt. As a result, there seems to have been a long-standing hatred between the two groups. On the other hand, the Kenites (who had been friendly to Israel and who lived in the same territory) were given warning of the attack so they could move out of the area (15:1-6).

When the attack took place, Saul did not keep all the holy war provisions. For one thing, he did not kill Agag, the king of the Amalekites. Nor did he destroy their herds. Instead, he took them as the spoils of war (15:7-9).

When Samuel found out about Saul's disobedience, he rebuked Saul. Saul's excuse was that he had taken only the best of the animals for a sacrifice to the LORD. Saul's motive may have been to win the favor of his soldiers, whose faith in him was badly shaken. Sacrifices other than the whole burnt offering allowed the offerers the rare chance to eat all the meat they wanted. Sacrifice days were literally feast days, and they were looked forward to with great anticipation by the average man. Samuel's rebuke, however, was based on the principle that Israel was to live in total commitment to the LORD, including the carrying out of the holy war (15:10-20).

Saul tried to excuse himself by saying that the people had taken the animals to offer a sacrifice. Samuel's reply was perhaps the best-remembered statement in the Saul stories:

> Has the LORD as great delight in burnt offerings and sacrifices,
>   as in obeying the voice of the LORD?
> Behold, to obey is better than sacrifice,
>   and to hearken than the fat of rams (15:22).

This questioning of the meaning of sacrifice without the proper attitude was to be repeated with even stronger emphasis by Israel's great prophets. Some would even go so far as to question the need for sacrifice[5] (15:21-23).

With this final act of rebellion, Samuel withdrew his support from Saul. Furthermore, he refused to see him again, although it is said that he "grieved for Saul" (15:35). Saul might be likened to a son whose father wanted him to be strong and independent. When he strove to make his own decisions and to show his independence—in the eyes of one father, at least—he always made a mess of whatever he did. Because his father was always looking over his shoulder, both he and the father ended up wondering what went wrong (15:24-35).

Saul and David

THE ANOINTING OF DAVID (1 SAM. 16:1-13)

Samuel's work was not done. Having told Saul that his rule would be the end of his family's kingship over Israel, he set out to find the LORD's next choice to be king.

This time he went to Bethlehem in Judah to find the future king. He was led to the family of Jesse, a sheepherder. Here, Samuel called for Jesse to parade all his sons before him so he could select the one the LORD had chosen. Several young men appeared before him, but he did not feel that any of them was the correct choice. He asked if there were others and was told that only the youngest, who was watching the sheep, was missing. When David was brought, Samuel knew he was right and proceeded to anoint him (16:1-13).

[5]Isaiah 1:12-17.

SAUL AND DAVID MEET (1 SAM. 16:14-23)

The damage to Saul's ego inflicted when Samuel withdrew his support was too much for his weak personality. He was thrown into deep depression, caused by "an evil spirit from the LORD." His servants thought that music might help him, and they suggested that someone be found to play on the harp. David's reputation as a musician had reached Saul's court, with the result that David was brought in to play for Saul (16:14-23).

DAVID AND GOLIATH (1 SAM. 17:1-58)

The story of David and Goliath is well known, but it has problems. One of the chief ones is that 2 Samuel 21:19 says:

> Elhanan, the son of Jaareoregim, the Bethlehemite, slew Goliath the Gittite, the shaft of whose spear was like a weaver's beam.

The passage in which this verse appears (2 Sam. 21:18-22), however, may suggest a possible solution since it speaks of four giant Philistine soldiers. Thus, the most logical solution is that both Elhanan and David slew giants, but that the name of one of them has been lost from the Samuel tradition. Furthermore, I Chronicles 20:5 says that Elhanan slew "Lahmi the brother of Goliath the Gittite."

Another problem seen by scholars is that 17:55-58 seems to suggest that Saul did not know David. One explanation given is that the story of David's playing for Saul is based on a different tradition from that of the Goliath story and that they are actually two different versions of how David met Saul. Another possible explanation is that Saul's unbalanced mental state could account for his failure to recognize David as the one who played for him.

The story itself is a familiar one. Things were going bad for Israel in a battle with the Philistines in the Valley of Elah. The Valley of Elah was located in southern Judah and was one of four such valleys that provided access into the hill country from the coastal plain. Without the access that these valleys provided, going from the coast to the hills would have been virtually impossible. The control of the valleys, then, was essential to the defense of the Israelite positions in the hills.

The armies of the Israelites and the Philistines had taken up positions opposite each other, with a valley between. The Philistines challenged the Israelites to send one of their men to fight their challenger, the giant Goliath, who was about 10 feet tall. No one from Israel dared to take up the challenge, even though Saul had offered his daughter to anyone who would successfully fight Goliath (17:1-10,25).

David, who had come to the battlefield to bring supplies to his brothers who were serving with the army, was astounded to find that no Israelite was willing to risk his life for the honor of his people (17:11-27). As a result, David, despite the sneering of his brother Eliab (17:28-30), volunteered to fight Goliath.

Saul, relieved to have someone to meet Goliath's challenge, offered David his armor. David refused, however, choosing not to sacrifice his mobility for whatever protection Saul's armor might offer. After all, a 10-foot giant would be considerably less agile than the much-smaller David (17:31-39). Instead, he chose to use his favorite weapon, the sling, to fell his victim (17:40).

The sling consisted of a leather pouch to which two leather strings were attached. A stone weighing several ounces was placed in the pouch. The strings were held in such a way that when the slinger whirled the sling rapidly, he could turn loose one string and send the rock toward the target. One practiced in the use of the sling could be quite accurate.

David's well-placed rock hit the giant between the eyes, knocking him to the ground unconscious. It was then a simple matter to take Goliath's sword and finish the job by beheading him. David's success led the Israelites to an Israelite rout of the Philistines (17:41-58).

DAVID IN THE FAMILY OF SAUL (1 SAM. 18:1-30)

Things changed radically for the Bethlehem shepherd boy when he entered the king's court. First, he gained a friend. Jonathan, Saul's son and general, was instantly attracted to David (18:1-5). David's success as a warrior had preceded him, for the women of the village were dancing in the streets and singing his praises. Saul, insecure as he was, became jealous of David (18:6-9). Slipping again into a period of mental disturbance, he attempted to kill David while David was playing music for him (18:10-11).

Saul then attempted to get rid of David by putting him in charge of an army squadron, hoping he would be killed. This just gave David further opportunity to add to his exploits and to gain more admiration from the people (18:12-16).

After reneging on the promise to give David his older daughter's hand in marriage, Saul then proposed that David marry Michal, his younger daughter. To earn this right, however, he had to kill 100 Philistines and bring their foreskins as proof of what he had done. David believed in doing a thorough job; he brought back 200 foreskins (18:20-30).

DAVID FLEES FROM SAUL'S MURDEROUS INTENTIONS (1 SAM. 19:1-21:15)

After a while David began to feel Saul's rejection of him, especially after Jonathan told him of Saul's orders that he was to be killed (19:1-7). Continued attempts were made on David's life (19:8-17), causing him finally to flee to Samuel at Ramah. When Saul sent messengers to capture David, the awesome sense of God's presence with Samuel made them unable to carry out Saul's orders. Finally, Saul himself went. But he, too, was overcome just as he had been after his anointing by Samuel (19:18-24).

Finally, David saw that the situation was impossible and decided to separate himself from Saul's household. Jonathan agreed to take word to Saul that David had gone to Bethlehem for a feast day (20:1-6). Furthermore, Jonathan was to note Saul's reaction to David's absence and then give David a signal about whether he felt it safe for David to return. When David did not return, Saul became violent, showing Jonathan that David could not return safely. By the prearranged signal, therefore, he let David know that Saul was determined to kill him (20:7-42).

In his flight from Saul, David came to Nob, just east of Jerusalem. Pretending he was on a mission for the king, he persuaded the priest Ahimelech to give him some of the stale bread left over from the service, that only the priests were to eat. He also persuaded the priest to give him the sword of Goliath that was kept at the shrine. Leaving Nob, he went to the Philistine territory, but he was recognized there. To avoid being killed, he acted like a madman (21:1-15).

David, the Outlaw

The years that followed his escape from Saul saw David in the rather questionable position of being an ally to the Philistines while, at the same time, proclaiming his loyalty to his own people. His power base was Judah, whose rough terrain furnished an abundance of hiding places for his forces, which were continually being reinforced by people who were becoming disillusioned with Saul.

PREPARATIONS FOR THE STRUGGLE WITH SAUL (1 SAM. 22:1-5)

The word that David was a fugitive from Saul brought many discontented men to his side (22:1-2). As a precaution against an attack on his family, David took his father and mother and asked the king of Moab to protect them (22:3-5).

THE MASSACRE AT NOB (1 SAM. 22:6-23)

In the meantime, Saul was intensifying his efforts to kill David. Unfortunately, he heard that the priests at Nob had aided David and, as a result, ordered their deaths. But he did not stop with the priests. He also ordered that Nob be treated as an enemy city in the holy war; it was to be completely wiped out. When the Israelite soldiers refused to do it, he hired mercenaries led by Doeg, an Edomite, to carry out his orders. Only one survivor, Abiathar, a priest, escaped to tell David what had happened (22:6-23).

RUNNING FROM SAUL (1 SAM. 23:1–24:22)

David and his men attacked the Philistines, who were about to seize Keilah, a Judean village. Instead of being grateful for David's help, however, the villagers were ready to surrender him to Saul in order to spare themselves from Saul's wrath (23:1-14).

David fled, with Saul in pursuit, to the area south of Hebron. There Jonathan found David and assured him that he would keep his whereabouts secret from Saul. They reaffirmed their personal friendship by a covenant (23:15-18). In the meantime, spies brought word of David's hiding place, causing Saul once again to set out after him. Just as he was closing in on David in the rough, hilly country of the Arabah, word came of a Philistine attack, which drew Saul away (23:19-29).

Next, Saul heard that David was at Engedi, an oasis on the western side of the Dead Sea. While Saul pursued David, he stopped in a cave "to relieve himself" (24:3), not knowing that David was hiding in the cave. While he was there, David crept up and cut off a piece of the robe that Saul probably had taken off. He resisted the temptation to kill Saul, however.

When Saul had left the cave, David called after him and told him that he had not taken the opportunity to kill him. Saul was so shaken by the event that he admitted he had wronged David. He exacted a promise from David not to kill his family after David became king (24:1-22).

DAVID, THE OUTLAW (1 SAM. 25:1–28:2)

Gaining two wives and losing one (1 Sam. 25:1-44). If one translated a description of David's activity into our modern idiom, it could be said that he was president and chairman of the board of the South Judah Protection Agency. He furnished the Judean villages and the more nomadic Israelites of the area with protection from raids by the Amalekites and other non-Israelite groups who also traveled about in the area. For this service he expected gratitude in the form of food and other provisions for his rather sizable personal army. Some contributed willingly, if not cheerfully, while others were more difficult to convince of their need for David's services. One such attempt to collect eventually ended rather surprisingly.

That the biblical storytellers had a great sense of humor is often reflected in the names they give certain characters. Like our nicknames, such as "Slim" or "Stone Face," the names they used were part of the meaning they wanted to convey in the story. Such a name was given to a sheepman from Carmel on the edge of the Judean wilderness which borders the Dead Sea. The narrator calls him Nabal, meaning "a vile thing." While this could have been his name, it it quite possible it is just a descriptive term applied to him because of his nasty personality.

Nabal had large herds of sheep and goats—3000 sheep and 1000 goats—that David had protected from raiders. When he sent word to Nabal that he would appreciate a nice gift in gratitude for the services rendered, all he got was an insulting message to the effect that he had nothing to give a renegade who had broken away from his master (25:1-13).

David, who was proud and hot-tempered also, immediately set out to pay back the insult by a show of force. At this point in the story, Abigail, a woman of intelligence as well as beauty (25:3), decided something must be done to head off David. She was wise enough to realize that (1) David's request was reasonable, and (2) he would not stand such an insult without retaliation (25:14-17).

Unknown to her husband, who was probably busy counting his sheep, she prepared a generous gift of food and drink and set out with her servants to head David off before he descended in fury upon their camp.

Abigail had figured correctly. When she met David, she used an unbeatable combination of flattery, food, and an appeal to his religious instincts. She convinced David that what he was about to do was foolish. Since he received the supplies he had originally sought, he returned to his headquarters (25:18-35).

When she returned, she found Nabal having a drinking bout. The next morning when his hangover was upon him, she told him what had happened. The shock caused a sudden attack in the form of a paralytic stroke. The text says, "He became as a stone" (25:37). He died ten days later (25:36-38).

When David heard of Nabal's death, he thanked the LORD for keeping him from a foolish attack on a fellow Judean. Such a thing would have given his detractors fuel for the flame and would have alienated others who looked on him as a hero.

Abigail, now a wealthy widow with 3000 sheep and 1000 goats, became so attractive that David felt obligated to marry her to show his gratitude for her thoughtful action on his behalf. Abigail was willing, so the marriage was carried out. He also married Abinoam from Jezreel, but lost Saul's daughter Michal, whom Saul had given to another man after David fled. This was an act designed to insult David, since to invade a man's harem could cost one his life.[6] At the time, David could do little about the insult (25:39-44).

ANOTHER VERSION OF SAUL'S ESCAPE FROM DAVID (1 SAM. 26:1-25)

This story has many parallels to 24:1-22, but it differs in important details. David and two of his men slipped into Saul's camp and took Saul's spear and water jug. As in the previous story, David refused to kill Saul. David went to the top of a nearby mountain and shouted down to Abner, Saul's general, and accused him of being careless in protecting Saul. Saul answered and admitted he had wronged David.

David joins the Philistines (1 Sam. 27:1–28:2).   This story, telling of David's alliance with the king of Gath, takes care to put David's action in as good a light as possible. It shows how David walked a thin line in claiming to have the interest of his people at heart while acting as the bodyguard for the Philistine king. In addition, it did keep him safe from Saul.

The End of Saul's Reign

SAUL AND THE WITCH OF ENDOR (1 SAM. 28:3-25)

Saul was desperate. The Philistine army had moved from Aphek (on the central coastal plain) to Shunem (near Mount Gilboa), where Saul's troops were assembled. There was an air of doom about Saul as he watched the Philistine armies gather for the battle that would come the next day. Samuel was dead, David was in the camp of the enemy, and Saul was overwhelmed by his lifelong sense of helplessness. When he tried to get some sort of leadership from the religious officials, no word was

---

[6]See Solomon's treatment of his brother Adonijah when Adonijah asked for permission to marry Abishag, David's wife, who became a part of Solomon's harem (1 Kings 2:19-27).

available. He could not dream up a solution, the Urim and Thummin would not fall right, and his prophets claimed that the LORD had nothing to say (28:3-6).

Finally, he sought for a medium who supposedly could call up the dead. To find one was difficult since most of them had been banished by his own order (28:3). Finally, a medium or witch was found in the nearby village of Endor. He sought her out at night and asked her to call up Samuel for him. She claimed to be in contact with Samuel, but the message she conveyed to Saul was a message of doom. He was reminded of his failures as a king and was told that he and his sons would die the next day (28:7-19).

Saul was terrified and fell to the ground. Finally, the woman persuaded him to take some food. After resting for a time, he left (28:20-25).

WHERE WAS DAVID? (1 SAM. 29:1-11)

Instead of proceeding immediately to the story of the battle for Mount Gilboa, the narrative switched back to David, probably to make it clear that David had no part in the death of Saul. He had been asked by Achish, the king of Gath, to go with him to fight Saul. David had consented. The other Philistine kings, knowing of David's background and popularity among the Judeans, objected vigorously. As a result, David and his forces were sent back to their base (29:1-11).

A RAID ON DAVID'S CAMP (1 SAM. 30:1-31)

While David was away, there was an Amalekite raid on his camp at Ziklag in the Judean foothills (30:1-6). David set out to pursue the raiders. When he returned from a successful attack on the raiders, some of his men did not want to share any of the spoils of the battle with those who stayed behind to guard the camp. David ruled that every man should receive an equal share. Furthermore, he shared the spoils with elders of Judah (30:7-31).

THE DEATH OF SAUL (1 SAM. 31:1-14)

Saul and his sons died in the battle on Mt. Gilboa. Saul, mortally wounded, committed suicide. The Philistines hanged the bodies of Saul

Figure 7–2. "They put [Saul's] armor in the temple of Ashtaroth; and they fastened his body to the wall of Beth–shan" (1 Sam. 31:10). Tell Beth–shan, in the Valley of Jezreel, was the site of an ancient city that guarded an important crossing point on the Jordan River.

Photograph by John H. Tullock.

and his sons on the wall of Beth-Shan. The people of Jabesh-gilead stole the bodies during the night and properly disposed of them.

David: King over Judah, 1000–993 B.C.

DAVID'S REACTIONS TO SAUL'S DEATH
(2 SAM. 1:1-27)

David was at Ziklag when the news of Saul's death on Gilboa came to him. The messenger told David he had found Saul still alive and that he had killed Saul, as Saul had requested. Furthermore, he had brought Saul's crown and armband as proof that Saul was dead.

David's reaction to the story was severe. He ordered the messenger's death because he had claimed to kill Saul, "the LORD's anointed" (1:14).

The messenger was not helped by the fact that he was an Amalekite. In view of the different story told in 1 Samuel 31, it would seem that this version either (1) is from another tradition, or, (2) that the Amalekite made up his role in Saul's death to gain David's reward for eliminating the last barrier to David's becoming king (1:1-16).

David's lament over Saul and Jonathan came from the book of Jashar. This book, which now is lost, seems to have been a collection of traditional songs used by biblical writers. While the lament speaks of both Saul and Jonathan, the feelings expressed for Jonathan were in keeping with the accounts of their strong bonds of friendship (1:17-27).

DAVID AS KING OF JUDAH (2 SAM. 2:1-11)

By popular consent, David was anointed king of Judah at Hebron (2:1-4a). David commended the people of Jabesh-gilead for their bravery in stealing the bodies of Saul and his sons and giving them an honorable burial (2:4b-7).

In the meantime, Abner (Saul's general) had placed Ishbaal (Saul's son) (1 Chron. 8:33) on the throne. The Israelite narrators, however, changed Ishbaal's name to show their opinion of him. Ishbaal means "Baal's man," since he was a worshiper of the god Baal. Ishbosheth means "man of shame." He ruled from Transjordan over the northern part of the country (2:8-11).

Civil war (2 Sam. 2:12-32). Before long, a civil war broke out at Gibeon. The site of the initial battle was a huge circular hole carved in solid rock. It contains a rock stairway leading down to a spring, where the people got water. It has been uncovered in recent years by archaeologists. The battle started when twelve men from each group met in a sort of wrestling match that turned deadly when swords began to be used. Among those killed was Asahel, a brother of Joab (David's general), who ran after Abner. Abner warned him to stop. When he did not, Abner killed him. The northerners rallied around Abner, causing Joab to withdraw (2:12-32).

Abner asks for peace (2 Sam. 3:1-22). Abner soon became disillusioned with Ishbosheth. This was shown in two ways. First, he committed treason by taking one of Saul's harem as his slave wife. Ishbosheth could do nothing because he was too weak (3:1-11). Second, Abner went to David and offered to surrender to him the rest of the country. He wanted to make a covenant with David, but David first demanded that Michal (his

Figure 7–3. "And Joab . . . and the servants of David met [Abner and the servants of Ishbosheth] at the pool of Gibeon" (2 Sam. 2:13). This circular hole, cut into solid limestone, contained a rock-hewn staircase leading down to a water source many feet below the surface.

Photograph by John H. Tullock.

former wife) be given back to him. Abner did this, and the covenant was made (2 Sam. 3:12-22).

Joab murders Abner (2 Sam. 3:23-39). As Abner was leaving the meeting with David, Joab met him. Calling him aside as though to have a conversation, Joab stabbed and killed Abner. His justification was that Abner had killed his brother and he was acting as his avenger. This was a violation of custom, however, since killing in war was not subject to the rule of blood vengeance. David and Abner had a covenant that made David responsible to avenge Abner's murder. While he lamented Abner, David did not act against Joab. Probably, he was afraid of Joab (3:39).

The murder of Ishbosheth (2 Sam. 4:1-12). With Abner dead, Ishbosheth's kingdom fell apart. Two men murdered him as he slept. They cut off his head and carried the gory trophy to David at Hebron. David reacted as he had at the report of Saul's death—he had the murderers executed.

David: King over All Israel, 993–961 B.C.

DAVID MAKES JERUSALEM HIS CAPITAL
(2 SAM. 5:1-10)

After ruling for another five and one-half years from Hebron (5:1-5), David captured Jerusalem. This heavily fortified Jebusite city, according to tradition, was built on the site where Abraham attempted to sacrifice Isaac (Gen. 22). The invaders got into the city by entering a tunnel which carried the waters of a spring under its walls. A shaft was cut down to the tunnel so that people could reach the water. David's men got inside the city and then opened the gate so others could come in.

The choice of Jerusalem was just one of a number of shrewd political moves that David made before and after he became king. While he was still a fugitive from Saul, David drew people to him who were unhappy with Saul. He also was careful to present himself as champion and protector of the common man in Judah. Furthermore, he wooed the village chiefs by presents when he took spoils in battle (1 Sam. 30:26-31).

In all his opportunities to kill Saul, David had never raised his hand against him. Even when opportunists tried to gain his favor by claiming to kill Saul and Ishbosheth, David had acted correctly—he put the admitted murderers to death. As a gesture to the memory of his friend Jonathan, he made Jonathan's crippled son, Mephibosheth, a ward of the state. This is one of the earliest-known examples of government aid to the handicapped! (2 Sam. 9:1-13).

The choice of Jerusalem for the capital was a good move because it was a neutral site. It never had been held permanently by Israel and thus belonged to no tribe. To have made Hebron, a city of Judah, the permanent capital would have stirred up considerable resentment, especially from Ephraim, Judah's rival for first place among the tribes.

A most important factor was that David came through to the people as a man of integrity, whose dedication to the LORD, the God of Israel, was without question. In his leadership they saw fulfilled the ideal of possession of the land promised to the patriarchs. This success on David's part was so impressive as to cause the covenant at Sinai to fade into the background. It was replaced with the concept of the covenant with David, which said that David's descendants would sit on the throne of Israel into the ages to come.

THE TASK AHEAD (2 SAM. 5:11-25)

After briefly mentioning (1) David's alliance with Hiram, king of Tyre who furnished builders and materials for David's projects (5:11-12), and (2) David's wives and children (5:13-16), the narrator turns to the

153

first problem which faced David when he became king; namely, the Philistine threat. How he dealt with the Philistines would determine his success as the king over all Israel. Saul's chief failure was his lack of success with the Philistines.

The Philistines were not long in testing him. Twice they attacked in the Rephaim Valley. Twice David, after consulting the LORD, defeated them (5:17-25).

BRINGING THE ARK OF THE COVENANT TO JERUSALEM (2 SAM. 6:1-23)

The ark, the sacred symbol of the LORD's presence with Israel, had been kept in a private home for over twenty years. David was determined to bring it to Jerusalem. The first attempt ended in tragedy, when Uzzah, one of the men who was moving it by cart, died when he touched the ark. The text says, "And God smote him because he put forth his hand to touch the ark" (6:7). The awe of the holy object caused an immediate halt to David's plans for three months (6:1-11).

During the three-month period, Obed-edom (in whose house the ark was kept) had evidence of God's blessing upon him. David concluded it would be safe to try again to move the ark. This time, a sacrifice was made after the ark was moved only six steps. David played the role of priest, wearing the priestly garment and dancing before the ark as it was brought into the city (6:12-15).

Michal, who had been returned against her will to David's harem as a condition to David's covenant with Abner (3:13), watched the events from her window. The next time she saw David, she told him he had acted like a dirty old man. David argued that he was dancing to honor the LORD. Because of her outspokenness (6:16-23), Michal was demoted in the harem.

NO TEMPLE BUILDING BY DAVID (2 SAM. 7:1-29)

After David's palace was complete, the question arose about a temple to the LORD where the ark could be permanently housed. Nathan, who functioned as David's spiritual adviser, encouraged him at first. Later, however, he came back and told David that he had had a vision that stated: (1) The LORD had always dwelt in the tabernacle from the exodus to that present time (7:5-7). (2) He had made David what he was (7:8-11). (3) He would make David's descendants rulers over Israel (7:12-17). David praised the LORD and prayed that the promise spoken by Nathan would be fulfilled (7:18-29).

know — Davidic Covenant is located here

DAVID'S MILITARY SUCCESSES (2 SAM. 8:1-18)

Israel controlled more territory during David's reign than at any other time in its history. Beginning with the defeat of her mortal enemies (the Philistines), David led his armies to conquer the territory east of the Jordan (8:2,12-14); north to the upper reaches of the Euphrates River, which included all the Syrian territory (8:3-11); and south to the borders of Egypt.

He ruled his kingdom well. Suggestions have been made that one reason for this was that when he captured Jerusalem, he captured people who had been trained by Egypt in the running of the government. Instead of killing them, he put them to work organizing and running his own empire.[7]

The Court History of David

Second Samuel 9:1–20:26 and 1 Kings 1 and 2 contain what is said to be one of the finest pieces of literature that has survived from ancient times. Its author had a first-hand knowledge of the inner workings of David's court. This enabled him to give an unusually frank picture of an Oriental king and his family problems. This literature could be called "David's Watergate tapes" because of the kinds of things it reveals about Israel's greatest king.

DAVID'S KINDNESS TO JONATHAN'S SON
(2 SAM. 9:1-13)

David's loyalty to the promises made to Jonathan resulted in taking care of Mephibosheth, Jonathan's crippled son, as a permanent responsibility.

THE WAR AGAINST THE AMMONITES
(2 SAM. 10:1-19)

Because of a covenant David seems to have made with the Ammonite king during his outlaw days, he sent messengers to the new king of Ammon, offering to continue the covenant relationship. The king was suspicious (10:1-5), however, and disgraced David's representatives. A war

---

[7]For a fuller discussion of this theory, see George E. Mendenhall, "The Monarchy," *Interpretation* XXIX, 2 (April, 1975), 155–170.

resulted, with the Ammonites calling the Syrians in to help them. It was in vain because David's armies, led by Joab, defeated them (10:6-19).

THE KING'S ROVING EYES: DAVID AND BATHSHEBA
(2 SAM. 11:1–12:25)

During the Ammonite wars, David stopped going out to battle with his men. There may have been two reasons for the change: (1) With the enlarged kingdom, David probably felt that he had to pay more attention to matters of government. (2) His advisers may have insisted that he no longer go to battle because, had he been killed, it would have been an irreplaceable loss to the kingdom. In any case, he stayed home (11:1).

With time on his hands, he had a chance to look around, and when he did he saw a beautiful woman taking a bath. It may well be that she meant for him to see her. In any case, the end result was pregnancy for Bathsheba and a problem for David (11:2-5).

What followed is a vivid example of how a deeply religious man can be so concerned with protecting his reputation that he can forget his religious principles. First, David tried by various means to make it possible that Bathsheba's husband, Uriah, would believe he was the father-to-be. But Uriah, a loyal soldier in David's army, would not cooperate. He felt it was unpatriotic to enjoy the pleasures of wife and home while his friends were fighting. Finally, in desperation, David sent Uriah back to the battle, with a secret order to Joab to put him in the front lines so he would be killed (11:6-21). Soon, the word came back that Uriah was dead. After a proper period of mourning, Bathsheba entered the king's harem (11:22-27).

David must have breathed a sigh of relief, but it was not for long. Nathan, prophet and spiritual adviser to the king, confronted David with what he had done. In that confrontation something of the character of David was revealed. Instead of banishing or even killing Nathan for his audacity, David faced his guilt and admitted his wrong (12:1-15).

From the time of its birth the baby was ill, causing David to mourn. When told of the baby's death, David, after having prayed for the child to live, ceased mourning (12:16-23). Not too long afterward, a second child, Solomon, was born (12:24-25). After Solomon's birth, David returned to the battle against the Ammonites and the war was won (12:26-31).

TROUBLE IN THE KING'S HOUSE (2 SAM. 13:1-39)

David's moral failures, coupled with his failure to control his children, brought a bitter harvest. Absalom and Tamar were David's children by one of his wives, while Amnon was the son of another wife. Amnon fell in love with his beautiful half-sister, but there seemed to be no way he could marry her. Following a suggestion of a cousin, the love-sick Amnon persuaded David to send Tamar to his house to cook for him while he pretended to be ill. While she was there, he raped her. After he had got what was wanted, he refused to marry her (13:1-19). This meant, then, that Tamar would never be able to marry for virginity was considered to be essential for marriage. David did not take any action against Amnon for his abuse of his sister.

Two years later, after all seemed to be forgotten, Absalom invited Amnon to a party. Under orders from Absalom, his servants waited until Amnon was drunk and then stabbed him to death. Absalom, with Joab's help, fled the country and stayed away for three years (13:20-39).

THE WIDOW'S TALE (2 SAM. 14:1-24)

Moab, knowing that David wanted an excuse to let Absalom come home, took an old woman from Tekoa to David. She told him a sad story of her two sons. According to the imaginary story, one of the widow's sons had murdered the other. Her relatives were ready to kill the surviving son to avenge the death of the dead son. Since this would leave no living male to carry on the family name, she was appealing to the king for protection for the murderer. David ruled that the need for an heir to carry his father's name was more important than punishment for the murderer (14:1-17).[8]

When David had so ruled, the grieving mother suddenly turned and rebuked David for not allowing Absalom to come home. David was immediately suspicious that Joab had planned the performance of the "widow." Even so, he commanded Joab to bring Absalom home, but on the condition that he not be allowed to see David (14:18-24).

ABSALOM, THE TROUBLE-MAKER
(2 SAM. 14:25–15:6)

Absalom was not content just with being allowed to return to Jerusalem. He asked Joab to come to see him, but Joab refused twice. To get Joab's attention, Absalom set his barley field on fire. Joab then agreed to persuade David to allow Absalom to return to the court. David agreed (14:25-33).

Then, Absalom began a systematic campaign to undermine his father. He would stand at the palace entrance. When someone came to bring a

[8]For a fuller discussion of this passage see John H. Tullock, *Blood-Vengeance*, pp. 198–200.

problem before the king, he would call them aside. Then he would tell them that they were just wasting their time, even though they were in the right in their complaint. He would assure them that if *he* were the king, they would get justice. He would allow no man to give the traditional bow of respect, but he would warmly embrace them like a brother.

> Thus Absalom did to all Israel who came to the king for judgment; so Absalom stole the hearts of the men of Israel (15:6).

ABSALOM'S REBELLION (2 SAM. 15:7–17:23)

After four years, Absalom made his move. He sent word to his supporters to gather at Hebron, David's first capital. He told David he was going there to celebrate a feast and received David's blessing on the trip. Once there, however, he had himself proclaimed king. Among those who joined him was Ahitophel, who had been one of David's advisers (15:7-12).

On hearing the news, David chose to run away rather than to fight his own son. He made plans to leave Jerusalem. He instructed ten of his wives to stay behind to take care of his house, but all his servants and his personal bodyguard went with him. Most of them were foreigners who were more loyal to David than to the nation of Israel. Typical of these was Ittai, a Philistine from Gath (15:13-23).

David was not without eyes and ears in Jerusalem, however. Zadok and Abiathar started to take the ark of the covenant with David, but he sent them back and told them to stay in Jerusalem. Furthermore, Husai (one of David's counselors) agreed to be a spy in Absalom's camp. Among the three of them, they managed to keep David informed of Absalom's moves (15:24-37).

Leaving Jerusalem, David went across the Kidron Valley, which separates the eastern boundary of the city from the Mount of Olives (15:30). As he crossed the mountain, he was joined by Ziba, the servant of Mephibosheth (Jonathan's son), who brought an offering of food and drink, and donkeys for David and his household to ride. Mephibosheth had deserted to Absalom's side (16:1-4).

Further on, he was roundly cursed and stoned by Shimei, a supporter of Saul's family. When one of his men offered to kill Shimei, David kept him from doing so. Instead, he continued on toward the Jordan River (16:5-14).

Meanwhile, Absalom entered Jerusalem. Hushai greeted Absalom and convinced him that he had deserted David. One of Absalom's first acts was to have sexual relations with one of David's concubines in full view of the people. This was meant to show that he had taken over his father's kingdom (16:15-23).

Conflicting advice was given to Absalom by Hushai and Ahitophel. Ahitophel advised immediate pursuit of David, but Hushai suggested that they wait. Furthermore, he suggested that Absalom personally lead the pursuit. This would prove his leadership ability to the people (17:1-14). Absalom took Hushai's advice. When he did so, Husai got word to Zadok and Abiathar, who, after some difficulty, managed to get word of Absalom's plans to David (17:15-22). In the meantime, Ahitophel committed suicide when he saw that Absalom would no longer listen to him (17:23).

CRUSHING THE REBELLION (2 SAM. 17:24–19:8)

David stopped when he reached Mahanaim in Transjordan. Mahanaim was located near Penuel, which was associated with the tradition of Jacob's wrestling with the angel (Gen. 32:22-32). Loyal followers in the area brought necessary supplies (17:24-29).

In preparation for the battle, David split his army into three parts, putting a commander over each. David wanted to lead, but his commanders refused to let him go. As they left, David asked that they "deal gently" with Absalom (18:1-5).

The battle raged in the forest of Ephraim. A patrol spotted Absalom riding a mule and took after him. As Absalom's mule ran under an oak, Absalom was caught by his head in a tree branch and was left hanging. When Joab heard, he came and ordered soldiers to kill Absalom. When they refused, Joab personally killed him and had his body thrown into a hole in the ground (18:6-18).

When messengers brought the news to David, he wept loudly, lamenting Absalom's death (18:19-33). When the people heard his lamenting, their shouts over the hard-won victory turned to a shamed silence. Joab's power over David was never more vividly illustrated than when he told David that if he wanted the support of those who had saved his life, he had better shut up his yelling and praise the people for their support. "For," he said:

> You have made it clear today that commanders and servants are nothing to you; for today I perceive that if Absalom were alive and all of us were dead . . . then you would be pleased (19:6).

David arose and did as Joab told him to do (19:1-8*b*).

PUTTING THINGS TOGETHER AGAIN
(2 SAM. 19:8*c*-43)

As David returned to Jerusalem, those who had supported Absalom either fled or tried to get back into David's good graces. Thus Shimei, who had cursed David as he left, met him and begged his forgiveness.

David promised that he would not kill Shimei, but he did not promise that someone else might not do it (19:8c-23).

Mephibosheth, Jonathan's son, came begging; but David divided his property and gave half of it to Ziba, Mephibosheth's servant, who had brought food to his men (19:24-30). David offered a place of honor to Barzillai, the Gileadite who had also brought supplies to him. Barzillai asked David to give the place to his servant (19:31-40).

When he arrived in Jerusalem, the elders of the northern tribes and the elders of Judah got into a dispute over who had the right to bring David back to Jerusalem. The Judeans claimed it was their right by kinship and the northerners claimed it was their right by majority rule (19:41-43).

SHEBA'S REBELLION (2 SAM. 20:1-26)

Taking advantage of the friction between the Israelites (northerners) and the Judeans, Sheba started another revolt against David, which gained a number of followers. David put Amasa in charge of the army, replacing Joab after he killed Absalom, and gave Amasa orders to put down the rebellion. Before he could get organized, Amasa was murdered by Joab (20:1-10c). Joab took over the army, and soon he had the rebellion under control (20:10d-26).

ODDS AND ENDS (2 SAM. 21:1–24:25)

The last three chapters of 2 Samuel do not fit into the story of the ins and outs of David's court. First, there is the story of a famine that lasted three years. Through prayer David became convinced that an atrocity that Saul had committed against the Gibeonites (Josh. 9) had not been forgiven by the LORD. He went to the Gibeonites and asked them if there were anything he could do to make things right with them for the harm Saul had done them. They replied that the only thing he could do was to turn over to them seven of Saul's sons. He did as they asked, and the Gibeonites hanged them (21:1-9). Rizpah, the mother of two of the victims, guarded their bodies from being attacked by birds of prey until only the bones were left. Then David had Saul and Jonathan's bones returned from Jabesh-gilead and buried Saul and his sons together.

The point of this story is that the ancient Israelites believed that murder (in this case, Saul's unjust killing of the Gibeonites) had to be punished by the death of the murderer. Since Saul was already dead, then his sons had to bear the blame for him. When justice was not done, the whole land suffered. One way that suffering came was through such natural disasters as drought and famine. The only way to bring such natural disasters to an end was to see that justice was done (21:10-14).

The next block of material mentioned the giants who might be called the heavyweight champions among the Philistines. The Israelites who defeated them are listed (21:15-22).

Chapters 22 and 23:1-7 are what is known as orphan psalms—that is, psalms found outside the books of psalms. Both are said to have come from David, and both are hymns of praise. Following the psalms is a series of episodes describing the heroic actions of David's mighty men. These men were his personal bodyguards and were fiercely loyal to him. As a matter of fact, David's army was largely a private army, recruited by David and paid by him (23:8-37).

Chapter 24 describes David's taking of the census, probably for purposes of taxation. Then, as now, the power to tax was the power to control. The LORD was said to have moved David to take the census. First Chronicles 21:1 corrects this by saying that Satan caused David to take a census. A plague came. To ease the plague, David bought Araunah's threshing floor on top of the mountain overlooking Jerusalem. Later, the Temple would be built there; and the large rock that formed the threshing floor would become a sacred spot for three great universal religions— Judaism, Christianity, and Islam. When David bought the site and offered sacrifices, the plague was lifted (24:1-25).

THE OLD ORDER PASSES (1 KINGS 1:1–2:12)

Like vultures waiting for a sick animal to die in the desert, so David's sons watched his strength slip away. Even a beautiful new concubine brought in to give David her warmest attention could not stir him. When that failed, the air began to be filled with plots and counterplots (1:1-4).

After Absalom was killed, Adonijah was David's oldest surviving son. No longer was there a prophet with the power and influence of Samuel who could anoint a man and place him on the throne. David had that power, but he was almost past the stage when he could use it.

Adonijah, probably sensing that David would not choose him, decided to take matters into his own hands. He enlisted help from powerful people: Joab (the long-time commander of David's army) and Abiathar (the priest who had been with David since his days as a fugitive). Like Absalom, he had been pleased and pampered by David. He invited many important people to a sacrifice and self-coronation, much like modern politicians invite prospective voters to a barbecue.

He failed to invite Nathan (the prophet), Bathsheba (Solomon's mother), Zadok (the priest), Benaiah (the chief of David's bodyguards), nor any of the bodyguards. He especially ignored Solomon, his chief rival for the throne (1:5-10).

Word of Adonijah's attempted coup set in motion a counterplot by those who supported Solomon. Nathan and Bathsheba plotted together to force the aged king to choose Solomon. Bathsheba was to tell David of Adonijah's plot and then remind him that he had promised the kingship to Solomon. Nathan would then come in and confirm what Bathsheba had said.

The plan worked to perfection. Nathan confirmed Bathsheba's news and questioned whether David had encouraged Adonijah to have himself proclaimed king. David had Bathsheba called back and swore a solemn oath to her that Solomon would succeed him. There is great irony in her parting words, "May my lord King David live forever!" She did not mean it! (1:11-31).

Action was taken immediately to insure that David's wishes were carried out. Solomon was placed on David's mule (an animal that no person except the king could ride) and taken to the Gihon Spring. He was accompanied by Nathan, Zadok, Benaiah, and David's bodyguard. There he was proclaimed king. Afterward he was led through the streets of Jerusalem, where the people, seeing that he was David's choice, filled the streets shouting, "Long live King Solomon!" (1:32-40).

Meanwhile, back at Adonijah's party, people began to wonder what all that noise in uptown Jerusalem was about. A messenger came running in! When he told what was happening, all Adonijah's guests suddenly remembered that they had something to do somewhere else. Adonijah, fearing that Solomon would have him killed, went to the great altar where sacrifices were made and remained there. The reason was that the altar was a sacred place and, supposedly, one would be safe there from punishment for any crime as long as he did not leave the sacred area. Solomon demanded and got a pledge of loyalty from Adonijah. In return, he promised to let Adonijah live unless some "wickedness" be found in him. Solomon, of course, would determine what "wickedness" was (1:41-53).

Soon afterward, David gave instructions to Solomon about what he should do when David died. After instructing him about spiritual matters (2:1-4), David turned to more practical instructions. On the one hand he gave instructions about Joab, who had been David's general and hatchet man, and whose atrocities David was either unable or unwilling to control. Joab was to be executed. On the other hand, Solomon was urged to treat Barzillai of Gilead kindly for his help to David during Absalom's rebellion. Shimei's fate was left to Solomon's discretion, but the strong implication was that Shimei would die. David said nothing about Abiathar. When David died, Solomon became the first Israelite king to come to the throne as the successor to his father (2:1-12).

AN EVALUATION OF DAVID

David's accomplishments as king have caused him to rank with Moses in importance in Israelite tradition. While it was true that there were no major challenges to his rule from Egypt, Asia Minor, or Mesopotamia, the fact that he could take a rather disorganized and divided people (such as Israel) and achieve what he did in the short span of forty years marked the man as a genius in military organization and administrative skill. While Solomon's kingdom would be more spectacular in its display of wealth and power, it was only because David's conquests were complete. Solomon had a period of peace in which to develop the kingdom economically.

Beyond the period of the united monarchy, David's influence was felt in three areas. First, in his choice of Jerusalem as his capital, he gave to the world its most revered city. To Jew and Christian alike it would become the earthly version of God's heavenly city. This is why the writer of the New Testament book of Revelation spoke of the ideal age as beginning when "the holy city, new Jerusalem," would come down from heaven to earth (Rev. 21:2).

Today (3000 years later) Jew, Christian, and Muslim make their way to a city whose influence far outweighs any importance that it should have. Many cities are larger; more influential economically; have more to offer in culture, education, and the arts; but none has about it the special quality and drawing power that Jerusalem has.

Second, the monarchy established by David would last more than 400 years; but its influence would extend even further. The secret of its longevity lay in the conviction that the LORD made a covenant with David to see that his descendants would rule over Israel. That covenant replaced the Sinai covenant in the thinking of the average Israelite (especially those who lived in Judah). Following David's time, when a covenant was mentioned it was assumed the covenant with David was being discussed.

When the monarchy ended with the Babylonian exile, the hope for its restoration lived on, especially as it was and had been proclaimed by the great prophets (Isa. 9, 11; Mic. 5:2-4). In the midst of the postexilic period, the hope for an ideal king who exemplified the best qualities of David grew into the doctrine of God's Anointed One, the Messiah. Jesus' disciples saw him as the fulfillment of that ideal, while Jewish interpreters continued to look for the new David who would deliver his persecuted people.

Third, David left his mark on the poetic literature of Israel. How many of the psalms he wrote is subject to much debate, but that he wrote some of them is sure, enough to cause him to be looked upon as the father of Israelite hymns. The psalms are different from other literature in the Old Testament because they are man's deepest emotions addressed to God. Since David is represented as such a deeply emotional man it is fitting that he would be connected with the most emotional literary form in the Old Testament.

Solomon: Riches, Wisdom, and Foolishness, 961–922 B.C.

If Saul was a judge who tried to be king and David was an empire builder, then Solomon introduced Israel to the rule of a typical Oriental despot.

GETTING RID OF POTENTIAL RIVALS (2 KINGS 2:13-46)

Solomon moved quickly to consolidate his power. Where David had nothing directly to do with the elimination of anyone who might be his rival, Solomon had no qualms about dealing with his enemies. Adonijah was his first victim. When he asked Bathsheba to persuade Solomon to let him have Abishag, David's last concubine, for his wife, Solomon found the wickedness in Adonijah that he had been looking for as an excuse to kill him. The request Adonijah made was actually an insult. David's harem became Solomon's on David's death, even though they probably were not considered to be Solomon's wives, since his own mother was in the group. Adonijah's request was his death warrant (2:13-25).

Solomon dealt more leniently with Abiathar, the priest. He removed him from serving at the Jerusalem shrine and exiled him to Anathoth, a small village near Jerusalem. From that village would come the great prophet Jeremiah in the latter part of the sixth century B.C. (2:26-27).

Solomon probably considered Joab as one of his more dangerous rivals. Even though he was old, Joab was a cunning and ruthless man who had managed to hold power in the army even when David tried to fire him. But his luck had run out. Solomon was just as ruthless, or more so, than Joab. He ordered Joab's execution. When Joab fled to the sanctuary for refuge and refused to come out, Solomon defied the taboo against killing anyone in a sanctuary and ordered Joab killed as he held onto the horns of the sacred altar. His place as general of the armies of Israel was taken by his executioner, Benaiah, the son of Jehoiada (2:28-35).

The last to be dealt with was Shimei, who was placed under a form of house arrest whereby he was not to leave the city of Jerusalem. Shimei observed the rules for three years; but, when one of his slaves ran away, Shimei went after him. Solomon had not forgotten—Shimei died also (2:36-46).

Figure 7–4. "Joab fled to the tent of the LORD and caught hold of the horns of the altar" (1 Kings 2:28). The "horns of the altar" (as illustrated by this tenth century B.C. limestone altar from Megiddo) were supposed to keep a fugitive safe as long as he clung to them. This was not true in Joab's case.

Courtesy of the Israel Department of Antiquities and Museums.

SOLOMON, THE RELIGIOUS MAN
(2 KINGS 3:1-27; 4:29-34)

The Israelite historian, in his evaluation of Solomon as a religious man, could not be quite as complimentary as he was about David. Perhaps he was hinting at one of the obstacles to Solomon's devotion to the LORD when he mentions his Egyptian wife. She and others of his wives influenced him to worship pagan gods.

In describing a prayer Solomon prayed, the narrator tells of God appearing in a dream and telling Solomon to ask what God could give him (3:5). Instead of asking for great riches, Solomon asked for wisdom to govern his people. God, in turn, promised both wisdom and riches (3:1-14).

An illustration of Solomon's wisdom is the famous story of the two women who claimed the same child. After the women had argued before him, he ordered the child cut into two pieces, one piece to be given to each woman. One woman agreed, but the true mother asked Solomon to let the child live and to give it to the other woman. Solomon awarded the baby to its true mother (3:16-28).

A summary statement concerning Solomon's wisdom (4:29-34) describes Solomon as wiser than all the eastern wise men. He was a speaker and collector of proverbs, a zoologist and a biologist, and a marvel to all who heard him (4:29-34). The queen of Sheba came from North Africa (Ethiopia) to marvel at his wisdom. Ethiopian tradition has it that she carried away more than wisdom since later rulers of the country were called in part, "The Lion of Judah" (1 Kings 10:1-13)!

SOLOMON, THE ORGANIZER (1 KINGS 4:1-28)

In organizing his kingdom, Solomon seems to have had two purposes in mind: (1) to divide the land as evenly as possible to provide for the systematic support of his elaborate court and for other taxation purposes; and (2) to break down the old tribal distinctions by paying little or no attention to tribal lines when dividing the country up into tax districts. In his first purpose, he succeeded—in the second, he failed (4:1-28).

SOLOMON, THE BUILDER (1 KINGS 5:1–7:51)

While David built an empire by conquest, Solomon covered it with buildings. Of all the building projects carried on by Solomon, the Temple at Jerusalem ranked first in importance for the Israelite historian.

Preparations for building the Temple (1 Kings 5:1-18). To build as Solomon did takes skilled workmen and quality materials, neither of which was abundant in Israel. The one thing Israel had in abundance was stone, but she lacked the forests to supply the woods needed.

To supply the needed material and skilled workmen, Solomon turned to David's ally, Hiram (King of Tyre in Phoenicia). Hiram agreed to supply cedar and cypress wood, as well as skilled workmen, to carry out the building of the Temple and palace complex in Jerusalem. Solomon agreed to supply food to Hiram. Also, he furnished Israelites to do the labor in cutting the wood in Lebanon and quarrying stone in Israel. Solomon's men had to contribute without pay one month's labor in three to the state.

The Temple is built (1 Kings 6:1–7:5). Like Jerusalem itself, the Temple—first built by Solomon, destroyed, and rebuilt again in the postexilic period and finally by Herod the Great—has managed to seize the imagination of countless millions of people for nearly 3000 years. Its remains, except for portions of the wall that once surrounded the area where it stood until its final destruction in A.D. 70, are under an area containing two Islamic mosques—the Dome of the Rock and the el Asqa Mosque. As a result, archaeological work is forbidden on the Temple Mount.[9]

By taking the biblical description, however, and by comparing it with similar temples found in Israel and Pheonicia, a fairly accurate idea of the Temple's appearance can be gained. One such building was a Canaanite temple found at Hazor in the northern part of Israel. It had the three-room plan used in the Jerusalem Temple. A later temple, from the period of the Israelite monarchy, was found at Arad, south of Jerusalem. There was found also at Beersheba a horned altar, such as is mentioned in the Old Testament (1 Kings 1:50; 2:28).[10]

First Kings 6:1 says that the Temple was built 480 years after Israel left Egypt. This poses a problem in chronology since it does not agree with other evidence of the date of the exodus. One possible explanation is that the figure 480 represents 12 generations. Biblical writers figured a generation as lasting 40 years, while today, 25 years is considered to be a generation. If this were the case, $12 \times 25 = 300$ years, which would place the exodus at about 1300 B.C., in keeping with present evidence.

According to all descriptions, both biblical and archaeological, the Temple was divided into three parts: (1) A porch or vestibule, which was 15 feet deep by 30 feet wide; (2) the Holy Place, which was 60 feet long and 30 feet wide; and (3) the Holy of Holies, which was a perfect cube—30 feet long by 30 feet wide by 30 feet high. The interior height of the rest of the building was 45 feet. Along the outside of the Temple were three levels of rooms, used for storage and other purposes. The interior of the building was decorated with elaborate carved woodwork. Gold also was used extensively in decorating the interior (6:2-36).

The Holy Place contained three principal items: the altar for incense, the seven-branched candlestick (menorah), and the table for the sacred bread (shew bread or bread of the Presence). The menorah actually was used later. In the earlier Temple, the lights were lamps with seven wicks. Priests entered the Holy Place daily in the performance of their duties.

The Holy of Holies originally contained the sacred box, the ark of

[9]See Cornfeld, *Archaeology,* p. 104ff.

[10]On the Hazor temple, see Yadin, *Hazor,* pp. 79–99. For the discoveries at Arad and Beersheba, see Cornfeld, *Archaeology,* p. 80, and Yohanan Aharoni, "Nothing Early and Nothing Late: Rewriting Israel's Conquest," *The Biblical Archaeologist,* 77, no. 4 (March 1976), 55–76.

Figure 7–5. "[Solomon] began to build the house of the LORD" (1 Kings 6:1). The floor plan of Solomon's Temple was similar to a number of Phoenician temples. This is understandable since the architects and artisans Solomon used were Phoenicians.

SOLOMON'S TEMPLE

I. GROUND PLAN

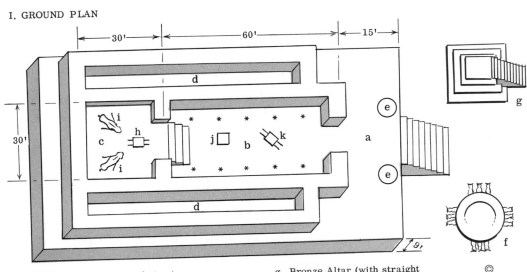

a. Vestibule or Porch (*'ûlām*)
b. Holy Place or Sanctuary (*hêkāl*), 60'x30'x40'
c. Holy of Holies (*debîr*), 30'x30'x30'
d. Side Chambers - three stories, each level 1.5' wider than the lower story
e. Two Free-standing Pillars of Jachin and Boaz
f. Bronze Sea

g. Bronze Altar (with straight steps of Albright-Wright)
h. Ark of the Covenant
i. Cherubim
j. Altar of Incense
k. Table for Loaves of Proposition
* Ten Candlesticks—five on each side

II. FRONTAL VIEW

d. Side Chambers: Treasury
e. Jachin and Boaz (40' high)
f. Bronze Sea (15' diameter)
g. Bronze Altar (Garber's ziggurat)
h. Flat Roof (Garber's Egyptian cornice) (Albright shows crenelations)

N.B.: No towers.

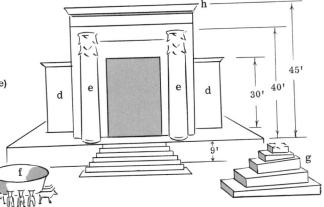

From the *Jerome Biblical Commentary* by Brown, Fitzmyer and Murphy. Copyright © 1968. Reprinted with permission of Prentice-Hall, Inc., Englewood Cliffs, N.J.

the covenant. At either end stood a winged figure, 15 feet high. It was carved from olive wood and plated with gold. It probably had both human and animal features, designed to represent all living creatures giving praise to the LORD, whose dwelling place was the Holy of Holies. Once a year, on the solemn Day of Atonement (Yom Kippur), the high priest could enter the Holy of Holies. Even he had to undergo an elaborate ceremony of cleansing before he could enter the room. His purpose was to bring before the LORD the sins of the people so they might be forgiven. Thus, the Holy of Holies represented to Israel the meeting place between God and man.

In the Temple courtyard stood the great altar made of uncut stones, upon which the sacrifices were made. Two huge bronze columns, named Jachin and Boaz, stood to the north and south of the entrance to the Temple. Their meaning and purpose are unknown (7:15-22). An elaborate bronze bowl resting on a base made from twelve bronze bulls also stood in the courtyard. It held about 10,000 gallons of water and may have been a reminder of the watery chaos mentioned in the creation story and of how God overcame it to create the world (7:23-26).

All the furnishings and equipment for the Temple were made by the Phoenicians. It should not be surprising, then, that the descriptions given in the Bible match the things discovered in Phoenician temples. The major difference seems to be that Israel's Temple contained no image of the Deity, while Phoenician temples contained many such images (7:27-51).

The dedication of the Temple (1 Kings 8:1-66).   After years of labor, the Temple was finished. The first act of Solomon was to have the ark of the covenant moved into its permanent home, the Holy of Holies. It was moved with elaborate precautions and with many sacrifices being offered (8:1-13).

The address and prayer of Solomon (8:14-53) emphasizes the importance of the covenant with David and the building of the Temple as carrying out Solomon's responsibility in the light of that covenant (8:14-21).

The prayer was a plea for God to keep his side of the covenant. First Kings 8:28-30 is particularly important because it emphasizes what many Israelites forgot in later years—namely, that God did not just dwell in the Temple in Jerusalem. No mere building could hold him. The prayer lists the conditions that would bring people before the LORD in prayer: (1) sin against one another; (2) defeat in war because of sin; (3) drought; (4) famine caused by pestilence, blight, mildew, or locusts; (5) foreigners who came to the Temple to worship; (6) holy war; (7) sin against God. With each there was a plea for forgiveness based on God's choice of Israel as his people (8:31-53).

In this section, then, the principle of the covenant was in operation. God, who gave the covenant though not required to do so, obligated himself to Israel because he was merciful. An Israelite could call upon God to exercise the mercy in his behalf when he came to God in repentance. He could not expect forgiveness without the proper attitude on his part. This theme was repeated by the great prophets and was prominent in the book of Deuteronomy.

After the people were led in praise to the LORD, elaborate festivities were observed in finishing the dedicatory services. The seven-day feast (held at the time of the Feast of the Tabernacles) sent away proud, happy, and filled with roast beef and mutton all those who came (8:54-66).

The LORD appears to Solomon again (1 Kings 9:1-9). After the dedication of the Temple, the LORD appeared again to Solomon. The promise of the continuance of David's line was made, but it was to be based on faithfulness to the LORD. If Solomon or those who followed him turned away from the LORD, however, judgment would come upon Israel.

Solomon's other building projects (1 Kings 7:1-12; 9:10-28; 10:14-29). Solomon spent even more time building an elaborate system of palaces and government buildings. Thirteen years were spent in building his palace, which had several sections: (1) the House of the Forest of Lebanon, built almost entirely of cedar; (2) the Hall of Pillars; (3) the Hall of the Throne where justice was administered; (4) Solomon's house; and (5) a house for his Egyptian wife.

Furthermore, he carried on other extensive building programs (including projects in Jerusalem, Gezer, Hazor, and Megiddo). At the latter three, identical city gates have been found. This indicates that the same architect probably planned and constructed all three. Furthermore, each of these cities show indications of other extensive building programs during Solomon's time. Elaborate shafts were constructed to enable the people to reach the city water supply. At Megiddo, for instance, stone steps led down into the shaft to a tunnel, which led outside the city wall to the water source, in a cave.[11]

Another building project consisted of a merchant fleet of ships, which were based in the Gulf of Aqaba at Ezion-geber, where the gulf reaches its northernmost point. Again, Hiram furnished the vital know-how, as well as sailors to operate the fleet (9:26-28). The Phoenicians were the supreme sailors of the ancient world, while Israel (with no suitable ports) developed little interest in the sea, except in Solomon's time. The

---

[11]For details, see Wright, *Biblical Archaeology,* p. 129ff. On the city gate and the Hazor water system, see Yadin, *Hazor,* pp. 187–247, which gives excellent drawings, plus black and white photographs.

trade was probably with countries along the east coast of Africa and the Arabian Peninsula.

Solomon's building projects were costly in more ways than one. For one thing, they cost him part of his empire. Hiram demanded payment in the form of territorial grants for all the work he had done. Though Solomon gave him twelve cities in the Plain of Acre, he was unhappy with what he got. The name Cabul, possibly meaning "that is nothing," was given to the region. Even then, Hiram had to pay for the territory (9:10-14).

The cost in money was great also. Solomon got money from several sources, the most obvious of which was taxes. But that was not enough. He would have also collected tariffs from caravans that used the international highways, the *Via Maris* and the King's Highway. Another source of income was international trade. Among other things, Solomon traded houses and chariots (10:29). He seems to have been the middleman in the trade between Egypt and the Asian and Mesopotamian states. An elaborate description of Solomon's luxuries (10:14-29) helps us to understand why so much money was needed in addition to his building programs.

THE SEEDS OF DESTRUCTION
(1 KINGS 9:15-23; 11:1-43)

The greatest cost in maintaining Solomon's elaborate kingship was the cost in human freedom. That cost would eventually destroy the united monarchy. Slavery made the building projects possible. It is said that Solomon "raised a levy of forced labor out of all Israel" (5:13), and that the non-Israelite population of the land was put into slavery to carry on the building projects (9:15, 20-23). As to the Israelites, "They were the soldiers, they were his officials, his commanders, his captains, his chariot commanders, and his horsemen" (9:22). Whether Israelites were enslaved by Solomon or not is unclear, but it does seem certain that they worked in labor gangs one month out of three as their contribution to the glory of the state.

Another destructive force was Solomon's large harem. Composed of more than 1000 women, the harem functioned primarily as a status symbol. Just as a wealthy man today may collect expensive automobiles as a way of showing off his wealth, so Oriental kings collected beautiful women. With the women, many of whom were married to Solomon to symbolize a covenant relationship with a foreign ruler, came the various deities they worshiped. Solomon's tolerance of foreign gods did not set well with devout Israelites, especially when he had altars built for foreign gods and even participated in worshiping them, in defiance of the LORD's commands (11:1-13).

Solomon's last years saw the seeds of destruction begin to take root and grow. People on the fringes of his empire began to rebel and break away. First, it was Edom, led by Hadad, a member of the royal house who had escaped to Egypt when David conquered his country (11:14-22). Soon, a Syrian leader named Rezon took control of Damascus (11:23-25).

More serious than either of these were the stirrings of rebellion within Israel itself. The old rivalry between Ephraim and Judah had been suppressed during David's and Solomon's time, but it was still very much alive. In Ephraim especially the old idea of charismatic leadership still survived, and with it the belief that the LORD through his prophet should designate the ruler, not some old king who passed on the kingdom as an inheritance to his son. That idea, once thought to be sound teaching by all Israel, became a heresy to those who believed the LORD had made a covenant with David.

The charismatic figure around whom the dissidents rallied was Jeroboam, an Ephraimite. He had been in charge of all of Solomon's forced labor. A prophet who was also a northerner, Ahijah the Shilonite, met Jeroboam one day. Taking a cloak, he tore it into twelve pieces to symbolize that an emergency existed. Ten of the pieces he gave to Jeroboam, telling him that he was chosen by the LORD to be leader over ten tribes, leaving only two to Solomon's house. Ahijah said that the LORD was bringing judgment upon Solomon for following foreign gods (11:26-39).

Word got to Solomon of Jeroboam's disloyalty. Fortunately, Jeroboam was able to escape to Egypt before Solomon could arrest him. There he found refuge. Shishak, the new pharaoh of Egypt, seems to have encouraged and protected Jeroboam as he had other rebels and fugitives from Solomon (11:40).

THE END OF SOLOMON'S REIGN (1 KINGS 11:41-43)

Finally, after 40 years of magnificence, Solomon died. He had acquired wealth, built buildings, and gained fame from his wisdom. It was during Solomon's time, furthermore, that Israelite literature began to flourish. Wisdom literature undoubtedly was rooted during Solomon's reign, making him the patron saint of Israelite wisdom. The long period of peace probably saw the first attempts to write down Israel's history. A good example of such an attempt would be the Court History of David.

But Solomon also lit the fuse for the bombs that would soon blow the kingdom apart. Excessive taxation, denial of human freedom, and religious apostasy were but a few of the problems left for Solomon's egotistical son and successor, Rehoboam, to solve. Rehoboam, unfortu-

Figure 7–6. David's Kingdom and the United Monarchy.

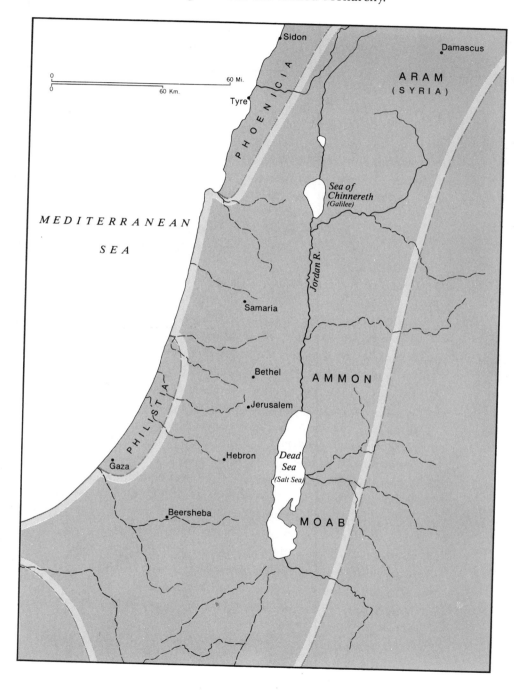

nately, was so self-centered that he did not even realize that there were any problems.

STUDY QUESTIONS

1. What was the attitude toward the monarchy in the Early and Late sources of the books of Samuel and Kings?
2. What was the Court History of David? How was it different from the usual accounts of the reigns of ancient kings?
3. What similarities are there in the birth story of Samuel (1 Samuel 1:1–2:11) and the story of the birth of Isaac (Genesis 19 and 21)?
4. Why was Samuel turned over to Eli the priest at such a tender age?
5. What roles did Samuel play as a leader in Israel?
6. What great series of events forced Israel to unite and eventually to choose a king?
7. What was the religious significance of the ceremony of anointing?
8. Why could Samuel be described as a "king-maker" and a "king-breaker"?
9. Why was Saul chosen to be king over Israel?
10. What were Saul's strengths as king? What were his weaknesses?
11. What did Saul do to gain Samuel's disfavor?
12. How soon after his anointing by Samuel did David become king?
13. What are the two different versions of how Saul and David met? What does this seem to indicate about the materials used in writing the Deuteronomic history?
14. What was David's relationship to Saul?
15. Why didn't David kill Saul and take over the kingdom?
16. What does the story of David and Abigail (I Samuel 25) tell us about David's relations to the people of the land during his outlaw period?
17. Why did David join forces with the Philistines?
18. How did David react to the death of Saul and Jonathan?
19. How did David eventually become king over all Israel?
20. Why did David make Jerusalem his capital?
21. Why was it important that David bring the ark of the covenant to Jerusalem?
22. What were the long-term results of David's affair with Bathsheba?
23. How did Absalom undermine David and what were the results of his rebellion?

24. How did David show that his choice as king was Solomon after Adonijah's attempted coup?

25. Evaluate David's reign as king.

26. How did Solomon profit from David's success as king?

27. What were Solomon's strengths and weaknesses as a king?

28. Describe the major parts of Solomon's temple and tell what the function of each was.

29. How did Solomon pay for all his extensive and expensive building projects?

30. How did Solomon's reign set the stage for the destruction of the united kingdom of Israel?

FOR FURTHER STUDY

CAIRD, GEORGE B. "1 and 2 Samuel: Introduction and Exegesis" in *Interpreter's Bible,* II. New York: Abingdon, 1953.

GRAY, JOHN. *I and II Kings,* 2nd ed. Old Testament Library. Philadelphia: Westminster, 1970.

HERTZBERG, H.W. *The Books of Samuel.* Trans. by J. S. Bowden. Old Testament Library. Philadelphia: Westminster, 1964.

MALY, EUGENE H. *The World of David and Solomon.* Englewood Cliffs, N.J.: Prentice-Hall, 1965.

PHILBECK, BEN F., JR., "1-2 Samuel" in *Broadman Bible Commentary,* III. Nashville: Broadman, 1970.

RAD, GERHARD VON. *Old Testament Theology,* Vol. 1. Trans. by D. M. G. Stalker. New York: Harper & Row, 1962. See pages 312ff for a discussion of the Court History of David.

CHAPTER EIGHT

Israel Becomes Two:
Israel and Judah
to the Fall of Israel

Introduction

An American company that specializes in wrecking buildings advertises that it can tear one down in a minute's time without breaking the glass in nearby buildings. By studying its structure, the company's experts can place explosives at strategic places which, when detonated, will cause the building to come crashing down into one huge pile of rubble. The nation of Israel was not destroyed by experts, but experts could not have done a much better or quicker job of destruction than Solomon's successor did!

METHOD OF APPROACH

One of the problems in studying the divided monarchy is how one should approach it. The method followed by most texts is to have a chapter on the Northern Kingdom from its division to its fall in 722–721 B.C. Yet, this is not the way it is discussed in the Bible. Since the purpose of this book is to follow the order of the biblical material as closely as possible, especially in the historical books, the discussion will be divided as follows: (1) from the division to the middle of the eighth century (but including the fall of the Northern Kingdom in 721 B.C.); (2) from the mid-eighth century to the death of Hezekiah (750–686); and (3) from the reign of Manasseh to the fall of Judah.[1]

THE PROBLEM OF CHRONOLOGY

If one reads several books on the Old Testament, one may find different dates for the same person or event. The reason is that biblical calendars, unlike modern calendars, followed no universally agreed-on starting point. All calendars today, especially in the Western world, use the birth of Jesus as the starting point. Before the coming of Christ, every nation had a different way of figuring the date. For the Israelites, time was figured from the beginning of the king's reign. Thus, a given event was said to have occurred "in the eighth year of King Hezekiah." How do we know, then, when the eighth year of King Hezekiah was by our way of reckoning time?

It is necessary to pinpoint a few dates in the history of Israel and calculate from those key dates. Fortunately, the Assyrians and Babylonians kept accurate calendars based on the rule of their kings. The king's reign always began on New Year's Day. Furthermore, each year was named after a court official to keep it separate and distinct. In addition, important happenings were recorded for each year. For scholars, the most important events used for dating are eclipses, the mention of contacts with the Israelite kingdoms, and the mention of Israelite rulers. As a result, two key dates, 853 and 605, can be established. The first was the Battle of Karkar, which involved the troops of Ahab, King of Israel. The mention of an eclipse within a few years of this battle is important because eclipses can be dated with precision if one knows where they occurred. Karkar is not mentioned in the Old Testament, but Ahab is; so the time of his reign can be pinpointed. The same is true of the Battle of Carchemish in 605 B.C. The records mention Jehoiakim, King of Judah. An eclipse again was the vital factor in dating the event.

That does not solve all the problems, but it helps. The Israelites were not careful to give the length of a king's reign. For instance, Uzziah was said to have reigned for 52 years. Yet, when Uzziah got leprosy, his son Jotham came to the throne as his coregent and reigned for 16 years. If you add the two together, you get 68 years. In reality, the total time was somewhere between 52 and 55 years, depending on the date of Uzziah's death. This creates difficulties for one working on chronologies and is the

[1]To help students keep the kings and their countries straight, (I) will follow the names of Israel's kings and (J) will follow the names of Judah's kings, where there might be confusion.

major reason why dates vary from one scholar's scheme to another. Most authors pick what seems to be the best chronology and stay with it.

The Division of the Kingdom (922–783)

REHOBOAM'S FOLLY (1 KINGS 12:1-19)

Trouble was not long in coming. Solomon was powerful enough to keep things under control while he lived; but his successor, Rehoboam, lacked the sound judgment needed to deal with the problems he inherited from his father.

After a coronation in Jerusalem, Rehoboam went to the old northern shrine at Shechem for another coronation by the northern tribes. The people appeared before him and asked for relief from the harsh requirements laid on them by Solomon. Rehoboam, instead of taking the advice of his senior counselors to lighten their burdens, listened to his younger friends. His arrogant answer was that if they thought things had been harsh under Solomon, then they had not seen anything harsh (12:1-15).

The northern tribes, led by Jeroboam, revolted. Rehoboam tried to put down the rebellion by sending his labor foreman to threaten the people. He was stoned to death, and Rehoboam himself just barely escaped in his chariot. Thereafter, the kingdoms would be known as Israel and Judah.

JEROBOAM (I, 922–901) BECOMES KING OF ISRAEL (1 KINGS 12:20–24)

Jeroboam was installed as king of the northern tribes, leaving only the tribe of Judah and perhaps the tribe of Benjamin under Rehoboam's control (12:20). Rehoboam raised an army to take back the northern territory, but a prophet named Shemaiah warned that such an attempt would be unsuccessful.

Jeroboam got the better part of the kingdom by most any standard. Israel, stronger economically, had a larger population, controlled the major roads, and had the best and most productive land. Its greatest weakness was the instability of its government. No sure way had developed for moving from the rule of one king to another. Its material assets also made it more attractive to outside powers, to whom Israel was accessible by its roads.

Judah, on the other hand, had the poorest land and the smallest part of the population. It was isolated. These characteristics made it less attractive to invaders. Its greatest assets were Jerusalem, with its already-rich traditions, and the Davidic monarchy, which assured stability in government.

JEROBOAM'S REIGN (1 KINGS 12:25–14:20)

In reading the history of the divided kingdom, one must be aware of certain things. For one thing, the writer was from Judah and was an admirer of David. Since Israel opposed the Davidic monarchy and the Davidic covenant, the historian had negative feelings about anything connected with the northern kingdom. For another thing, Jerusalem (to the Deuteronomic historian) was the only place where true worship could be carried on. When Jeroboam led the revolt and set up worship centers at Dan and Bethel, he used golden calves to replace the ark of the covenant as the symbol of the LORD's throne. For this reason, he became

Figure 8–1. "So the King . . . made two calves of gold . . . and he set one in Bethel" (1 Kings 12:28, 29). Tell Bethel, some ten miles north of Jerusalem, was where Jeroboam I set up a shrine to keep the Israelites from going to Jerusalem to worship.

Photograph by John H. Tullock.

the devil incarnate to the religious men of Judah. All who followed Jeroboam were put in the same category.

It did not take Jeroboam long to gain the disapproval of the prophets in Israel. By choosing calves as symbols of the throne of God, he chose the symbol of Hadad, the chief god of the Baal religion (12:25-33). This brought down upon him the wrath of the prophets. A Judean prophet came to Bethel and pronounced the LORD's judgment upon it (13:1-3). Jeroboam tried to punish the prophet, but paralysis struck him and caused him to back down. Then he offered to pay the prophet, but the prophet refused (13:4-10).

On his way back to Judah, the prophet was stopped by another prophet who invited him to a meal. The Judean refused, saying that the LORD told him not to eat in Israel. The Israelite persuaded him to do so by telling him he had a message from the LORD that he should eat. While they were eating, the Israelite prophet told the Judean prophet he would be killed for disobeying the LORD. When he died, the Israelite buried him and commanded that he, too, should be buried in the same tomb. (13:11-32).

As further evidence of the LORD's displeasure with Jeroboam, the prophet Ahijah told Jeroboam's wife that their son Abijah would die. Furthermore, he said that Jeroboam's dynasty would be replaced. All this is an indication of the important roles that prophets played in relation to the kings of both Israel and Judah. When Jeroboam died, he was succeeded by another son, Nadab (13:33–14:20).

REHOBOAM'S REIGN (1 KINGS 14:21-29)

Rehoboam (J, 922–915) had a notably unsuccessful reign. Not only did he have to deal with the revolt of the northern tribes, but he also had a war on his southern border. Shishak of Egypt had dreams of reviving the glory of the Egyptian empire. To do that, he had to control Palestine, which had vital highways. He attacked in the south, penetrating the hill country and the coastal plain. He extended his conquests all the way northward to Megiddo, as both Egyptian records and an inscription found at Megiddo show. Jerusalem, as well as a number of cities in the hill country, came under attack. This caused Rehoboam to pay an enormous bribe to keep Shishak from destroying the city (14:21-28).[2] At his death, Rehoboam was succeeded by his son Abijam (14:29-31).

[2]See Martin Noth, *The History of Israel*, 2nd English ed., rev. by P. R. Ackroyd (New York: Harper & Row, 1960) p. 239 on Shishak's invasion.

ABIJAM AND ASA OF JUDAH (1 KINGS 15:1-24)

Rehoboam was succeeded by Abijam (J, 915–913), but his reign was negative and short. According to 2 Chronicles, he enjoyed considerable military success over Jeroboam. He captured Bethel, Jesanah, and Ephron. This pushed Israel's front lines back some 6 to 8 miles in places (2 Chron. 13:1-22).

His brother Asa (J, 913–873) had one of the longest reigns of any king of Judah. He was credited with at least a halfway attempt to abolish pagan religions, but he did not go so far as to get rid of the local worship centers. The historians gave him an A for his personal religious attitudes. The war with Israel continued during Asa's reign. Baasha (I) of Israel was able to move within 5 miles of Jerusalem, where he fortified Ramah, a town on the main road through the hills. In desperation, Asa (J) sent an expensive bribe to Ben-hadad, the king of Syria, to persuade him to attack Israel. Ben-hadad obliged Asa (J), invading the northern and eastern territories of Israel, capturing a number of cities, including Dan and Hazor. This forced Baasha (I) to retreat. Asa (J) took advantage of the retreat to use the materials in the fortifications at Ramah to fortify Mizpeh and Geba. The fortress has been found in recent years by archaeologists[3] (15:9-24). Second Chronicles 14:9-15 tells of another military attack on Judah by Zerah the Egyptian, but Asa was successful in defeating his armies.

THE PARADE OF KINGS IN ISRAEL
(1 KINGS 15:25–16:20)

After the death of Jeroboam, Israelite kings came and went with surprising rapidity. Before taking the kingship, the only anointing that many of the kings received was a personal anointing of greed and lust for power. Nadab (I, 901–900) succeeded his father, Jeroboam, only to be murdered by Baasha (15:25-28). Baasha (I, 900–877) did not stop with Nadab but also hunted down the rest of Jeroboam's family and murdered them. As discussed previously, Baasha (I) continued the wars with Asa (J). Because of his military power he lasted more than 20 years and died in an unusual way for an Israelite king–of natural causes (15:29–16:7)!

There followed three kings in less than two years. Elah (I, 877–876), Baasha's son, was murdered by Zimri (I, 876). Zimri likewise killed all Baasha's kinfolk. His reign set a record—he was king for seven days

---

[3]On the military movements of Israel and Judah, see Johanan Aharoni and Michael Avi-Yonah, *The Macmillan Bible Atlas* (New York: The Macmillan Company, 1968), pp. 122–123. For a description of the fortress, see G. Ernest Wright, *Biblical Archaeology*, p. 151ff.

before he went out in a blaze of glory by burning the palace down upon himself. Zimri's suicide had been provoked by an attack by Omri, an army commander who decided that he, too, had the royal look about himself (16:8-20).

The Dynasty of Omri (876–842)

ISRAEL AND HER NEIGHBORS

Israel and Judah had been fortunate to survive the first 50 years following the collapse of the united monarchy in 922 B.C. The key to their survival came from the outside, since Egypt was powerless and no one state had achieved dominance in Mesopotamia. For a brief time, it looked as though the quiet period would end when Assyria, led by Asshur-nasir-pal (884–860) rose to power and pushed all the way to the Mediterranean. His conquests probably did not reach as far south as Israel, nor were they permanent. His cruelties set the tone for succeeding Assyrian rulers, causing the Assyrians to be among the most dreaded conquerors in the ancient Near East.[4]

The more immediate problem for Israel was its relationship with Syria (called Aram in the Hebrew text). Ben-hadad, whose reign extended from about 884 to 842 B.C., was strong enough to be a constant problem to Omri and his son Ahab. As a result, the two small countries alternated between being at war and being allies. When no one else threatened them, they fought each other. But whenever a threat arose from Assyria, they joined for mutual protection.

Omri also renewed with Phoenicia the old alliance that had been so profitable to both David and Solomon. To seal the covenant, Omri's son Ahab was married to Jezebel, the daughter of the king of Tyre. That marriage would have far-reaching effects upon Israelite society and religion.

Israel's relations with Judah changed for the better during the Omrid dynasty. The two kingdoms became allies, Israel being the dominant party in the alliance. Athaliah, who probably was Ahab's daughter (2 Kings 8:18,26), was married to Jehoram of Judah to symbolize the union between the two kingdoms.

THE INFLUENCE OF OMRI (1 KINGS 16:21-28)

Omri (I, 876–869) had brief opposition from another contender named Tibni. Moving quickly to organize his kingdom along the lines of the Davidic and Solomonic kingdoms, he renewed old alliances; began

---

[4]John Bright, *A History of Israel*, p. 236ff.

building programs, which Ahab carried on; and moved the capital to the hill of Samaria from Tirzah.

Moving the capital from Tirzah in the Valley of Jezreel to Samaria (1 Kings 16:23-24) showed something of Omri's sense of judgment. The hill of Shemer on which Omri and Ahab built Samaria was an excellent city site from a military standpoint. Later, it would take the Assyrian army several years to capture it.

By Omri's time, water was no longer the problem it had been, since in the tenth century the Israelites had developed the cistern. A cistern was an underground jug, dug into the rock and plastered with lime to keep it from leaking. During the rainy season, runoff water was channeled to the cisterns to be stored for the dry months.

The remains of Omri's and Ahab's palace have been found at Samaria. The exceptionally fine masonry work enclosed an area 582 feet long by 424 feet wide. The palace, which Ahab built for Jezebel, was 89 feet by 79 feet. In this palace were found many ivory pieces, fitting the description in 1 Kings 22:39 as "the ivory house which he built." Extensive building programs were carried on at other cities, including Megiddo, during the Omri-Ahab years.[5] Omri's power and influence can also be seen in the fact that many years after his death Israel was known in Assyrian records as "the land of Omri." Furthermore, the Moabite stone (found in 1868) speaks of how Moab was conquered by Omri and lists the annual tribute or bribe the Moabites had to pay to Israel. Mesha, the king of Moab who erected the stone, threw off Israelite control during Ahab's wars with Syria.[6]

Despite his achievements, the biblical writer only mentions the fact that Omri built Samaria and that "he did more evil than all who were before him" (1 Kings 16:25-28).

THE REIGN OF AHAB (I, 869–850)
(1 KINGS 16:29–22:4)

Introduction (1 Kings 16:29-34). As far as the biblical writer was concerned, the news about Ahab was bad—first, last, and always. He was worse than his father, Omri (16:30). He married Jezebel, an ardent worshiper of the Canaanite god Baal, and worshiped her gods. Furthermore, he built altars to Baal and made an idol to represent Asherah, Baal's

---

[5]Gaalyah Cornfeld and David N. Freedman, eds., *Archaelogy of the Bible: Book by Book,* (New York: Harper & Row, 1976), pp. 119–121. See also Martin Noth, *The History of Israel,* (New York. Harper & Row, 1960), p. 231.

[6]James B. Pritchard, ed., *The Ancient Near East:* An Anthology of Texts and Pictures, (Princeton: Princeton University Press, 1965), p. 209.

Figure 8–2. "[Omri] fortified the hill, and called the name of the city which he built, Samaria" (1 Kings 16:24). The ruins of the Omri–Ahab palace complex at Samaria reveal unusually fine construction for that time. Ivory decorations were discovered in the excavations.

Photograph by John H. Tullock.

mistress. The implication is that he gave approval to human sacrifice as a part of worship (16:31-34).

The Canaanite fertility religion. One of Israel's major problems from the day it entered Palestine was what it was to do about the Canaanite culture and religion. The harsh demands for a holy war was one attempt to deal with the problem. Israel's leaders were intelligent enough to know that the sexually oriented religion of the Canaanites would make the more demanding requirements of the worship of the LORD harder to live by. For this reason, the uncompromising demands of a holy war, if carried out, would eliminate not only the religious shrines but all who taught the religion.

But things did not happen that way. Israel failed to conquer the land completely. Instead, the Canaanites were absorbed into the population, even when Canaanite lands were taken. With the Canaanites came their culture and religion.

Imagine what it would be like to be Sam Israelite, who comes from the desert where his principal occupation has been that of a shepherd.

Suddenly, he finds himself in possession of a house and land of his own. He is now a farmer. He plants his crops, but they fail. He has a Canaanite neighbor who plants his crops and succeeds.

He goes to his neighbor, Joe Canaanite, and says, "Say, Joe, how is it that your barley looks so much better than mine?"

Joe answers, "Why, Sam, the problem with your crops is that you are worshiping the wrong god. Your god was OK when it came to warfare, but he is just not experienced enough in growing crops. Come with me tomorrow to the Shrine of Hadad. We are having our spring fertility dance and, man, are those temple girls beauties! After all, Baal really knows how to make that barley grow." It is not hard to imagine what many Israelite men would do in that case.

Baalism was based on the wet–dry cycle of the year, which is common in Palestine. According to the Baal myth, Baal and Anat were brother and sister, but also lovers. Baal was killed by his enemy, Mot, the god of death. Mot ate Baal. Because Baal made the earth produce, his death caused vegetation to die (the dry season). Anat, or Asherah as the Old Testament calls her (1 Kings 16:33), went looking for Baal. Anat seized Mot, killed him, and made hamburger of him. She scattered the bits of his flesh over the fields for the birds to eat. Baal came alive when Mot died. Sexual union between the lovers then brought fertility to the land once more (the rainy season).[7]

It was this religion that Jezebel was so ardently promoting in Israel. She also donated money to it. In the court alone there were 450 prophets of Baal and 400 prophets of Asherah (1 Kings 18:19). Baalism threatened to sweep over the land, but one man—the prophet Elijah—stemmed the tide.

Elijah among the prophets.   Elijah was the first prophet who could be ranked with the great prophets. In later Jewish tradition he became the symbol of the ideal prophet as Moses was the symbol of the ideal law-giver (Luke 9:30,33). Before he is discussed, it might be well to look at the whole idea of prophecy as it was practiced in Israel (and Judah) in the time of the Hebrew kingdoms. (In this discussion, the term Israel will apply to all the people, north and south, not just those in the Northern Kingdom.)

Israel was not alone in having prophets. Balaam (Num. 22:1–24:25) was not an Israelite, as both the Bible and a recently found inscription show.[8] Mari, a city in the northern part of Mesopotamia, had prophets who gave oracles (sayings) in much the same manner that the Israelite

---

[7]This, and many other stories about Baal were a part of the Ugaritic materials from the fourteenth century B.C. They are translated in Pritchard, *The Ancient Near East*, pp. 92–118.

[8]Jacob Hoftijzer, *The Biblical Archaeologist*, 39, 1 (March, 1976), 11–17.

Figure 8–3. "Ahab took for wife Jezebel . . . , and went and served Baal, and worshipped him" (1 Kings 16:31). Baal was the god of the storm, and thus the god of fertility, since water was essential for the growth of crops. This stele of Baal, which is from the nineteenth–eighteenth century B.C., is from the Ras Shamra Museum and shows the god holding a bolt of lightning.

The Louvre. Photograph by David Rogers.

prophets did.[9] Furthermore, as later study will show, not all Israelite prophets were admirable men. Some were simply yes-men to the kings. But the true prophets of Israel were men who were in a class by themselves.

Three Hebrew terms were used to describe the prophet. Two of them are translated "seer." The third word is *navi'*, which probably meant "one who speaks for another." So Aaron was the *navi'* for Moses since he was the one who spoke for Moses (Exodus 7:1). "Seer" was a term used earlier to describe the prophets, but by the time of the great prophets (eighth to sixth centuries B.C.) it was more of a derogatory term.

[9]Herbert B. Huffmon, "Prophecy in the Mari Letters," *The Biblical Archaeologist*, 31, 4 (December, 1968), 101–124.

Two other descriptive but nonbiblical terms applied to prophets were "ecstatic" and "diviner," referring to the way the prophet received his message. Ecstatics were prophets whose prophecy came as part of a psychological experience, such as a trance or highly emotional state. This was what was meant when Saul was described as being among the prophets (1 Sam. 10:10-13). Ecstatic prophets did strange things and had strange experiences.

Diviners, on the other hand, read the signs in nature—the pattern of the clouds or the patterns of the intestines of a bird or animal—in short, the equivalent of reading palms or tea leaves today. None of the great prophets were diviners in this sense of the word, but a number of them (especially Ezekiel) did have some characteristics of the ecstatics.

These characteristics marked Israel's prophets as spiritual giants:

1. They were God-moved men whose message was, "Thus says the LORD."

2. They were courageous men, unafraid to deliver their message regardless of the personal danger involved.

3. They were honest men, always concerned with the truth.

4. They were moral men who preached a message that demanded the highest in moral living from their hearers.

5. They were compassionate men, sensitive to the cry of the oppressed.

6. They were sensitive men, aware of what was happening in the world around them and convinced that the LORD was in control of what was happening.

7. Great literary writings - better than others

Not all who claimed to be prophets were true prophets. Not all true prophets made the headlines so they could appear in the Bible. Some undoubtedly died in obscurity. None of the true prophets enjoyed great popularity, even though some of them were counselors to kings. Some prophets lived together in a communal society, such as Elisha's "sons of the prophets." Some were on the payroll of the court, as Ahab's prophets were (1 Kings 22). Isaiah was a royal counselor, whether invited to be or not (Isa. 7:3-9). Others were loners like Elijah, fiercely independent and critical of the established order.   connected w/ Real crisis

Two other matters need to be mentioned. For one thing, the prophets were, first of all, concerned with their own time and what was about to happen to their people. Their message has meaning for today because they were applying divine principles to human problems. This is still the task of religion. In the second place, time was the sure test of the validity of a prophet's message. Many times it was very difficult to distinguish between contradictory messages of two prophets. Naturally, the people preferred the word of the prophet with the more positive message. The same problem is with us today.

Elijah confronts Ahab (1 Kings 17:1-24).

While there is no book of the Bible that bears Elijah's name, he is given more space in the Deuteronomist's history of Israel than any other prophet, including Isaiah and Jeremiah.

Elijah was a mysterious person. He would appear, give a pronouncement (oracle), and disappear just as suddenly. He was a prophet of doom and a man who could be both courageous and cowardly. His first confrontation was with Ahab. He appeared before Ahab to tell him that there would be a three-year drought in Israel. The point was that Baal, whose worshipers claimed he could bring rain, was to be challenged at his own game (17:1). Elijah finished his immediate task and returned to the eastern side of the Jordan, where he was in familiar territory and safe from Ahab's clutches (17:2-5). When the drought began to devastate Transjordan, at the LORD's command, Elijah went to Phoenicia, where he stayed with a widow and her son. The presence of the man of God in her home brought prosperity to her and restored her son to life after he died (17:8-24).

The contest on Carmel (1 Kings 18:1-46).

Things were bad in Israel—so bad, in fact, that the king himself went out looking for water for the royal animals. Accompanying Ahab was Obadiah. Unknown to Ahab and Jezebel, Obadiah had been responsible for saving 100 prophets of the LORD during a purge by Jezebel (18:1-6).

When Obadiah and Ahab separated to increase their chances of finding water, Obadiah met Elijah. Elijah asked Obadiah to tell Ahab that he wanted to see him. Obadiah was afraid that if he did, Elijah would disappear again. Finally, he was convinced and agreed to do as Elijah asked (18:7-16).

King and prophet confronted each other, both accusing the other of being a "troubler of Israel." Then Elijah issued a challenge: Bring the people and all the Baal prophets to Mt. Carmel for a test of strength (18:17-19).

Ahab took up the challenge and did as Elijah proposed. Mt. Carmel was an ancient worship site, a mountain that juts out into the Mediterranean Sea on Palestine's northern coast. Its height causes clouds blowing in from the sea to release their moisture, so that vegetation stays green longer there than in any other place in Israel. The sure sign of severe drought was when the vegetation on top of Mt. Carmel withered (Amos 1:2). Thus, it was a favorite shrine for Baal worshipers. Like Moses' challenge to pharoah by the Nile, Elijah was issuing a challenge from the LORD to play the contest on Baal's home court (18:20).

The people gathered. Elijah challenged them to follow either Baal or the LORD. Then he challenged the 450 Baal prophets to prepare a sacrifice. They were to call on Baal to ignite the fire, since he was god of the storm and fire (lightning). Elijah would do the same thing and would call on the LORD. The god who answered by fire would be the winner. The people agreed and pledged to follow the god who revealed his power (18:21-24).

The Baalites prepared their sacrifice and began a day-long ritual, designed to evoke Baal's response. Doing a sort of limping dance, they circled the altar, crying, "O Baal, answer us!" Noon came, but there was no response from Baal. Elijah made sarcastic remarks and suggested that they were not crying loud enough, that Baal was meditating, relieving himself, traveling, or perhaps just sleeping. The frenzy among the prophets increased. They cut themselves, hoping that the flowing of blood would cause the falling of rain. "But there was no voice, no answer, no heed" (18:25-29). The rain did not come. Baal had failed.

When evening came, the exhausted Baalites gave up their futile efforts. Elijah went into action! He built an altar, prepared the sacrificial bull (which, ironically, was the symbol of Baal), and then soaked everything thoroughly with water. Elijah's prayer was simple:

> "O LORD, God of Abraham, Isaac, and Israel, let it be known this day that thou art God in Israel, and that I am thy servant, and that I have done these things at thy word. Answer me, O LORD, answer me, that this people may know that thou, O LORD, art God, and that thou hast turned their hearts back." Then the fire of the LORD fell (18:36-38).

What happened on Mt. Carmel? Some say lightning; others say that the water contained petroleum or gas. What happened really defies explanation, but it was a vital moment in the history of a people. The LORD had beaten Baal at his own game; he, not Baal, had brought the rain. Elijah took a practical approach to limiting the power of Baalism. He called upon the people, who seized the Baal prophets and killed them, even as Jezebel had killed the prophets of the LORD. Elijah did not stop Baalism completely; but he dealt it such a severe setback that it, at least, did not envelop Judah as much as it had Israel (18:30-40).

When the rains came, Ahab had to ride furiously to get down from the mountain. Elijah showed his ability as a distance runner by outrunning Ahab's chariot to Jezreel, some 17 miles away. It was just a warm-up for his encounter with Jezebel (18:41-46).

A mad woman and a scared prophet (1 Kings 19:1-21). Courageous Elijah soon changed to cowardly Elijah when Jezebel heard what he had done to her prophets. She sent him word that when she got her hands on him, it would be the end of him. Elijah decided it was time for him to beat a hasty retreat.

Being an experienced runner, he lost no time in putting distance between himself and Jezebel. His servant could not keep up, so Elijah left him in Beersheba and continued southward toward Sinai. In the wilderness, where he had stopped for rest, he prayed for the LORD to take his life. Instead, he awoke to find food. After eating, he continued his journey (19:1-8).

Arriving at Horeb (Sinai), Elijah rested in a cave. While there, the LORD appeared (theophany) with an accusing question, "What are you doing here, Elijah?" (19:9). Instead of answering the question, Elijah complained that he was the only faithful servant of the LORD left. Told to go stand on the mountain, he experienced wind, earthquake, and fire; but the LORD did not appear in any of the natural catastrophes. Instead, in the quietness following the tumult, a still, small voice asked the same accusing question, "What are you doing here, Elijah?" (19:13). Elijah gave the same whining excuse (19:14). The answer came back, "Get up and get busy. There are 7000 people in Israel who are still faithful" (19:9-18). On his return, he found a new disciple named Elisha (19:19-21).

Ahab and Ben-hadad[10] ***(1 Kings 20:1-43).*** The most dangerous enemy Ahab had was Ben-hadad of Syria. Warfare between the two kingdoms was frequent, each side winning some and losing some. Ben-hadad laid seige to Samaria and took tribute, as well as Ahab's wives and children. Ahab, on the advice of an unknown prophet, launched a surprise attack and routed the Syrians. Later, in a battle at Aphek in Transjordan near the Sea of Galilee, Israel defeated Syria and took Ben-hadad prisoner. Ben-hadad pleaded for his life and agreed to grant Ahab business concessions in Damascus. Ahab agreed to let Ben-hadad go. The prophet rebuked the king for freeing Ben-hadad to fight again. The prophet had seen the war as a holy war in which Ben-hadad should have been killed (20:1-43).

Ahab, Naboth, and Elijah (1 Kings 21:1-29). A classic example of the prophet's role as the conscience of the nation can be seen in the story of Naboth's vineyard. Naboth, a native of Jezreel (where the king had his winter palace), had a vineyard that joined the royal lands. Ahab decided he needed the land for a garden, but Naboth refused to sell it. As an Israelite citizen, his refusal of Ahab's offer was within his right. He, as a typical Israelite, had a feeling of kinship and responsibility for his land. Supposedly, it had been assigned to his family in the time of the conquest and was a legacy to be passed on from generation to generation.

When Naboth refused, Ahab went home and sulked. Jezebel found

---

[10]On the threat of Syria to the Israelite Kingdoms see Martin Noth, *The History of Israel*, pp. 240–241.

out the cause of his unhappiness and set about to get Ahab what he wanted (21:1-7).

Skillfully using the law to the advantage of the royal house, she bribed the village elders to call a meeting of their group, of which Naboth was probably a part. Then, she hired two of the most dishonest witnesses that money could buy to swear that they had heard Naboth curse God and the king. The reason for two witnesses was that the law required at least two witnesses to prove any charge (Deut. 17:6). The penalty for blasphemy was death by stoning. After Naboth was accused, the sentence was carried out (21:8-14).

With the last obstacle out of the way, Ahab took over Naboth's land. When he went to inspect it, however, the first person he saw was Elijah. Elijah pronounced the LORD's judgment upon Ahab and his family and more specifically upon Jezebel, whom he said would be eaten by dogs. This was the most disgraceful thing that could happen to a person. Ahab repented, but it only stayed the execution for a little while (21:15-29).

Two kings and a courageous prophet (1 Kings 22:1-40).   Before the incident described here, an important historical event had taken place. In 853 at Karkar on the Orontes River in northwestern Syria, Shalmaneser III of Assyria fought against an alliance of western kings, including Ahab of Israel and Ben-hadad of Syria. They, along with other small kingdoms, patched up their differences along enough to face a common enemy. A measure of Ahab's prosperity can be seen in the fact that he furnished 2000 war chariots, half of the total chariots used by the western alliance. Shalmaneser said that he won the battle, but that was as far as he got in his conquest. The importance of this battle lies in the fact that it can be dated precisely, and thus it is an invaluable aid in dating events in the Old Testament.[11]

Three years later (850), Ahab and Ben-hadad were ready to go at it again. The bone of contention was Ramoth-gilead, a border city in Transjordan. Ahab (I) called on Jehoshaphat (J) to go to battle with him to recapture Ramoth-gilead (22:1-4).

After assembling his troops and making it obvious what he was about to do, Ahab took Jehoshaphat's advice and consulted his 400 court prophets. They saw what the king wanted to do and, since he fed and clothed them, they were not about to contradict his wishes. So, with one accord the 400 told Ahab to go to battle and the LORD would give him victory. Jehoshaphat could not accept that much agreement and asked if there was another prophet. Ahab replied that there was one, Micaiah ben Imlah, but that he was a negative thinker who was always predicting doom (22:5-12).

---

[11]Aharoni and Avi-Yonah, *Atlas*, p. 81.

Figure 8–4. Israel and Judah—850 B.C.

Sidon

Damascus

Leontes R.

PHOENICIA

Tyre

Dan

DAN

ARAM
(SYRIA)

0   60 Mi.

0   60 Km.

Acco

Sea of
Chinnereth
(Galilee)

MEDITERRANEAN
SEA

Megiddo

ISRAEL

Ramoth-
Gilead

Samaria

Jordan R.

Jabbok R.

Joppa

AMMON

Bethel

Ashdod

Jerusalem

PHILISTIA

Gaza

Hebron

Dead
Sea
(Salt Sea)

JUDAH

Beersheba

MOAB

EDOM

Kadesh-Barnea

At Jehoshaphat's urging, Micaiah was called. When he seemed to agree with the 400, Ahab was suspicious. Then Micaiah gave an oracle predicting the death of the king. He told of being in the heavenly council (a way of emphasizing that the message he gave was the LORD's, not his) and hearing the LORD say he would cause Ahab's prophet to lie to him (22:13-23).

Ahab accepted the advice that he wanted to accept and went to war. He left orders for Micaiah to be jailed and fed bread and water until he returned from battle. Micaiah's last word was that if Ahab did return, the LORD had not spoken by him (22:24-28).

Ahab died in the battle, bleeding to death from a chance shot by a Syrian archer. When they returned his body to Samaria, harlots washed themselves in the water made bloody from washing his chariot. This presumably was supposed to give them some special kind of appeal. The fate of Micaiah is unknown (22:29-40).

JEHOSHAPHAT (J, 873–749), A GOOD KING
(1 KINGS 22:41-50)

After the incident involving Micaiah, Jehoshaphat's reign is summarized briefly. For the most part, his was a positive rule that rooted out corrupt religious practices, made peace with Israel, took control of Edom, and tried to reestablish sea trade through Ezion-geber. He was succeeded by Jehoram (J, 849–842).

foremost of early prophets

Ahaziah (I, 850–849), Elijah and Elisha (1 Kings 22:51–2 Kings 2:25). The only reason Ahaziah rated any notice was that he was consulting a pagan god about an injury he had received. When Elijah heard of it, he sent word to Ahaziah that he would die. When Ahaziah sent soldiers to arrest Elijah, they met disaster. Finally, he pleaded for Elijah to come. When Elijah went, he simply repeated his judgment—that Ahaziah would die because he had consulted a pagan god (2 Kings 1:1-18).

Shortly afterward, Elisha (Elijah's assistant) was told by a group of prophets that Elijah was going to be taken away in a whirlwind. Elisha did not want to accept this prophecy. When it happened, Elijah's cloak was left for Elisha, symbolizing his role as Elijah's successor. Other prophets saw Elisha as Elijah's successor and joined in with him. Unlike Elijah, who had been a very private person, Elisha was much more of a public figure and political activist. As a result, many miracle stories are told about him (2:1-25).

JEHORAM (JORAM) OF ISRAEL (849–842)
(2 KINGS 3:1-27)

The relation of Mesha of Moab to Israel was that of vassal, as described in the Moabite Stone. During the Israelite-Syrian wars, he broke away. Jehoram (I) and Jehoshaphat (J) went on an expedition against Mesha. When they saw him sacrifice his son to his pagan god, they were horrified and turned back.

STORIES ABOUT ELISHA (2 KINGS 4:1–9:14)

Numerous stories grew out of Elisha's ministry. Like Elijah, he was said to have helped a poor widow (4:1-7). His prayer to the LORD was credited with making fruitful a barren woman who had befriended him and restoring her child to life when it died (4:8-37). He was credited with making poisonous stew safe to eat and multiplying loaves of bread (4:28-44).

One of the most famous stories is about healing Naaman, a Syrian army commander, of leprosy. Naaman had heard of Elisha through an Israelite slave girl. When Naaman came to Elisha, he offered to pay for the cure. Elisha refused but instructed Naaman to wash seven times in the Jordan River. When he did, the leprosy disappeared. He again tried to pay Elisha, but payment was refused. Then Elisha's servant, Gehazi, saw a chance to make some easy money. He followed Naaman and, telling him that Elisha had changed his mind, he took Naaman's money. When Elisha found out what Gehazi had done (5:1-27), he pronounced on him Naaman's leprosy.

When Ben-hadad, the king of Syria, tried to attack Israel, Elisha warned the Israelites and frustrated Ben-hadad's plans. Ben-hadad gave orders for Elisha's capture, but they were frustrated (6:8-23). Then Ben-hadad attacked Samaria and laid seige to it. Food began to get so scarce that the people resorted to cannabalism. Because Elisha had provoked the king (probably Jehoram), he blamed him for the problems in Samaria and went out with his men to arrest Elisha. When they came to his house, Elisha told them that food would be plentiful in the city by the next day. During the night, the Syrian army fled, having been frightened by noises of what they thought was an army about to attack them. Three Israelite lepers found their abandoned camp and brought the news to the city (6:24–7:20). The supplies left by the Syrians fell to the Samarians. Thus the prophet's prediction of plenty was fulfilled.

The final mention of Elisha shows him as a political activist. Called by the ill Ben-hadad of Syria to predict whether he would die, Elisha confirmed that he would, sending word by the messenger Hazael, and telling him that Hazael would be king in his place. Hazael returned to Ben-hadad and made Elisha's prophecy come true—he smothered Ben-hadad and seized the throne (8:7-15).

In the meantime, Judah also had a king named Jehoram (J, 849–842), who managed to lose control of Edom. He was married to Athaliah, Ahab's daughter. When he died, their son Ahaziah (J, 842) succeeded him. Ahaziah died that year (8:16-29). Jehoram of Israel (Joram) was killed in a battle the same year by Jehu, a chariot commander in his army. His death and Ahaziah's death were the direct result of an action of Elisha. He chose Jehu to be king of Israel and commissioned him to destroy the family of Ahab. Jehu's army unit supported him and proclaimed him king (9:1-13).

Jehu to Jeroboam II (842–746)

The century from 842 to 746 began with a violent purge and ended with the Northern Kingdom's most glorious days, under Jeroboam II. Although the Assyrians flourished for a short time and forced Israel's kings to pay tribute, their last serious threat came with Adad-Nirari II. He destroyed Syrian power in 802, but he was unable to follow up his advantage. Syria and Assyria both were weak for the next fifty years.[12]

took kingdom from father by force

BLOODY JEHU (I, 842–815) (2 KINGS 9:1–10:34)

After Jehu was anointed king (9:1-13), he immediately set out to establish his power. King Jehoram (Joram) of Israel was recovering from wounds received in the Syrian war at Jezreel. King Ahaziah of Judah (842) was visiting the king of Israel. Jehu met the two kings at Naboth's vineyard. Jehoram (I) was killed immediately by an arrow through his heart. Ahaziah (J) was chased down and shot. He managed to get to Megiddo before he died (9:14-29).

Going on to Jezreel, Jehu came to the house of Ahab's wife, Jezebel, and threw her out a second story window into the street. When the soldiers came by later to pick up her body, all but her hands had been eaten by dogs (9:30-37). Then Jehu systematically slaughtered all the relatives of Ahab, as well as his close friends and advisers. Furthermore, he killed relatives of the Judean king who had come north to visit (10:1-17). Pretending that he was a Baal worshiper, he called a meeting of all Baal worshipers. When they were gathered together, they were killed too (10:18-31).

[12]Bright, *A History of Israel*, p. 252ff, gives the details.

What Jehu did was the equivalent of a new president's taking office and ordering all the former president's family, all his advisers, and all government workers killed. It also had the same effects that such a purge would have on our government—Jehu's new government was very poor. Later on, Hosea (an eighth-century prophet of Israel) would condemn the bloodthirstiness of Jehu. Jehu lost territory to Syria (10:32-36) and paid tribute to Shalmaneser III of Assyria in 841.[13]

ATHALIAH (J, 842–837) (2 KINGS 11:1-21)

The only woman to rule either kingdom was Athaliah of Judah, the mother of Ahaziah, whom Jehu had killed. She seized power and started a purge of her own, but failed, however, to kill prince Joash, a small boy who was hidden by his aunt. Eventually, Jehoida (the chief priest) led a coup that overthrew Athaliah and put seven-year-old Joash on the throne (11:1-21).

JOASH (J, 837–800), THE BOY KING (2 KINGS 12:1-21)

Joash's long reign was comparatively peaceful except for an attack by Syria under Hazael. He had to bribe Hazael to withdraw with monies which he had collected for a temple-repair fund and all the other money he could get (12:1-21).

TWO ISRAELITE KINGS AND THE DEATH OF ELISHA (2 KINGS 13:1-25)

The next two Israelite kings were not particularly distinguished. Jehoahaz (I, 815–801) was reduced by the Syrians to a military weakling. His successor, Jehoash (801–786), had a bit more success than his father, since the Assyrians had virtually destroyed Syria in 801. It was during his reign that Elisha died (13:1-25).

AMAZIAH OF JUDAH (800–783) (2 KINGS 14:1-22)

Amaziah came to the throne after his father, Joash, had been assassinated. This in itself was a testimony to the stability of Judah's government in that the succession to the throne of the Davidic line could even survive attempted coups. Warfare once more broke out between

[13]Bright, *A History of Israel*, p. 251.

Figure 8–5. "The time that Jehu reigned over Israel in Samaria was twenty-eight years" (2 Kings 10:36). Jehu's reign began in a blood-bath and ended in submission. "Jehu, son of Omri," is shown in an artist's representation of a panel of an obelisk on display in the British Museum. He is paying tribute to Shalmaneser III of Assyria.

The British Museum. Drawn by Buford Winfrey.

Israel and Judah, resulting in Amaziah's (J) capture by the army of Jehoash (I) (14:1-22).

JEROBOAM II (I, 786–746) (2 KINGS 14:23-29)

Israel's last burst of prosperity came during the reign of Jeroboam II (I, 786–746), who combined with Uzziah of Judah (783–742) to extend the limits of the Hebrew kingdoms to those achieved during the days of David and Solomon. Such prosperity was made possible by two things: (1) Assyria's knockout blow to Syria in 801 B.C., combined with Assyria's own fifty-year weakness after that event; and (2) the talents of Jereboam as a military leader and civil administrator. Uzziah of Judah seems to have been equally as talented. While condemning his religious failures, the narrator speaks volumes in one verse about Jeroboam:

> He restored the border of Israel from the entrance of Hamath as far as the sea of the Arabah [Dead Sea], according to the word of the LORD, the God of Israel, which he spoke by his servant Jonah the son of Amittai, the prophet, who was from Gath-hepher (14:25).

Even the Syrian capital of Damascus came under Israelite control.

UZZIAH OF JUDAH (783–742) (2 KINGS 15:1-7; 2 CHRON. 26:1-23)

Uzziah is given no more notice than Jeroboam. Yet he also brought to his kingdom unparalleled prosperity. In the Chronicler's history his accomplishments are more fully told: (1) He conquered the Philistine territory and once more established Judah's control of the vital coastal highway. (2) He pushed back the Ammonites and the Arabs of Transjordan, as well as the Negev, to the traditional borders of Egypt. (3) He fortified Jerusalem and cities in the Negev, as well as in the foothills of Judah and the coastal plain. (4) He promoted agriculture. (5) He modernized his army, equipping it with the latest weapons (2 Chron. 26:1-15).

During the reign he became a leper. The Chronicler blamed the disease on Uzziah's pride, which caused him to try to take over the priestly role. When he became angry because of the priests' opposition, "Leprosy broke out on his forehead, in the presence of the priests in the house of the LORD" (2 Chron. 26:19). The leper was segregated from all public contact. This meant that even though Uzziah was still called the king, his son Jotham actually carried out his duties as king until Uzziah's death in 742 B.C.

1st of the Classical Prophets

Israel's Eighth-Century Prophets: Amos and Hosea

In the Israelite kingdoms, between the mid-eighth century and approximately 500 B.C., there arose a remarkable group of men whose words furnished a large portion of the materials found in the Hebrew Bible. What is all the more amazing is that most of those words were spoken in short, to-the-point sayings called oracles. They were designed to be heard, not read. It is to disciples who memorized and passed on the oracles until they were written down that we owe their preservation (Isa. 8:16). A later generation realized that what the prophets had spoken was true. This led to the writing of the books of the prophets. The prophets, for the most part, were quite unpopular in their own time.

Two of these prophets, Amos and Hosea, preached in Israel in its last days. Amos brought to bear the viewpoint of an outsider, while Hosea revealed the heartbreak of a native who saw his beloved country sliding toward the brink of destruction.

AMOS: THE SHEPHERD FROM TEKOA

The times. Amos preached in Israel after Jeroboam II had completed his wars of conquest. The nation was riding the crest of a superficial prosperity. There was a merchant class whose motto must have been:

"Buyer, beware!" Short-weight, shoddy merchandise and inflated prices were the rule and not the exception. The small farmer was cheated when the merchants bought his surplus grain. They used an oversized measure and weighed out the farmer's money on rigged scales. When they, in turn, sold grain to the common people, they used a substandard measure and charged an inflated price. The grain, furthermore, was rotten and full of trash. The demand of the law: "Love your neighbor as yourself" (Lev. 19:18) was forgotten in their greed for gain.

Religion was very popular. The shrines were filled with worshipers, and feast days were numerous. The king had his personal shrine at Bethel. Sacrifices were offered in abundance, and many people even slept by the altar at night to demonstrate their devotion to the LORD. But for all their religiosity, it had little effect on dealings in the marketplace.

Society was divided into the haves and have-nots. The rich were getting richer, and the poor were becoming poorer. The rich man could care less about the poor man. If the poor man starved to death, it would just decrease the surplus population.

While things were tranquil on the domestic scene, things were beginning to change on the international front. Within a few years from the time of Amos's appearance at Bethel, Assyria (like a sleeping giant) would rouse itself and begin a westward march that would crush the small western kingdoms, including Israel.

The man.   There has been much discussion about Amos. After all, he was the first prophet whose words became an Old Testament book. Nothing is known about his family or whether he even had one. He was a Judean, a native of Tekoa, a small village about 12 miles south of Jerusalem in the hill country.

He was a shepherd. Much of the debate about Amos is over the term used to describe him, since it was not the usual term for a shepherd. The only other time the word was used in the Old Testament was in 2 Kings 3:4, where Mesha, king of Moab, was described as a "sheep breeder" (Amos 1:1, RSV). Amos also described himself as a "dresser of sycamore trees" (7:14). The sycamore was a kind of low-quality fig, used for food for cattle and poor people. To "dress a sycamore tree" seemed to involve pinching or puncturing its fruit to hasten the ripening of it. The sycamore would not grow at Tekoa, so Amos had to go either to Jericho or westward to the Shephelah (foothills) to do that job.

Scholars draw opposite conclusions from these known facts about Amos. (1) He was a poor man who had to have two jobs to make a living; or (2) he owned flocks and lands that others looked after, freeing him to take the wool from his sheep to Bethel and Samaria, where there were more traders and the prices would be better.

Whatever the truth was, he did go north and what he saw provoked his imagination. He was a passionate believer in the LORD, the God of

Figure 8–6. "Amos who was among the shepherds of Tekoa" . . . (Amos 1:1). In this barren, rocky country Amos heard God's call to "Go, prophesy to my people Israel" (Amos 7:15).

Photograph by David Rogers.

Israel. What he saw taking place in the cities of Israel did not agree with what he knew of the requirements of the covenant the LORD had made with his people at Sinai. He went to preach, not because he wanted to, but because he felt compelled by the LORD: "The LORD *took* me . . . and the LORD said to me, '*Go*, prophesy to my people Israel' " (7:15) [emphasis added].

The book. While the book of Amos, as it stands, was probably put in its final form during the Babylonian exile, the messages were spoken sometime near 760 B.C., but not later than 750 B.C.

The introduction (Amos 1:1-2). After an introduction somewhat standard for the prophets, the theme of the book " the LORD roars from Zion" emphasizes the source of the prophet's message.

Look at what the neighbors are doing (Amos 1:3–2:5). Amos's sermon started out by painting a lurid picture of the sins of Israel's neighbors. Syria had committed unspeakable atrocities in war by tearing captives to pieces under iron threshing sledges (1:3-5); the Philistines were slave traders (1:6-8); the Phoenicians also traded in slaves and were covenant breakers (1:9-10); Edom had maintained an undying hatred for Israel (1:11-12); the Ammonites had mercilessly ripped open the stomachs of pregnant women (1:13-15); Moab had desecrated the bones of the Edomite king (2:1-3); and Judah had rejected "the law of the LORD" (2:4-5). Each section or oracle opened with the phrase "For three transgressions of ———and for four, I will not revoke the punishment"; and ends with "I will send a fire."

You are even worse, Israel (Amos 2:6-16).   While Amos charged Israel's neighbors with one major sin, the charges against Israel were many. The rich put the poor into slavery for the least of debts (2:6). They pushed the poor man down at every opportunity (2:7*a*). Father and son patronized the same prostitute at the shrine where the LORD was supposed to be worshiped (2:7*b*). In violation of Israelite law, they took a man's only garment and kept it overnight (Deut. 24:13) with the excuse that they needed it for a religious purpose (2:8*a*). The priests and their friends had drinking parties, using religious funds to buy wine (2:8*b*).

They did these things despite the LORD's blessings upon them (2:9-11). In fact, they even went further. They demanded that the prophets not prophesy and tried to get Nazirites to violate their vows not to drink wine (2:12). Because of these sins, judgment would be swift and certain (2:13-16).

Hear this word (Amos 3:1–5:17).   These chapters contain three sermons, introduced by the phrase, "Hear this word." In chapter 3 the theme of the sermon is "privilege brings responsibility." The reason for the severity of Israel's punishment was that it had been blessed more than any other people by being chosen by the LORD (3:1-2). As a result the LORD God was bringing a judgment that would destroy shrine and altar, winter house and summer house (3:3-15).

Chapter 4 was directed to the women of Samaria. Amos compared them to the fat, sleek cows of the pastures of Bashan. They, like their husbands, were greedy drunkards concerned only with their own desires. When the invader came, instead of being given an honorable burial, their dead bodies would be speared with hooks and dragged through the broken city walls to be cast out for the animals to devour (4:1-3).

Religion had become sin because it was false worship (4:4-5). The LORD had warned the people by famine (4:6), drought (4:7-8), blight and locusts (4:9), war (4:10), and natural catastrophe; but none of these had turned them back to the LORD. Thus, judgment was certain (4:12). In 4:13 there is a hymn to the power of the LORD:

> For lo, he who forms the mountains, and creates the wind,
>   and declares to man what is his thought;
> who makes the morning darkness,
>   and treads on the heights of the earth—
> the LORD, the God of hosts, is his name!

The prophet set before Israel the alternatives in 5:1-17—death or life. He sang a funeral song in the limping halting rhythm of the dirge:

> Fallen, no more to rise,
>   is the virgin Israel;
> forsaken on her land,
>   with none to raise her up (5:2).

Its only hope for life was to seek the LORD, for life could be found in him (5:4,6,14). Otherwise, judgment would be so severe that farmers would have to be pressed into service as wailers since there would not be enough professional wailers to go around (5:16-17).

The day of the LORD is upon you (Amos 5:18-27).   In some of the most vivid imagery found in prophetic literature, Amos described the day of the LORD. In popular thought, the day of the LORD was to be a day of

Figure 8–7.   "Hate evil, and love good, and establish justice in the gate" (Amos 5:15). The city gate, shown in the plan of the Solomonic gate at Megiddo, was the courthouse in ancient Israel. The city elders met in the alcoves to conduct the business of the city, which included trials.

Photograph by John H. Tullock.

triumph and celebration, when the LORD would give Israel victory over its enemies (5:18). Not so, said Amos. It would be a day of

> darkness, and not light;
> as if a man fled from a lion,
>   and a bear met him;
> or went into the house and leaned with his hand against the wall,
>   and a serpent bit him.

Their religious services were such farces that they had no effect on the way they lived. The only thing that could satisfy the LORD was to

> let justice roll down like waters,
> and righteousness as an ever-flowing stream (5:24).

This verse sums up the major theme of Amos's preaching—that a righteous God demanded righteousness from those who worship him. Right living involved giving every man his due. When viewed from the standpoint of mercy, justice can have an almost negative quality; mercy means that personal merit does not come into consideration. So the rich men of Israel preferred mercy. The poor, however, looked at justice as a positive quality. They had never rated that high on the scale of human values. When a person suffering injustice achieves justice it is a blessing.

Amos also raises the question of the value of sacrifice (5:25). What he seemed to say that was wrong about the system was not sacrifice as it was the sacrificer. A wrong attitude changes worship of any kind into blasphemy.

Woe to the wealthy (Amos 6:1-14).   Amos saw pride and self-indulgence as major problems in Israel. Because of the nation's military successes, its leaders pictured themselves as the great leaders in the world. The LORD had brought down other nations, so Israel should not think it could not fall (6:1-3).

The upper classes spent time in drunken carousing, bragging on their greatness, and caring nothing for their fellow Israelites. They were celebrating while their ship was sinking, unaware of the danger around them (6:4-7). Because of their pride, judgment was inevitable (6:8-14).

The visions of Amos (7:1–9:4).   The visions of the prophets were a major part of their prophetic experiences. Five visions are described in the book of Amos: (1) the locust plague; (2) the judgment by fire (drought); (3) the plumbline; (4) the basket of summer fruit, and (5) the LORD by the altar.

What was the nature of these visions? The visions of Amos—as well as later prophets, especially Isaiah, Jeremiah, and Ezekiel—seemed to begin with some ordinary circumstance of the prophet's life. But in a particular situation the ordinary event took on extraordinary meaning and significance for the prophet. He drew from it a lesson that had an application to the situation with which he was dealing. This could mean that the prophet never went through any trancelike state or extreme emotional condition as the ecstatics did. Rather, it may well be that the vision was played out in a sort of "glorified" imagination. Ezekiel's visions by the River Chebar (Ezekiel 1) would seem to be an exception to this. Even so, those visions, strange as they were, began when Ezekiel observed the approach of a thunderstorm (Ezekiel 1:4).

Amos's first two visions are different from the other three. They threatened judgment; but when the prophet pleaded for the people, judgment was suspended (7:1-6). With the vision of the plumbline, there was no suspension of judgment—it was inevitable. These visions may say something of the stages of Amos's thinking about Israel. For a time he had hope. As time went by, however, be became convinced that there was no hope—judgment had to come.

The account of the visions is interrupted by a prose description of a confrontation between Amos and Amaziah, the head priest at the king's shrine at Bethel. Amos was told to go back to Judah and mind his own business. Amos replied, in effect, that he was minding the LORD's business and that Amaziah would not escape the judgment, even though he was the religious leader (7:10-17).

The fourth vision (8:1-3) contains a pun or play on words. Written Hebrew words contain only consonants. The consonants for "summer fruit" are KTS, and the consonants for "the end" are KTS. So when Amos was asked, "What do you see?" he replied, "A basket of KTS (summer fruit)." The LORD said, "The KTS (end) is coming for my people." This word of judgment formed the text for a sermon on judgment on those who could not worship because they were thinking of how they could cheat their neighbors in the market when the religious holiday was over. For such, judgment would include famine for those whose habit it was to gorge themselves on food. Furthermore, there would be a famine of the word of the LORD when men wanted most to hear it (8:4-14).

The final vision spoke of judgment coming upon the religious shrine. Amos probably saw a priest standing by the altar, and that scene led to the vision of the LORD himself standing by the altar calling for judgment (9:1). No matter how men tried to escape, there would be, in the words of the spiritual "No hiding place down here" (9:2-4). Following another hymn (9:5-6) comes one of the most remarkable statements in the book:

> "Are you not like the Ethiopians to me,
>   O people of Israel?" says the LORD.
> "Did I not bring up Israel from the land of Egypt,
>   and the Philistines from Caphtor and the Syrians from Kir?" (9:7).

This question attacked a commonly held view among the Israelites—that the LORD was their God alone and was not concerned with any other people. Other people had their own gods. A conflict between two nations also meant a conflict between the respective dieties of those nations. But, both here and in the the opening words of judgment on Israel's neighbors, Amos was saying that the LORD, the God of Israel, was the God of all nations. Because of that, the LORD was just as concerned about the Syrians and the Philistines as he was the Israelites.

A better day (Amos 9:10-15).   The book of Amos ends with a hopeful note that may have been added in the dark days of the Babylonian exile by a Judean editor (9:11-15). By that time, the judgments spoken of by Amos were a reality and the role of the prophets had changed from pronouncers of doom to ones who held out hope. None of the prophets, however, saw God's judgment as the complete wiping out of the people. Instead, they saw it as the means whereby the nation would be cleansed of its corruption and purified for a new and better day.

Amos: a summary.   Why was Amos important?

1. He was the first of the so-called writing prophets, although the writing was probably done by later disciples.
2. He represented what was best in the prophetic tradition—courage, honesty, compassion, and the ability to see the inevitable result of the things that were going on in Israelite society.
3. The ideas he preached were these:
   a. The LORD, the God of Israel is the God who is concerned with all people.
   b. The LORD is a righteous, highly moral deity who demands right living by those who worship him.
   c. No man who is right with the LORD will treat his fellow man like a thing to be abused.
   d. The inevitable result of the abuse of privilege will be judgment. Though man may be unjust, the LORD of all the earth will see that justice is done.

HOSEA: THE PROPHET WITH THE BROKEN HEART

Amos had preached during the days of Israel's glory, but now those days of glory were over. When Jeroboam died in 746 B.C., the government, which had seen forty years of stability and progress, fell apart like a sand castle before the ocean waves. The causes were both internal and external.

As Amos had seen the internal rottenness which had created a situation that made it impossible for the kingdom to exist much longer, Hosea was the witness to the disintegration of the kingdom brought on by that rottenness. If that was not enough, the giant who had been sleeping between the Tigris and Euphrates rivers woke up hungry and began to look in all directions for countries it could gobble up. The nightmare the prophets were talking about was on its way to becoming a frightening reality.

The rise of Assyria.   Assyria, the Mesopotamian state that had driven across the small west Asian states before, but had not been able to maintain its hold on them, had a new and vigorous king, Tiglath-pileser III (745–727). Tiglath-pileser III had an empire as his goal, and he set out to get it. His armies went in all directions, conquering as they went. He conquered the Babylonians and took the name "Pulu" (or Pul as the Old Testament speaks of him). More important for this story, he moved westward in 743, invading the Syrian city-states. It seems that Uzziah of Judah led the opposition to Tiglath-pileser but had no permanent effect on his march of conquest. By 738 the northern Syrian states were paying heavy tribute to him.

But money was not the only price Tiglath-pileser demanded of his victims. Determined to crush rebellion before it started, he had a policy of taking all the survivors in the upper levels of society, along with the skilled workers, and moving them to another country. Then he would bring in captives from other areas and settle them in the captured lands. Of the original population only the poor people, the elderly, and the sick were left behind—none of whom were able to provide leadership for a rebellion.[14]

Israel (745–721)

The parade of kings in Israel (2 Kings 15:8-31).   After Jeroboam's death, if one became king in Israel it was almost a sure guarantee that he would be murdered. Had there been an insurance company to insure the lives of kings, it most certainly would have been bankrupted.

The first king in the parade was Zechariah (I, 746–745), Jeroboam's son (15:8-12). He lasted about six months before he was murdered by Shallum. Shallum (I, 745) managed to hold onto the prize for one whole month before he was murdered by Menahem, a particularly brutal man. Because some of his fellow Israelites were not too happy at the prospects of having him as king, Menahem attacked their cities and cut open the stomachs of all the pregnant women (15:13-16).

---

[14]On the attraction that the western lands had to the Mesopotamian rulers, see Martin Noth, *The History of Israel*, pp. 253–254.

Menahem (I, 745–738) was on the throne for a longer period of time because he surrendered to the armies of Tiglath-pileser (Pul) and paid a heavy bribe to keep Assyria from destroying the country. He seems to have been able to escape assassination and to put his son Pekahiah on the throne in his place (15:16-22).

Pekahiah (I, 738–737) was not so fortunate. His reign was ended shortly by an army commander, Pekah, who killed him in his own house (15:23-26).

Pekah (I), Jotham (J), Ahaz (J), and the Syro-Ephraimitic War (2 Kings 15:27–16:20; see also Isa. 7:1-25).   In the beginning of the reign of Pekah (I, 737–732), the Assyrians struck the northern region of Israel (later known as Galilee), probably because Pekah had failed to pay the required money into the Assyrian treasury. At the same time, Jotham (J, 742–735) was ruling in Judah, having been coregent with Uzziah many years. A coregent was one who actually carried out the king's duties when the king was unable to do them.

Jotham was succeeded by Ahaz (J, 735–715), his son. Pekah, smarting under the Assyrian rule, tried to stir up a rebellion against Assyria. In that action he was supported by Rezin, king of Syria. When Ahaz refused to join, Pekah and Rezin threatened to invade Judah and put their own man on the throne.

An attack was made in 734 but it was unsuccessful, as the prophet Isaiah had told Ahaz it would be (Isa. 7:1-25). Ahaz, however, figured that Assyrian armed might was a better refuge in time of trouble than a prophet's promises. He carried a huge bribe to Tiglath-pileser to buy his favor. Like a disobedient little boy trying to get back his parents' good graces, Ahaz went out of his way to prove his loyalty to Tiglath, even to the extent of setting up a bronze altar to the chief Assyrian deity in the Temple court. In addition, he commanded that regular sacrifices be made to the Assyrian deity (16:1-20).[15]

Meanwhile, back in Israel, disaster was developing. Tiglath probably needed no encouragement from Ahaz to invade. In 734, he followed the international highway southward, knocking out Philistine cities that also were involved in the plot. Then, he reduced Israel to a few square miles of territory in the central hill country surrounding Samaria. In 732 he destroyed Damascus, killed Rezin, and added Syria to his empire (16:9).

Hoshea (I, 732–722/21): Israel's last king (2 Kings 17:1-41).   Hoshea, like most of his immediate predecessors, became king by murder. Pekah became his victim in the year 732. Hoshea played the role of the obedient servant to Assyria for a time, but when Tiglath-pileser III died in 727,

---

[15]John Bright, *A History of Israel*, p. 271ff.

Hoshea got ideas about rebellion. The change of kings was always a testing time, since major empires like Assyria also had those who coveted the kingship enough to murder for it. The vassal states hoped that there would be a struggle for power. This would give them an opportunity to regain their freedom from the overlords, who were beset with internal problems.

Hoshea chose a broken stick to lean on. He appealed to Egypt for help. Egypt, however, was like an aged man who had been living on a starvation diet. It could hardly support itself, much less offer help in a rebellion against Assyria. Shalmaneser V (726–722) struck Samaria in 725 and set up a seige of the city. The seige showed that Omri had chosen well when he moved the capital to Samaria. It took the armies of Assyria three years finally to capture the city in 722/21 (17:1-6).

With the fall of Samaria, the kingdom of Israel disappeared, never to rise again. The biblical writers saw the LORD at work in its downfall, just as Amos and Hosea saw its inevitable ruin. The narrators named Jeroboam I as the chief culprit. He had brought about the division of the kingdom and had introduced the golden calves as objects of worship (17:7-23).

Assyria's policy of switching populations among its vassal states was carried out in the Northern Kingdom. That action would produce a mixed race of people, known in later times as the Samaritans. That result came about when the new inhabitants intermarried with the poor people who were left in the land. The mixing of cultures included a mixing of religions. This mixed religion would be looked down upon by later Jews with contempt because they felt that the true worship of the LORD had been corrupted (17:24-41).

The man.   Unlike Amos, who came from outside Israel to pronounce judgment, Hosea was a native of the Northern Kingdom. While his judgments were as severe as those of Amos, they were spoken with tearful pleading instead of in a tone of righteous indignation. The book of Hosea is one of the most difficult Old Testament books to translate from Hebrew. This has led some scholars to suggest the reason as being the highly emotional nature of the prophet.

Hosea had enough to make him emotional. Not only was his nation in a mess, but his marriage also was. His marital problems were used to present a unique view of the LORD's relationship to Israel. Prophets, like ministers today, could not resist the temptation to use their families as sermon illustrations!

The book.   Since the first three chapters of the book deal with Hosea's relations to his wife and family, his life can be discussed as a part of the discussion of the book.

Figure 8–8. "Pul [Tiglath-pileser III] the king of Assyria came against the land" (2 Kings 15:19). Ancient kings were more interested in booty than territory. Assyria wanted both. In this drawing, officials of Tiglath–pileser III are recording spoils after a victory: sheep, goats, cattle, prisoners. The reign of Tiglath–pileser III, Central Palace at Nimrud, eighth century B.C.

Courtesy of *Biblical Archaeologist.* Drawn by Valerie M. Fargo.

Marriage and a family (Hos. 1:1–2:1). The introductory verse suggests that the time of Hosea was after 750 B.C., to the downfall of Israel in 722–721 B.C.

On the LORD's command, Hosea married Gomer, the daughter of Diblaim:

> Go, take to yourself a wife of harlotry and have children of harlotry, for the land commits great harlotry by forsaking the LORD (1:2).

Did the LORD actually command his prophet to marry a common prostitute? This question has been answered in several ways:

1. The LORD actually commanded Hosea to marry a prostitute, which he did.
2. Gomer was not a prostitute physically. Instead, she was a Baal worshiper and, as such, was spiritually unfaithful. Whether she was ever physically unfaithful was not important.
3. Gomer was a virgin when Hosea married her, but she became unfaithful after marriage. Later, when he looked back upon the experience, he realized that she already had such tendencies when he married her.
4. The whole story is an allegory, which had no real relationship to Gomer's morals (1:2).

The first three possibilities are the ones most often advanced. The fourth is usually rejected on the grounds that no self-respecting prophet would tell such a story about his wife if it were not true. If he did, he surely would be in trouble at home!

Hosea's children not only had to bear the burden of their mother's disgraceful conduct, but also their names became a part of their father's sermon illustrations. The first-born, Jezreel, reflected Hosea's opinion of the bloody purge of Jehu, which had been commissioned by the prophet Elisha. Since Jeroboam II was of the Jehu dynasty, Hosea saw the LORD's judgment coming upon Israel because of Jehu's indiscriminate slaughter of people (1:3-5).

The second child was a daughter, Lo-ruamah, or "Not pitied." This meant that judgment would come upon the sinful nation, and no pity would be shown it by the conquerors (1:6-7).

The third child's name may have had a double meaning. It was a son named Lo-ami, or "Not my people." Primarily, the name was meant to say that the LORD would no longer claim Israel as his people. It may also reflect Hosea's suspicions of his wife's indiscretions by saying, "This one is not mine!" (1:8-9).

In 1:10–2:1 the prophet spoke a word of hope that the day would come when the message of the children's names would be changed. In that day instead of the LORD saying to Israel, "You are not my people," he would call them "sons of the living God." Lack of pity would give way to pity, and Jezreel would be a place of joy, not destruction.

Unfaithful wife—unfaithful people (Hos. 2:2-23). In an oracle calling for his children to plead with their mother that she change her ways, Hosea compared his relations with Gomer to the LORD's relations with Israel. As Gomer had followed her lovers and been unfaithful, so Israel had gone after the Baal cult and had forsaken the LORD. Israel praised Baal for making the land fruitful, when, in reality, it was the LORD who had brought fertility to the land. The LORD would punish Israel, therefore, for her unfaithfulness (2:2-13).

But punishment was not all. Once Israel had been punished, the LORD would woo her as he had when he brought her from Egypt to the wilderness, in hopes of bringing back the love of her youthful days. Again, a play on the names of Hosea's children was used to emphasize the LORD's hope for his people (2:14-23).

The purchase (Hos. 3:1-5).   Whereas chapter 1 tells Hosea and Gomer's story in the third person, chapter 3 tells how the story ended in the words of the prophet himself. Few details are given, but it can be assumed that Gomer was probably being sold as a slave because she had been abandoned by her lovers. Hosea bought her for the price of a slave— fifteen shekels of silver and about ten bushels of barley. He did not restore her immediately to the place of a wife, however. She had to undergo a period of probation before that could happen. So the LORD would do for Israel. She, too, would be bought back, but not without penalty on her part (3:1-5).

Judgment must come, but there is hope (Hos. 4:1–14:9).

1. *The LORD's lawsuit (Hos. 4:1-3).*   The prophets often used the language of the court to give their message of judgment. This is usually indicated in English translations by the term "controversy" or "contention." This was not just an argument—it was a legal charge. Three key terms stand out in the accusation in 4:1: "There is no *faithfulness* or *kindness* and no *knowledge of God* in the land." The lack of these three qualities was the basis for all the other failures of the people. Faithfulness meant carrying out promises that were made. Kindness was a sense of compassion that had depth and meaning. Knowledge referred to an intimate, personal kind of knowing, such as was shared by husband and wife, and the word was used for this kind of relationship. These terms recur frequently in the oracles of Hosea and are the key to understanding the book.

The failure to have faithfulness, kindness, and knowledge had resulted in

> swearing, lying, killing, stealing, and committing adultery; they break all bounds and murder follows murder (4:2).

2. *The guilt of the religious leaders (Hos. 4:4-10).*   The first ones indicted in the LORD's lawsuit were the priests and prophets. They were dispensers of the knowledge of God so vital to the survival of the people. As a result of their failure, the people were being destroyed because of their lack of knowledge (4:4-6).

Religious prosperity had brought increased sin. More priests and prophets just meant more to lead the people astray, since the people followed the priests. The LORD's priests had led the people to the worship of Baal (4:7-10).

3. *The harlotry of the people (Hos. 4:11–5:2).*   Baalism had the people in its grip. They worshiped the poles, sexual symbols of Baal. The young women of Israel, married and unmarried, became involved in the sexual rites at the shrines (4:11-13) with the knowledge and approval of the men of the family (4:14). As a result, worship at the traditional shrines was a mockery. They paid no attention to the LORD and stubbornly went on their way (4:15-19). False leaders had brought them to destruction and punishment (5:1-2).

4. *The result of idolatry (Hos. 5:3-7).*   Israel had become so mired in the muck of Baal worship that the people could no longer find their way back to the LORD. Even though they might seek him, they could not find him. He had withdrawn from them because of their sin.

5. *War on the horizon (Hos. 5:8-14).*   Another device of the prophet was to speak of the approach of an invading army, announcing its progress from town to town (5:8). Judah and Ephraim, the two strongest tribes, symbolized for Hosea the two kingdoms. They sought the aid of the great powers when they were in trouble, but they ignored the LORD, who would turn from healer to destroyer. The only hope was that their suffering would bring them to their senses (5:8-14).

6. *False repentance (Hos. 5:15–7:2).*   Even though Israel repented, it was a false repentance. It had no more permanence than a fog in the morning (5:15–6:4). The key verse of Hosea is this:

> For I desire steadfast love and not sacrifice, the knowledge of God, rather than burnt offerings (6:6).

As was true of Amos, Hosea's understanding of the LORD's demands was that acts of worship within themselves were not enough to please him. Sacrifice as an attempt to bribe the LORD was useless, for he would not be bribed. Only a commitment of love whose endurance was based on knowing and doing what the LORD demanded could satisfy him.

Instead of steadfast love and knowledge of God, Israel's worship was a flagrant violation of everything good. At every shrine, sin was multiplied. At Adam, the covenant was broken; at Gilead, there was bloodshed; even the priests at Shechem were murderers, and harlotry was the accepted thing (6:7-10). Every time the LORD would bless Ephraim, there was more evidence of corruption uncovered (6:11–7:2).

7. *Anarchy in the country (Hos. 7:3-7).*   This passage reflects the period when kings came and went in rapid succession. There were plots and counterplots in the palace, and one king had hardly taken the throne when he was murdered and another took his place. Hosea compares the plotting to an oven filled with hot coals, ready to burst into flame when they get sufficient oxygen (7:3-7).

8. *Ephraim is a half-baked cake (Hos. 7:8-16).*   Hosea was a master of figures of speech. Bakers had to turn the flat, thin pieces of bread for them to cook properly. Israel was compared to a cake left unturned—it was burned on one side and doughy on the other and was unfit to eat. Israel was like the dove, a bird easily snared in a net. So Israel had fallen into the trap of its powerful neighbors by trying to play the game of international politics. In religion, the people turned to Baal, even though the LORD was the one to whom they owed their blessings (7:8-16).

9. *False worship and false friends (Hos. 8:1-14).*   The enemy was hovering over Israel like a bird of prey. The kings it had chosen were not the LORD's choice. The idols the people worshiped were false gods. They had sown "the wind and they shall reap the whirlwind" (8:7). The friends they had tried to buy were false. The numerous altars they had built were for sinning, not worshiping. They sacrificed so as to gorge themselves on meat; not to truly worship the LORD. Israel and Judah both faced the LORD's judgment (8:1-14).

10. *The judgment to come (Hos. 9:1-17).*   Because Israel had forsaken its God and been a harlot for Baal, Egypt and Assyria would destroy it (9:1-3). All worship would end and be replaced by mourning. The days of punishment had arrived. Even the prophet, who was supposed to be the LORD's spokesman, was listened to no longer. The people called him a fool and tried to destroy him. But God would bring judgment upon them (9:4-9).

Israel had once been faithful. When it entered Canaan, however, it took up Baal worship. Now barrenness would afflict Israel. "No birth, no pregnancy, no conception" would be the rule (9:11). Baal could not make Israel fertile. And, even when she did give birth, the children would die in infancy or be slaughtered by the invaders (9:10-17).

11. *Increased altars—increased sin (Hos. 10:1-8).*   Like a grapevine heavy with grapes, Israel was filled with places of worship; but these would be destroyed (10:1-2). The people were liars, making covenants with no intention of keeping them. Their major concern was to preserve their licentious worship, but it would be destroyed by the armies of Assyria (10:3-6). There would be no place for them to hide when judgment came (10:7-8).

12. *Judgment must come (Hos. 10:9-15).*   Hosea refers to the atrocity of the Benjaminites at Gibeah (Judg. 19) as the kind of sin that continued to his day in Israel. The LORD was pleading with them to sow good crops—righteousness and steadfast love—and seek him (10:9-12). Instead, they were sowing iniquity and reaping injustice. They were trusting in military power and not the LORD. They would have war, but they would suffer destruction instead of enjoying victory (10:13-15).

13. *The LORD still loves Israel (Hos. 11:1-11).*   Despite its sins, the LORD still loved Israel.

> When Israel was a child, I loved him,
>   and out of Egypt I called my son.
> The more I called them,
>   the more they went away from me.
>
>   . . .
>
> Yet it was I who taught Ephraim to walk,
>   I took them up in my arms;
> I led them with cords of compassion
>   with the bands of love (11:1-4*b*).

Despite the LORD's love, Israel turned away. Now, it faced judgment at the hand of Assyria. Those people who escaped Assyria's clutches would flee to Egypt (11:5-6). But this was not what the LORD wanted:

> How can I give you up, O Ephraim!
>   How can I hand you over, O Israel!
> How can I make you like Admah!
>   How can I treat you like Zeboiim!
> My heart recoils within me,
>   my compassion grows warm and tender.
> I will not execute my fierce anger,
>   I will not again destroy Ephraim;
> for I am God and not man,
>   the Holy One in your midst,
>   and I will not come to destroy (11:8-9).

Hosea had hope for the survival of the nation despite the fact that it had to go through judgment. This applied to the people as a whole, including Judah (11:10-12).

14. *Judgment must come (Hos. 12:1–13:16).*   Judgment had to come. The people had sinned too much to avoid it. From Jacob's deception to the prophet's day, the record was one of sin and broken promises (12:1-6). There was cheating in the marketplace (12:7-9); there was no attention paid to the warnings of the prophets—which were all to no avail. Even though a prophet (Moses) brought them out of Egypt, the people turned away (12:10-14). Idols were made in abundance, and sin piled on top of sin (13:1-2). So the nation would vanish like the morning mist or like the chaff of the wheat before the wind (13:3).

The LORD, who would be Israel's saviour, had to be its destroyer instead. Like the beast of prey when it is provoked, he would destroy Israel. No king could save it, for they too were destroyed (13:4-11). Only the LORD had power to defeat even death and the power of Sheol (the grave). But, because of Ephraim's sin, he would not do so (13:12-16).

15. *A plea to return (Hos. 14:1-8).* Hosea made one last plea to the people to return to the LORD and to depend upon him and not Assyria. Only the LORD could heal them of their "wickedness." He would be to them like water to thirsty plants; like a tree under whose shade they could dwell.

16. *A wisdom saying (Hos. 14:9).* Hosea closes with a wisdom saying:

> Whoever is wise, let him understand these things;
>   whoever is discerning, let him know them;
> for the ways of the LORD are right,
>   and the upright walk in them,
>   but transgressors stumble in them.

17. *Summary on Hosea.* Like Amos, Hosea was a prophet of judgment; but he emphasized that the LORD still loved Israel. The chief culprits in Israel's downfall were the religious leaders. They were supposed to be experts in the knowledge of God, but they were leading the people to worship Baal. Instead of lives marked by compassion and concern for their fellowman, most of the Israelites were selfish, corrupt, and immoral. While the remnant idea of the later prophets was not a part of Hosea's theology, it was strongly implied in his emphasis on the LORD's love for his people and the suggestion that there would be those who would survive the judgment.

STUDY QUESTIONS

1. What two dates are the basis for Old Testament chronologies and how were they arrived at?
2. How did Rehoboam handle the Israelites' request for more freedom? What resulted from his answers?
3. What advantages and disadvantages did Jereboam have as he began to rule over Israel?
4. Why was Rehoboam not able to regain the territories that revolted against him?
5. Why was Israel referred to as "the land of Omri" for many years after that king's short reign?
6. Why was Samaria chosen by Omri as his capital?
7. What was the basis upon which Baalism appealed to the Israelites?
8. What characteristics did all the great prophets of Israel share?
9. How were the prophets concerned about the future?
10. What was the significance of Elijah's contest with the Baal prophets on Mt. Carmel?

11. What was Elijah's relationship to Ahab and Jezebel?

12. Why could Jezebel get away with having Naboth murdered?

13. Identify: ecstatic, diviner, court prophet.

14. Why should Micaiah ben Imlah be considered important?

15. Compare Elijah and Elisha.

16. In what way did Jehu's purge of the house of Omri contribute to instability in Israel?

17. What international conditions made it possible for Israel and Judea to flourish during the reigns of Jereboam II and Uzziah?

18. The Deuteronomic historian gave Jereboam II low marks. How would a secular historian rate him?

19. List the accomplishments of King Uzziah of Judah.

20. What kinds of conditions gave rise to the prophetic ministry of Amos?

21. What do Amos's oracles against the nations (1:3–2:5) say about his doctrine of God?

22. What was the major theme of Amos's preaching?

23. Name Amos's five visions and give a statement about the meaning of each one.

24. Define: oracle, vision.

25. Why was Amos important?

26. How did Hosea's attitude toward Israel differ from the attitude of Amos?

27. Identify: Tiglath-pileser, Sargon II, Pekah, Hoshea.

28. How can the LORD's command for Hosea to marry a harlot be interpreted?

29. How did Hosea relate his troubled marriage to his message to Israel?

30. What was the significance of the names of Hosea's children?

31. What does Hosea 4:1-3 show as to the influence of the courts on the language of the prophet?

32. Memorize Hosea 6:6.

FOR FURTHER STUDY

Chronology

THIELE, E. R. *The Mysterious Numbers of the Hebrew Kings.* Chicago: University of Chicago Press, 1951. An in-depth study of the problems of biblical chronology.

The Prophets

ANDERSON, BERNHARD W., and WALTER HARRELSON, eds. *Israel's Prophetic Heritage.* Essays in honor of James Muilenburg. New York: Harper & Row, 1962.

GRAY, JOHN. *I and II Kings.* Philadelphia: Westminster, 1963.

HESCHEL, ABRAHAM J. *The Prophets.* New York: Harper & Row, 1963. One of the truly great books on the prophets.

HYATT, J. PHILIP. *Prophetic Religion.* New York: Abingdon-Cokesbury, 1947. A simple, yet informative book on the prophets.

LINDBLOM, JOHANNES. *Prophecy in Ancient Israel.* Philadelphia: Muhlenburg, 1963. A comprehensive work.

NAPIER, B. DAVIE. "Prophet, Prophetism" in *Interpreter's Dictionary*, Vol. III. pp. 896–919.

RAD, GERHARD VON. *The Prophetic Message.* Trans. by D. M. G. Stalker. London: S.C.M., 1968. Paperback.

SCOTT, R. B. Y. *The Relevance of the Prophets*, rev. ed. New York: Macmillan, 1968. A classic work now in paperback.

WASTERMANN, CLAUS. *Basic Forms of Prophetic Speech.* Trans. by Hugh E. White. Philadelphia: Westminster, 1967.

WINWARD, STEPHEN. *A Guide to the Prophets.* Richmond: John Knox, 1969. A good introduction to the prophets available in paperback.

Amos and Hosea

BRUGGEMAN, WALTER. *Tradition for Crisis: A Study in Hosea.* Richmond, John Knox, 1968.

CRIPPS, A. S. *A Critical and Exegetical Commentary on the Book of Amos.* London: S.P.C.I.C., 1929. An old but good commentary.

MAYS, JAMES L. *Amos.* Old Testament Library. Philadelphia: Westminster, 1969.

———. *Hosea.* Old Testament Library. Philadelphia: Westminster, 1969. One of the best commentaries on Hosea.

SMITH, GEORGE ADAM. *The Book of the Twelve*, I, rev. ed. New York: Harper & Row, 1940. One of the truly great works on the prophets.

WARD, JAMES M. *Amos and Isaiah: Prophets of the Word of God.* New York: Abingdon, 1969.

———. *Hosea: A Theological Commentary.* New York: Harper & Row, 1966. His translation of Hosea is especially enlightening.

WOLFF, H. W. *Joel and Amos.* Hermeneia. Philadelphia: Fortress, 1977. Especially helpful for those who know the biblical language.

———*Hosea.* Hermeneia. Philadelphia: Fortress, 1974.

CHAPTER NINE

And Then There Was One: Judah Alone

The glories of the Davidic and Solomonic era had faded into the mists of the past. All that was left was the tiny state of Judah, powerless before the juggernaut from Mesopotamia. But Judah chose a wiser course of action than her sister state—she gave in to Assyria, paid the required tribute, and continued to exist for another century and a half.

Judah during Israel's Last Days

When Tiglath-pileser III came to the throne, Judah at first tried the hero's role but soon decided that such was not a wise course of action. In 743, Judah under Uzziah had led a coalition of western states in opposition to Assyria that was unsuccessful in its attempts at stopping Tiglath-pileser III. When Ahaz (J, 735–715) came to the throne, he faced a more immediate threat from Israel (led by Pekah) and Syria (whose king was Rezin). These two kings tried to persuade Ahaz to join in opposing Tiglath, but, unlike his grandfather Uzziah, he chose to join Assyria rather than to fight it. He therefore appealed to Assyria for help against the threats by his neighbors. Tiglath-pileser III readily obliged, taking tribute from Ahaz and blotting out Syria and Israel.

The Eighth-Century Prophets from Judah

Just as Amos and Hosea had preached the word of the LORD in Israel, so Isaiah and Micah were prophets in Judah. These remarkable men undoubtedly knew of each other since they came from such a limited area, but neither their writings nor the historical books give any indication of this fact, except for one oracle common to both (Isa. 2:2-4 and Mic. —*exactly alike* 4:1-3). Each was unique and each in his ministry emphasized the important issues of the day. Isaiah, a native of Jerusalem with access to the royal court, viewed things on an international scale. Micah, in contrast, was limited in his vision to the Israelite kingdoms and was a rural conservative. Both men were sensitive to the cries of the poor and downtrodden. They believed that the true man of God could not ignore the cries of the oppressed. Religion that made no difference in one's sensitivity to his fellow Israelite was an insult to the LORD.

Isaiah and the Kings of Judah

Just as Israel was going to its grave, Judah was about to be blessed with Hezekiah (715–687/86), one of its best kings. The prophet Isaiah served as his wise and respected counselor. Previously, Isaiah had advised Hezekiah's father, Ahaz, who did not value his advice so highly.

ISAIAH AND AHAZ (ISA. 6:1–8:21)

Isaiah was a man of Jerusalem, *of the upper class* obviously from the upper classes of society. Some have even suggested that he might have been related to the royal family. In any case, he seemed to have an access to the royal court that few people enjoyed.

He was a family man with a wife and at least two, and perhaps three, sons. His wife was referred to as the prophetess (Isa. 8:3). This may mean that she, too, functioned as a prophet; or it may mean simply that she was Mrs. Prophet Isaiah.

The call of the prophet (Isa. 6:1-13).   Isaiah's call came in the year of King Uzziah's death. The young Isaiah was in the Temple, possibly watching the pomp and pageantry surrounding the coronation of Jotham, Uzziah's son. The king was supposed to be God's representative on earth. But Isaiah saw more than the earthly representative of God—instead, he saw the LORD himself sitting on the throne. In his vision, the LORD was flanked by two bright, six-winged creatures called "seraphim" (RSV) or "flaming creatures" (TEV), who called out, "Holy, holy, holy is the LORD of hosts, the whole world is full of his presence" (6:3). The formula "Holy, holy, holy" was the Hebrew way of saying "the most holy" or "holiest of all," since repeating an adjective took the place of our comparative and superlative degrees (holy, holier, holiest). This was not a reference to the Trinity (Father, Son, and Holy Spirit) since such an idea was unknown in Isaiah's day (6:1-3).

The Temple foundations shook under Isaiah's feet, and the smoke from the altar gave the scene an eerie appearance. The vision of the holy God overwhelmed the young man with a sense of sin and guilt. In his spiritual agony, he cried out in confession of sins: "Woe is me, for I am unclean!" (6:4-5).

In his vision, he saw one of the flying creatures take a fiery coal and touch his lips, symbolic of the cleansing power of the LORD in forgiveness. Then he heard a call, "Whom shall I send, and who will go for us?" Isaiah answered, "Here am I! Send me" (6:6-8).

Mayo disagrees

He was then given a strange commission: he was told to go preach to people who would not pay attention to him. When he questioned how long he was to preach, he was told to preach until the land lay desolate, stripped of its inhabitants. Only a remnant would remain. In short, Isaiah was called to be faithful, not successful (6:9-13).

This chapter contains two unique features of Isaiah's preaching. Like the other prophets, before and afterward, he would be a prophet of judgment and doom. But among the things that were different about his preaching were the ideas concerning the holiness of God and the righteous remnant of Israel.[1] The importance and meaning of the ideas will be discussed later.

Isaiah and Ahaz: the Syro-Ephraimitic War (734–732) (Isa. 7:1–8:21).

The first appearance of Isaiah as a prophet is described in chapter 7. Isaiah and his son Shear-jashub met Ahaz in Jerusalem. The son was taken along because his name represented a part of his father's message. The name was symbolic of Isaiah's doctrine of the remnant. It meant, "A remnant shall return." As such, it reflected a hopeful theme in Isaiah's preaching (7:1-4).

Ahaz was troubled by the threat of Syria and Israel. Isaiah gave him a message from the LORD to ignore the threats. Instead, he should "Take heed, be quiet, do not fear," for the little tyrants threatening him would soon vanish. The prophet showed his contempt for King Pekah by referring to him only as the "son of Remaliah" (7:5-9).

Isaiah challenged Ahaz to ask for a sign from the LORD that what he was saying was true (7:11). Ahaz refused to do so (7:12). Isaiah then said that the LORD would give a sign anyway. That sign was that a young woman would have a child whose name would be Immanuel. The name meant "God with us" (7:14). It was in keeping with the earlier promise to Ahaz that what he needed to do was trust in the LORD, not Assyria.

Isaiah 7:14 is one of the most controversial passages in all Scripture. Following the basic principle of biblical interpretation that says a verse

---

[1] From now on, Israel will be used in the older sense of all the Hebrew people, not just the residents of the northern portion of the country.

should never be interpreted apart from its surroundings or context, the verse said a child would be born in a few months to a woman who was then pregnant. Before the child would be capable of making his own decisions (7:15, TEV), Judah's persecutors would be gone (7:10-16).

This interpretation is not accepted by many Christians because they see in it a direct reference to the virgin birth of Jesus Christ. This view is based on the King James Version, which translates, "Behold, a virgin shall conceive, and shall bear a son, and shall call his name Immanuel." For them, it was a messianic prophecy. In support of this view, they cite Matthew 1:23, which quotes Isaiah 7:14 to support the teaching concerning Jesus' virgin birth.

The Hebrew word translated "virgin" (KJV) or "young woman" (RSV) is not the technical term for a morally upright, unmarried young woman. Rather, it is the more general term that describes all young women, married or unmarried. In that sense, it was a neutral word. It had nothing to say about the young woman's character. This is why most modern versions of the Old Testament translate the word as "young woman" (RSV and TEV, for example). Matthew's Gospel followed the Greek text of the Old Testament, not the Hebrew text. The Greek text has the technical word for "virgin." Matthew quoted the only Bible he had (which was the Greek Old Testament) to reinforce his doctrine that Jesus was born of a virgin.

To summarize: Isaiah said a child would be born to a young married woman in his day and the child would be named "Immanuel" (God with us). That would be a sign to a stubborn king that he needed to trust in the LORD's power, not in the power of the Assyrian army. Many hundreds of years later, a new child was born to a virgin girl in a cave in Bethlehem. As the child grew, men began to realize that in him they sensed the presence of God among them. When the writer of Matthew's Gospel was searching the Jewish Scriptures (the LXX or Septuagint version), he read Isaiah 7:14. In that ancient promise of Isaiah to Ahaz, he sensed a deeper and more meaningful fulfillment in the life of Jesus of Nazareth. He truly was Immanuel, "God with us." To that writer, the old promise had been fulfilled in a new and magnificent way.

Who was the original child? Some believe that it was Ahaz's own son, Hezekiah, who was to become one of Judah's most devout and able kings. Another possibility was that the child was Isaiah's own son. This would seem to find support in the fact that the two other children mentioned in this passage (7:1–8:15) are Isaiah's children.

Ahaz ignored the warnings, even though Isaiah continued to issue them. Isaiah named another son by the ominous name Maher-shahal-hash-baz. (Someone has suggested that he was nicknamed "Hash" since his name was so long.) The name means, "Quick loot, fast plunder" (TEV) and describes the greed and destructiveness of the Assyrians. Isaiah told

Ahaz that if he refused the LORD's peaceful waters he would find himself floundering in the Assyrian flood (8:1-15).

Finally, in frustration, Isaiah told his disciples to record what he had said since the people would not listen to him. If they were more interested in listening to fortune-tellers than they were to listening to the word of the LORD, then that was their responsibility (8:16-21).

ISAIAH AND HEZEKIAH (2 KINGS 18:1–20:20, ISA. 20:1-6; ISA. 36:1–39:8)

Isaiah found a more receptive ear in Hezekiah (715–687/86), who succeeded his father, Ahaz. Isaiah was Hezekiah's friend and counselor in at least two major crises during his reign—the Ashdod Rebellion and the invasion of Sennacherib.

Hezekiah's reform and the Ashdod rebellion (2 Kings 18:1-12; Isa. 20:1-6). Hezekiah came to the throne when Assyria's attention was diverted from the western states. Given a bit of breathing room, he set out to bring about a reform in the religious practices in Judah. He moved vigorously to destroy the pagan altars built by his father, destroyed shrines where Baal worship still persisted, and even destroyed the bronze serpent made by Moses and kept in the temple as a reminder of Israel's days in the wilderness. The serpent had become an object of worship, with people burning incense to it as if it were divine. The evaluation of Hezekiah was that

> He trusted in the LORD the God of Israel; so that there was none like him among all the kings of Judah, nor among those who were before him.

He slightly enlarged his kingdom, especially at the expense of the Philistines. For a short period of time, he also refused to pay tribute to the Assyrians (18:1-12).

Soon the Assyrian tiger was on the prowl again. The people of Ashdod, a Philistine city, tried to lead a rebellion against the Assyrians in 714. Egypt, who had a strong king for a change, encouraged the rebellion since the Assyrians were so close to Egypt's borders. Hezekiah was invited to join the leaders of other small western states.

Isaiah advised Hezekiah to steer clear of the fight. To emphasize the gravity of what he said, Isaiah walked about Jerusalem naked and barefoot for three years to stress what could happen to Judah if Hezekiah were foolish enough to fight the Assyrians. While such an action might seem strange to us today, Isaiah was portraying an all-too-familiar sight to the Judeans, who had seen naked war captives paraded through the streets (Isa. 20:1-6).

Sennacherib's invasion (2 Kings 18:13–19:36; 20:12-19). Hezekiah seems to have stayed out of the rebellion that was crushed in 711. But trouble would not stay away for long. Near the end of Sargon's life, revolt flared again in the Assyrian empire. Babylon, under Merodach-baladan, led the revolt. Egypt stirred up the western states, including Judah, hoping to regain a foothold for itself in Palestine. The description in 2 Kings 20:6-19 of envoys from Merodach-baladan who came to Hezekiah from Babylon may represent an attempt to persuade Hezekiah to join the revolt. Isaiah protested that dealings with Babylon would bring trouble in the future.[2]

Hezekiah was drawn to the conflict like a moth to a flame—and with much the same results. Expecting an invasion by Sennacherib (704–681), he set about strengthening the defenses of Jerusalem. Among other things, to insure a safe water supply, he had a tunnel dug from the Gihon Spring in the Kidron Valley to a pool inside the city. The source of the spring was then covered so the enemy could not find it. The pool into which it flowed was known as the Pool of Siloam in New Testament times. The tunnel was more than 1700 feet long and represents an unusual feat of engineering for such an early time. In the tunnel an inscription describing how it was dug was found by accident in the late 1800s by a young Arab boy who was wading through it. It is still possible to go through the tunnel today.[3]

One water tunnel was not enough to stop Sennacherib. In 701, he attacked the coast and the land east of the Jordan, taking forty-seven Judean cities and, in his words, shutting Hezekiah up in Jerusalem "like a bird in a cage." Hezekiah emptied his treasury, the Temple treasury, and even stripped the gold decorations from the Temple to pay Sennacherib off (2 Kings 18:13-16; Isa. 36:1).

Yet a different picture of Sennacherib's success is presented in 2 Kings 18:17–19:37. After threats were made by Sennacherib's officers about what the Assyrians would do to the city (2 Kings 18:17-37; Isa. 36:2-22), Hezekiah consulted Isaiah. Isaiah assured him that Sennacherib would withdraw and would be killed in his own country (2 Kings 19:1-7; Isa. 37:1-7).

In the meantime, when the Egyptian King Tirhakah threatened Sennacherib's southern flank, Sennacherib withdrew long enough to put down the threat. When that was finished, he returned to renew the siege of Jerusalem. He once again sent threatening letters to Hezekiah (2 Kings 19:8-13). Hezekiah once more went to the Temple to pray, and Isaiah, as spokesman for the LORD, brought the answer to that prayer. He reassured

[2]On Hezekiah's role in the rebellion against Sennacherib see Martin Noth, *The History of Israel*, pp. 265–267.

[3]James B. Pritchard, *Ancient Near East in Pictures, 2nd ed.* (Princeton: Princeton University Press, 1955), pp. 85, 232, 280, 338.

Figure 9–1. "[Hezekiah] rebelled against the king of Assyria, and would not serve him" (2 Kings 18:7). Hezekiah had this tunnel, which brought water from the Gihon Spring into Jerusalem, dug as a defensive measure.

Courtesy of George L. Kelm.

Hezekiah that Jerusalem would not fall. In fact, he said that not one arrow would be shot into Jerusalem nor any siege mound be built around it. He repeated the prediction that Sennacherib would return home and be murdered (2 Kings 19:14-34; Isa. 37:8-35).

Some scholars think that there were two invasions by Sennacherib. The main reasons they give are as follows:

1. The account in Kings says Hezekiah submitted and paid a heavy bribe to Sennacherib (2 Kings 19:13-16).
2. Yet Isaiah said that Sennacherib would not take Jerusalem nor would he even lay siege to it (19:32-34; Isa. 37:33-35).

3. Second Kings 19:9 says that "Tirhakah king of Ethiopia" opposed Sennacherib. But according to Egyptian records Tirhakah became coregent in Ethiopia (Egypt) only in 690/89 and did not become king until 685/84. He probably was no more than ten years old in 701.

Some simply say that the differences can be accounted for by realizing that the biblical account and Sennacherib's account are told from two different points of view. Others are led to conclude that there were two invasions by Sennacherib. The first, in 701, devastated Judah, causing Hezekiah to pay heavy tribute. The second, coming around 690/89, was the one in which Isaiah made the prediction that Sennacherib would never take Jerusalem. Second Kings 18:17 and following would describe that invasion. Sennacherib started to attack Jerusalem, only to be drawn away by Tirhakah's threat. With that taken care of, he came back, only to meet disaster in the form of a devastating plague that struck his army. As the historian writes:

The angel of the LORD went forth, and slew a hundred and eighty-five thousand in the camp of the Assyrians; and when men rose early in the morning, behold, these were dead bodies (19:35; Isa. 37:36).

Later Sennacherib was murdered by his own sons (19:36-37; Isa. 37:37-38).[4]

One other narrative (other than the visit by the Babylonian representatives, who probably preceded the Sennacherib invasion) concerns Isaiah and Hezekiah. Hezekiah was ill. The prophet came and told him he would die. Hezekiah prayed, requesting that he be permitted to live longer. Isaiah then returned and said Hezekiah would live another 15 years. As a sign that Hezekiah would recover, the shadow on the sundial was to go back 10 steps (20:1-11).

THE BOOK OF ISAIAH

The book that bears Isaiah's name was one of four scrolls of the prophets in the Jewish scriptures: Isaiah, Jeremiah, Ezekiel, and the Twelve (the minor prophets). It has two major divisions: chapters 1–39 and chapters 40–66.

[4]John Bright, *A History of Israel*, pp. 296–308, has an extended discussion of this problem. Martin Noth, *The History of Israel*, pp. 268ff, sees only one invasion which left Hezekiah as an Assyrian vassal.

Figure 9–2. The Assyrian Empire.

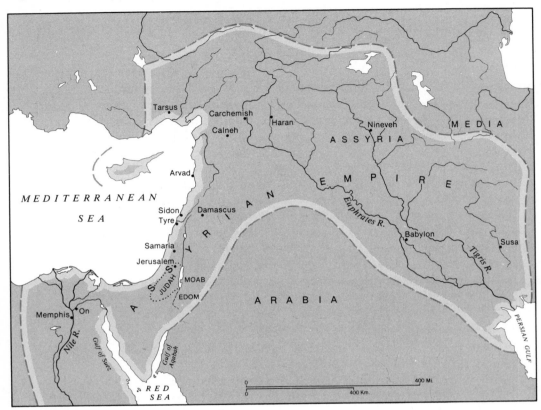

The book: its background. There are two major views about the authorship and the unity of the book. Those who argue for a single author and for the unity of the book hold the following:

1. The oldest form of the book, the Dead Sea Scrolls manuscript, had the entire 66 chapters much as it stands today.
2. The primary emphasis in prophecy was on prediction. God enabled the prophets to see what would happen hundreds of years in the future.
3. The author of the whole book, therefore, was Isaiah of Jerusalem in the eighth century B.C.

Those who argue for more than one author make the following points:

1. The prophets were primarily spokesmen for their own time. The future they were most concerned with was the immediate future.[5]

2. Isaiah 1–39 and 40–66 are different in a number of ways:

   a. They differ in historical background: 1–39 was set in an eighth-century background, while 40–66 was set in the Babylonian exile.

   b. They differ in style: 1–39 is narrative and typical prophetic oracles, while 40–66 is very elaborate poetry.

   c. They differ in their view of God: 1–39 speaks of the holiness of God, while 40–66 speaks of God as Creator.

   d. They differ in speaking of God's representative: 1–39 speaks of the Messiah, while 40–66 speaks of the Suffering Servant.

On this basis, those who hold to a multiple authorship see the work of at least two different prophets in the book of Isaiah, the second of whom looked upon himself as a disciple of Isaiah of Jerusalem, even though 100 years separated the two men.

While there is disagreement about the authorship of the book, most of those who study it will agree that chapters 40 to 66 reflect an exilic and postexilic background. For that reason, those chapters will be discussed in the historical context of the Babylonian exile and the years immediately following it.

The book: its contents.   What follows will be an attempt to describe the contents of Isaiah 1–39.

Oracles concerning Judah and the Messiah (Isa. 1:1–5:23; 8:22–12:6)

1. _Hear, O heavens (Isa. 1:1-9)._   The men of Judah were indicted as rebellious sons who did not have a personal knowledge of the LORD (1:2-3). The people were sinful and completely separated from the LORD. They were rebels who, despite repeated punishment, still continued to rebel. Even when the country was devastated by war (Sennacherib's invasion), they still had not repented. Their sinfulness would bring destruction, such as happened to Sodom and Gomorrah (1:4-9).

2. _Luxurious religion (Isa. 1:10-23)._   Sodom and Gomorrah also symbolized the sinfulness of Judah in its more prosperous days. There was no lack of religion. Sacrifices were made in multitudes, services were piled on top of services, and prayers were plentiful, but they were hypocritical—

---

[5]As far as the writer of this text is concerned, the point at issue in this statement for either view is not God's ability to do what he willed with the prophet. The central question then was, "What _did_ God do?" not "What _could_ God do?" I believe the prophets spoke primarily about their own time and circumstance.

they had no effect on personal conduct (1:10-16c). They only thing that would please the LORD would be that the people:

> Cease to do evil,
>> learn to do good;
> seek justice,
>> correct oppression
> defend the fatherless,
>> plead for the widow (1:16d-17).

The LORD was still pleading with Judah to be obedient. If she continued to rebel, however, judgment would come (1:18-20). Jerusalem, the LORD's city, was a harlot, a refuge for murderers, and a place of corruption where justice was denied to the helpless (1:21-23).

3. *There is hope (Isa. 1:24-31).*   The LORD's judgment had to come; but it would be a cleansing, not a killing, judgment. It would be like smelting ore to remove its impurities. Redemption would come through justice. Rebellion would be severely dealt with (1:24-31).

4. *There's a great day coming (Isa. 2:1-5).*   This remarkable oracle was so famous that it was included in two prophetic books: Isaiah (2:1-4) and Micah (4:1-3). This means (1) the LORD gave the same oracle to both, or (2) Isaiah got it from Micah, or (3) Micah got it from Isaiah, or (4) they both got it from somewhere else. Be that as it may, it looks to an ideal age when judgment is past and the LORD has established his kingdom of peace.

5. *The day of the LORD (Isa. 2:6-22).*   The LORD rejected his people because they had depended on the wrong things. They depended on soothsayers (2:6); money, horses and chariots (2:7); and handmade idols (2:8). Their pride would be humbled because the day of the LORD was coming. Like Amos, Isaiah saw the day of the LORD as a time of judgment on the proud men of Israel. In 2:11 and 2:17 the refrain is repeated:

> And the haughtiness of man shall be humbled,
>> and the pride of men shall be brought low;
>> and the LORD alone will be exalted in that day.

6. *Trouble in Jerusalem (Isa. 3:1-15).*   The setting for this oracle was either the time of Ahaz, when the Assyrian forces were devastating the land (734) or the time of the Sennacherib invasions (701). There was famine in the city (3:1) and a breakdown in the rule of law (3:2-5). Everyone looked for leadership, but no one wanted the responsibility (3:6-8). The condition had been brought on the city by the failure of leaders to lead (3:9-15).

7. *Those Jerusalem women (Isa. 3:16–4:1).*   In a scathing attack on the haughty women of Jerusalem, Isaiah gives a look at what the belles of

Jerusalem society wore. But when judgment came, their finery would be destroyed. They would be so humiliated at not having a home that they would be willing to support themselves if they only could say they were married (4:1). Women's liberation had not reached Jerusalem in 700 B.C.

8. *The righteous remnant (Isa. 4:2-6).*   This oracle gives a good example of how the words of the prophets were arranged. The previous oracle spoke of the women of Jerusalem. This one, though entirely different in tone, also mentions the "daughters of Zion" (4:14) just as 3:16 had done. The phrase served as a catchword to tie the two passages together.

This oracle looks beyond the judgment to the righteous remnant the prophet believed would redeem the nation. It recalled the wilderness days by referring to the cloud by day and the fire by night (4:5). For the prophets, the wilderness days, at times, were the "good old days" when Israel was right with the LORD.

9. *The LORD's love song (Isa. 5:1-7).*   Using the form of a wedding song, the prophet tells of the LORD's love for Israel. The nation was like a vineyard that the LORD had carefully prepared and planted with the choice Sorek grapes, the best grape grown in Palestine. But when the harvest time came, instead of fine wine grapes, the vines yielded small sour grapes that set one's teeth on edge. The LORD destroyed the vineyard, therefore, and let it go to rack and ruin (5:1-6).

The song was explained in 5:7 as an allegory:

> For the vineyard of the LORD of hosts
>   is the house of Israel,
> and the men of Judah
>   are his pleasant planting;
> and he looked for justice,
>   but behold, bloodshed;
> for righteousness,
>   but behold, a cry!

10. *Woe! woe! woe! (Isa. 5:8-23).*   For the sins, six woes were pronounced on the sinners of Judah. (1) Covetousness was shown by the greed for land (5:8-10). (2) Drunkenness started early in the morning and lasted into the night. It made men insensitive to the LORD's demands (5:11-12). Furthermore, this lack of knowledge of the LORD was destroying the nation (5:13-17). (3) Cynicism caused men to say that the LORD really would not do anything about their sin (5:18-19). (4) Some even went so far as to glorify evil and to say it was acceptable (5:20). (5) Conceit caused men to overvalue their own wisdom (5:21). (6) The judges were more anxious to show their prowess as wine drinkers than they were concerned about giving justice. Instead, decisions favored those who paid the biggest bribe (5:22-23).

11. *The LORD's Messiah (Isa. 8:22–9:7; 11:1-16).* An important theme for Isaiah was the teaching concerning the LORD's Anointed One, the Messiah. The messianic teachings arose in times of great trouble when the people were looking for a deliverer. If this idea originated with Isaiah, the reign of Ahaz (or the time of the Sennacherib invasions) would seem to be a likely time for the idea to have developed.

Such seems to be the background of 8:22–9:7. The Assyrian invaders had seized that part of northern Palestine known as "the land of Zebulun and the land of Naphtali . . . the land beyond the Jordan, Galilee of the nations" (9:1). But the prophet believed the nation was on the threshold of a better day. Darkness would be brightened by a great light; the nation would grow, and war would be no more (9:2-5). The reason for this was that a child had been born who was of David's line who would outshine David as king. Extravagant titles would be given him:

Wonder of a Counselor, Mighty God, Father Forever, Prince of Peace.

He would practice justice in his dealings and live a life based on the will of the LORD (9:6-7).

It may well be that this glorified vision of the ideal king was inspired by Hezekiah, whose religious reforms were more thorough than those of anyone before him. In later years, however, these verses took on new meaning when the nation ceased to be. Then, they were interpreted as looking forward to a time when the nation would be restored by the Messiah. Israel's idea of the Messiah was always connected with national hopes and dreams.

The other strong messianic passage in Isaiah is 11:1-16. This passage saw the Messiah (1) in terms of his connection with the Davidic lines (11:1) and (2) in terms of his outstanding personal characteristics (wisdom, understanding, counsel, might, knowledge, and fear of the LORD) (11:4-5). It would be an unusual time, when even those animals that were natural enemies would be at peace (11:6-9). Most importantly for Israel, it would be a time of gathering the scattered people from the nations and of giving them control over their enemies (11:10-16).

12. *Miscellaneous oracles (Isa. 9:8–10:4; 5:24-30; 10:27b-34).* Sometimes prophetic sayings got divided, one part appearing at one place in the text and the rest appearing somewhere else. In 9:8–10:4 is a sermon on judgment that has a recurring theme:

For all this his anger is not turned away and his hand is stretched out still (9:12,17,21; 10:4).

This conclusion of this sermon seems to be found in 5:24-30. It naturally follows 10:4 and has the same theme verse (5:25).

The sermon begins with a word of judgment against the proud

Israelites who thought they could save themselves. But the LORD had raised up enemies who would devour them (9:8-12). Judgment had come because the leaders had failed to lead. Neither the civic leaders nor the religious leaders had fulfilled their responsibilities (9:13-17). The judgment would be like fire in a dry thicket. Each man was concerned only with his own selfish interest. Brother stood against brother (9:18-21). The lack of concern and compassion for the helpless was especially bad. The judgment would be like a violent storm (10:1-4). It would devour the sinners like a fire in dry stubble because they had "rejected the law of the LORD of Hosts, and have despised the Holy One of Israel" (5:24-25). The LORD would use a fierce nation, therefore, as the instrument to punish his sinful people (5:26-30).

The second of these oracles describes in vivid terms the approach of the Assyrian army. Like an announcer describing a race, the cities along the route were called out by the prophet. Nearer and nearer drew the Assyrian army of either Tiglath-pileser III or Sennacherib. Finally, the soldiers were close enough for the Jerusalem populace to see them in all their might. The promised judgment was about to become a horrible reality (10:27b-34).

13. *Words of hope and joy (Isa. 10:20-27; 12:1-6).*   Israel would be destroyed, but not completely. A righteous remnant would survive the Assyrian destruction, and the destroyers would feel destruction themselves (10:20-27).

The first major section of Isaiah, chapters 1–12, ends with two short songs of praise (12:1-3 and 4-6).

Oracles against foreign nations (Isa. 13:1–19:24; 21:1–23:18).   These oracles were directed to nations beyond Israel's borders. This shows how the prophet saw himself as the LORD's spokesman to all mankind, not just to Judah alone.

1. *Against Babylon (Isa. 13:1–14:23).*   Babylon revolted against Assyria in 704 but had only limited success. A century later, however, it destroyed the Assyrian power, took over its empire, and destroyed Judah for the final time in 587/86. Many thousands of Judeans were taken into exile in Babylon. It was against such a background that this oracle was set.

What Babylon had done to others would be done to it. The prophet pictured the LORD as gathering an army to destroy Babylon. In 13:17 that army was specifically mentioned as being the Medes, who were led by Cyrus the Great, the destroyer of Babylon. Many of the prophets spoke to the LORD's using the nations like checkers, moving them at will to do his bidding. Babylon, used as an instrument of punishment for Judah, would, in turn, be punished for its sinfulness by Cyrus and the Medo-Persian armies (13:1-22).

One of the results of Cyrus's conquest would be the restoration of Israel to its land (14:1-2). The sermon ends with an extended taunt song in which the prophet lords it over the conquered enemy (14:3-23). Of particular interest is 14:12:

> How you have fallen from heaven,
> O Day Star, Son of Dawn!
> How you are cut down to the ground,
> you who laid the nations low!

This is often taken from its context by Christian interpreters and applied to Satan. As it stands here, it referred to Babylonian or Canaanite gods who had been shown to be powerless.

2. *Against Assyria (Isa. 14:24-27).*   This short oracle promised that the Assyrian conquest would be short-lived.

3. *Against Philistia (Isa. 14:28-32).*   Philistia will not be safe from the conqueror.

4. *Against Moab (Isa. 15:1–16:14).*   While Moab, located on the eastern side of the Dead Sea, was a traditional enemy of Israel, there was not the strong antagonism between the two countries that existed between Judah and other of her traditional enemies. The prophet called the roll of the cities in Moab that had felt the heel of the conqueror's boot (15:1-9). He described the refugees (15:5) and pleaded with the Israelites to give them refuge (16:4). Such a courtesy had been extended to David's family when he was a fugitive from Saul. So the prophet mourned the hardships endured by the conquered people (16:1-14).

5. *Against Damascus (Syria) and Israel (Ephraim) (Isa. 17:1-6).*   It is somewhat difficult to tell where this oracle ends. A clue to its ending (and for many other oracles, for that matter) is the phrase "says the LORD God of Israel" (17:6). It was spoken by the prophet during the Syro-Ephraimitic war (734–732) and foretold the failure of that ill-fated venture.

6. *Against idols (Isa. 17:7-14).*   The prophets were especially hard on idols and idol makers because the worship of idols represented for them a denial of the LORD's action on behalf of his people (17:7-11). Idols were helpless, but the LORD could rout the armies of the nations (17:12-14).

7. *Against Egypt (Isa. 18:1–20:6).*   Isaiah was particularly strong in his opinions about Egypt (sometimes called Ethiopia as in 18:1). This oracle probably was associated with the Ashdod rebellion as was Isaiah's symbolic action of parading through Jerusalem for three years unclothed like a captive (20:1-6). The prophet warned that the Assyrians "a people feared far and near" (18:2) would bring an end to the rebellion as the LORD looked on (18:1-6). The Assyrians then would bring gifts to the LORD (18:7).

Another saying (19:1-15) described a civil war the leaders would be unable to put down in Egypt. Finally, a strong king would impose an iron rule over them (19:1-4).[6] Egypt had not consulted the LORD, so all her so-called wisdom had only brought confusion.

A third saying concerning Egypt and Assyria has a theme phrase "in that day" (19:16,18,19,23,24) and looks to a time when Egypt and Assyria would follow the LORD (19:16-25). Isaiah 20:1-6 has been discussed previously.

8. *Against Babylon again (Isa. 21:1-10).*   Another oracle set in the time of the Babylonian exile catches something of the terror the people felt in the midst of war. Babylon fell before the Medo-Persian forces like grain before the reaper (21:1-10).

9. *Against Dumah (Edom) (Isa. 21:11-12).*   Located here is one of the most famous passages in Isaiah:

> "Watchman, what of the night?
> Watchman, what of the night?"
> The watchman says:
> "Morning comes, and also the night.
> If you will inquire, inquire;
> come back again" (21:11-12).

Edom was noted for its tradition of wisdom, but its wisdom could not save it. Deliverance would come (morning), but so would destruction (night).[7]

10. *Against Arabia (Isa. 21:13-17).*   Little was said in the Old Testament about Arabia. The prophet seems to be speaking of raids on caravans that the LORD opposed.

11. *Against Jerusalem (Isa. 22:1-14).*   During the invasions by Assyria, either in 714 or 701, Jerusalem faced the possibility of being captured and destroyed. The leaders would depend upon their own strategy and armies to defend themselves, but not upon the one who could give real protection. Because of this failure to recognize the LORD, the people celebrated their own funerals with the attitude:

> "Let us eat and drink,
> for tomorrow we die" (22:13).

And die they would (22:14)!

12. *Against Shebna (Isa. 22:15-25).*   In the midst of sermons against the nations stands a saying against Shebna, who was Hezekiah's right-hand man. His emphasis on military might and his advice to Hezekiah to revolt against Assyria provoked the wrath of the prophet, who said that the

---

[6]John Bright, *A History of Israel*, p. 279, tells of such a strong ruler in the person of Piankhi who founded the "Twenty-fifth (Ethiopian) Dynasty" in 710 after a period of anarchy. His rule was preceded by a period of anarchy.

[7]Oxford Annotated Bible, RSV, Isa. 21:11-12 note.

LORD would throw him out like a ball in a large field (22:15-18). He would be replaced by Eliakim, who would be more willing to listen to the LORD. Even so, he would fail to carry out his responsibilities (22:19-25).

13. *Against Tyre (Phoenicia) (Isa. 23:1-18).*   The Phoenicians were the merchant princes of the ancient world. As such, they rarely ever were warlike. As traders, they wanted to stay on good terms with all the countries surrounding the Mediterranean, where they had their trading posts. The Mesopotamian powers, both Assyria and Babylon, coveted her good harbors and fleets of ships, since that gave them access to the Mediterranean Sea. Because of its position as middleman for the nations, Tyre managed to survive for many centuries. Furthermore, it was built on an island, which made it virtually impossible to conquer. Tyre finally was destroyed by Alexander the Great in the fourth century B.C.

The Isaiah apocalypse (Isa. 24:1–27:13).   In these chapters is found a kind of writing known as apocalyptic literature. It appears in only a few places in the Bible: here, in Ezekiel and Daniel, and in the Revelation in the New Testament. It grew out of prophetic literature but was different in a number of ways:

> It spoke of the earth and the universe being in turmoil.
> It used highly figurative language, often describing strange creatures unknown on earth.
> It made generous use of number symbolism.
> It was written to be read, not spoken to be heard.
> It was designed to comfort the faithful in a time of trouble, not to rebuke the sinners.

The Isaiah apocalypse does not share all these characteristics, but it does speak of the LORD at work in the universe to bring deliverance to the faithful.

1. *Destruction is coming (Isa. 24:1-13).*   The earth will be laid waste by the LORD. The earth and the heavens will writhe in pain because its inhabitants have violated the LORD's covenant. The polluted earth will be cursed, and desolation will come (24:1-13).

2. *Praise the LORD (Isa. 24:14-16a).*   Praise to the LORD will resound from the ends of the earth.

3. *Judgment will be universal (Isa. 24:16b-23).*   There will be no escape from judgment. The earth will stagger like a drunk man. Judgment will be upon men and gods—all will be prisoners when the LORD reigns (24:16b-23).

4. *Praise to the triumphant LORD (Isa. 25:1-12).*   This passage opens with a psalm praising the LORD, who has triumphed over the strong powers of the earth, protecting the helpless and putting down the ruthless (25:1-5). The ideal age will come when death will be no more, and praise will be given to God who has brought salvation (25:6-9). Moab's defeat will be symbolic of the LORD's power to sweep aside any power that opposes him (25:10-12).

5. *A psalm of praise (Isa. 26:1-19).*   This psalm would have been used in a service celebrating a military victory. The LORD was praised for making the city secure and strong by helping the people defeat their enemies (26:1-6). The LORD would bless the righteous and those who sought him earnestly (26:7-9).

The wicked could learn nothing by letting them go on in their wickedness. The foreigners who had ruled Israel were wicked. Now they were destroyed, but Judah had prospered (26:10-15).

That had not always been so, however. In the time of trouble, the people had cried to the LORD. Without the LORD, the enemy would triumph over them (26:16-19). In 26:19 there may be one of the few Old Testament references to life after death.

6. *The LORD comes in judgment (Isa. 26:20–27:1).*   This passage mentions Leviathan, a mythological sea monster spoken of in Canaanite literature. The apocalyptist saw the LORD's triumph as universal, including all powers of land and sea.

7. *The LORD will deliver his people (Isa. 27:2-13).*   The LORD would be the vinedresser of his vineyard (Israel). It would blossom and bear fruit enough under his care to supply the whole world (27:2-6). The enemies of Israel would be put down and idolatry would be crushed (26:7-11). Israel would be gathered from exile and restored to the land (27:12-13).

Oracles from various times (Isa. 28:1–35:10)

1. *The drunkards of Ephraim (Isa. 28:1-13).*   Alcoholism, like homosexuality, is not a modern problem, as this passage shows. Isaiah particularly directed his ire at the priests and prophets of the Northern Kingdom who were famous for their wine-bibbing (28:1-8; see Hos. 4). Their drunken state had so clouded their minds that they could not function as teachers of the law of the LORD. Those who followed their example would be destroyed as they would be (27:9-13).

2. *The leaders of Jerusalem (Isa. 28:14-22).*   The leaders of Jerusalem had become cynics, scoffing at the idea that the LORD could deliver them. In so doing they had left the LORD's covenant that would bring life and had made a covenant with death. They substituted lies for truth (28:14-15). The LORD stood by his demands for justice. When judgment came,

the things the leaders trusted would fail and they would be destroyed (28:16-22).

3. *A parable (Isa. 28:23-29).*   Like a farmer, the LORD does everything at the proper time.

4. *Judah's future (Isa. 29:1-8).*   Mount Zion, where David had built his city, was called by other names. Here the prophet speaks of it as Ariel. It stood as a symbol for Judah, whose decline would not be permanent (29:1-4). The day would come when the LORD would put down Judah's foes, and its former strength would be like a dream (29:5-8).

5. *Spiritual stupidity (Isa. 29:9-24).*   When men thought they were at their wisest, they usually were the most stupid because they did not realize how little they did know. The prophet's vision was meaningless, and the LORD's warnings fell on deaf ears. Their religion was man-made, not God-given (29:9-12).

But the LORD would still do marvelous things. He would confound the wise and bring joy to the meek and poor. Jacob would rejoice and would come to stand in awe before his God, willing to be taught once more (29:13-24).

6. *Do not trust Egypt—trust the LORD (Isa. 30:1-17).*   This oracle came when Sennacherib was threatening the western states. Hezekiah had sent envoys to Egypt to ask for help, but the prophet strongly opposed Hezekiah's effort to play one big power off against the other. Egypt's help would be worthless (30:1-7).

Isaiah's stand won him no ribbons for popularity. He was told to stick to being religious and not to try to apply it to everyday life (30:8-11). But the LORD's reply through the prophet was that those who tried to shut the prophet up would be smashed like a clay vessel (30:12-14). One of the key ideas in Isaiah's theology is found in 30:15:

> For thus said the LORD God, the Holy One of Israel,
>   "In returning and rest you shall be saved;
>   in quietness and in trust shall be your strength."

But the plea to trust the LORD was in vain. Instead, military power had become the god and by military power would the nation be destroyed, left

> like a flagstaff on top of a mountain,
> like a signal on a hill (30:17*b*).

7. *The LORD will be gracious (Isa. 30:18-26).*   The people would have to go through affliction before they would be willing to pay attention to him who would be their teacher, who would say, "This is the way, walk in it" (30:21). Then, the people would get rid of their idols (30:18-22).

Prosperity would come, and land would produce bountiful crops, and the LORD would bind up the wounds of the people (30:23-26).

8. *Assyria's affliction (Isa. 30:27-33).*   The major cause of joy in Israel would be the downfall of the Assyrians. They had been marked for destruction by the LORD.

9. *Trust the LORD—not Egypt (Isa. 31:1-3).*   Egypt was not to be trusted for:

> The Egyptians are men, and not God;
> and their horses are flesh, and not spirit (31:3a).

Anyone who trusted in them and not God would be destroyed.

10. *Sennacherib cannot harm you (Isa. 31:4-9).*   This passage accompanies the story in 2 Kings 19:32-34, in which Isaiah said that Sennacherib would protect the city of Jerusalem. In the time of Jeremiah, Isaiah's promise of the LORD's protection for Jerusalem would be taken from its context and used to promote the idea that Jerusalem could never fall. While promising the LORD's protection for Jerusalem in a specific situation, the prophet still emphasized the need to follow the LORD (31:6-9).

11. *Justice will prevail (Isa. 32:1-8).*   This saying looked to a time when balance would be restored in society. Justice would prevail, and men of judgment would rule (32:1-8).

12. *Watch out, foolish women (Isa. 32:9-20).*   The matrons of society were warned that hard times were coming, when they would lose their luxurious way of life (32:9-14). But the LORD's spirit would be poured out, and prosperity and justice would once more prevail in a peaceful land (32:15-20).

13. *A prophet's grab-bag (Isa. 33:1-24).*   This chapter contains a mixture of materials beginning with a rebuke to a destroyer (probably Assyria) (33:1). Verses 2-4 are a prayer addressed to the LORD and pleading for his grace. Verses 5-6 praise the LORD for what he will do in bringing the times back into balance.

Verses 6-9 describe the situation as it existed: a time of trouble, broken convenants, and lack of concern for one's fellow man. But the LORD addressed himself to the situation, declaring that judgment would come. He who lived by the way of the LORD had nothing to fear, but he who disregarded that way was doomed (33:10-16).

But the future would be glorious (33:17-24). The arrogant and rude ones would be gone. Jerusalem would be a quiet peaceful city because of the presence of the LORD in his majesty:

> For the LORD is our judge, the LORD is our ruler,
> The LORD is our king; he will save us (33:22).

14. *The LORD's vengeance (Isa. 34:1-17).*   Many scholars think that this chapter and the one that follows belong with chapters 40–66, since they seem to speak of a time near the end of the Babylonian exile. The subject of 34:1-17 is the LORD's warfare against the nations that oppose him. The LORD is spoken of as a dread warrior whose sword "is sated with blood . . . is gorged with fat" (34:6). The expression, "the day of the LORD's vengeance" (34:8), was a term used in primitive justice, which means the day when the LORD sets things right. Vengeance, in the biblical sense, meant "bringing things back to even that were uneven" or "balancing what was unbalanced" (34:1-8).

Edom was used as an example of those nations who opposed the LORD and thus opposed Judah. There seems to have been a particularly strong hatred between the Edomites and Israel, because Edom took every opportunity to hit at Israel when she was weak. Thus the LORD's enemies will be left as desolate as Edom (34:9-17).

15. *Joy for Zion (Isa. 35:1-10).*   The other side of the coin of the LORD's judgment upon the nations would be the restoration and prosperity of Israel in the land. This is why vengeance and salvation are mentioned together in 35:4:

> Behold, your God
>   will come with vengeance,
> with the recompense of God.
>   He will come and save you.

> The sick would be restored to health, the deserts would bloom,
> and the ransomed of the LORD shall return,
>   and come to Zion with singing;
> everlasting joy shall be upon their heads;
>   they shall obtain joy and gladness,
>   and sorrow and sighing shall flee away (35:10).

The final chapters, 36–39, were discussed under "Isaiah and Hezekiah," earlier in this chapter.

Summary on Isaiah.   As we have seen, Isaiah 1–39 contains a wide variety of materials, some of which may not be from Isaiah of Jerusalem. There is also much in the book that sounds like the other prophets. An example would be the day-of-the-LORD idea that comes from Amos. Like the other prophets of the eighth century B.C., Isaiah was a prophet of judgment. There are, however, four major ideas that have been discussed as being distinct in the message of Isaiah. They are as follows:

1. *The holiness of God.* Holiness has about it the idea of separation, of difference, or of distinction. Some speak of God's otherness. For

Isaiah, God's holiness or difference from man was a moral difference. He was a moral being who demanded morality from those who worshiped him.

2. *A quiet, confident faith.* God was not only holy, but he was trustworthy. Isaiah's advice to both Ahaz and Hezekiah in times of crisis was to trust God, not military power (7:4,15; 30:15).

3. *A righteous remnant.* Judgment was sure to come upon Israel, but its purpose was not to destroy but to purify the nation. A small group of holy people would survive who would form the basis of a new and righteous society.

4. *The Messiah.* The new age would be ruled by the ideal David. Isaiah may have hoped that Hezekiah would fulfill this dream, but later interpreters looked into the future for the LORD's Chosen One.

Micah: The Country Preacher

While Isaiah was counselor to the kings of Judah, a prophet from the country village of Moresheth-gath in the Philistine territory was also preaching the word of the LORD.

THE MAN

Little is known of Micah beyond what can be discovered from the book that bears his name. His father was not important enough to be mentioned. His village was far different from the bustling metropolis of Jerusalem. Unlike Isaiah, who loved Jerusalem, Micah considered it and Samaria to be "sin cities," ripe for the judgment of the LORD.

THE BOOK

The small book that bears Micah's name falls into four parts: oracles against Jerusalem (1:1–3:12); a new day for Israel (4:1–5:16); oracles against Israel (6:1–7:7); and a final section of Israel restored (7:8-20).

Oracles against Jerusalem (Micah 1:1–3:12). Micah preached before the Northern Kingdom fell, so part of his preaching was directed toward Samaria and its sins. But the main use he made of Samaria and its sins was to say that Jerusalem was just like it. Just as the LORD's judgment was coming on Samaria, so it would come on Jerusalem (1:1-9).

Micah, like the other prophets, enjoyed using puns. In a series of puns in Hebrew, which cannot be easily translated into English, he described the destruction of the small cities and towns in the path of the invaders (1:10-16).

Micah reserved his most scathing comments for the upper classes of society. He accused them of lying awake, plotting to steal from the common man (2:1-5). They tried to stop the prophets of the LORD from prophesying the truth, preferring a prophet who would

> go about and utter wind and lies,
>   saying, "I will preach to you of wine and strong drink,"
> he would be the preacher for this people! (2:11)

The oracle was softened by a later addition, which spoke of the righteous remnant (2:12-13).

Particularly biting was an oracle about the leaders of Judah. They hated good and loved evil. They were like cannibals,

> who tear the skin from off my people,
>   and their flesh from off their bones;
> who eat the flesh of my people,
>   and flay their skin from off them,
> and break their bones in pieces,
>   and chop them up like meat in a kettle,
>   like flesh in a caldron (3:2-3).

The LORD would not hear them on the day of judgment (3:1-4).

Prophets, too, felt the lash of Micah's tongue, especially those prophets who curried the favor of the rich. They would be disgraced, but the true prophet would be vindicated (3:5-7). Micah, of course, considered himself to be a true prophet:

> But as for me, I am filled with power,
>   with the Spirit of the LORD,
>   and with justice and might,
> to declare to Jacob his transgression
>   and to Israel his sin (3:8).

Where Isaiah had said Jerusalem would not fall to the armies of Sennacherib in 701, Micah had no such faith in the future. The sins of the city's leaders were sure to bring doom. He foresaw a day when Zion would "be plowed as a field" and Jerusalem's hills would be covered with trees instead of houses (3:9-12).

A new day will come (Micah 4:1–5:15). In startling contrast to chapters 1–3, this section of Micah speaks of restoration and a glorious future, leading many interpreters to say another prophet at a later time was responsible for it. The first passage (4:1-3), in particular, has questions raised about it because it also appears in Isaiah 2:2-4. It speaks of a time when universal peace would come and all nations would come to worship the LORD, the God of Israel. It would be a time when weapons of war would be turned into instruments of peace because war would be ended. In that time, each man would dwell in his own home in peace and safety (4:1-5). The crippled and rejected peoples of the earth would receive special attention from the LORD (4:6-8).

The next oracle speaks of the Babylonian exile and how the LORD will rescue his people from it. Under the LORD's plans, Israel would triumph over her enemies and live by the LORD's will. The present condition, however, was an enemy siege (4:9–5:1).

One of Micah's most famous sayings was the Bethlehem oracle (5:2-6). Since the messianic concept was connected with the Davidic monarchy, it would be quite natural to expect the birth of the future king to be connected with David's city, Bethlehem. This was quoted in the New Testament as a messianic prophecy (Matt. 2:6).

The remainder of chapter 5 deals with the defeat of the Assyrians and the restoration of the remnant of Jacob, who will be scattered "like dew from the LORD." The remnant would be purified from its worship of idols (5:7-15).

Oracles against Israel (Micah 6:1–7:7).   If only one sermon from Micah had survived, Micah 6:1-8 would be sufficient to cause him to rank among the great prophets of Israel. In this oracle, he managed to sum up the important point of the message of each of the three other eighth-century prophets.

The oracle is a classic example of the use of court language by the prophet to present the LORD's case against Israel. The essentials of a trial are present:

1. *The court is called to order (Micah 6:1-2).* The LORD who is judge, jury, and prosecuting attorney calls on the mountains and hills to be spectators at the trial and announces that the court is in session.
2. *The indictment and evidence is presented (Micah 6:3-5).* The indictment against the defendants is presented in a series of questions (6:3) charging the people with being tired of the LORD. The LORD's past dealings with Israel are recalled to show that Israel has no right to complain.
3. *The defense pleads its case (Micah 6:6-7).* Protesting their innocence, the people ask, "What more can we do? Does the LORD require

more offerings?" If so, they would be willing to sacrifice even their first-born children.

4. *The verdict is delivered (Micah 6:8).* What the defense had said was that, whatever bribe the LORD demanded, the people would pay. But that was the heart of the problem. Material offerings, even first-born children, were meaningless when that was all that was offered.

> He has showed you, O man, what is good;
>   and what does the LORD require of you
> but to do justice, and to love kindness,
>   and to walk humbly with our God? (6:8)

In this verse, Micah summed up the teaching of the eighth-century prophets: Amos's theme of justice; Hosea's theme of love (kindness); and Isaiah's theme of the quiet, confident walk with the LORD.

Following this oracle, Micah spoke against the cheating in the marketplace and oppression by the rich. These sins would bring the LORD's judgment in the form of famine and desolation (6:9-16). He lamented the fact that good men had perished and that the ungodly seemed to be everywhere, ready to murder at every opportunity. Bribery was rampant; no one could be trusted; and children were disobedient to parents. The only hope was to look to the LORD for salvation in such an evil time (7:1-7).

Israel's triumph over her enemies (Micah 7:8-20).   Israel would not always be under the enemy's heel. The time would come when the LORD would deliver his people and the enemy would be destroyed (7:8-10). The nations that despised Israel would be drawn to her (7:11-13).

Micah 7:14 is a prayer to the LORD to be a shepherd to his flock; a response from the LORD follows in 7:15-17, promising a repeat of the marvels of the Exodus days. The nations will be subject to Israel instead of Israel being subject to the nations (7:14-17).

Finally, Micah's book closes with a short psalm of praise to God:

> He will again have compassion upon us,
>   he will tread our iniquities under foot.
> Thou wilt cast all our sins
>   into the depths of the sea.
> Thou wilt show faithfulness to Jacob
>   and steadfast love to Abraham,
> as thou hast sworn to our fathers
>   from the days of old (7:19-20).

1. How did Judah manage to survive the Assyrian invasions which destroyed Israel and Syria in the latter part of the eighth century (745–721)?
2. What was Isaiah's relationship to Ahaz? to Hezekiah?
3. What was the nature of Isaiah's call to be a prophet?
4. What was Isaiah's advice to Ahaz in the Syro-Ephraimitic crisis?
5. What was the significance of the names of Isaiah's children?
6. What did Isaiah advise Hezekiah to do during the Ashdod rebellion?
7. How did Hezekiah prepare for the Assyrian invasion during Sennacherib's reign?
8. Discuss the theory that there were two invasions by Sennacherib.
9. Give the arguments concerning the authorship and the unity of the book of Isaiah.
10. Summarize the four major teachings of Isaiah 1–39 and cite one passage where each of these teachings appears.
11. What was Isaiah's attitude toward Jerusalem?
12. How did Micah look at Jerusalem?
13. What did Micah see as the great evils of Israelite society?
14. Show how Micah 6:1-8 reflects the procedures of an ancient law court.

FOR FURTHER STUDY

Isaiah

BLANK, SHELDON H. *Prophetic Faith in Isaiah*. New York: Harper & Row, 1958. Isaiah as viewed by a leading Jewish scholar.

CHILDS, BREVARD S. *Isaiah and the Assyrian Crisis*. Studies in Biblical Theology. 2nd ser., no. 4. Naperville, Ill.: Alec R. Allenson, 1967.

KAISER, OTTO. *Isaiah 1–12*. Trans. by R. A. Wilson. The Old Testament Library. Philadelphia: Westminster, 1974.

———. *Isaiah 13–39*. Trans. by R. A. Wilson. The Old Testament Library. Philadelphia: Westminster, 1974.

KELLY, PAGE H. "Isaiah" in *The Broadman Bible Commentary*. Nashville: Broadman, 1971.

LESLIE, ELMER A. *Isaiah*. New York: Abingdon, 1963.

SCOTT, R. B. Y. "Isaiah 1–39: Introduction and Exegesis" in *Interpreter's Bible*, V. New York: Abingdon, 1956.

SMITH, GEORGE ADAM. *The Book of Isaiah*, rev. ed. New York: Harper & Row, 1927.

VRIEZEN, TH. C. "Essentials in the Theology of Isaiah" in *Israel's Prophetic Heritage*. Ed. by Bernhard Anderson and Walter Harrelson. New York: Harper & Row, 1962.

WARD, JAMES M. *Amos and Isaiah*. New York: Abingdon, 1969.

Micah

MARSH, JOHN. *Amos and Micah*. London: S.C.M. Press, 1959.

SNAITH, NORMAN. *Amos, Hosea and Micah*. London: Epworth, 1956.

See also the general books on the prophets cited following chapter 8.

CHAPTER TEN

And Then There Was None: Judah's Last Days

Judah's last century started badly with the reign of Manasseh, saw some of the nation's best days under Josiah, and ended with the death of Judah under Zedekiah. One hundred years from the death of Hezekiah, the nation died in the flames of Jerusalem; but the remnant survived on the banks of the Tigris and Euphrates rivers.

The International Situation

The rivalry between Assyria and Egypt continued and, as usual, Judah was caught in the middle. After Sennacherib's murder by two of his sons, a third son, Esarhaddon (680–669), became king and proved to be more than able to bring his vast empire under control. Babylon was his first victim. Egypt was soon to follow in 671. Asshur-banapal, Esarhaddon's son and successor, had to deal twice with a rebellion in Egypt. It was finally smashed when the ancient capital of Thebes, which was located in southern Egypt, was captured in 663. Egypt was left almost helpless for a period of time.

The Situation in Judah

BAD DAYS UNDER MANASSEH (2 KINGS 21:1-18; 2 CHRON. 33:1-20)

Israel's historians had little that was positive to say about Manasseh. Both the Bible and Assyrian records indicate that he was a puppet of the

Assyrians. Second Chronicles 33:11-13 tells how he was one time bound in chains and taken before an Assyrian king at Babylon.[1]

His reign saw a rebirth of Baal worship in Judah. He rebuilt the high places, where he set up altars to the Canaanite fertility gods and goddesses. Furthermore, he built altars in the Temple area for the worship of the star deities ("the host of heaven"), also showing Assyrian influence. He practiced human sacrifice, even burning his own son on an altar to a pagan god; and he encouraged the practices of black magic and fortune-telling. Those who opposed him were severely persecuted:

> Manasseh shed very much innocent blood, till he had filled Jerusalem from one end to another. (2 Kings 21:16)

JOSIAH, THE BOY KING (2 KINGS 22:1–23:30)

When Amon (642–640) tried to continue the policies of his father, Manasseh, he signed his own death warrant. After ruling for two years, he was assassinated. His eight-year-old son, Josiah, was placed on the throne in his place (21:19-26).

Josiah's early years.   Josiah (640–609) came to the throne at a time when Assyria was fading as a world power, Egypt was still weak, and Babylon had not yet become a threat to the western states. Since he was only eight years of age, the government was actually controlled by the high priest, who was the chief religious official of the kingdom (2 Kings 22:1-2).

First attempts at reform (2 Chron. 34:1-7).   Hilkiah, the high priest, influenced Josiah to take strong action early in his reign to destroy the pagan religions that Manasseh had so ardently promoted. This activity extended even into the cities of the old Northern Kingdom (2 Chron. 34:1-7). This seems to have begun in 627, the year that Asshur-banapal, the last strong Assyrian king, died.[2]

The prophet Zephaniah (Zeph. 1:1–3:20).

1. *His life.*   Before Josiah's reform had made too much headway, the prophet Zephaniah seemed to have been active. Little is known about Zephaniah except for the fact that his ancestry was traced back to Hezekiah. It is probably safe to assume that this was King Hezekiah. This

---

[1]John Bright, *A History of Israel*, p. 310, suggests that Manasseh was accused of taking part in a revolt. The Chronicler saw it also as punishment for his sins.

[2]John Bright, *A History of Israel*, pp. 312–314, gives the details of Assyria's decline. See also Martin Noth, *The History of Israel*, pp. 269–271.

Figure 10–1. The Kingdom of Judah–seventh century B.C.

would mean that Zephaniah was related to the royal family. Although he preached during Josiah's reign (1:1), the nature of his preaching would indicate that his ministry was probably in the early years of Josiah, perhaps from 640 to 630.

2. *The book*.   The major idea in the book of Zephaniah is the day of the LORD, which indicates that he had been influenced greatly by the traditions about the prophet Amos. Many of the phrases in Zephaniah's description of the day of the LORD were almost direct quotations from Amos, especially Amos 5:18-20 and 8:9-14.

a. *The LORD's sweeping judgment (Zeph. 1:2-6)*.   The LORD's judgment would devastate land and sea. The special object of that judgment would be Judah's idols and those who worshiped them—the Baalites; the worshipers of the heavenly bodies; the followers of Milcom, an Ammonite deity; and any others who had turned from the LORD.

b. *The high and mighty of Jerusalem (Zeph. 1:7-13)*.   Judgment would begin at the top, where responsibility was the greatest. It was Judah's leaders who had led the people astray, and judgment would reach even to the royal family itself. Some leaped over the threshold or doorsill because they believed a demon lived there; if one stepped on it, evil would result. The custom of carrying the bride over the threshold probably had its origin in a similar belief (1:7-9).

From the palace the judgment would sweep on through the city, where the merchants hawked their wares. The LORD is pictured as going through the city with a lamp, looking in every nook and cranny, trying to find the cynical men of Judah who had said that he would not do anything to them. They were compared to wine that had become thick and useless because of the lees (small sandlike particles that settled to the bottom of the wineskin as the wine aged) (1:10-13).

c. *The great day of the LORD (Zeph. 1:14-18)*.   In tones like Amos's, Zephaniah described the day of the LORD that was rapidly approaching. It would be a day of wrath,

> a day of distress and anguish,
> a day of ruin and devastation,
> a day of darkness and gloom,
> a day of clouds and thick darkness,
> a day of trumpet blast and battle cry
> against the fortified cities
> and against the lofty battlements (1:15-16).

d. *Hope for the righteous (Zeph. 2:1-3)*.   Zephaniah did see hope for the humble people of the land, who would come to the LORD and "seek righteousness" and "seek humility."

e. *Devastation on the nations (Zeph. 2:4-15)*.   As was common among the prophets, Zephaniah did not see the day of the LORD's judgment as being limited to Judah. Judgment would come as well as Judah's enemies, for they too were rebels against the LORD. The Philistines (2:4-7), Moab and Ammon (2:8-11), Ethiopia (Egypt) (2:12), and Assyria (2:13-15) would know the wrath of the LORD. Of Assyria, he said:

> Herds shall lie down in the midst of her,
>   all the beasts of the field;
>
>   . . .
>
> the owl shall hoot in the window
>   the raven croak on the threshold;
>   for her cedar work will be laid bare.
>
>   . . .
>
> What a desolation she has become,
>   a lair for wild beasts!
> Every one who passes by her
>   hisses and shakes his fist (2:14-15).

f. *Woe to Jerusalem (Zeph. 3:1-7).*   Having pronounced the LORD's judgment on Judah's enemies, Zephaniah once more turned his attention to Jerusalem and her officials. He compared her officials to beasts of prey (the lion and the wolf). Her prophets were immoral men, disgraces to the name of the One whom they claimed to represent. Only the LORD himself was concerned with justice. He could not depend on his human representatives to see that it was done.

g. *A better day is coming (Zeph. 3:8-13).*   The net effect of the LORD's judgment would be to cleanse the earth. The defiled speech that began with man's rebellion at the Tower of Babel would be purified when the people were brought back to the land (3:8-10). Sins would be forgiven, and pride would be no more. In its place the people would be humble and lowly, teachable and truthful (3:11-13).

h. *Jerusalem shall be restored (Zeph. 3:14-20).*   The climax of the new day would be the restoration of Jerusalem. Judgment would achieve its purpose of cleansing the nation; days of mourning would become festival days when the people were once more gathered in the land.

Changes under Josiah (2 Kings 22:3–23:27).[3]

Finding the scroll (2 Kings 22:3-20).   If the chief priest hoped to shape the young king's thinking to cause a return to the basic religious foundations of the nation, he did a good job. Efforts at reform may have begun as early as 630 and gained in intensity as the years passed.

In 622 an important event took place. On instructions from Josiah,

---

[3]The traditional date for the beginning of the prophet Jeremiah's ministry is 626 B.C. However, since the major portion of his ministry followed the reign of Josiah, discussion of it will be reserved until the reigns of Jehoiakim, Jehoiachin, and Zedekiah.

a major repair job on the Temple began under the direction of Hilkiah, the chief priest (22:3-7). In the process of cleaning out the building, a scroll containing a version of the law of Moses was found. The manuscript was taken to the king's secretary, Shaphan, who in turn reported its discovery to the king (22:8-10).

Deuteronomy

When the scroll was read to Josiah, he was greatly upset and tore his clothes to express his sense of anxiety. He immediately gave orders that Huldah, a prophetess, should be consulted about the course of action that should be taken (22:11-13). The oracle that Huldah gave spoke of the LORD's displeasure at the idol worship in Judah, but it promised that Josiah would prosper because of his penitent attitude (22:14-20).

Covenant renewal and religious reform (2 Kings 23:1-27). When Josiah received word of Huldah's oracle, he led the people in a ceremony of covenant renewal (23:1-3). But he went further than just pledging to keep the law of the LORD; he applied the law practically to the situation. Josiah's actions, based on the law that had been discovered, have led scholars to conclude that the scroll was the major part of what is known today as the book of Deuteronomy. Thus they refer to Josiah's reform movement as the Deuteronomic reformation.

His first major step was an attempt to rid the land of pagan cults. In Jerusalem many altars to pagan deities had been erected in Manasseh's time. These were destroyed, along with various images that were a part of the worship. Extending the purge further, orders were given that not only were altars in Judah to be destroyed but also the altars in cities, such as Bethel in the old Northern Kingdom. Those who were priests at the pagan shrines were slain to rid the land of their influence (23:4-20).

Next, Josiah ordered the celebration of a great passover, calling to the minds of the people the LORD's mighty acts in bringing them out of the land of Egypt (23:21-23). This reminder of the LORD's covenant with Moses was a sort of call for revival of the old-time religion that had for the most part been forgotten, with the emphasis on the covenant with David. So impressive were the passover services that the historian said of them:

> No such passover had been kept since the days of the judges who judged Israel, or during all the days of the kings of Israel or the kings of Judah (23:22).

A most important aspect of the reform was the gathering of all the priests of the LORD in Jerusalem for the purpose of centralizing all worship services in the Jerusalem Temple. The reason for this was to assure that the worship be kept pure, not mixed with elements of pagan worship. While this was a noble idea, one major result of the action would prove fatal to the whole reform. Out of the centralizing of worship developed the idea that (1) the Temple was the LORD's dwelling place;

(2) the LORD would never permit his dwelling place to be destroyed; and (3) since the Temple was located in Jerusalem, Jerusalem could never be destroyed because the LORD lived there in the Temple. The conclusion that Jerusalem was safe from all attack, furthermore, seemed to be supported by Isaiah's words, spoken in the days of Sennacherib's invasions, to the effect that Jerusalem was protected by the LORD (Isa. 37:33-35; 2 Kings 19:32-34).

Meanwhile, in the rest of the world.   Josiah had been able to operate so freely because Assyria was a weakling on the verge of being completely eliminated from the international scene. The beginning of the end came when the Babylonians gained their independence and joined with the Medes in an attack on the Assyrians. The Egyptians came to Assyria's aid, but it was a case of too little and too late. In 614, the Medes captured Asshur, Assyria's early capital. In 612, the combined forces of the Medes and Babylonians captured and destroyed Ninevah. The final blows came with the fall of Haran in 610 and an attempt by the Assyrians to recapture it in 609. The giant was dead.[4]

The death of Josiah (2 Kings 23:28-30; 2 Chron. 35:20-27).   Josiah, the brightest star among the Judean kings, died a tragic death on the famous battlefield of Megiddo. Pharaoh Neco of Egypt was pushing his army northward along the international highway to try to stop the advance of the Medo-Babylonian armies at Carchemish. For some unknown reason, Josiah chose to try to stop Neco; but he only succeeded in getting himself killed. The year was 609. His death set in motion a chain of events that would end in the death of the nation itself.[5]

Two Prophets and King Jehoiakim

Of these two prophets, only Habakkuk was directly concerned with the fortunes and misfortunes of Judah, while Nahum concerned himself with the destruction of Nineveh, the capital of Assyria.

NAHUM: PROPHET OF THE LORD'S VENGEANCE ON NINEVEH

Almost nothing is known about Nahum. He is called "Nahum of Elkosh" in 1:1. Speculation about the location of Elkosh suggests that it was in either Judah, the Galilee region, or Mesopotamia. The name of the

---

[4]For details see John Bright, *A History of Israel,* p. 314ff.

[5]Martin Noth, *The History of Israel,* p. 278, discusses possible reasons for Josiah's challenge of Neco.

Figure 10–2. "King Josiah went to meet him; and Pharaoh Neco slew him at Megiddo, when he saw him" (2 Kings 23:29). Josiah lost his life on this famous battlefield, called the Plain of Megiddo or Esdralon, when he tried to block Egypt's invasion of the Babylonian empire.

Photograph by John H. Tullock.

city of Capernaum, famous in Jesus' day, literally means "village of Na(h)um." This probably is the basis for believing Elkosh was located in Galilee. The one thing that could be said with certainty about Nahum is that he hated the Assyrians. The book dates from about 612. It mentions the plunder of Thebes (Nah. 3:8), which took place in 663 and thus could not be earlier than that date. Nineveh was destroyed in 612. That would seem to be the latest year one could date the book.

The LORD is a jealous God (Nah. 1:1-11). The book starts with an ancient poem on the LORD as an avenging God. It is an acrostic—that is, different letters of the alphabet start each line. Since not all the letters in the Hebrew alphabet were used, it is an incomplete acrostic. The poem may be original with Nahum, or he may be quoting it from some other source.

The LORD punishes those who have set themselves against him (1:2-3a). The forces of nature do his bidding (1:3b-5). No one can endure his wrath because his judgments are complete (1:6-11). Behind this idea of the LORD as an avenging God is the basic idea that he is the God of justice, the One who can set things right in the universe. The enemies of the LORD are those who would destroy the principle of justice in the earth, and only He is able to set things right. His vengeance is directed toward punishing the guilty and righting things that have been made wrong.

You are doomed, Nineveh (Nah. 1:12–3:19).   In what is probably the most powerful poetry in the Bible, Nahum described the fate of Nineveh, the capital of the hated Assyrian Empire. There is little that is positive in the poem except the words of assurance to Judah in 1:12-13 and 1:15, where Judah was told that it would be delivered from the Assyrian threats. Between these words of assurance were words of doom for Assyria (1:14).

In vivid language, Nahum described the fall of the doomed city. First came the warning of the approaching armies (2:1), followed by a description of the invaders. The scarlet-clad soldiers were accompanied by the gleaming metal war chariots that flashed like torches under the dazzling Mesopotamian sun (2:3-4). The defenders of the city were caught unprepared for the attack. They rushed about in confusion, trying to organize the defense; but it was all in vain (2:5). The invaders were already inside the city, even in the king's palace, carrying off the queen. The poet saw the fall of the city as being compared to a dam breaking, releasing the waters of a pool (2:6-8). The city was plundered—the strong man became a weakling (2:9-13).

In another powerful poem (3:1-19), the poetry catches the sound of the pounding of the horses' hooves and the rumble of chariots on cobblestone streets (3:1-3). Nineveh was like a harlot who had laid many low with her diseases. Now she would be stripped naked and assaulted with manure while everyone looked on with contempt (3:4-7).

Nineveh was reminded that other great cities had fallen, including Thebes, the ancient capital of Egypt. No matter how strong Nineveh's defenses might be and no matter how numerous her population, she was doomed. Her unceasing evil would soon end because she would be wiped from the face of the earth (3:8-19).

THE REIGNS OF JEHOIAKIM AND JEHOIACHIN (2 KINGS 23:31–24:17)

Josiah's death brought radical changes in Judah. The reign of his son Jehoahaz (609), who had succeeded him, was cut short by Pharaoh Neco of Egypt. Once more Judah was put under a foreign overlord. Jehoahaz was imprisoned and died in Egypt (23:31-34).

In his place, the Egyptians made his brother Eliakim king. When Eliakim became king, his name was changed to Jehoiakim (23:24). Among some peoples, the king always took a new name when he became the ruler.

Such may have been the custom in Israel, but this is the only direct evidence of it.

Jehoiakim (609–597) paid heavy tribute to the Egyptians the first few years of his reign. That did not keep him from spending rather extravagantly for his own comfort, however. At Beth-kerem, just south of Jerusalem, he had an elaborate palace built, which was to draw the fire of the prophet Jeremiah:

> Woe to him who builds his house by unrighteousness,
>   and his upper rooms by injustice;
> who makes his neighbor serve him for nothing,
>   and does not give him his wages;
> who says, 'I will build myself a great house
>   with spacious upper rooms,'
> and cuts out windows for it,
>   paneling it with cedar,
>   and painting it with vermilion.
> Do you think you are a king
>   because you compete in cedar? (Jer. 22:13-15*a*)

The remains of his palace have been found, and some of the stones still have traces of the bright red paint.[6]

Jehoiakim's loyalties changed in 605, when the Babylonian army defeated Egypt at the battle of Carchemish in Northern Mesopotamia. The only thing that kept the Babylonians from sweeping southward through Palestine was the death of Nabopolassar, the ruler of Babylon. He was succeeded by Nebuchadnezzar, who demanded and got Jehoiakim's submission with the resulting money payment.

Hosea's description of Israel as a "silly dove" (Hos. 7:11), flitting first to one great power and then to the other, was an apt description of Jehoiakim. By 601 he had switched his loyalties back to Egypt. The Babylonians, having seized control of the Coastal Plain by 602, fought a battle with Pharaoh Neco's forces in 601. Both sides had heavy losses, causing Nebuchadnezzar to withdraw from Palestine for a time to lick his wounds. Jehoiakim quickly switched his allegiance to Egypt. It was a fatal mistake.

In 598, the Babylonians invaded Judah in force. It was a convenient time for Jehoiakim to die, which he did—either from natural causes or with the assistance of an assassin (2 Kings 24:1-6). His son Jehoiachin (597) succeeded him, coming to the throne just in time to be captured when the city fell early in 597. Several thousand people—including the king, his mother, many of Jerusalem's leading citizens, and an enormous amount of booty—were taken to Babylon. Most of the people, among them a priest named Ezekiel, were settled in villages along a large irrigation

---

[6]See Cornfeld, *Archaeology*, p. 171ff.

canal called the River Chebar (Ezek. 1:1). Babylonian records describe the event and speak of the spoils of the victory. Jehoiachin would remain as a captive until 560, when he was released and made a ward of the Babylonian royal court (2 Kings 25:27-30).

HABAKKUK: THE PHILOSOPHER PROPHET

If philosophers are people who ask important questions, then Habakkuk must be called a philosopher. While most prophets said, "Thus says the LORD," or "thus the LORD is about to do," Habakkuk said, "Why, LORD, are you about to do what you are about to do?"

The man.   Nothing personal is known about Habakkuk. Unlike some of the other prophets, no mention is made of family or birthplace. Other than a brief mention in a book of the Apocrypha, no other mention was made of him in any Jewish religious literature. What can be learned of him has to come from the way he approached his work as the LORD's spokesman.

The book.   Set in the time when the Babylonians were threatening to overrun Judah, Habakkuk raised some searching questions about the meaning of God's activity in the events of his day, the period from about 609 to 597. The writers of the Dead Sea Scrolls interpreted the prophet's words as bearing directly on their own situation (165 B.C.–A.D. 70). A commentary on Habakkuk 1–2 interprets the reference to the Chaldeans as meaning the Romans.

The book falls naturally into three sections: 1:1–2:5, Habakkuk's questions; 2:6-20, woes; and 3:1-19, a psalm entitled "Habakkuk's prayer."

Habakkuk's questions (Hab. 1:1–2:5).   The first question was this: "LORD, how long must this flaunting of your will go on?" (1:1-4). Habakkuk's question has raised the question of who was flaunting the LORD's will. Was it the people of Judah? Or was it the Babylonians? Probably he was referring to the situation in Judah that had developed after Josiah's death.

The answer to the question came: The LORD was sending the Chaldeans (Babylonians) to punish the Judeans for disobeying the will of the LORD (1:5-11).

That answer shocked Habakkuk and brought forth a second question: "LORD, how can you punish us with people who are more unrighteous than we are?" After all, the Babylonians were cruel and merciless pagans who were catching small nations in their nets as fishermen catch fish (1:12-17).

Since the answer did not come immediately, the prophet mounted a watchtower to see what the LORD would do (2:1). Then the answer came: The LORD did things in his own good time. The man who would survive and live was the man who was faithful to the LORD. The great Christian Apostle Paul quoted Habakkuk 2:4 in his letter to the Galatians: "The righteous shall live by his faith." Later, in the sixteenth century A.D. this verse was instrumental in setting Martin Luther on his way to the beginning of the Protestant Reformation.

"Woe to him" (Hab. 2:6-20).   The woes, a common feature of prophetic oracles, are directed toward five groups: (1) Woe to him whose greed drove him to plunder to get riches. (2) Woe to the violent man. (3) Woe to the bloody man. (4) Woe to the drunkard. (5) Woe to the idol maker.

Habakkuk's prayer (Hab. 3:1-19).   This psalm has the name of a tune by which it was to be sung, indicating that it was used in the worship services of the Temple. It was used to praise the LORD, recalling his mighty work (3:1-15). The exodus events are described in highly figurative language:

> The mountains saw thee, and writhed;
>   the raging waters swept on;
>
>   . . .
>
> Thou didst bestride the earth in fury,
>   thou didst trample the nations in anger.
>
>   . . .
>
> Thou didst trample the sea with thy horses,
>   the surging of mighty waters. (3:10,12,15)

The psalmist was overcome by what he had seen of the LORD's activity and waited expectantly for what he would do to the invaders (3:16). This caused him to rejoice, even though all else failed around him, for:

> God, the LORD, is my strength;
>   he makes my feet like hinds' feet,
>   he makes me tread upon my high places (3:19).

Jeremiah, Zedekiah, and the Last Days of Judah

To have to preach about men's sins and shortcomings made the lot of the prophet a hard one. But to have to advocate surrender to the hated enemy and be called a traitor was the fate of Jeremiah, the last great prophet of the days of the Israelite kings.

HIS EARLY LIFE AND CALL (JER. 1:1-19)

Jeremiah was from a priestly family who lived in Anathoth. It was the village where Abiathar, David's friend who supported Adonijah as David's successor, had been exiled by Solomon. Jeremiah was probably a descendant of Abiathar.

He preached during the reigns of Josiah, Jehoiakim, and Zedekiah; and he continued until he was taken by a group of rebels in 582 to Egypt, where he died.

The call (Jer. 1:1-19). The traditional dating for the call of Jeremiah as a prophet is 626. This dating is based on the fact that 1:2 says, "To whom the word of the LORD came in the days of Josiah . . . in the thirteenth year of his reign." The only problem with the 626 date is that later on Jeremiah mentioned a threat by a northern nation against Palestine (1:13-19).

Advocates of the 626 date believe that Jeremiah's "foe from the north" were the Scythians, a people about whom little is known. The Scythians were from east of the Persian Gulf and were one of the many peoples who gave Assyria increasing problems in the declining years of its empire. If they did invade the west, as the Greek historian Herodotus says, it would have been about the time that Jeremiah was called. There is little evidence, however, that such an invasion actually took place.[7]

A more realistic threat from the north were the Babylonians. For this reason, some interpreters would date Jeremiah's call in 616 rather than 626. These interpreters argue that the Babylonians were the real "foe from the north." As to the dating in the "thirteenth year of Josiah," it is explained as a scribal mistake that should read "the twenty-third year of Josiah." This argument does not convince many scholars, however, with the result that most still date Jeremiah's call in 626.

Jeremiah's ministry compares to that of Isaiah's in length, especially if his call came in 626. It extended over part or all of the reigns of five kings, as well as the rule of Gedaliah, the governor of the Babylonian province that included Judah. His influence, both positive and negative, extended across all lines of society and even across national boundaries. In the call several interesting features appear:

1. He felt that the LORD had destined him to be a prophet even before he was born (1:5a,b).

2. He was called to minister across national boundaries (1:5c).

3. He was still quite young when he became conscious of his call (1:6). His protest that he was "only a youth" probably means that he was still in his teens.

[7]John Bright, *A History of Israel,* p. 314.

4. The LORD assured Jeremiah that he would be with him and take care of him (1:7-8).

5. Jeremiah was called to be a prophet to the nations whose ministry would be one of judgment that would lead to a positive result (1:9-10).

Two visions accompanied the call of Jeremiah: (1) the vision of the almond tree, and (2) the vision of the boiling pot. As with the visions of Amos, Jeremiah's visions involved ordinary things that took on deep spiritual meaning.

The vision of the almond tree (1:11-12) involves a pun, as did Amos's vision of the summer fruit. The noun *ṣqd* in Hebrew meant "almond tree" while the verb "to watch" also was *ṣqd*. Jeremiah said, "I see a rod of almond (*ṣqd*)." The LORD answered, "You have seen well, for I am watching (*ṣqd*) over my word to perform it" (1:12). The point was that the LORD would do what he said he would. The almond tree would remind Jeremiah of that assurance.

The vision of the boiling pot probably came when Jeremiah saw someone spill a pot of hot water. As he watched the water sweep along the twigs and pebbles before it the message came that a foe from the north would sweep over the land and sweep away its inhabitants (1:13-15). Jeremiah was told to preach that judgment courageously in the face of all opposition (1:16-19).

His early ministry.   What did Jeremiah think of the reform under Josiah? This is one of the mysteries surrounding the book of Jeremiah. Little is said of Jeremiah's relations to Josiah, either in the book of Jeremiah or in the history in 2 Kings. Whether Jeremiah preached at all during Josiah's reign is uncertain, although some would assign the oracles in chapters 2–6 to that period.[8] If that is so, he had a rather low estimate of the value of the reform movement. His personal evaluation of Josiah appeared in 22:15-16, where he compared Josiah and Jehoiakim:

Do you think you are a king
    because you compete in cedar?
Did not your father eat and drink
    and do justice and righteousness?
    Then it was well with him.
He judged the cause of the poor and needy;
    then it was well.
Is not this to know me?
    says the LORD.

[8]See notes on Jeremiah in the *Oxford Annotated Bible*, RSV.

The book.   Another mystery about Jeremiah relates to the arrangement of the book that bears his name. In chapter 36, there is a description of the writing of what was probably the first edition of the book. Jeremiah hired a scribe named Baruch to write down all the oracles that he had given to that date (605). When Baruch did so, he was instructed by Jeremiah to read them in the Temple. At that time, for some unknown reason, Jeremiah was barred from the Temple (36:1-8). When the scroll was read, it caused quite a reaction. Officials of King Jehoiakim's court who were still friendly to Jeremiah thought it should be taken to the king. When Jehoiakim heard it, he burned it, a sheet at a time. Jeremiah then redictated the scroll, adding a number of oracles to it (36:9-32). That edition may be chapters 1–25, since chapter 26 starts with a second version of a story found in chapter 7.

The mystery about the book is that it appears that someone had each chapter written on a single sheet, threw them down the stairs, and then arranged them in the order in which they were picked up. There seems to be little purpose in the way the book was arranged. For this reason, the dated prose sections will be discussed in chronological order as nearly as possible; then the oracles will be discussed as they appear.

JEREMIAH AND JEHOIAKIM

If Jeremiah admired Josiah, his admiration did not carry over to his son Jehoiakim. From the beginning of Jehoiakim's reign, Jeremiah was in big trouble.

The Temple sermon (Jer. 7:1-15; 26:1-24).   In the year 609 Jehoiakim was placed on the throne of Judah by Pharaoh Neco of Egypt. In that same year Jeremiah appeared in the Temple during a festival to preach a scathing sermon. Its theme was as follows:

> Amend your ways and your doings . . . Do not trust in these deceptive words: 'This is the temple of the LORD, the temple of the LORD, the temple of the LORD' (7:3-4).

Versions of this sermon appear in both Jeremiah 7 and 26. Chapter 7 contains a fuller version of the sermon. It attacked the popular notion that the LORD would not permit Jerusalem to be destroyed because the Temple was located there. Instead, the people's only hope was to return to the great moral principles set forth in the Sinai covenant. If the people did not change their ways, Jerusalem's fate would be the same as Shiloh's, one of Israel's earliest shrines. It had been destroyed by the Philistines in 1050 (7:5-15; 26:2-6).

If Jeremiah hoped to move the people to action, he was not disappointed. The action, however, was directed toward him. He was seized and threatened with death (26:7-9). Word got to the community leaders about the commotion in the Temple. Jeremiah was saved from lynching, but he was put on trial for his life on the charge of blasphemy—that is, cursing the Temple, which was the LORD's dwelling place. This meant that he was cursing the LORD himself.

A formal trial followed. First, the evidence was presented against Jeremiah (26:11). Then, Jeremiah spoke in his own defense. He admitted saying what he had said and even repeated the essentials of his sermon (26:12-13). Having done this, he threw himself on the mercy of the court, but not without warning it that if he were put to death an innocent man would be dying (26:14-15). Finally, the verdict came. Jeremiah was declared "not guilty." The judges cited Micah 3:12, where Micah had predicted Jerusalem's destruction. They pointed out that Hezekiah did not put Micah to death; therefore Jeremiah should be freed (26:16-19).

Another prophet, Uriah, who had made a similar prophecy, was not so fortunate. He fled to Egypt, but Jehoiakim had him brought back and put him to death (26:20-23). Jeremiah still had powerful friends who protected him (26:24).

His conflict with Jehoiakim.

By 605 Jeremiah was in trouble with Jehoiakim. He criticized Jehoiakim for submitting to the Babylonians in a symbolic action that involved burying a linen waistcloth on the banks of the Euphrates River. When he dug it up later, it was soiled. Judah's relations to Babylon would cause her to be as soiled and as useless as the waistcloth (13:1-11).

Another action that aroused Jehoiakim's ire came when Jeremiah and a group of his supporters went to the valley of Hinnom. There Jehoiakim had set up altars to Baal and had practiced child sacrifice. Jeremiah condemned the pagan cults. He smashed a flask to symbolize how the LORD would smash Jerusalem and its inhabitants for following false gods (19:1-15).

Jeremiah was arrested by Pashur, a Temple official. He was beaten and placed in the stocks for public ridicule. When he was released the next day, Jeremiah denounced Pashur and repeated his warning, with a private word of judgment for Pashur (20:1-6). This may have been the action by Jeremiah that resulted in his being barred from the Temple. This would have been the time that Baruch became his secretary and wrote the first edition of his book.[9]

Finally, Jeremiah warned Jehoiakim that Babylon would come and destroy Judah. This warning may have come after the battle of Carchemish

[9]See p. 259.

in 605, or it could have been a warning that preceded the Babylonian invasion of 598, which led to the first fall of Jerusalem. In any case, Jeremiah saw it as the certain judgment on Jerusalem for the people's failure to follow the law of the LORD (25:1-15).

JEREMIAH AND JEHOIACHIN

Jehoiachin's reign (598–597) was so brief that Jeremiah said little about him. In an oracle in 22:24-30, Jeremiah spoke of Jehoiachin (whom he called Coniah) as being like a "despised broken pot." He was to be considered childless since none of his children would ever succeed him as king of Judah (22:30).

JEREMIAH AND ZEDEKIAH

Jeremiah's relations to Zedekiah were most unusual. When Jerusalem fell in 597, Zedekiah was put on the throne by the Babylonians. He was the brother of Josiah and thus the uncle of the two previous kings. The Babylonians seem not to have deported all the leadership in 597, but they left those they thought would be loyal to them. Their loyalty was short-lived! Soon there was a powerful group who was pressuring Zedekiah to declare his independence from Babylon or to switch his loyalties to Egypt. A group of "righteous ones," probably led by some of the prophets, kept insisting that the LORD had permitted the exile only as a temporary punishment. It would be ended in a year or so with a dramatic deliverance of the people. Zedekiah seems to have responded to whichever group was exerting the most pressure. He respected Jeremiah enough to ask him for advice, but he was too weak to carry out the advice he received.

The vision of the figs (597) (Jer. 24:1-10). Jeremiah's opinion of the exiles, as compared with those left in the land, is shown by the vision of the figs. To steal some lines from a nursery rhyme, the figs could be described as follows:

> The basket that was good was very, very good,
> But the one that was bad was horrid.

For Jeremiah, the good figs represented those who had been taken to exile; but the bad figs were those who had been left behind.

True and false prophets: the sign of the yoke (Jer. 27:1–28:17). Pressure began to mount on Zedekiah to break away from Babylon as soon as

Nebuchadnezzar, the Babylonian king, lessened the pressure on the city after its capture. Two things had led to this situation: (1) A revolt in Babylon involving some of Nebuchadnezzar's army. Some of the Jews who were in exile may also have been involved. (2) The accession of a new king, Psammetichus II (594–589), to the throne of Egypt. He and his successor, Hophra (589–570), both encouraged rebellion against Babylon.[10] The court prophets encouraged Judah to join the revolt, preaching that the LORD was about the deliver the exiles and bring them home. Those who opposed them were branded as traitors and unbelievers.

Jeremiah aroused the ire of the superpatriots by consistently insisting that Judah's only hope of survival lay in being loyal subjects of Nebuchadnezzar. To emphasize this point, he made a wooden yoke like that used to hitch oxen to a plow and wore it on his neck. This object was to emphasize the wisdom of Judah's wearing Babylon's yoke (27:1-22).

Hananiah, a leader of the superpatriots and a prophet from Gibeon, grabbed Jeremiah's wooden yoke and broke it. The LORD, he said, had broken Babylon's yoke and would return the people to the land in two years. Jeconiah (Jehoiachin), furthermore, would be restored to his rightful place as king (28:1-4; 10-11).

Jeremiah replied that he hoped Hananiah was right, but that the real proof would rest on whether his words actually came true (28:5-9). Later, Jeremiah came back with yoke bars made of iron. He told Hananiah that not only would Babylon's yoke not be broken, but that Hananiah himself would die (28:12-16).

In that same year, in the seventh month, the prophet Hananiah died (28:17).

The letter to the exiles (Jer. 29:1-32).   To help defuse the situation in Babylon and to help the exiles get a better hold on reality, Jeremiah wrote a letter. The time was about 593. In the letter Jeremiah made four major points:

1. Live as normally as possible. Do those things that would be done if you were at home and the country were at peace (29:4-6).
2. Be good citizens. What was good for Babylon was good for the exiles, for "in its welfare you will find your welfare" (29:7).
3. Pay no attention to the superpatriots and false prophets. They are just trying to deceive you. The LORD did not send them (29:8-9).
4. When the time is right, the LORD will bring you home (29:10-14). This is the meaning of the term "when seventy years are

[10]John Bright, *A History of Israel,* p. 328ff.

completed for Babylon." In the same connection, Ezekiel would use forty years as his symbol for a complete period (Ezek. 4:6).

Jeremiah specifically named two prophets who were stirring up trouble—Ahab and Zedekiah. Nebuchadnezzar would soon snuff out their lives, for they were nothing but liars and deceivers (29:15-23). He had a further word to say about Shemaiah, who had written to Zephaniah, a Jerusalem priest, telling him to arrest Jeremiah and put him in the stocks. Zephaniah, however, was Jeremiah's friend and shared the letter with him. When he heard it, Jeremiah predicted the doom of Shemaiah (29:24-32).

The last days of Judah (2 Kings 25:1-21). Zedekiah's rebellion brought disaster. Early in 588, Nebuchadnezzar struck Judah. He set up a siege of Jerusalem and began to overpower the smaller cities. By early 587 only Lachish and Azekah, small cities to the southwest of Jerusalem, were still standing. The Lachish letters, found in the ruins of that city a few years ago, describe the desperate situation. As a significant passage from one of the letters says,

> We are watching for the signals of Lachish, according to all the indications my Lord hath given, for we cannot see Azekah.[11]

This letter, written to the commander of the garrison at Lachish, indicated that Azekah had fallen and it would only be a matter of time until Jerusalem and Lachish would fall also. There may also be a reference to Uriah, the prophet mentioned in Jeremiah 26:20-24, or a reference to Jeremiah himself in the letters, although this is uncertain.

In the summer of 588, the Egyptians made a move to oppose the Babylonians, causing a temporary lifting of the siege. They were quickly defeated, however, and the siege began again. Conditions within the city worsened as the food supply sank lower and lower. Lamentations 4 described in gruesome detail the effects of the food shortage: the dry, shriveled skin of people who once were sleek and healthy (Lam. 4:8); mothers resorting to cannibalism, eating their own children (Lam. 4:10); and the danger of walking in the streets, for fear of being killed for food (Lam. 4:18).

During that trying time, Jeremiah kept encouraging Zedekiah to submit to the Babylonians to save the lives of the people. The superpatriots, on the other hand, were threatening Zedekiah or anyone else who suggested surrender. Zedekiah was unable to make any real decision on

[11]Pritchard, *The Ancient Near East*, p. 213.

his own. He stood helplessly by as the nation slid over the brink to its destruction.

False dealings with the slaves (Jer. 34:1-22). Jeremiah's influence was strong, even in Judah's last days. In 588, during the first part of the Babylonian siege, he delivered an oracle to Zedekiah, saying that Zedekiah would not be put to death when Jerusalem fell (34:1-5). This was the time of the Lachish letters; since Lachish, Azekah, and Jerusalem were the only Judean cities still unconquered by the Babylonians (34:6-7).

Zedekiah persuaded the people to free all the slaves in Jerusalem. This probably stemmed from both practical and religious motives. From a practical standpoint, the freed salves would more likely be willing to fight for the city if they were free. From a religious standpoint, Zedekiah was carrying out a provision in Israelite law that called for the freeing of all enslaved Israelites every seventh year (34:8-10).

Scarcely had the action been taken when it was withdrawn and the freed people were once more enslaved. The probable cause for this reversal was the lifting of the siege of Jerusalem when the Egyptians marched out to oppose the Babylonians. Feeling that the threat was removed from the city, the wealthy men seized their former slaves and enslaved them again. Jeremiah warned that because of their dishonesty, they would have charged to them "liberty to the sword, to pestilence and to famine" (34:17). The destruction of the city and its leaders was a foregone conclusion (34:11-22). ─outside Jerusalem

Purchasing the field at Anathoth (Jer. 32:1-44). One of the difficulties about Jeremiah's life is ascertaining when he was in custody and when he was free. The incident discussed in Jeremiah 32 may have preceded the incident involving the slaves or may have come at about the same time. Zedekiah imprisoned Jeremiah, as he had in Jeremiah 32; but it seems he had an attack of conscience and freed him.

At the time of this story, probably because of pressure from the pro-Egyptian superpatriot group, Jeremiah was in prison. The LORD told him that his cousin Hanamel wanted to sell a field at Anathoth to him and that he was to buy it. Hanamel was following the law of the redemption of property, which provided that any property had to be offered to one's kin if it were for sale. It was to be offered to the nearest of kin—beginning with brothers, then uncles, and then cousins, in that order (Num. 27:9-11).

When Hanamel came, Jeremiah bought the property and received a proper deed for it. The deed consisted of two copies, one that was kept sealed and another that could be opened for public inspection (32:1-15).[12]

---

[12]Such deeds were found in recent years among the Bar Kochba letters. Yigael Yadin, *Bar Kochba: The Rediscovery of the Legendary Hero of the Second Jewish Revolt Against Rome* (New York: Random House, 1971), p. 229ff.

Hanamel's purpose in selling the field was to get money that could be more easily held if the city fell. On the other hand, Jeremiah purchased the field to show his confidence that people would survive the coming exile and would once more inhabit the land (32:16-44). In that sense, it was a carrying out of the positive aspect of his call "to build and to plant." It illustrates quite vividly the prophetic view of judgment as redemptive and cleansing rather than annihilating—completely wiping out the people.

In prison again (Jer. 37:1–38:28). If this chapter follows chapter 32, Jeremiah must have been released from prison. The Babylonian withdrawal had taken place (37:1-5). Jeremiah warned Zedekiah that the withdrawal was only temporary. Nothing could stop the destruction of Jerusalem (37:6-10).

Taking advantage of the peaceful interlude, Jeremiah decided to go to Anathoth to look at the land he had bought from Hanamel. As he was going out of the city, he was seized by an overzealous guard and accused of trying to desert to the enemy. He was beaten and thrown into prison, where he remained for many days (37:11-15).

Finally, Zedekiah ordered that Jeremiah be brought out secretly so he could consult with him. He asked Jeremiah if there was any word from the LORD. Jeremiah told him that there was—it was the same word of judgment that he had pronounced before. Then Jeremiah, weakened by his prison experience, begged Zedekiah not to put him back into the dungeon. Zedekiah protected him for a time and saw that he got what food was available (37:16-21).

Jeremiah's enemies were persistent, to say the least. When they found Zedekiah had rescued Jeremiah from the dungeon, they pressured Zedekiah to turn the prophet over to them. Again, Zedekiah yielded; and Jeremiah was once more in the hands of his enemies.

The next place he found himself was in a cistern. Cisterns were underground containers for water, hewn out of the rock. They varied in size from those that would hold a few thousand gallons to others that would hold tremendous amounts of water. Jeremiah was thrown into a small cistern partially filled with mud that had been washed in. Jeremiah sank into the mire. If he had not been rescued by one of Zedekiah's servants, he probably would have died there (38:1-13).

Once again, Jeremiah came before Zedekiah. Once again, Zedekiah asked the prophet if there was any message from the LORD for him. Once again, Jeremiah told Zedekiah that his only hope was to surrender to the Babylonians. Otherwise, death and destruction awaited him and the inhabitants of Jerusalem (38:14-23). But in contrast to their previous meeting, when Jeremiah had pleaded for his life (37:20), Zedekiah was now pleading to Jeremiah not to let the leaders know that Zedekiah had consulted him because they would kill him if they found out. Jeremiah assured Zedekiah that he would not betray him. In exchange, Zedekiah kept him in prison in the royal quarters (38:24-28).

And then there was none: Jerusalem falls (Jer. 39:1-10; 52:1-34; 2 Kings 25:1-21).   Famine, pestilence, and the Babylonian army finally prevailed. Jerusalem fell, probably in the year 587, although some date the fall in 586. Ancient armies won more battles by patiently waiting for their enemy to starve than they did by direct assault. For almost two years, Nebuchadnezzar's army had cut off the inhabitants of Jerusalem from any source of food other than what had been stored in the city. Since there was no room within the city walls to grow food, the people inevitably faced the choices of surrender or starvation if the siege could not be lifted by other means. While the Babylonians had battering rams to break down the walls, Jerusalem had strong fortifications that enabled her to hold out until starvation and disease took their toll on the defenders of the city (39:1-2).

Zedekiah, realizing that further resistance was futile, fled the city at night. He was captured near Jericho, however, and carried before Nebuchadnezzar at Riblah of Hamath in the northern part of Syria. He was condemned to watch the slaughter of his sons and his chief officials. Then, his own eyes were punched out and he was taken to Babylon as a prisoner (39:3-7).

Meanwhile, Jerusalem was burned—including the palace complex and the Temple. The walls were broken down, and the talented people among the population were taken to Babylon. Only the poor and helpless people were left behind. The Babylonians gave them land to insure their loyalty (39:8-10).

The fate of Jeremiah (Jer. 39:11–40:6).   Jeremiah, still in prison as a result of his problems during the siege, was brought out and released. At first, it seems he had been included among those to be taken to Babylon. Later, when given the choice of remaining in the land, he chose to do so. He was put into the custody of Gedaliah, an official in Zedekiah's court who had been appointed governor by the Babylonians.

After the Fall (Jer. 40:7-44:30)

The murder of Gedaliah (2 Kings 25:22-26; Jer. 40:7–41:18).   The land was in ruins. The dreams of independence were shattered, and the people who were left were beaten and disillusioned. The Babylonians appointed Gedaliah as governor over the Babylonian province of which Judah was now a part. The seat of government was moved to Mizpah as Jerusalem was only a heap of blackened rubble (Jer. 40:7).

Gedaliah urged the people to serve the Babylonians (Chaldeans) and to gather what food they could from the vines and trees. People who had fled to Transjordan returned to their homes when they heard that the

Figure 10–3. "Nebuchrezzar, king of Babylon, came against Jerusalem and besieged it; in the eleventh year of Zedekiah, in the fourth month, on the ninth day of the month, a breach was made in the city" (Jer. 39:1,2). The ruins of a seventh century B.C. wall that was destroyed by the Babylonian invaders.

Photograph by David Rogers.

land was once more at peace. Fortunately for them, the fruit crops were abundant (40:8-12).

Unfortunately, Ishmael, who was of the royal house, plotted against Gedaliah. Gedaliah was warned of the plot, but he ignored it—to his own downfall. Ishmael killed not only Gedaliah in 582 but also a large number of Jews and Chaldean soldiers. Among those he attacked were eighty men from Shechem, Shiloh, and Samaria, who seemingly had come to the site of the ruined Temple to offer a sacrifice on that sacred spot. This would indicate that even though the Temple was destroyed, worship of a sort was still carried on there. Ishmael killed all but ten on the worshipers. They bought their lives with promises of food to Ishmael and his men (41:1-8).

Johanan soon raised a force to fight Ishmael. When the fight came, many of those people from Mizpah whom Ishmael had taken captive fled to join with Johanan. Ishmael beat a hasty retreat to the other side of the Jordan (41:11-18).

The flight to Egypt. Johanan, fearing that he would be blamed for Gedaliah's death, fled to Egypt. Jeremiah tried to persuade him not to do it, but Johanan did not heed Jeremiah's advice. Instead, Jeremiah was forced to go along (42:1–43:7). The last words of Jeremiah were predictions of doom for Egypt and for those who had fled to it for protection. Only Baruch, Jeremiah's faithful disciple, would escape with his life (43:8–45:5). So far as is known, Jeremiah died in Egypt.

THE ORACLES OF JEREMIAH

The oracles of Jeremiah are scattered throughout the book. Those found in chapters 2–6, 8–20, 30–31, and 46–52 will be examined.

Early oracles (Jer. 2:1–6:30).

These oracles, while representing different periods of Jeremiah's ministry, seem to come largely from the earlier years.

Remembering better days (Jer. 2:1-3). This oracle, addressed to Jerusalem, reminded the people of a better time. Like Hosea, Jeremiah was fond of using family illustrations to describe the LORD's relationship to Israel. In this oracle, Israel was the bride in wilderness days, but evil had changed that ideal situation.

Israel has been unfaithful (Jer. 2:4-37). Jeremiah, too, used the language of the legal system to describe the LORD's dealings with the people. He reminded them of the LORD's blessings in the past—how they had been brought through the deserts to a land where food grew in abundance. Yet they had taken the LORD's blessings but had given Baal credit for them (2:4-8).

Because of their sin, the LORD had a lawsuit against them because the people had changed the real God for a nongod. To use another figure, they had abandoned a spring that gave cool, clear, life-giving water. Instead, they were trying to get water from a cistern they had dug in the rock. It leaked because of cracks that had developed in its walls (2:9-13).

Israel's problems were increased by the fact that the leaders constantly tried to play the game of power politics when they had no power. They were like a high school football team playing in a professional football league. When Assyria and Babylon were strong, they ran to Egypt for help. But when Egypt got too strong, they switched their allegiance to the Mesopotamian power for protection against Egypt. As a result, they were always in trouble (2:14-19).

A further sin was their tendency to follow popular religion and to participate in the sensuous nature cults. They had abandoned the LORD's yoke to become slaves to Baal. They were like wild animals, unrestrained in their lust. Enslaved by their own sexual appetites, they could not break away (2:20-25).

They would not go unpunished. Like thieves caught in the act, they would plead for mercy. The gods they had trusted could not help, even though the people might call on them. The LORD had tried to correct them, but his efforts had been in vain. Instead, they had gone on their way, sinning at will but proclaiming their innocence when caught. But the evidence of their guilt was clear. Punishment would come from Egypt and Assyria, to whom they had fled for safety (2:26-37).

Repent, O Israel (Jer. 3:1–4:4). This oracle, or series of oracles, repeats the word "return" a number of times. By this word the prophets, including Jeremiah, spoke of the meaning of repentance. It meant a complete change of direction, a new way of doing things, or a coming back to a tried and tested way of life.

Israel was like a divorced wife. Israelite law forbade a man from taking back a wife from whom he had been divorced, especially if she had married another man in the meantime. Even so, the nation had been so defiled by following the Baals that it really had no right to expect the LORD to take it back. Israel was like a prostitute, taking one sexual partner after another. The assessment was this: "You have done all the evil you could" (3:5).

Israel and Judah were both like false sisters who played the harlot at every stone and tree (3:9). The reference to "stone and tree" means that these were sexual symbols for the Baal worshipers. The LORD had expected them to return to him, but Judah had turned out to be even worse than Israel. The LORD pleaded for both to return to him. He promised to give them faithful leaders who would feed them with "knowledge and understanding" (3:15). Jerusalem would be exalted, and the land would once more be united (3:6-18).

The LORD had hoped they would be like sons who would call him "My Father" (3:19). Instead, they had been like "a faithless wife who leaves her husband" (3:20). Instead of joy, there was weeping on the bare hills because they had perverted the LORD's blessings. Dishonor would cover them (3:21-25).

Like Hosea, Jeremiah pleaded to the LORD for Israel before it was too late. He called for the people to abandon their abominable ways and to return to the principles set forth in the Sinai covenant. Using the familiar figure of circumcision, Jeremiah gave it a figurative meaning by calling for them "to circumcise their hearts;" i.e., to allow themselves to be touched by his pleas for repentance. Otherwise, judgment would devour them like a fire (4:1-4).

Beware the foe from the north (Jer. 4:5-31). Some of Jeremiah's most vivid language is to be found in his oracles about the threat to Israel from the northern foe. In 4:5-10 he sounds a call to the people to flee to the fortified towns. From the north, an enemy was coming like a hungry lion ready to pounce on its victim. It would devastate the land. Leaders would fail, and promises of protection to the land made in Isaiah's day would prove useless.

Jerusalem was endangered. Like a hot wind from the desert, the enemy would come. Already from the northern provinces of Dan and the central region, warnings were coming: "Besiegers from a distant land; they shout against the cities of Judah" (4:16).

The prophet's own distress at the prospects are vividly described:

> My anguish, my anguish! I writhe in pain!
>   Oh, the walls of my heart!
> My heart is beating wildly;
>   I cannot keep silent,
> for I hear the sound of the trumpet,
>   the alarm of war (4:19).

Disaster was everywhere. There seemed to be no end of the enemy's marching armies. The people were stupid, lacking the knowledge of the LORD, which meant life. The only skill they possessed was skill in doing evil (4:11-22).

Everywhere the prophet looked he saw the desolation of war—crops destroyed, cities burned, and even the birds seemed to have abandoned the desolate land. But in the midst of the disaster the people were like a faded harlot, dressed in showy clothes and fancy jewelry, vainly trying to cover the ravages of age and abuse with more cosmetics, not realizing that no one desired her. Instead, they despised her enough to kill her (4:23-31).

Judah is hopelessly immoral (Jer. 5:1–6:30). Like Diogenes, who searched through Athens with a lantern looking for an honest man, Jeremiah was commanded to search Jerusalem for a man, "One who does justice and seeks truth; that I may pardon her." This undoubtedly referred to the story about Abraham who kept trying to save Sodom and Gomorrah by attempting to find enough righteous people in them. Jeremiah's search was as unsuccessful as was Abraham's (5:1-3).

At first, Jeremiah concluded that only the poor and ignorant were unjust and untruthful, simply because they did not know any better. But when he searched among the upper classes, the result was the same. Judgment, therefore, would come like a devouring animal from the forest or desert. There could be no pardon for their sins. They were like "well-fed lusty stallions each neighing for his neighbor's wife" (5:8). They were a faithless people, lying to one another, as well as to the LORD. Even the prophets were nothing but "windbags" (5:13, Moffatt). An ancient nation, speaking a strange language, would destroy their sons and daughters, their flocks and herds, their vines and fig trees, and their fortified cities (5:4-17).

Jeremiah 5:18-19 interjects a note of hope that the judgment will not completely wipe out the nation but will mean exile for the survivors.

What the people were doing was senseless. They were deliberately doing those things that brought bad results instead of good. The prophet used the figure of the bird trap to speak of how men oppressed others. A theme found in 5:9 is repeated in 5:29: "Shall I not punish them for these things? says the LORD; and shall I not avenge myself on a nation such as this?" This is followed by a word about the religious leaders: The prophets were giving false prophecies, the priests were following the advice of the prophets, and the people seemed to approve of what was happening. The end was coming (5:20-31).

Like the watchman at the wall, the prophet sounded the alarm to the people of Jerusalem and its nearby cities, Tekoa and Bethhaccherem. Jerusalem faced attack from the north. The prophet imagined he heard the orders given by the enemy commanders:

> "Prepare war against her;
>   up, and let us attack at noon!"
>
>   . . .
>
> "Up, and let us attack by night,
>   and destroy her palaces!" (6:4-5)

The LORD had given orders for siege to be laid to Jerusalem because of the sin within her. The LORD was tired of withholding his wrath. He was tired of prophet and priest who cried "Peace, peace" when there was no peace. He had pleaded with the people to walk in the right paths, but they would have none of it. Judgment would come at the hands of a northern invader:

> they are cruel and have no mercy,
> the sound of them is like the roaring sea;
> they ride upon horses,
> set in array as a man for battle,
> against you, O daughter of Zion! (6:23)

The prophet had been cast into the role of an assayer—a tester of the people. Just as man test metals for purity, so the prophet was to test the people. They failed the test (6:1-30).

Mixed oracles (Jer. 8:4–10:25)

The people have shown incredible stupidity (Jer. 8:4-17).   A man who falls should have sense enough to get up. The people had gone away from the LORD, but they did not have sense enough to return (8:4-7). Yet, they claimed to have wisdom and the law of the LORD with them. But their scribes and wise men had misled them. They had cried "Peace, peace" when there was no peace (see 6:13-15). Their doom was sealed. No fortified city would save them. They sought peace, but evil came; they sought healing, but terror came. The enemy's horses were sweeping into the northern provinces signaling the end of the nation (8:8-17).

The heartsick prophet (Jer. 8:18–9:1).   This oracle probably has earned Jeremiah the mistaken title of the "weeping prophet." It is undeniable that he was a very emotional man. This passage shows how deeply he was stirred by the events that he saw were to be the inevitable result of the people's sinfulness. His words were harsh, but the emotional strain of having to say them showed through. So he laments about the situation, expressing his grief; there seemed to be no healing for the sickness of the nation. In this passage are some famous lines: "The harvest is past, the summer is ended, and we are not saved" (8:20). This particular line expressed the kind of frustration the farmer felt when the harvest was too small to supply food for the winter months ahead. The reference to "balm in Gilead" (8:22), made doubly famous by a well-known spiritual by that name, referred to the region east of the Sea of Galilee that was famous for a kind of gum used for medicine. Another well known saying closes the lament:

> O that my head were waters,
>   and my eyes a fountain of tears,
> that I might weep day and night
>   for the slain of the daughter of my people! (9:1)

Beware of your neighbor's tongue (Jer. 9:2-9).   Tears turned to frustration, causing the prophet to want to get away from it all. The people were adulterous, liars, and deceitful, "Heaping oppression upon oppression, and deceit upon deceit, they refuse to know me, says the LORD" (9:6).

The oracle closes with a familiar theme, "Shall I not avenge myself on a nation such as this?" (see 5:9,29).

Cry for Zion (Jer. 9:10-22).   Funerals in ancient societies were a good clue to one's wealth. Mourners were hired. The noise made at a funeral was an indication of the wealth of the dead man. In this oracle, the prophet calls for mourning for the mountains and pastures, the areas essential to the flocks of the shepherds. The most skillful mourners were called for so they could teach others to wail for the calamity that had befallen Zion (Jerusalem). Death was everywhere, even in the palaces.

True glory (Jer. 9:23-26).   Neither wisdom, might, nor riches could match understanding and knowing the LORD who practiced "steadfast love, justice, and righteousness" (9:23-24). Israel, who thought it had wise men, would be punished along with the heathen nations (9:25-26).

A sermon on idols and those who make them (Jer. 10:1-25).   One of the things that astounded the prophets was Israel's fascination with idols. Some of their most scathing comments were reserved for idols and idol makers. As Jeremiah observed:

> Their idols are like scarecrows in a cucumber field,
>   and they cannot speak;
> they have to be carried,
>   for they cannot walk.
> Be not afraid of them,
>   for they cannot do evil,
>   neither is it in them to do good (10:5).

How the people could worship such creations of their own hands instead of the LORD, the true God, was beyond the prophet's imagination. In his words, they were "stupid and foolish" (10:8). The idols had not made the heavens and the earth—the creation was the work of the LORD. Man and his idols were powerless. The idols and their makers would perish in the time of judgment (10:1-16).

The judgment was upon them. The siege was in force. It was not the LORD's desire that it be thus, but the stupidity of Israel's leadership had made the judgment necessary (10:17-22).

The prophet's involvement was shown by a short prayer in 10:23-25. He prayed that he himself would be corrected. He also prayed for punishment on the nations who refused to recognize the LORD.

The confessions of Jeremiah and other oracles (Jer. 11:1–20:18).   This section of the book of Jeremiah provides an intimate look at the inner workings of Jeremiah's mind. Among the oracles in these chapters are six that have been called "the confessions of Jeremiah" because of their intimate nature. They are found in 11:18–12:6; 15:10-21; 17:14-18; 18:18-23; 20:7-13; and 20:14-18.

The first confession: Save me from those who would kill me, O LORD! (Jer. 11:18–12:6).   The first confession follows a sermon in which Jeremiah spoke words of judgment upon those who refused to follow the covenant. Jeremiah was told to pronounce judgment upon them. He was told, furthermore, not to even pray for them because of the vileness of their sins (11:1-17).

Such sermons did not earn Jeremiah the "Favorite Prophet of the Year" award from the board of trustees of the Jerusalem Temple. Instead of repentance, their reaction was threats of violence. When Jeremiah heard of their threats, he did not say, "O LORD, forgive them," either. Instead, he asked for the LORD to protect him from those who would kill him (11:18-20).

To make it even worse, Jeremiah was told that the leaders among the plotters were his own kinfolk, "The men of Anathoth" (11:21). Again, he pleaded for the LORD to take his side. He could not understand how such wicked men could prosper (12:1-4).

The answer was not too encouraging. The LORD said, in effect: "Jeremiah, if you think things have been bad up to this point, then cheer up—they will get much worse!" (12:5-6).

Miscellaneous oracles (Jer. 12:7–15:9). Following the first of the confessions are oracles of various times and circumstances. In 12:7-13 the prophet saw the land abandoned, left desolate because the LORD had given up the people who had forsaken him to their enemies. Not only would the LORD's people feel the heel of the oppressor, but also the neighboring states would feel it. The time would come when all would be restored because they would learn the way of the LORD (12:14-16).

The prophets were fond of allegory, and Jeremiah was no exception. In 13:12-14 he used the figure of a wine jar. As the wine jar was filled with wine, so the people were filled with drunkenness. But as the wine jar could be smashed to bits, so could the people be destroyed.[13]

The sense of conflict so vividly portrayed in the confessions appears also in an oracle found in 13:15-27. The prophet wept because the people had been too proud to admit their wretched condition. Exile was their fate because they had followed false ways and false friends, who now ruled them. They had become so accustomed to doing evil that they could no more change their ways than the Ethiopian could change his skin color or the leopard could erase his spots (13:23).

The prophets saw all events as the direct action of the LORD, either as an act of blessing or judgment. During a time of drought, Jeremiah spoke of the dryness as the LORD's punishment for the sins of the people (14:1-10).

One of the major sources of the trouble that afflicted the land was the false prophets. They were assuring the people that there would be peace, but those prophets were nothing but liars whose doom was certain (14:11-16). Jeremiah wept over the carnage of war that was evident both in the city and in the countryside. In the midst of it, ignorant priests and prophets "ply their trade through the land, and have no knowledge" (14:17-18).

Jeremiah prayed for the rejected nation, acknowledging her wickedness. He based his plea for mercy on the matter of God's honor and reminded him of his covenant with the people (14:19-22). The answer came that even if Moses and Samuel were making the pleas, Judah's doom would be the same. Sickness, the sword, famine, and captivity awaited the

---

[13]On the linen waistcloth (13:1-11) see p. 260.

people. The reference to the sins of Manasseh may suggest that this oracle
came early in Jeremiah's career (15:1-4).

*The second confession: Why do you treat me this way, LORD? (Jer. 15:10-
21).*   Following another oracle that continues the theme of Judah's doom
(15:5-9), Jeremiah's second confession begins. In words that echo Job's
lament (Job 3:1-10), Jeremiah bemoaned his fate. Nothing he did pleased
men, even though he had pleaded with the LORD on their behalf. The
assurance came to him that the doom of the sinners was certain (15:10-
14).

Jeremiah recalled the circumstances of his call to be a prophet:

> Thy words were found, and I ate them,
>   and thy words became to me a joy
>   and the delight of my heart;
> for I am called by thy name,
>   O LORD, God of hosts (15:16).

He had shunned the society of others, especially places of merry-
making, because he was so moved with indignation over the conditions in
the country. But that had only brought him pain. He felt that the LORD
had deceived him like a wet-weather spring that promised water all year
long but dried up when the rains ceased (15:15-18).

After that outburst, a word of assurance came to Jeremiah. If he
would faithfully preach the LORD's words, he would still have enemies;
but they would not overcome him. The LORD would be with him to
deliver him out of the hands of those who would harm him (15:19-21).

Mixed materials (Jer. 16:1–17:13).   One of the major sources of
Jeremiah's personal frustrations is found in 16:1-13. The primary personal
aim of every normal Israelite male was to marry and have children,
especially sons. In pre-exilic times, a doctrine of life after death was not
developed. As a result, one thought of living beyond this life in terms of
living through his children. If one did not marry, then he could not
legitimately carry out that basic desire. Or, if his marriage produced no
children, the desire also was frustrated. This was why barren women are
portrayed by the Old Testament as being persons who put out great
efforts to become pregnant.[14]

Jeremiah was told not to marry because it could only mean tragedy
for him. Any wife or children he had would die in the wars fought over
Jerusalem. He would be better off without any family than to have his
family destroyed by the war (16:1-4).

---

[14]Read again the story of Rachel and Leah in the Jacob stories for an example of this
(Gen. 30:1-24).

Furthermore, he was to avoid the normal social functions. He was to avoid funerals, parties, and weddings—three of the chief social functions of his day. When the people asked him why the judgment was coming on them, he was to tell them it was because of their idolatrous worship (16:5-13).

Inserted in the midst of oracles of doom was an oracle of assurance that the people would come back to the land following the exile (16:14-15).

After another oracle of doom (16:16-18), there follows an oracle looking to a time when idol worshipers will realize the futility of what they are doing and turn to the LORD (16:19-21).

Jeremiah 17 opens with an oracle on Judah's sin of idolatry (17:1-4). Then follows a series of proverbs, strongly resembling those proverbs found in the book of Proverbs. First, there was a curse pronounced on man who trusted in himself. He was compared to a desert shrub that never would amount to anything (17:5-6).

Next, a blessing was pronounced on the man who trusts in the LORD. He is like a tree, which regularly bears a crop of fruit, planted by a stream of water. If this sounds strangely familiar, there is good reason, since Psalm 1 makes the same comparison and may be based on this passage from Jeremiah (17:7-8).

A famous passage from Jeremiah is 17:9-10, where he raised the question about the deceitfulness of humanity: "The heart is deceitful above all things and desperately corrupt; who can understand it?" The LORD is the one who searched the heart and mind. He gives each man what he deserves.

These oracles conclude with the comparison of a man who gains wealth by unjust means with a bird whose eggs do not hatch. Just as the bird wastes her eggs, so he will lose such riches in the end (17:11). All who forsake the LORD will be put to shame (17:12-13).

The third confession: Heal me, O LORD (Jer. 17:14-18).   This confession was a prayer for healing and salvation. Jeremiah's enemies were cynics who would not believe him. He declared that he had not prayed for disaster on his enemies. If he had not before, he did then; and he called for them to be destroyed with "double destruction" (17:18).

The trip to the potter's house (Jer. 18:1-17).   Like the poet who saw "sermons in stones,"[15] Jeremiah saw a sermon in the house of the potter. As he watched the potter shape a pot, it was spoiled. He took the clay, reduced it to a formless mass again, and reworked it to form another vessel that met his standard of work (18:1-12).

In this everyday action, Jeremiah saw a lesson about the LORD's

---

[15]From *As You Like It,* Act II, Scene 1.

power to do what he chose to do with his people. If they refused to follow his way, he could rework them as the potter reworked the clay. Tragically, the people had become marred by their unwillingness to follow the requirements of the covenant. The LORD would turn his back on them to show his displeasure (18:13-17).

The fourth confession: Let them have it, LORD! (Jer. 18:18-23). This confession is introduced by a report of the plots against Jeremiah. What is of particular interest is the mention of the three major classes of religious leaders—the priests, the wise men, and the prophets. This is one of the few places where the "wise men" are classed with priests and prophets as leaders of the religious community. The wise men were particularly concerned with the practical matters of how to get along in human society. Their major interest was the day-to-day existence of humanity (18:18).

Jeremiah's enemies ganged up to counteract anything he said about them. They decided to "smite him with the tongue." In desperation, the prophet turned to the LORD to plead his case once again. Reminding the LORD how he had pleaded for those who were abusing him, Jeremiah appealed for justice for himself. In a scathing tirade against his enemies, he asked that the worst of calamities should befall them and their families because of their plots against him (18:19-23).

The fifth confession: You have made a fool of me, LORD (Jer. 20:7-13). This confession reflects the prophet's increasing sense of frustration as he tried to minister to the people of Jerusalem. The LORD had deceived him into being a prophet with promises of his presence. But the life of a prophet, even with the LORD's presence, was more than Jeremiah had bargained for. He got so tired of preaching about violence and destruction that he determined that he would quit. Instead, the urge from the LORD was so strong that he found himself preaching again in spite of his resolutions not to do so. Since even his closest friends were trying to destroy him, he did not need any enemies (20:7-10).

Suddenly, there was a shift in his mood. His complaints changed to praise as he realized that the LORD would take care of his enemies (20:11-13).

The sixth confession: Why was I ever born, LORD? (Jer. 20:14-18). This final confession probes the depths of the prophet's misery. Like Job (Job 3), he cursed the day he was born: "Why did I come forth from the womb to see toil and sorrow and spend my days in shame?" (20:18).

The significance of Jeremiah's confessions. In the confessions, the agony of Jeremiah's inner struggles were revealed. Here was an honest man whose faith in the justice of God led him to put aside all pretense in his prayers. He survived those horrible times because he was able to purge himself of his inner conflicts through prayer to the One whom he experienced as the personal LORD.

Oracles of consolation (Jer. 30:1–32:40). These oracles expressed the positive side of Jeremiah's call to prophecy. Judgment on Judah was not the final act of God. It was a cleansing fire, designed to burn away the impurities. The LORD would restore the purified people to the land (30:1-3).

Judgment is coming, but restoration will follow (Jer. 30:4-22). The men of the land were like women in the anguish of childbirth. They were distressed because it was the day of the LORD's judgment (30:4-7). The time would come, however, when the oppressor's yoke would be broken. The worship of the LORD God and the rule of David would be restored (30:8-9).

Because of those prospects, Jacob and Israel should be comforted. Even though they were suffering grievous illnesses under current conditions, the LORD would restore their health and bind up their wounds (30:10-17). Cities would be rebuilt, the king's palace would stand in its usual place, voices would be raised in praise to the LORD, and life would be normal once more: "And you shall be my people, and I will be your God" (30:18-22).

The storm of the LORD (Jer. 30:23–31:1). God's wrath would go forth as a storm. It would not be understood immediately, but later on it would. He would be God to all the families of Israel.

Israel returns and is restored (Jer. 31:2-22). The survivors of Israel would once more experience the LORD's everlasting love. They would know again their best days—days of happiness and plenty, days of praise and worship, days of gathering the exiles from earth's farthest corners (31:2-9).

He who had scattered Israel would gather them as a shepherd gathers his flock (31:10-11).

> They shall come and sing aloud on the height of Zion,
>   and they shall be radiant over the goodness of the LORD,
> over the grain, the wine, and the oil,
>
> . . .
>
> their life shall be like a watered garden,
>   and they shall languish no more (31:12).

The restoration would not be without a touch of sadness. There would be weeping for those who did not survive. But weeping was to be put aside in the expectation of a joyful future. Even Ephraim, representative of the Northern Kingdom, could still come back if he would (30:13-22).

A new people and a new covenant (Jer. 31:23-40).   As the LORD had watched over the people (Jer. 1:12) to "pluck up and break down, to overthrow, destroy and bring evil (31:28; see also 1:10), so he would now "watch over them to build and to plant" (31:28). In earlier times, the emphasis had been upon how the sins of one affected his whole family, so much so that a common proverb said, "The fathers have eaten sour grapes and the children's teeth are set on edge" (31:29). This would no longer be so. Each individual would have to answer for his own sin.

This concept of individual responsibility introduced by Jeremiah was one of his distinct contributions to biblical theology. Ezekiel would take the same idea and expand it (Ezek. 18,33).

An idea growing out of Jeremiah's teaching about individual responsibility was the new covenant (31:31-34). The old covenant had been written on stone tablets and, more often than not, had failed to make the transition from a written principle to a living practice. The principles had not become personal guidelines for life. Jeremiah looked for a day when the LORD's law would be the normal way of life. Each man would "know the LORD" and live by that knowledge.

Jeremiah illustrated the LORD's relationship to Israel by comparing it to the fixed order of nature (31:35-37). Jerusalem would be rebuilt and become the LORD's sacred city once again (31:38-40).

Oracles against foreign nations (Jer. 46:1–51:64.   A section on oracles against foreign nations was standard for many of the prophets. Jeremiah was no exception.[16] Many of Jeremiah's oracles were specifically dated as to time and situation, whereas other prophets' oracles were less certain as to their date.

Against Egypt (Jer. 46:2-28).   These two oracles, the first of which was dated in 605, taunted Egypt because of its defeat at Carchemish in northern Mesopotamia by the armies of Nebuchadnezzar of Babylon. Jeremiah saw it as a day when the LORD brought a well-deserved punishment to Egypt. No amount of medicine would heal its wounds (46:2-12).

The second oracle referred to one of the times when Babylon met Egypt on its own territory. Two possible times were 605 and 601. Jehoiakim switched his loyalties to Egypt in 601, when the two armies fought to a standstill. Jeremiah foresaw the eventual destruction of Egypt by the Mesopotamian power (46:13-26). The LORD would save his people. Even though they had to face judgment for their sins, they would survive (46:27-28).

Against Philistia (Jer. 47:1-7).   This brief oracle describes the march of the invading armies down the coast, isolating the Phoenician cities of

---

[16]See Amos 1–2, Isaiah 13–23, Ezekiel 25–32, Zephaniah 2:4-15.

Tyre and Sidon, then moving on down the *Via Maris* to knock out the main Philistine cities of Gaza and Ashkelon.

Against Moab (Jer. 48:1-47).   To read the oracle against Moab with real understanding, one needs a biblical atlas with detailed maps. It was a travelogue of Moabite territory listing most, if not all, of its major cities. Though it speaks of Moab's destruction, it ends on a promise of restoration to Moab "in the latter days." This reflected the fact that the Moabites and Israelites were not so antagonistic toward each other as Israel had been against others of its neighbors. The story of Ruth, told to support the claim that David had a Moabite grandmother, gave an indication of friendly relations between the two peoples.

Against Ammon (Jer. 49:1-6).   This short oracle was directed toward Israel's neighbor in the territory occupied by the modern country of Jordan. It, too, ends on a positive note of restoration.

Against Edom (Jer. 49:7-22).   There was no pity expressed for the Edomites. Noted for its wise men, Edom would lose all her wisdom. The city of Sela (but later known as Petra), located in a box canyon with only one narrow entrance, was exceedingly difficult to conquer. But even the rock fortress of Sela would not save Edom. Edom had kicked Judah when she was at her lowest ebb in 587, and the blows would not be forgotten. Much of this oracle is also found in the book of Obadiah. This may mean it originated with Jeremiah, with Obadiah, or with someone else.

Against Syria (Jer. 49:23-27).   No set of foreign oracles would be complete without mentioning Syria, Israel's long-time enemy. It ends with words that sound strangely like Amos:

> And I will kindle a fire in the wall of Damascus,
>   and it shall devour the strongholds of Ben-hadad. (49:27)

Against Kedar and Hazor (Jer. 49:28-33).   These were minor groups of people in the northeastern part of Palestine. At one time, Hazor had been a major city in the north.

Against Elam (Jer. 49:34-39).   Elam was east of Babylon in the region of the present-day country of Iran.

Against Babylon (Jer. 50:1–52:64).   The oracles of Jeremiah are concluded with a series of oracles against Babylon, since it was Israel's chief foreign enemy. There was a constant shifting of persons spoken to in these oracles. The oracles began with the LORD announcing to the nations that Babylon had been taken (50:2-4). The people of Judah would return to the LORD, asking the way to Zion (50:4-5). They had been like lost sheep, attacked by wild animals (50:6-7).

The LORD addressed the people and told them to flee from the land of Chaldeans (Babylon), for invaders were coming who would destroy everything in their path (50:8-10). Babylon was told that her doom was sure. She would be hissed at by all who passed her (50:11-13). Her enemies were invited to attack her, for they would be carrying out the LORD's vengeance against her (50:14-16).

Attention was then shifted to Israel. Israel was compared to a sheep hunted by lions. Assyria, then Babylon, had attacked Israel. Now the tables would be turned. Israel would be restored as Babylon was destroyed (50:17-20).

Then follows a series of oracles describing the destruction of Babylon. The hammer that had broken many was now broken (50:21-28). The archers were summoned to bend their bows at it. Fire would burn its cities (50:29-32); the LORD would redeem Israel, but the sword would devour Babylon (50:33-38); unrest would upset its inhabitants (50:39-40). As it had come from the north to devastate Palestine, so a northern foe would devastate it. Its king would be helpless for the enemy would be like a lion in a sheepfold (50:41-46).

Jeremiah 51 continues on the theme of the LORD's judgment against Babylon. It would be winnowed as a farmer winnows grain (51:1-7); its wounds would be so great that no balm would heal it (51:8-10). The enemy was summoned to prepare its weapons and mount an assault against the city, for the LORD had promised victory (51:11-14).

In the midst of the oracles of doom, there is a hymnlike section describing the LORD's power in nature. In contrast to that power, the idol was the powerless product of stupid men. It could not compare to the God of Jacob (51:15-19).

In 51:20-23 there is the oracle of the hammer. Babylon had been a hammer by which the LORD had meted out punishment to those who had sinned against him. Now, however, the destroyer would be destroyed. The LORD summoned the nations to make war against it, to make it a land of desolation and waste (51:24-33). What Nebuchadnezzar had done to Jerusalem would be done to Babylon (51:34-37). Its fall was like a land awash with the waves of the sea (51:38-44). Judah was warned to flee, for the LORD's wrath would be poured out on the land (51:45-46). Babylon's fall would come because of what it had done to Israel (51:47-51). The LORD would see to it that Babylon was laid waste for he was the God of justice (51:52-58).

According to 51:59-64, Jeremiah wrote on a scroll all the oracles against Babylon. He sent it to Babylon by Seraiah, the quartermaster in Zedekiah's court. Seraiah was told to read the oracles in Babylon. Having done that, he was to tie a stone to the scroll and throw it into the Euphrates. Just as the scroll would sink in the river, so Babylon would sink—to rise no more.

EVALUATION OF JEREMIAH

Jeremiah was a man of unusual courage. While he was not without supporters in Jerusalem during the dark days of Judah's decline, it required great fortitude to say what he felt was necessary in the face of strong opposition among the powerful men of Jerusalem. The full effect of what he said was only realized as the exiles looked back at what had happened and realized how right Jeremiah had been. Their appreciation of what he had said helped them make a more realistic evaluation of their situation and adjust to it.

STUDY QUESTIONS

1. How was Mannaseh's reign different from that of his father Hezekiah?
2. Describe the reform that took place during Josiah's time. Why was it called the Deuteronomic reformation?
3. What were the advantages and disadvantages of centralizing all of Israel's worship in Jerusalem?
4. State the themes of Zephaniah, Nahum, and Habbakuk.
5. What great international events were taking place in the last years of Josiah's reign?
6. How did the policies of Jehoiakim differ from those of his father Josiah?
7. Why is Habbakuk referred to as "the first Jewish philosopher"?
8. What was unusual about the call of Jeremiah to be a prophet?
9. What was the significance of the two visions that were associated with the call?
10. Why are chapters 1–25 referred to as the "first edition" of the book of Jeremiah?
11. What was the Temple Sermon and what were its results?
12. Describe Jeremiah's relations with King Zedekiah.
13. What was Jeremiah's advice to the exiles and why did he need to give such advice in the first place?
14. How did Jeremiah show his faith in the future of the nation?
15. What was Jeremiah's relationship to Josiah? Jehoiakim? Zedekiah?
16. Why was Jeremiah considered a traitor by many of the people of Jerusalem?
17. What happened to Jeremiah when Jerusalem fell?
18. Identify: Baruch, the New Covenant, 597, 587/6

19. What theme in the book reflects Hosea's influence on Jeremiah?
20. What were Jeremiah's confessions?

FOR FURTHER STUDY

Habbakuk, Zephaniah, Nahum.

See the general works on the prophets cited after chapter 8.

Jeremiah

BRIGHT, JOHN. *Jeremiah.* Anchor Bible. New York: Doubleday, 1965. The introductory material is especially helpful.

GOTTWALD, NORMAN. *Studies in Lamentations.* Studies in Biblical Theology, no. 14. Naperville, Ill.: Alec R. Allenson, 1954.

HYATT, J. PHILIP. "Jeremiah: Introduction and Exegesis" in *Interpreter's Bible,* VI. New York: Abingdon, 1956.

———. *Jeremiah: Prophet of Courage and Hope.* New York: Abingdon, 1958.

LESLIE, ELMER A. *Jeremiah.* New York: Abingdon, 1954. An Apex paperback.

ROBINSON, H. WHEELER. *The Cross in the Old Testament.* London: S. C. M. Press, 1955.

SKINNER, JOHN. *Prophecy and Religion.* New York: Cambridge, 1922. A standard work on Jeremiah.

CHAPTER ELEVEN

The Exile:
Judah's Dark Night
of the Soul

The land lay in ruins. Cities that once were alive with people now were blackened piles of rubble. Fields that once produced abundant crops of life-sustaining foods now lay idle, overgrown with weeds. Jerusalem, the once proud city of David and Solomon, was wrecked. Its houses, from the hovels of the poor to the palaces of its kings, were burned to the ground; its massive walls were filled with gaping holes; and the Temple, the building that popular religion was sure would be the magic charm to protect the city, was just another heap of rubble. And the people—they who had given life to the city—were gone. Many were dead in the city's ruins; others were exiles in neighboring lands. Those of the upper echelons of society who had survived had been carried to Babylon as prisoners of war. All who were left were poor farmers and shepherds, men incapable of leading any kind of revolt against the powerful armies of Babylon.

After the Fall

The fall of Jerusalem was a shattering blow to the people, who had thought the presence of the Temple would protect the city. The giddy optimism of a few years before was replaced by an air of gloom and despair. Nowhere was that spirit reflected more starkly than in the book of Lamentations.

284

LAMENTATIONS: FUNERAL SONGS FOR A DEAD CITY

This book, which is only five chapters long, is made up of five poems that mourn the fall of Jerusalem. Chapters 1, 2, and 4, especially, are written in such vivid language that they must have come from the pen of an eyewitness to the horrors described. Chapters 3 and 5 may well have come from the same author, but probably they were written at a later time when he had had opportunity to reflect on what had happened.

Characteristics of the book. There are two distinct characteristics to the poems. First, they are all in what is called the *qinah*, or dirge, rhythm. To understand this, one must understand a bit about Hebrew poetry. Hebrew poetry was based on the principle of parallelism. To have parallelism, each line of poetry had to have at least two or more parts. What was said in one part of the line was more or less answered in the second part of the line. Generally speaking, in English translation a verse in English is one line in Hebrew. For instance, Lamentations 5:20 says:

> Why dost thou forget us for ever,
> why dost thou so long forsake us?

What was said in the first part of the line was repeated in the second part of the line (the second line in English). More will be said about parallelism later.

Rhythm also was vital in Hebrew poetry. Each part of the line had certain stresses or strong words. As a general rule, no part of a line had less than two stresses or more than three stresses in it. In *qinah* there were three stresses in the first part of the line and two stresses in the second part of the line, creating a 3:2 rhythm. This 3:2, or *qinah*, rhythm was used for dirges (funeral songs) or laments over calamities that had occurred.

A second feature of the poems is that all of them were written as acrostics. An acrostic was formed by starting successive lines of poetry with the letters of a word of the alphabet. For example, early Christians used the fish as a symbol because they could form an acrostic on the Greek word for fish *(ichthus)* as a confession of faith:

*I*esous	(Jesus)
*Ch*ristos	(Christ)
*Th*eos	(God)
*U*ios	(Son)
*S*oter	(Savior)

[handwritten margin notes:] major feature of Hebrew poetry

[handwritten margin notes:] purpose – to reinforce the idea of the 1st line.

Lamentations has a series of alphabetic acrostics using the letters of the Hebrew alphabet. Since the Hebrew alphabet has 22 letters, chapters 1, 2, 4, and 5 have 22 verses each while chapter 3 has 66, or 3 times 22, verses.

Contents of the book. The mood of the book is set by a cry of anguish in the first word. The English word "How" translates a Hebrew expression of woe:

> *How* lonely sits the city
>   that was full of people!
> How like a widow has she become,
>   she that was great among the nations!
> She that was a princess among the cities
>   has become a vassal (1:1).

Jerusalem, the abandoned widow (Lam. 1:1-22). Jerusalem was like a widow, weeping bitterly, because she had been deserted by all who loved her (1:2). No one entered her gates anymore because the enemy had carried away her people (1:3-6). All she had left was memories of past glories. Now she was filthy and soiled, the victim of her enemies (1:7-10). Hunger stalked the land. The LORD had inflicted great sorrow upon her. He had afflicted her and abandoned her (1:11-13).

Jerusalem's sins had become a yoke on its neck. Its best soldiers had been helpless before the power of the invader. So Jerusalem wept. There was no one to comfort it. It was mocked and despised by its neighbors (1:14-17). Yet, the LORD had been just because Jerusalem had been disobedient. It had called for help from its allies, but they had refused its pleas. Now it was sorry for its sins because death and destruction were everywhere. Its enemies taunted it because of its condition. It wanted the LORD to punish them (1:18-22).

The punishment of Jerusalem (Lam. 2:1-22). The second lament falls more easily into natural divisions. Lamentations 2:1-9 describes the destruction of the land and city; 2:10-12 describes the emotional and physical effects of the siege; 2:13-19 was an address to Jerusalem reminding it of the causes of its condition; and 2:20-22 was a prayer to the LORD to be aware of what was happening in the city.

The destruction of the land (Lam. 2:1-9). The Temple, the LORD's dwelling place, was abandoned. The LORD had gone through the land, destroying without mercy both the villages and the cities. Forts and palaces alike were in ruins. The Temple was smashed—the services were ended. The strong walls that protected Jerusalem were broken down. The gates where justice was dispensed and where the ebb and flow of humanity was seen as it entered the city were buried in the rubble of the walls.

The effect on the people (Lam. 2:10-12).   Old men sat in an unbelieving daze while young girls bowed to the ground in sorrow. The author had wept until he could weep no more. Famine stalked the city so that hungry children fell like wounded men while others died in their mother's arms.

O Jerusalem, how can I comfort you? (Lam. 2:13-19).   Jerusalem's condition was hopeless. It had let itself be deceived by lying prophets. Now, people passed by and poked fun at its condition. Its enemies sneered at it. The LORD's patience had run its course, and destruction had come. The poet called for Jerusalem's walls to cry out to the LORD for mercy for its children, who were "starving to death on every street corner" (2:19).

LORD, look what you are doing (Lam. 2:20-22).   The poet pleaded with the LORD to look at the suffering. Mothers were becoming cannibals, eating their own children. Priest and prophet, young and old, were being slaughtered everywhere. Jerusalem's enemies were having a "carnival of terror" (2:22, TEV) at its expense.

A personal lament, advice about the God's righteousness and mercy, and a prayer for help against the enemy (Lam. 3:1-66).   This poem is two things. First, it actually is a combination of three poems, each with a different purpose. They are welded together into one triple alphabetic acrostic; that is, instead of each line starting with a different letter of the alphabet, here each set of three lines starts with a different letter of the alphabet.

1. A lament about life (Lam. 3:1-24).   The poet had known suffering. He had been quite ill or injured, having come close to death (3:1-5). He had cried to God, but there seemed to be no answer. Instead, like Job, he felt that God had used him for target practice because God's arrows had pierced his body. He had been pushed down into the dirt so many times he had lost hope (3:6-18).

Yet, in the depths of his bitterness, he remembered an important thing:

> The steadfast love of the LORD never ceases,
>   his mercies never come to an end;
> they are new every morning;
>   great is thy faithfulness.
> "The LORD is my portion," says my soul,
>   "therefore I will hope in him" (3:22-24)

2. The importance of trusting God (Lam. 3:25-51).   As if to answer and to add to the positive note sounded in the last stanza of the previous psalm, this poem speaks of the importance of patience. That it was a different poem can be seen in the shift from the singular to the plural in the use of the personal pronouns.

The goodness of the LORD was to all who trusted him. Patience should be practiced, therefore, in whatever situation life brought. The LORD might permit sorrow and pain, but he took no pleasure in doing so. He was aware of what was happening to everyone. His will would be carried out. The thing his people should do was to admit their sin. The calamities that had come upon them caused the poet sorrow for what had happened to the women of the city.

3. *Rescued from my enemies (Lam. 3:52-66).* This was a combination of a lament and thanksgiving. The poet spoke of his treatment by his enemies. He cried to the LORD and was assured that he would be rescued. The LORD kept his word. The poet then prayed for punishment for the enemy.

Conditions during the siege of Jerusalem (Lam. 4:1-22). The horrors of the siege of Jerusalem are nowhere more vividly portrayed than in this chapter. The holy objects of the Temple were scattered in the streets. The invaders smashed people like clay pots. Those who survived lost all sense of humanity in their wild urge to live. Children starved to death because adults would not share food with them. The upper classes, always the healthier people in the population because of a better diet, starved like the poor. Those who died by the sword were the fortunate ones. Things were so bad that mothers boiled and ate their own children (4:1-10).

The LORD had poured his wrath on the city with such violence that Jerusalem's neighbors were shocked. None of them believed that Jerusalem could be conquered. Prophets and priests who had misled the people were now shunned as though they were lepers. The city's leaders were ignored instead of being honored (4:11-16).

The survivors kept looking for help, but none came. It was not safe to walk in the streets; if a person fell, he could be eaten! (4:17-19).

The end came. Those who tried to flee were chased down. The king, trying to escape the city, was captured. The Edomites, Judah's neighbors to the southeast, taunted the victims, increasing the natural hatred the two peoples had for each other. Judah's punishment was complete (4:20-22).

Restore us, O LORD (Lam. 5:1-22). The people were under the oppressor's heel. Taken from their land, they were like motherless children. Everything they got had a price on it, even the water they drank. The punishment for their sin was upon them. The famine had produced diseases that had brought raging fevers; their women were abused physically by the invading soldiers; oppression was the rule and not the exception. Joy had been turned to mourning (5:1-18).

The LORD was their only hope. The only question was whether or not he had completely rejected them (5:19-22).

THE FATE OF THE SURVIVORS

Not everyone who survived the war was taken to Babylon. As has been noted previously, a number of people, including Jeremiah, were left in the land under the governorship of Gedaliah. When Gedaliah was murdered in 582, those who were his supporters fled to Egypt, thinking they would be blamed. They, and others who went to Egypt from time to time, would become the basis of a strong Jewish community in later centuries.

In Judah the population was low. It was estimated by some to be as low as 20,000, less than one-tenth of what it had been in the days of the eighth-century prophets.

Of those taken to Babylon in three deportations (597, 587, and 582), the grand total was probably less than 5000. This indicates something of the large number of people who had died in the Assyrian and Babylonian wars.[1]

With the Exiles in Babylon

The Babylonian exile had a profound effect upon the future of the people who had been known as the Israelites. It affected every area of their life, from how they were to live in relation to their God to how they were to live in relation to their fellow man.

THERE WERE SOME CHANGES MADE

The people who went into the Babylonian exile survived not only as individuals but also as an identifiable group of people. Their religion, though tested in the fires of war and surrender, also survived. But there were some important changes that took place.

A new name. Since the survivors of the Babylonian wars were principally from the tribe of Judah, from that time forth they have been known as Jews, a short form for Judahites.

A new way of life. While some of the people had lived in cities and were merchants, the majority of the survivors basically were rural people, dependent upon pastoral and agricultural occupations for a living. After

---

[1]Bright, *A History of Israel,* p. 344 ff. See Martin Noth, *The History of Israel,* pp. 287–288, on the nature of the deportations and Gedaliah's reign.

Figure 11–1. The Babylonian Empire–sixth century B.C.

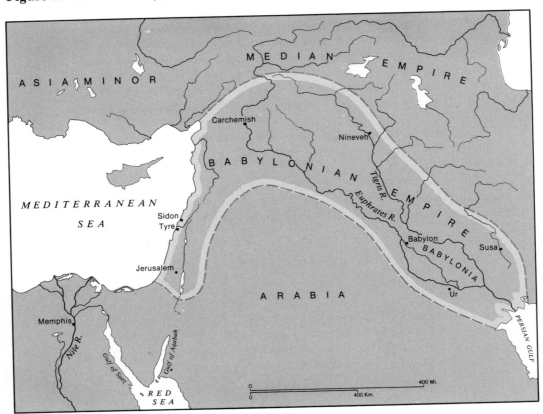

the exile, the Jews were predominantly an urban people, living in cities and making their living in various commercial enterprises.

A new language. The people who went to exile spoke Hebrew; those who returned spoke Aramaic, the language of the Babylonians. Aramaic was the most widely spoken language in the Near East. It was similar to Hebrew, so that the change was not a difficult one to make. Hebrew continued to be used to some extent, especially in religious services.

A new way of worship. Exile brought separation from the Temple and its system of sacrifices. Devout Jews, however, found that the LORD was with them, even in a foreign land. Whether the synagogue was actually founded in the period from 587 to 538 cannot be determined with certainty. Undoubtedly, the conditions that led to its founding were present in the exile. Services of prayer, praise, and reading of sacred writings surely must have been carried on. From the worship services, it was only a short step to the formal structure that made up synagogue worship.

A new emphasis on the traditions of Israel.   The exile brought the threat of the loss of the sacred traditions of Israel. Since many of them were unwritten, there was a matter of urgency involved that they be committed to writing before those who knew them died. Many of those who possessed such traditions in their memories had perished already in the siege of Jerusalem. The exile must have been a time of unusual literary activity. That at least the final materials were added to Israel's history which has been preserved in 1 and 2 Samuel and 1 and 2 Kings (the so-called Deuteronomic History) can be seen from the account of the release of King Jehoiachin from prison in 560 (2 Kings 25:27-30). Writing down the traditions became a project of the priests during the exile, especially since they had no sacrifices to offer. It would continue for many years.[2]

A new emphasis in theology.   The Israelites who went into exile were not true believers in one God alone (monotheists). Evidence suggests that the devotees of popular religion, while paying lip service to the worship of the LORD (the God of Israel), actually were worshipers of numerous gods (polytheists). Or, at least they believed that other gods existed, even though they only worshiped one God (henotheists). The Jews who returned from the exile were devout monotheists, so much so that they wanted nothing to do with the people of the old northern territories who still considered themselves to be worshipers of the God of Israel. Their religion, however, had incorporated too many foreign elements to please the Jews. Because of this, there would be increasing friction between the two groups.

[handwritten annotations: "→ only one God exists", "→ more than 1 God exists", "→ several Gods, but they only worshipped one"]

THE PROPHET OF THE TRANSITION: EZEKIEL

Jeremiah had done his part to prepare the people for the exile, as well as to help those who were in exile to take a realistic view of their situation. Even so, religiously, the exile was a shock, as the book of Lamentations so vividly illustrates. The inevitable question, "Why did it happen to us?" must have been asked of the religious leaders in the exilic community. Some wanted to believe the pious predictions of the false prophets that the exile would be ended soon, when the LORD brought about a miraculous overthrow of the Babylonians. In line with that belief,

[2]But see Martin Noth, *The History of Israel,* p. 292, who says the Deuteronomic History was written in Palestine.

indications are that a number of people plotted to overthrow the government and were executed.[3] It was to counter such false optimism that Jeremiah's letter to the exiles had been written (Jer. 29). Others of the community undoubtedly were not willing to accept any explanations and gave up any idea of God. For a third group, two prophets made sense and enabled them to survive the exile with a more mature faith founded in a deepened understanding of the LORD, the God of Israel. Ezekiel was the first of these prophets.

Ezekiel, the man.   Ezekiel was a priest before he became a prophet (Ezek. 1:3). His father was Buzi, about whom nothing is known. We know Ezekiel was married, as Ezekiel 24:15-18 tells of the death of his wife. Nothing was said in the book about any children. From the first chapter of his book, it is evident that he was a most unusual man. He had strange and bizarre visionary experiences, he acted out many of his messages to the people instead of delivering them, and he had a mathematician's delight in precise detail. A modern psychiatrist would have a field day trying to figure what made him function.

He had been taken to Babylon in the deportation of 597. At that time he was still a priest. In 593 he experienced a call of the LORD to be a prophet. For the next twenty years or so he carried out that responsibility.

He was exclusively a prophet to the exiles, doing in Babylon what Jeremiah was trying to do in Jerusalem—that is, trying to prepare the people for (1) the inevitable fall of Jerusalem and (2) trying to put a damper on the false hopes for an immediate return to Palestine, which some of the prophets were promoting. Once Jerusalem fell in 587, however, Ezekiel became a prophet of hope, trying to prepare the people for their return to the land. He laid out a blueprint for a restored Temple and worship system.

The book of Ezekiel.   The book, with more precisely dated oracles than any of the major prophets, falls naturally into three major divisions: Chapters 1–24: oracles against Jerusalem; chapters 25–32: oracles against foreign nations; and chapters 33–48: oracles of restoration.

Oracles against Jerusalem (Ezek. 1-24)

1. *The call of Ezekiel (Ezek. 1:1–3:27).*   The call of Ezekiel was similar to that of earlier prophets, such as Isaiah and Jeremiah, in that visions were associated with it. It was different in the nature and extent of the visions.

a. *The prophet called (Ezek. 1:1-28).*   Ezekiel was by the River Chebar, which actually was a major irrigation canal on the Euphrates River (1:1).[4] The young priest probably was in a meditative mood when the dark clouds

---

[3]Bright, *A History of Israel,* p. 346 (Jer. 29:21).

[4]Walter Eichrodt, *Ezekiel* in *Old Testament Library* (London: SCM Press, 1970), p. 52.

of an approaching thunderstorm caught his attention (1:4). The mention of "brightness round about it," "fire flashing forth continually," and the reference to "gleaming bronze" (1:4) all suggest a particularly violent storm with much lightning and possible hail associated. Up to that point, Ezekiel's description would fit any violent summer storm.

From then on, the storm becomes the backdrop for an astounding vision, which for Ezekiel seemed to be normal. Unlike Amos, who saw messages from the LORD in ordinary events, Ezekiel saw extraordinary sights that became the bearers of the divine message.

First, there were the creatures of the vision. They had four faces, four wings, and the legs of bovine animals with hoofs like calves (1:5-7). Under the wings were human arms and hands. The faces were those of an eagle, an ox, a lion, and a man. The eagle suggested mobility, the ox suggested strength, the lion suggested lordliness, and the man suggested intelligence (1:8-10). Their wings permitted them to fly in any direction without turning around. Fire (suggested by lightning?) was in the midst of the creatures, symbolic of the cleansing power of the LORD (1:11-14).

The creatures were accompanied by wheels arranged somewhat like a gyroscope. In other words, there were two wheels, one of which was arranged at a 90° angle from the other. Or, they were like a ball with quarter sections cut out all except for a small band of the material. This permitted them to roll in any of the four major directions (1:15-17). The eyes that decorated the rims were suggestive of the all-knowingness or *omniscience* of God. Wherever the living creatures went, so did the wheels (1:18-21).

Above the creatures—symbols of all living creation at the service of the LORD—and the wheels Ezekiel saw a vision of the LORD himself sitting on a throne just as Isaiah did (Isa. 6). The creatures covered their bodies with two wings in the LORD's presence (Ezek. 1:22-23; see Isa. 6:2). As they flew, the sound of their wings was like the thunder of the storm. When they came into the LORD's presence, they stopped flying (11:24-25).

The prophet-to-be saw the LORD from the waist down. The upper part of the body was obscured by fire, the brightness of which reminded him of the rainbow that followed the storm (1:26-28). "Such was the appearance of the glory of the LORD" (1:28). The word "glory" as used here might also be translated as the "overwhelming presence" of the LORD.

What the first chapter describes is basically the same thing Isaiah 6 describes—that is, a theophany or appearance of the LORD to the one who was being called. Behind all the elaborate symbolism was the prophet's basic conviction that the LORD who had called him to be a prophet was master of the universe, not just master of a little narrow strip of land called Palestine. As such, the LORD could be anywhere he chose to be, even among the forlorn exiles by the River Chebar in Babylon.

b. *The prophet commissioned (Ezek. 2:1–3:27).*   Ezekiel, who had fallen on his face when he realized that he was in the presence of the LORD, was commanded to stand on his feet. He was addressed as "son of man," which, for Ezekiel, simply means "Man," a form of address (2:1-3). He was given a fivefold commission:

(1) *As a prophet to a rebellious people (Ezek. 2:1–3:3).*   They were an "impudent and stubborn" people (2:4), but he was not to let that stop him from doing his job. In an action symbolizing the receiving of the LORD's message of lamentation, mourning, and woe, Ezekiel ate a papyrus scroll that tasted as sweet as honey. He would enjoy speaking the LORD's message.

(2) *As a prophet to a stubborn people (Ezek. 3:4-9).*   Although the word was sweet to Ezekiel, it would be distasteful to those to whom it would be preached. Their failure to understand would not be because of a language difference, but because of a lack of willingness to hear.

(3) *As a prophet to the exiles (Ezek. 3:10-15).*   Ezekiel's mission was directed specifically to the people who were in exile, more specifically to the exiles at Tel-abib (from which the modern Israeli city of Tel-aviv derives its name) on the Chebar canal. He went there and sat silently in the midst of the community for seven days.

(4) *As a watchman for the house of Israel (Ezek. 3:16-21).*   The emphasis in this commission laid the responsibility upon Ezekiel to carry out his call as a prophet. Like Isaiah, he was called to be faithful whether or not he was successful (Isa. 6:11-13).

(5) *As a portrayer of the LORD's judgment (Ezek. 3:22-27).*   Ezekiel, more than any other prophet, was the master of symbolic action. By such pantomimes, he acted out what was about to happen rather than describing with words the LORD's impending judgment. As a part of this phase of his ministry, he was to remain silent until the LORD told him to speak.

2. *The prophet in action (Ezek. 4:1–5:17).*   Almost immediately, it seems, Ezekiel began to prophesy by pantomime.

a. *Let's play war (Ezek. 4:1-3).*   First, he played war, using a large sun-dried brick. Using it as a symbol for Jerusalem, he set up miniature camps and siege lines around it, built dirt ramps up to it, and made miniature battering rams as if to knock down the imaginary walls. He took a small piece of iron to make a movable shield such as was used by attacking armies as they tried to get near city walls to attack them. Then he enthusiastically played war.

b. *The long rest (Ezek. 4:4-8).*   Next, Ezekiel was commanded to lie on his side 390 days as a sign of the length of Israel's punishment. For Judah's punishment, he was to lie on his side 40 days. While each day was to indicate a year's exile, the significance of the numbers was not explained further. The period of 390 years may simply indicate that Israel's exile would go on indefinitely; 40 years would seem to indicate for Ezekiel what

70 years represented for Jeremiah—a symbol of the completion of the LORD's time. When things were right, the exiles would return.

c. *Food is scarce! (Ezek. 4:9-17).*   A third action involved the mixing of various grains, beans, and peas to make flour for bread. Under ordinary circumstances, such a thing was not done; but when a siege was on, one ate anything available. The command to cook the food over dried human manure was too much for Ezekiel's priestly instincts. When he pleaded for an exception, the LORD permitted dried cow manure for the cooking fires. All of this demonstrated the extreme conditions that existed during the siege of Jerusalem.

d. *The prophet's haircut (Ezek. 5:1-17).*   A man's hair was his pride. The prophet got a lesson in humility when he was told to cut his hair like a captive of war. Then, he took the hair from his shorn head and divided it into three parts. A third was burned, a third was chopped to pieces with the sword, and a third was scattered to the wind. A few hairs left clinging to his garments were divided in the same way. In the explanations that followed, the symbolism of this action was explained. Like the prophet's hair, so the inhabitants of Jerusalem would be divided:

> A third part of you shall die of pestilence and be consumed with famine in the midst of you; a third part shall fall by the sword round about you; and a third part I will scatter to all the winds and will unsheathe the sword after them (5:12).

Although the LORD had made Jerusalem the center of the universe, she was doomed (5:5).

3. *The prophet preaching (Ezek. 6:1–7:27).*   A spoken sermon follows the descriptions of the pantomimed sermons. Its title might be "Judgment on the Mountains." This sermon was directed against the mountains where the Baal cults had their worship centers. The sermon had four parts, each closed by the refrain, "I am the LORD." The first division was spoken to the mountains as if they were living persons, describing how the pagan altars that were supposed to be for the celebration of life and fertility would be the scene of death and barrenness (6:1-7).

The second part spoke of the scattering of the people into foreign lands. They would remember how they had grieved the LORD and would realize his threats had not been in vain (6:8-10).

The third division called for mourning to take place because men would die of pestilence and famine. When corpses were found on the altars, the high hills, and every place they had worshiped the pagan gods; when the land was made desolate, then, "they shall know that I am the LORD" (6:11-14). The sermon closes with oracles of doom for the land (7:1-27).

4. *Heresy in the Temple (Ezek. 8:1–11:25).*

a. *Those abominable idols (Ezek. 8:1-18; 11:1-21).*   Pages have been written about these visions of Ezekiel found in chapters 8–11. One of the major questions relates to whether they were visions or whether Ezekiel actually was present in Jerusalem to witness the things he described. Travel back and forth to Jerusalem from Babylon was not unknown. Ezekiel's intimate knowledge of the Temple, growing out of his training as a priest, however, would explain his detailed descriptions. Furthermore, his powers of discernment and previous visionary experiences would seem to argue for these being visions on the order of extrasensory perception.

As Ezekiel described it, he was transported to Jerusalem by a hand that held him by a lock of hair. He was brought in vision to the northern gateway of the inner court, where there seemed to be some sort of pagan image. Immediately, he was aware of the overpowering presence of the God of Israel (8:1-4).

After having the pagan image and the ceremonies celebrating its presence pointed out to him (8:5-6), he was shown a hole in the wall. Following instructions, he dug in the hole and found a door. Entering the door, he saw seventy of Judah's leaders, led by a Temple official, worshiping pictures of animals drawn on the walls (8:7-13). They may have been evidence of the worship of Egyptian deities.[5]

Going to the north gate of the Temple, there Ezekiel found women weeping for Tammuz, the Babylonian god of vegetation (8:14-15).[6] Next, he went to the east side of the Temple where he found twenty-five men worshiping the rising sun. Thus in the house where the LORD alone was to be worshiped, all sorts of services to pagan gods were being carried on (8:16-18). Jerusalem's doom was pronounced:

> Therefore I will deal in wrath; my eye will not spare, nor will I have pity; and though they cry in my ears with a loud voice, I will not hear them (8:18).

This passage seems to have been continued in 11:1-21. There specific people who were leaders in the worship of pagan deities were named. In his vision, Ezekiel saw one of them (Pelatiah, the son of Beniah) die. The hope for a righteous remnant was mentioned, along with certain judgment for the sinners of Jerusalem.

b. *Marked for destruction (Ezek. 9:1-11).* The LORD called for the executioners to make ready. Six men, prepared to act as the LORD's executioners, stepped up with their weapons ready. A seventh man with a writing case was with them (9:1-2). The LORD instructed the seventh man to go through the city and to put a mark on the foreheads of those who were disturbed by the abominations that were being parcticed in the Temple. They were the righteous who would survive the siege. This was in keeping with the commonly held theological view that the righteous

[5] *Oxford Annotated Bible,* RSV note on Ezek. 8:10.
[6] See Pritchard, *The Ancient Near East,* pp. 76–79.

would enjoy blessings and a long life, while sinners would die young. Ezekiel would have said that those who died during the siege were sinners (9:3-4).

Once the righteous were marked, the executioners were ordered to do their job. Beginning with the unfaithful leaders, they were to slaughter the unmarked people. As Ezekiel experienced this vision, he, like Amos, prayed to the LORD, asking him if he was going to destroy all the people. The LORD answered that the guilty would not be spared. The scribe reported that he had done his job (9:5-11).

c. *No more glory in the Temple (Ezek. 10:1-22; 11:22-25).*   When Ezekiel looked, he saw a repeat of the vision by the River Chebar with the LORD on the throne, the winged creatures (now called cherubim), and the wheels. The LORD commanded the scribe to take fire from the fire under the cherubim, which he did (10:1-8). He scattered them over the city to burn it (10:2).

In 11:22-25 the glory of the LORD (his overpowering presence) left the Temple, accompanied by the cherubim and the wheels. This was Ezekiel's way of saying to the exiles that the Temple and Jerusalem could no longer claim the LORD's protective presence. Thus the vision ended. The time was 592, only five years before Jerusalem would be destroyed.

5. *In action again (Ezek. 12:1-20).*   In an action closely related to his word about the withdrawal of the presence of the LORD from Jerusalem, Ezekiel acted out before the people what would happen to the survivors in Jerusalem. He gathered up his portable possessions like one who was being taken to exile. He dug through the mud wall of his house at night and crawled through the hole, taking his baggage with him (12:1-7). He was then instructed to tell the people that his action symbolized what King Zedekiah would do in attempting to escape from Jerusalem. He would not be successful, however. He would be captured, blinded, and taken to Babylon as a captive (12:8-16).

Ezekiel then drank water and ate, quaking and trembling like one who was mortally afraid. This would be the condition of the people in Jerusalem as they awaited the fall of the land (12:17-20).

6. *Hard words for false prophets and unfaithful people (Ezek. 12:21–14:23).*   Some people made fun of Ezekiel, saying that he kept predicting doom, but it never came. He was told to warn the people that judgment no longer would be delayed. His words were not for a sweet by-and-by; they were about a harsh here-and-now (12:21-28).

a. *The fate of false prophets (Ezek. 13:1-16).*   The prophets of popular religion were not concerned with the LORD's message. Instead, they were busy thinking up messages that would soothe the people and cause them to react favorably to the messenger. Instead of building a wall of truth behind which Israel could be secure, they had built a faulty wall. Then they covered their mistakes with whitewash. When the flood of judgment came, the whitewash would not hold the wall together. So the prophets who kept on crying peace when war was unavoidable would be destroyed like the faulty wall.

b. *The fate of fickle women (Ezek. 13:17-23).*   Ezekiel condemned women "who sew magic bands upon all wrists and make veils for heads of persons of every stature" (13:18). This referred to some sort of witchcraft or magical practice that was condemned in Israel in the time of the early monarchy (1 Sam. 28:3). They had led righteous people astray. As a consequence, judgment upon them would be severe. A favorite theme of Ezekiel closes the oracle, "Then you will know that I am the LORD" (13:20-23).

c. *The fate of idol worshipers (Ezek. 14:1-23).*   When certain leaders of the people came to Ezekiel, it was revealed to him that they were idol worshipers. The LORD would not permit such a person to have a correct message through a prophet because of his false worship (14:1-5). The only hope for the idol worshiper was to repent and put away his idols. Idol worshipers would be cut off by the LORD even if they tried to appear righteous by consulting a prophet. Both he and the prophet he consulted would be false and would face the LORD's judgment (14:6-11).

Such unfaithfulness would condemn the land—even if Noah, Daniel, and Job still lived in the land. Their righteousness would only save them. The righteous could only save themselves. (This idea of individual responsibility was further discussed by Ezekiel in chapters 18 and 33.) Jerusalem was about to face four severe acts of judgment—"sword, famine, evil beasts and pestilence to cut it off from man and beast" (14:21). Any who survive would testify that the LORD had acted out of a just cause (14:12-23).

7. *The prophet and his allegories (Ezek. 15:1–17:24).*   Ezekiel was particularly fond of allegories (stories in which some actual person or event is represented by a symbol). For instance, in 15:1-8 Jerusalem was represented by a grapevine. The grapevine was no good except as a fruit-bearing plant. Its wood was useless as wood and could only be burned. Jerusalem had become useless as a dead vine and therefore had to be burned.

a. *Jerusalem: the faithless wife (Ezek. 16:1-63).*   Again Jerusalem was like an unfaithful wife. Ezekiel suggested that the racial background of the Jews was mixed. "Your father was an Amorite and your mother was a Hittite." The LORD found her (the people of Israel) when she had been abandoned to die at birth, and he brought her up. When she was a grown woman, he wooed her and won her as his bride. He gave her all the luxuries that a beautiful woman desired (16:1-14).

Unfortunately, she became a harlot, selling her favors to every one who passed by. She gave to others the blessings the LORD (her husband) had given her. She even sacrificed their children to her lovers. Egypt and

Assyria had been her lovers, but she had been so lustful that she had paid them to take her favors instead of them paying her (16:15-34).

Her days were numbered. She would be stripped naked before the world and held up to shame. Her land and possessions would be given to others. She would be cut to pieces by the swords of those who had patronized her (16:35-43). Samaria and Sodom had been her sisters. They had been bad, but not nearly so bad as Jerusalem. She had used Sodom as a byword in the days when things had been going well for her. Now Jerusalem had become like Sodom (16:44-58).

The LORD would restore Jerusalem. The very act of restoration would cause her to blush in shame when she remembered how she had acted in the past (16:59-63).

b. *The great eagles (Ezek. 17:1-24).* This allegory of the two eagles concerned the royal house of Judah and its attempts to play one power off against another. The first eagle represented Babylon, who took Jehoiachin to Babylon and set Zedekiah in his place. But Zedekiah— instead of doing as the Babylonians wanted, and in so doing, preserving the lives of the people—sent envoys to Egypt (the second eagle). The result would be the destruction of the kingdom and Zedekiah's deportation. This allegory applied to the intrigues that led to the second Babylonian invasion of Palestine in 589.

8. *The soul that sins shall die (Ezek. 18:1-32).* One of the new features of Ezekiel's theology was his doctrine of the individual's responsibility for his own actions. The dominant view in Israel was the idea of corporate responsibility. In such a view the emphasis was on the group rather than the individual. Out of it grew the concept that a child could suffer for his father's sins or vice versa. A proverb that expressed this idea had arisen: "The fathers have eaten sour grapes, and the children's teeth are set on edge." It was also enshrined in the law in Exodus 20:5: "Visiting the iniquity of the fathers upon the children to the third and fourth generation." Now things had changed. The new rule was this: "The soul that sins shall die" (18:1-4).

The remainder of the chapter was spent in illustrating that basic point. A righteous man who kept the covenant provisions would live. If he had a son who broke every law in the book (of the covenant), the son would die for his sins; but the father would be blameless (18:5-13).

The reverse of that situation was also true. The righteous son of a covenant-breaking father would live, but the unrighteous father would die for his sins. If the sinner turned to righteousness or the righteous man turned to sin, he who turned to righteousness would gain life while he who turned to the wrong would lose it. Some were saying that the LORD was not doing right, but they were the ones who were wrong. He was the judge, but he preferred to give life rather than death. What they must do was to turn from their sins so the LORD could give them life (18:14-32).

9. *Two poetic allegories (Ezek. 19:1-14).*   Reverting to the allegory form again, Ezekiel combined it with the lament, or dirge, rhythm. The allegory was of a lion who had two cubs whom she raised in proper "lion fashion" to adulthood. One (Jehoahaz, Josiah's successor) was captured and taken to Egypt. The second was either Jehoiachin (598–597) or Zedekiah (597–587), who both were taken as prisoners to Babylon (19:1-9).

Then he spoke of Judah's mother as a grapevine whose branches were strong and became the rulers of the land. But the vine was pulled up by its roots and planted in the desert where it would never be strong again. So the royal house of Judah would never be strong again (19:10-14).

10. *Three sermons (Ezek. 20:1–22:31)*

a. *The will of God (Ezek. 20:1-49).*   In 590, some of the community leaders came to Ezekiel to ask him what the LORD's will was for the people. Undoubtedly, this was a perplexing question since they had been getting contradictory advice from the other prophets in the community as opposed to the advice given them by Ezekiel's and Jeremiah's letters to them. In answer to their questions, they were reminded of the long and sordid history of disobedience their forefathers had lived. Time after time, the LORD had affirmed and reaffirmed his commitment to be their God and lead them to a good life and his demand that they put aside other gods and worship him only (20:1-6). They had violated his covenant and gone after other gods in Egypt, from which he had delivered them (20:7-9); in the desert, where he had given them the sabbath as the sign of the covenant (20:10-26); and in the land, which he had promised to give them (20:27-30). The LORD was disgusted with such behavior. They asked what his will was, but they had been told his will. Yet, they were committing the very same sins that their fathers had committed (20:30-32).

The LORD was determined to weed out the sinners from among the people. Only the righteous would be allowed to return to Palestine. If they were going to serve idols, they had better do it while they could. Such would not be allowed when the return came about. Then they would worship him and him alone. The LORD was acting to protect his honor. For that reason, he could not deal with the people as severely as their wickedness deserved (20:33-44).

This sermon ends with a short oracle about a fire in the south. Judah (the southern kingdom) would be devoured by a northern foe. Instructed to deliver this warning, the prophet protested having to speak in riddles (20:45-49).

b. *The sword of the LORD (Ezek. 21:1-32).*   The sense of urgency that frequently appeared in Jeremiah's prophecies as the end of Judah neared can also be seen in these oracles on the sword. As one of the most common weapons of war, the sword symbolized death and destruction. The LORD spoke of himself as the enemy, drawing his sword to kill the people of Jerusalem (21:1-4). The prophet was told to groan and cry out in despair. When the people asked why he was groaning, he was to give them the news of what was to happen. The news was about a sword, sharpened and polished for the battle, ready to slaughter whoever got in its way (21:5-13). The prophet was to act as a soldier, using his sword in battle to bring home the truth of his message (20:14-17).

The prophet then was told to draw a map, portraying the roads from Mesopotamia to the west. There was a fork in the road—the west fork leading to Jerusalem and the east fork leading to Rabbah, the capital of Ammon. The King of Babylon was described as standing at the fork, consulting his gods about which city to strike. Taking a handful of arrows, he shook them and threw them down. He hoped the pattern they made would give some indication of which road he would take.[7] By means of divination or casting lots, he consulted his gods and examined an animal's liver, another mode of divination. The arrows pointed to Jerusalem (21:18-22).

This would shock the people of Jerusalem who had made treaties with Babylon, but they had forgotten how they had sinned against the LORD. They were guilty, and Babylon was the sword of the LORD's righteous anger. The rulers would be exiled, and the land would be given to the poor. Ruin! Ruin! This would be the fate of Jerusalem (21:23-27).

Although the Ammonites had been spared, they had no reason to gloat. Their day was coming. The sword and fire would destroy them in their own land (21:28-32).

c. *The sins of Jerusalem (Ezek. 22:1-31)*.   This sermon contains a laundry list of the sins of Jerusalem. The commandment said, "You shall not murder," but they were murderers (22:1-4a). The commandment said, "You shall make no graven images," but they worshiped idols (22:4b). The commandment said, "Honor your father and your mother," but they dishonored their parents (22:7a). The commandment said, "You shall not steal," but they stole from foreigners, widows, and orphans (22:7b). The commandment said, "Remember the sabbath," but they did not keep the sabbath and desecrated holy things (22:8). The commandment said, "You shall not lie," but they lied about one another so they would be put to death (22:9a). The commandment said, "You shall not commit adultery," but they not only committed adultery, they also committed incest (sexual relations with a relative) (22:9b-11). Beyond the Ten Commandments, they loaned money at interest and took bribes to murder. They had forgotten the LORD (22:1-12)

[7]See note on Ezek. 21:21 in *Today's English Version*.

Those sinners would not go unpunished. They would be scattered among the nations as evidence that the LORD was the ruler (22:13-16). Ezekiel compared what would happen to the people to the refining of metal. The impure metal is put into a hot furnace, where heat is used to separate the pure metal from the waste or slag. The people of Jerusalem would he refined in the fires of the exile as sinners would be separated out for destruction (22:17-22).

The major problem was the leaders of the land: the upper classes, the priests, and the prophets. They were like voracious animals, seizing by force things that were not theirs. The priests had become so materially minded that spiritual things were meaningless to them. The rulers had become thieves, while the prophets had become purveyors of false oracles. The people, too, had followed the examples of their leaders. They were extortioners and robbers. The LORD had looked for someone to stem the tide of corruption, but he had found no one. Judgment was certain (22:23-31).

11. *Those wild, wild sisters (Ezek. 23:1-49).*   In this allegory Samaria and Jerusalem were represented as two sisters, Oholah and Oholibah. Together they represented all of the Israelite people, both north and south. They had already been guilty of sexual immorality in Egypt. Like the prophet Hosea, however, the LORD had made them his wives, despite their previous record of sexual looseness. Children came, but the sisters could not stay away from other men. First, it had been Egypt and Assyria. Oholah (Samaria) became a victim of Assyria, who had disgraced her and killed her (23:1-10).

Oholibah (Jerusalem) was even wilder. She cavorted with Assyria and the Babylon. She was expecially attracted to the Babylonian officials. But, as was generally the rule, they abused her so much she sought other lovers. She became even more immoral as she offered herself to any who would take her (23:11-21).

Her former lovers, the Babylonians, would be her executioners. Their well-equipped armies would pour down the northern invasion routes and rape the land. She would be handed over to people who hated her. Soon her fate would be that of her sister Oholah (Samaria) (23:22-35).

The oracles close with a restatement of what had been said previously and with the theme, "You shall know that I am the LORD God" (23:36-49).

12. *The rusty pot (Ezek. 24:1-14).*   The allegory of the rusty pot was dated in January 588, as Nebuchadnezzar's army laid siege to Jerusalem.[8] Ezekiel was using this figure to say that Jerusalem's "goose was cooked"— that is, its fate was sealed. Its inhabitants would be destroyed because of the bloody atrocities committed that had gone unpunished. The reference

---

[8]The date follows that of the *Oxford Annotated Bible*, RSV note on Ezekiel 24:1.

to blood poured out on a rock (24:7) comes from the idea that one's life was in the blood. If blood were shed, as in a murder, the victim was usually left unburied. The ancients believed that the spilled blood cried out to God for the murder to be punished. Blood poured on a rock would be especially conspicuous since it would stain the rock.

The rusty pot spoke of the filthiness of Israel's sin. The only way to get rid of it was to burn it out, so the destruction of Jerusalem was a part of the cleansing process (24:1-14).

13. *The prophet's wife dies (Ezek. 24:15-27; 33:21-22).*   Ezekiel's final oracle of doom was the most difficult of all. It was an acted oracle. He was told that his wife would die, and when she did, instead of following the usual customs of wailing, going without a turban, going barefooted, having the mouth covered, and eating only "the bread of mourners" (24:17), he was to act as if nothing had happened (24:15-18).

After his wife's death, the people asked the reason for his strange and unnatural behavior, and he told them, as instructed, that the news of Jerusalem's fall would soon reach them. When it did, they were to make no special note of it. Instead, they were to go on with life as usual. As Ezekiel had done at his wife's death, so they were to do when Jerusalem died (24:19-24).

Ezekiel was told that when a fugitive came to bring the news of Jerusalem's fall, a new phase of his ministry would begin (24:25-27). The sequel to this passage appears in Ezekiel 33:21-22. In January 586[9] a messenger arrived in Babylon to tell of Jerusalem's fall. Ezekiel had been silent since the evening before, but when the news came he began to proclaim a new message.

Oracles against foreign nations (Ezek. 25:1–32:32).   As was standard, at least for the more prominent prophets, Ezekiel had a fairly long section on oracles against foreign nations. At times his arrangement of oracles suggests the influence of the Amos traditions, about which Ezekiel undoubtedly knew. His oracles were confined to the nations immediately surrounding Israel, and Egypt. Notably absent are oracles against Babylon and Syria. Syria was probably omitted since it had long ceased being a threat to Judah.

1. *A roll call of the neighbors (Ezek. 25:1-17).*   A series of short oracles was directed against Judah's immediate neighbors—Ammon, Moab, and Edom in Transjordan, and Philistia, on the southwestern Mediterranean Coast. Ammon (25:1-7) had gloated over Judah's misfortune, but its time would soon come (compare Ezek. 21:18-23). A similar charge seems to have been lodged against Moab (25:8-11). Edom had been particularly

---

[9]According to *Oxford Annotated Bible,* RSV note on Ezekiel 33:21.

vindictive, taking advantage of Judah's weakness to enrich itself at Judah's expense. This was especially galling in the light of previous bad relations between the two peoples (25:12-14). The Philistines also seemed to have acted in a similar manner, as had Edom (25:15-17). All these would fall victim to the Babylonians just as Judah had.

2. *Many words against Tyre and the Phoenicians (Ezek. 26:1–28:26).* Ezekiel had a multitude of oracles against Tyre. The Phoenicians, for whom Tyre was the most representative city, had played an important role in the history of the Israelite people. Although the fact is not mentioned in biblical history, the Phoenicians had a vital impact on the language and thoughts of the Hebrews. Furthermore, during the Israelite monarchy Tyre was an important ally of the Israelites. For David and Solomon, as well as for Omri and Ahab at a later time, the Phoenicians furnished building materials and expert help to carry out the huge building program of those kings. They also furnished a sea arm for the Israelite kingdoms. Since Israel had no suitable ports, their alliance with the Phoenicians served Israel well. Throughout most of their histories, the Phoenician and Israelite kingdoms were united by covenants. There is no mention of any military activity between the two peoples.

Despite their previous history of peaceful relations, Ezekiel said that Tyre tried to profit from Jerusalem's troubles. As a result, they would feel the hand of judgment and "They will know that I am the LORD" (26:1-6). Nebuchadnezzar would besiege the city for thirteen years. Finally, its surrender to him would bring an end to Phoenician national life. It would finally be joined to the mainland by Alexander the Great in 333, when he built a causeway to the city in order to conquer it. It continued to exist as an important city down into the New Testament era.[10]

Ezekiel saw the LORD's punishment for Tyre growing out of its gloating over Jerusalem's fall (26:2). He went on to describe in vivid detail what would happen to the city and especially to cities on the coast around Tyre. All this was to demonstrate the LORD's power (26:7-21).

Chapter 27 was a lament or funeral song for Tyre. A description of its ships, the vehicles of commerce which made it the great trading center, is found in 27:1-9. It's armies were mercenaries, hired from other nations (27:10-11). A directory of goods, services, and clients gives an insight into the wide range of Tyre's merchant ships (27:12-24). But all that would be lost, like a ship wrecked in a stormy sea. A funeral song would be sung, while shocked mourners would stare in disbelief at the fate of the great merchant city (27:25-36).

Ezekiel then turned his attention to the king of Tyre. The king was pictured as being puffed up with pride, ripe for the calamity that was

[10]A. S. Kapelrud, "Tyre," *Interpreters' Dictionary of the Bible,* IV, 721–723.

about to befall him (28:1-10). No matter how rich and handsome he was, his evil conduct would be his undoing. He would be hurled to the ground and his city destroyed (28:11-19).

3. *A short word about Sidon (Ezek. 28:20-23).*   As with Tyre, so with Sidon.

4. *Blessings on you, Israel (Ezek. 28:24-26).*   Israel would return to its land, but none of these enemies would bother it again.

5. *The fall of Egypt (Ezek. 29:1–32:32).*   These chapters contain a number of oracles about Egypt, dating from 587 to 571.

a. *That Egyptian crocodile (Ezek. 29:1-16).*   Egypt was like a giant crocodile lying in the Nile River and waiting for a victim to come within its range. The LORD was going to take a large hook and catch the crocodile. Then he would throw it, covered with fishes, into the desert to die (29:1-6*a*).

Israel had gone to Egypt for support, but it was attacked instead. The LORD was going to make Egypt a wasteland because of the way Israel had been treated. The people would be scattered, and only a weak kingdom would continue to exist there (29:6*b*-16).

b. *Egypt is given to Nebuchadnezzar (Ezek. 29:17-21).*   This oracle, dated in 571, was the last dated oracle of the prophet. Nebuchadnezzar had laid siege to Tyre in 585. After thirteen years, Tyre surrendered; but it was a hollow victory for Nebuchadnezzar, since what he gained was not worth the cost.[11] Ezekiel, whose earlier oracles had spoken of the devastation that was coming upon Tyre at Nebuchadnezzar's hand (26:17-21), spoke this oracle that recognized the realities of the situation regarding Tyre. Nebuchadnezzar's army had fought hard, so much so that "Every head was made bald and every shoulder was made bare" (29:18). Since he had failed at Tyre, he was given Egypt as his pay for hard work against Tyre (29:20). Nebuchadnezzar took advantage of a change of kings to invade Egypt in 568, but what he did is uncertain since records of the action have been lost. During the last days of Babylon, there was peace between the two.[12]

c. *Egypt is doomed (Ezek. 30:1-19).*   Continuing the theme of Egypt's conquest by Nebuchadnezzar, Ezekiel compares it to the "day of the LORD" (Amos 5:18). Egypt and all her allies would fall (30:1-9). Nebuchadnezzar was about to carry off all Egypt's wealth and devastate the land (30:10-12). Along with the other destruction would be the destruction of Egypt's idols. Its strong cities would no longer protect it. From one end of the land to the other, devastation would come (30:13-19).

[11]For a fascinating article on Tyre and Phoenicia, see S. W. Matthews, "The Phoenicians: Sea Lords of Antiquity," *National Geographic,* Vol. 146, 149–189.
[12]John Bright, *A History of Israel,* p. 352.

d. *Oracles against the Pharaoh (Ezek. 30:20–32:32).*   Turning from the land in general, the oracles are directed toward the ruler of Egypt, Pharaoh Apries, otherwise known as Hophra (589–570). In 587 Ezekiel said that the LORD would weaken the king of Egypt ("break his arms," 30:22) and strengthen the king of Babylon (30:20-26).

In an allegory of the cedar tree, Pharaoh Hophra was compared to a cedar in Lebanon. In that country the cedar grew to magnificent size, making the country famous for that particular kind of wood. In the allegory, one particular tree outgrew all the rest because it had more water (the Nile River). It was so big that it towered over the other trees. Even the trees of the garden of Eden could not match it (31:1-9).

But the woodcutter came (Babylon). The tree was cut down and left. Its valuable wood became nothing more than a brush pile where the birds nested. That would be the pharaoh's fate. He would die and go to Sheol (the grave), where all men went. Hophra was assassinated in 570 (31:10-18).[13]

A lament was sung for Pharaoh Hophra (32:1-16). He had been a lion among the nations, but God would throw a net over him and cast him to the ground. His body would become food for the birds. Babylon would come with the sword and make the land of Egypt desolate.

The prophet pictured Egypt in the grave with the other nations that had perished—Assyria, Elam, Meshech and Tubal, Edom and the Sidonians. The Pharaoh might not like it, but that would be his end (32:17-32).

Hope for a better day (Ezek. 33:1–48:35).   From chapter 33 on, the oracles of Ezekiel were directed toward encouraging the people to plan for the future, when they would be restored to the land of Palestine. Chapters 33–39 deal with oracles of restoration, while 40–48 deal with the rebuilding of the Temple and the restoration of worship.

1. *Oracles of restoration(Ezek. 33:1–39:29)*

a. *The watchman's responsibility (Ezek. 33:1-20).*   This oracle took a principle and illustrated it by a number of examples. The principle was that a watchman bore the responsibility to warn the community of danger. If he did his job well and the community failed to heed his warning, then the community as a whole bore the blame for whatever happened. If, however, the watchman failed to be alert and to warn the community of imminent danger, then they had to bear the responsibility for his failure (33:1-6).

So it was with a man and his sins. If the prophet warned him, then the man was responsible for his sins. If the prophet failed to warn him, then the prophet had to share the responsibility (33:7-20; see also chapter 18).

[13]John Bright, *A History of Israel,* p. 352.

b. *Oracles against the inhabitants of the land (Ezek. 33:23-29).*   The people who had been left in the land had claimed the abandoned properties for themselves. But that would not be so because they had sinned by continuing to act in the way they had before the exiles had been taken away.

c. *They don't believe you, Ezekiel (Ezek. 33:30-33).*   The people were listening to Ezekiel, but they took him as seriously as they would an entertainer who sang songs to them.

d. *The responsibility of shepherds (Ezek. 34:1-31).*   Shepherds who enjoyed all the benefits derived from their flocks but who failed to take care of them soon would lose them. So it was with the spiritual shepherds of Israel. In looking out for themselves first, they had lost their flocks (34:1-10).

In contrast, the LORD would go out and search for his lost sheep until he found them. He would bring them back and care for them. He would take care of the sick. He would separate the good from the bad. He would protect the poor and mistreated from the strong who would oppress them. A Davidic king would be restored to the throne, and Jerusalem would prosper once more. Then they would know the LORD (34:11-31).

e. *You are going to get it, Edom (Ezek. 35:1-15).*   This sounds like a misplaced oracle against a foreign nation. It probably indicates, however, the depth of the feeling of antagonism that existed between the Israelites and the Edomites, especially after the Edomites seemed to have taken advantage of Judah during the Babylonian war. Edom was accused of saying that it would rule both Judah and Israel (35:10), but the LORD would see that Edom was left desolate (35:15).

f. *Blessings on you, Israel (Ezek. 36:1-38).*   This really is a continuation of the oracle against Edom. The nations surrounding Israel had made fun of it in its time of calamity. The situation was about to change, however. Israel would prosper while they would be humiliated. Israel's cities would be rebuilt when the people returned to Palestine. The land had devoured them before, but that would no longer be so (36:1-15).

When Israel had lived in Palestine before the exile, they had defiled it. They disgraced the name of God. What the LORD was about to do then was for the sake of his own name and reputation. The implication of this was that it was an act of grace toward Israel, something it did not really deserve:

> A new heart I will give you, and a new spirit I will put within you; and I will take out of your flesh the heart of stone and give you a heart of flesh. And I will put my spirit within you, and cause you to walk in my statutes and be careful to observe my ordinances . . . You shall be my people, and I will be your God (36:26-28)

g. *O dry bones, hear the word of the LORD (Ezek. 37:1-14).*   The most famous of Ezekiel's visions perhaps was the vision of the dry bones. The prophet, either physically or in vision, was taken to a battlefield. The corpses of the slain had been left to rot in the sun or to be devoured by animals. As a result, bones were scattered everywhere. The prophet was commanded to preach to the bleached bones. As he preached, the bones came together. In the words of the spiritual

> The toe bone connected to the foot bone;
> the foot bone connected to the ankle bone;
> the ankle bone connected to the leg bone. . . .

When the bones were connected into a skeleton, the prophet was told,

> Prophesy to the breath *(ruach)* . . . and say to the breath *(ruach)* . . . come from the four winds *(ruchoth)*, O breath *(ruach)* and breathe on whose who are slain.

As can be seen by the words in parentheses, there is a play on words or a pun here.

The point of the whole oracles was to continue to express the idea that the Jews would be restored. The nation that was dead and scattered, like the bones, would be brought alive again by the LORD's action.

h. *The two shall be one (Ezek. 37:15-28).*   The prophet was told to take two sticks and to write the word "Judah" on one and "Israel" on the other. Then, he was to hold them in his hand as though they were one. His action would symbolize the reunion of the two parts of the nation under one king.

i. *The LORD and Gog of Magog (Ezek. 38:1–39:29).*   With these oracles, Ezekiel moves into the realm of the apocalyptic. Apocalyptic literature was different from prophetic literature in a number of ways:

It aimed at encouraging the faithful of the LORD's people in a time of trouble instead of telling sinners among the LORD's people that judgment was coming.

It usually was written first and read later instead of spoken first and written later.

It used unusual imagery and numbers in a sort of code, which the readers for whom it was intended understood but which outsiders could not understand.

It spoke of God being directly involved in conflict with the enemy. This was different from the common Old Testament idea of God working through human and natural means.

It was concerned with the triumph of God over the forces of evil in the universe.

The author was usually anonymous since he did the work under the name of a famous person.

Not all these elements were present in the oracles about Gog. They were present in later apocalyptic literature, such as Daniel and the New Testament book of Revelation, as well as in extrabiblical apocalyptic works.

Attempts have been made to identify Gog of Magog (38:2) with some ruler of Ezekiel's time. The best that can be said is that with our present knowledge, no satisfactory identification can be made. This has led to numerous attempts to identify Gog with various nations over the centuries by those who see these oracles purely in a futuristic sense with unfortunate results.

Perhaps the best that can be said is that Gog was representative of those forces that have opposed, and will continue to oppose, the LORD's rule in the world. This would seem to be supported by the fact that the description of Israel (whom Gog was to invade) was an idealized description that had not existed before Ezekiel's time, nor has it since. Ezekiel expected it in the near future (39:1-20).

The invasion would be the signal for the LORD to intervene by unleashing the forces of nature against him. "Then they will know that I am the LORD" (38:23). The devastation of the armies of Gog would be so great that Israel would be burning abandoned weapons (those with wooden handles) as firewood, thus saving their own trees. It would take them seven months to bury all of Gog's dead soldiers as they attempted to clean up the land.

That Ezekiel was talking about something in the near future would seem to be indicated by the closing part of the oracle, where he once again spoke of Israel's restoration to the land. This would be done to show the LORD's holiness. "Then the people will know that I am the LORD" (39:21-29). *never equaled what it was before*

2. *The restoration of the Temple (Ezek. 40:1-48:35).* The remainder of the book of Ezekiel deals with the rebuilding of the Temple and its related buildings, along with the altar for sacrifices (40:1-43:27); the priests (44:1-31); the division of the country (45:1-6); the prince's lands and rules of the conduct (45:7-46:18); the Temple foundations (47:1-12); the division of the land (47:13-48:29); and the names of the gates of Jerusalem (48:30-35).

This interest in priestly things was in keeping with Ezekiel's interest in the priesthood. He of all the prophets would be the most likely to try to put the principles preached by the prophets into practical activities. For him, this would not only include social action but also worship activity.

The Temple would continue to be the center of such worship activity in a restored community. Thus the vision of the Temple, with details of its dimensions, would be of interest to Ezekiel. He, as a former priest, would be receptive to such a vision (40:1–42:20).

As he saw the overpowering presence of the LORD leave the Temple (11:22-25), so he envisioned its return to the restored community and the rebuilt Temple. It was to be a new day when the people with new hearts of flesh would be obedient to the LORD's commands (36:26), would be ashamed of their old ways, and would serve the LORD alone in faithfulness (43:1-12).

The responsibility of priestly service would be limited to those priests who were the descendants of Zadok. All other Levites would serve as helpers, but they would not be allowed to serve as priests because of their unfaithfulness (44:10-31).

Special lands were to be set aside for the LORD, including the area around the Temple (45:1-6). The ruler, now called the prince instead of king, was also allotted certain territory; but he was given severe warnings about his conduct toward the people (45:7-9). Instructions were given about what the prince was to receive in the way of offerings from the people. He, in turn, was to furnish animals and materials for national offerings in important festivals and other holy days (45:10–46:15).

Among the unusual features of this series of visions was the description of a stream of water flowing from the base of the Temple toward the Jordan Rift and the Dead Sea. The farther it flowed, the deeper the stream was. When it reached the Dead Sea, the Dead Sea's stagnant waters came to life with all kinds of animals and fish.

One of the features of the Garden of Eden was that it was well watered. To people who lived in a dry land, a stream of fresh water was priceless. For Ezekiel in his idealized vision of the restored land, the "LORD in his holy Temple" would be the source of life for a land and a people who had been to the grave of exile but had returned from the dead. Even the Dead Sea would live in that ideal time (47:1-12).

Ezekiel: a summary.   Ezekiel was a prophet with a number of differences:

1. While he, like Jeremiah, had been a priest, his priestly background seems to have had more effect upon him than Jeremiah's had upon him.
2. The visions of Ezekiel were much more elaborate and numerous than were those of earlier prophets. As such, he was a connecting link between the prophets and the later apocalyptic writers.
3. He made extensive use of allegory as a teaching device.
4. He made a major contribution, with Jeremiah, to prophetic thought in his teaching of individual responsibility.

5. Perhaps his most important contribution was to give meaning to Jewish religious life after the calamity of 587. His work served as a bridge between the pre-exilic religion of Israel and later Judaism.

The End Has Come for Babylon

The Babylonian (or Chaldean) Empire was like a shooting star. It flashed across the heavens briefly and then burned out.

THE DECLINE OF BABYLON

When Nebuchadnezzar died in 562, Babylon began to die. His successor Evil-merodach (562–560) released King Jehoiachin of Judah from prison, but he died in the same year. Other kings came to the throne, Nabonidus (556–539) being the last one. He aroused great antagonism by trying to make major changes in the national religion. Nabonidus was interested in excavating and exploring ruins and abandoned temples—a sixth-century B.C. archaeologist! He left the running of the kingdom to his son Belshazzar. He even refused to come to Babylon for the New Year's Festival, the chief religious festival of the year and one in which the king played the leading role. This brought a major division among the people just as a new power was rising in the East.

CYRUS THE PERSIAN

Babylon's "most dangerous rival" was Media. When a revolt led by the Persian king Cyrus broke out in the Median empire, Nabonidus may have supported it. But Cyrus rapidly became a dangerous force to be reckoned with. By 550 Media was under his control. He defeated an alliance of Egypt, Babylon, and Lydia by conquering Lydia in 546, Babylon in 539, and penetrating all the way to the Egyptian frontier by 538.[14]

The Exile's Great Unknown Prophet

Cyrus was to be the instrument of Israel's restoration to the land. The very fact that the people were sent back home was an unusual action by an unusual ruler. A prophet in the exile saw Cyrus as the LORD's

[14]For further details, see John Bright, *A History of Israel*, pp. 353–354, 360–361, and Martin Noth, *The History of Israel*, pp. 300–302.

Figure 11–2. The ruins of the Ishtar Gate suggest the magnificence of Babylon at the height of its power.

Courtesy of Ewing Galloway.

instrument to bring about his aim to restore Israel to its land. He was the second prophet who, with Ezekiel, helped the people to adjust to their situation.

THE MAN

In a discussion of Isaiah of Jerusalem,[15] the arguments were advanced for the belief that the book of Isaiah was the product of the ministry of more than one prophet. Many dispute such a theory, but it also has an equal number of strong advocates. An acceptance of a multiple authorship is assumed here. As a result, the prophet will be referred to as Deutero-Isaiah (Second Isaiah).

When one assumes that there was at least one other prophet whose work is found in the book of Isaiah (Isa. 40–66), little can be said about him. The Second Isaiah was among the exiles, as was Ezekiel. He obviously

[15]See pp. 218–239.

was an admirer and probably considered himself to be a disciple of the prophet Isaiah of Jerusalem, even though 100 years separated them.

Much can be said about his work, for he, along with Ezekiel, gave the Jews reasons to continue to believe in their God. Without their work, the religion of Israel would have had difficulty in surviving. They gave the devout Jews a reason for their devotion.

THE BOOK   *2ⁿᵈ Isiah*

The book, in reality, is not a separate book as the Old Testament now stands; it is chapters 40–66 of the book of Isaiah. It falls naturally into two parts: 40–55 and 56–66. The first was set in Babylon; the second seems to be set in the restored community in Jerusalem.

Comfort to Israel (Isa. 40–55)

The prophet's call (Isa. 40:1-11).   The keynote of Isaiah 40–55 was reassurance to a nation who had been trampled underfoot by Babylon, reviled and scoffed at by her neighbors, and exiled in a distant land. Rebuke enough had been flung at them. The LORD, through the prophet, sent a word of comfort:

> Speak tenderly to Jerusalem,
>   and cry to her
> that her warfare is ended,
>   that her iniquity is pardoned,
> that she has received from the LORD's hand
>   double for all her sins (40:2).

Such a condition could have existed only after the fall of Jerusalem. Only then could it be said, "She has received from the LORD's hand double [punishment] for all her sins" (40:2).

A dialogue follows the opening lines. It would seem to be the prophet's unique way of describing the LORD's call to him. He was told to be like a king's herald, going through the land and announcing the king's imminent appearance. He was to see that the rough places in the road were smoothed down and that the chuckholes were filled in. The LORD's overpowering presence was about to make itself known in the midst of the people as he led them from exile in a new exodus back to Palestine (40:3-5).

A command came to "cry" or preach. When the prophet-to-be asked what the nature of his message would be, he was told that he was to say that everything would pass away like the grass and the flower except the word of God. It would "stand forever" (40:6-8).

He was to herald the good tidings to Jerusalem from the high mountains that the LORD was about to return to rule the land with strength, justice, and compassion:

> He will feed his flock like a shepherd,
>   he will gather the lambs in his arms,
> he will carry them in his bosom,
>   and gently lead those that are with young (40:11).

In praise of the LORD, the Creator (Isa. 40:12-32).   The prophet's job was not an easy one. He faced the questions of the cynics who said, "My way is hid from God and my right is disregarded by my God" (40:27). They could understand punishment for their sins, but what had happened to them seemed to have gone far beyond the punishment due for their sins. The prophet's answer was a magnificent poem on the LORD as Creator.

The poem consisted largely of rhetorical questions—that is, questions whose answers were already known both to the asker and the one to whom they were asked. By those questions he pointed out that the LORD had created the universe (the waters, the heavens, and the earth). He consulted no one, for the nations were as nothing to him (40:12-17).

He could not be compared to idols, for they were only wooden gods created by a puny man (40:18-20).

> Have you not known? Have you not heard?
>   Has it not been told you from the beginning?
>   Have you not understood from the foundations of the earth?
> It is he who sits above the circle of the earth,
>   and its inhabitants are like grasshoppers;
> who stretches out the heavens like a curtain,
>   and spreads them like a tent to dwell in;
> who brings princes to nought,
>   and makes the rulers of the earth as nothing (40:21-23).

A king was hardly seated on his throne before he passed away, and his place was taken by another (40:24).

There was no one to whom the LORD could be compared; he had created the universe, giving each heavenly body its name and placing it in the created order (40:25-26). His people, therefore, had no reason to question whether he was concerned for them for:

> The LORD is the everlasting God,
>   the Creator of the ends of the earth.
> He does not faint or grow weary,
>   his understanding is unsearchable (40:28-29).

The LORD gives power to every age. He gives power to the aged ("him who has no might"), children ("youths"), and those at the peak of their physical strength ("young men"):

> They who wait for the LORD shall renew their strength,
>   they shall mount up with wings like eagles,
> they shall run and not be weary,
>   they shall walk and not faint (40:31).

The young children still have time to reach their full potential ("mount up . . . like eagles"); the young men can still reach high goals ("run and not be weary"); while the elderly can still have a meaningful life ("walk and not faint") (40:29-31).

The nations on trial (Isa. 41:1-29). The LORD was calling the nations to judgment, where they would have a chance to defend themselves (41:1). While he was not named, the prophet described the rapid advances Cyrus was making. But Cyrus was an agent of the LORD.

> Who has performed and done this,
>   calling the generations from the beginning?
> I, the LORD, the first,
>   and with the last; I am He (41:4).

The nations were trembling at the news of the Persian advances. The idol makers were trying to encourage one another, hoping their idols would save them. But the LORD had taken Israel from the ends of the earth. Israel was the LORD's servant and could be assured of his presence and help (41:2-10). Israel's enemies would be put to shame, for the LORD would help Israel triumph over its enemies (41:11-16). Furthermore, he would make the desert bloom for Israel.

The false gods were challenged, therefore, to submit evidence of their ability to produce results. They could not, of course, since they were nothing. Only the LORD had the power to move nations and men at his command. The coming of Cyrus (still not named) had been announced to Israel. When one looked to the idols for any help, they found nothing (41:17-29).

Pg. 279

The first Servant Song (Isa. 42:1-4)

1. *The Servant Songs.* One of the unique features of Second Isaiah is the Servant Songs. These are four poems (42:1-4; 49:1-6; 50:4-11; 52:13–53:12). These are called the Servant Songs because they introduce a figure who is referred to as the LORD's Servant. Each poem adds more information about the Servant, the climax coming in Isaiah 52:13–53:12, where the Servant's trial and death are described.

Numerous questions are raised about the poems, especially in two major areas: (1) What is their relationship to the rest of 40–55? Did they originate separately from 40–55 or as a part of it? (2) Who was the Servant?

As for the first of the questions, whether they originated separately or not, they are so skillfully blended into the rest of the material that they do not seriously interrupt it. The first poem, for example, climaxes the section on the LORD's judgment of the nations. The Servant was portrayed as the instrument of that judgment.

The question of the Servant's identification will be left until the last of the four poems is discussed.

2. *The Servant's mission (Isa. 42:1-4).*   In this poem, the LORD describes the mission of the Servant, who would "bring forth justice to the nations" (42:1). Unlike conquerors, he would do his work quietly; but his gentle manner would not deter him in his object.

> He will not fail or be discouraged
>   till he has established justice in the earth;
>   and the coastlands wait for his law (42:4).

I am the LORD your God (Isa. 42:5–46:13).   Oracles in these chapters constantly return to a single theme: "I am the LORD your God." Like the theme notes of a symphony, they recur time and time again. Different subjects are discussed—idols and idol makers, Cyrus, the restoration of Israel—but they all come back to the theme.

God created heavens and earth with all of its inhabitants. His Servant had been given to bring light to the people. He alone would do it, for no idol could share his glory (42:5-9).

The prophet broke out in a hymn of praise, calling on the whole creation to praise God for his fight against his enemies (42:10-13). In the battle he would help his people, even though they had been blind to what he did for them. Even so, the LORD would keep his promises (42:14-17).

Unfortunately, all that Israel had seen had been meaningless to the people. The LORD had wanted to save them, but they had been led from the land. The LORD had given them over to the enemy because they had sinned against him. They had learned nothing from their experience (42:18-25).

Yet the LORD would rescue his people, because they were his.

> When you pass through the waters I will be with you;
>   and through the rivers, they shall not overwhelm you;
> when you walk through fire you shall not be burned,
>
>   . . .
>
> For I am the LORD your God,
>   the Holy One of Israel, your Savior (43:2-3).

Others would be given in exchange for Israel. A new exodus would take place, when the people were brought back to the land; they were the LORD's people, created for his glory (43:1-7).

In using the figure of a trial again, the prophet portrayed God as summoning the nations to demonstrate that he was God above all others. No god was formed before him; none would be formed after him. They were witnesses to the fact. He had saved Israel before any other God came along. He was the only one who could deliver them now (43:8-13).

To prove his power, he was sending an army to conquer Babylon. Many years before, he had led the nation in the first exodus from Egypt; but that was past history. A new thing was about to happen. A new exodus was about to take place (43:14-21).

Yet Israel had sinned against God by failing to worship him properly; but he would not hold their sins against them. Instead, he challenged those who accused him of wrongdoing to bring their witnesses to court (43:22-28). He had created Israel. Israel was his servant, the people he loved. He would bless them so that they would thrive like plants that had plenty of water. Gradually they would come to recognize that he was the first, last, and only God (44:1-8).

In contrast to the living God were the idols. In a scathing satire on idols (44:9-20), the prophet said that both idols and idol makers were nothing! After all, a man chose a tree or metal and fashioned it with his hand to look like himself. The maker of wooden idols took a tree, burned part of it to cook his food and to warm himself, and used the other part to make a god to worship. Such a person was stupid! "He feeds on ashes; a deluded mind has led him astray, and he cannot deliver himself or say, 'Is there not a lie in my right hand?' " (44:20).

The LORD had swept away Israel's "transgressions like a cloud" (44:21-22). The prophet broke out into song at the prospect of the LORD's redemption of the people. He who was doing this had created heavens and earth, had confounded the wisdom of men, and had promised that Jerusalem would be rebuilt. He was the one, furthermore, who raised up Cyrus the Persian to be his servant to rebuild Jerusalem (44:21-28).

In an address to Cyrus[16] (45:1-7), the LORD promised to go before him and prepare the way for his conquests. What Cyrus was about to do was for the sake of the LORD's people. He had been chosen as the LORD's servant.

> I call you [Cyrus] by your name,
>   I surname you, though you do not know me.
> I am the LORD, and there is no other,
>   besides me there is no God.
> I gird you, though you do not know me.

. . .

[16]Cyrus is called *Meschiach* (Messiah) according to the *LXX* in 45:1.

> I form light and create darkness,
>   I make weal and create woe,
>   I am the LORD, who does all these things (45:4-5,7).

Using a figure from Jeremiah, the prophet pronounces woe on one who strives against his maker, like a pot against the potter (Jer. 18). The created ones cannot question the Creator's actions. The man Cyrus was created to do the LORD's work in freeing his people. The nations would acknowledge that Israel's God was supreme. He was the creator, and he spoke the truth. No idol could take his place. The judicial decision must be made, therefore. Who was the Creator? Who is the only true God? Who could save the people? The LORD, the God of Israel. In him is salvation for to him, "Every knee shall bow, every tongue shall swear" (45:8-25).

In contrast, the gods of Babylon had to be carried on the backs of donkeys! They could not go from place to place, much less create anything. Their makers had to move them from one place to another. They could even be captured and carried away. Yet the LORD had cared for Jacob from the beginning; and he would be with them to the end. Could he be compared, then, to a god made of gold by a human craftsman? An idol that had to be carried about on men's shoulders? Absolutely not:

> For I am God, and there is no other;
>   I am God, and there is none like me,
> declaring the end from the beginning
>   and from ancient times things not yet done (46:9-10).

He was the one who would soon deliver Israel (46:1-13).

Sing a sad song for Babylon (Isa. 47:1-15).   The prophet sang a lament for Babylon. It would be reduced to slavery. Even though the LORD had permitted it to take Israel into exile, it had been proud. It thought it would rule forever, but its end would come (47:1-7). Though it thought that it would never be like a childless widow, it would be (47:8-9). It thought it could do evil and no one would know it, but ruin would come upon it quickly (47:10-11). Its sorcerers and wise men who claimed they could save it were like stubble and would fail because they could not deliver it (47:12-15).

You have heard, now see all this (Isa. 48:1-22).   The prophet sums up in this chapter what he had said in chapters 40–47. The chapter marks a dividing point in chapters 40–55. In it the LORD reminded the people that he had revealed the past to them long ago. Now, he was about to reveal new things to them—things they did not know. These things had been kept from Israel because of its previous inclinations toward unfaithfulness. Because of that record, what the LORD was about to do was for his own sake. He would not give his glory to anyone else. It was the LORD who had created the heavens and the earth (48:1-13).

No one would have predicted that Cyrus would have attacked Babylon; yet the LORD had been behind his success. The prophet adds a note of reminder: "And now the LORD god has sent me and his spirit" (48:16). If the people had followed the LORD,

> Then your peace would have been like a river,
>
> . . .
>
> your offspring would have been like the sand,
>   and your descendants like its grains;
> their name would never be cut off
>   or destroyed from before me (49:18-19).

The oracle ends with the prophet urging the people to begin the new exodus, to shout it to the ends of the earth, "The LORD has redeemed his servant Jacob." He would lead them through the deserts, making water flow from the rocks (48:14-22).

The second Servant Song: the Servant's responsibility (Isa. 49:1-6). This second Servant poem goes further than the first in describing the Servant and his role in the world. Instead of being written in the third person, this poem was written in the first person as the Servant described his call from God. Like Jeremiah, he felt that from birth he had been chosen by the LORD for his role. The LORD spoke of him as being like a secret weapon (49:1-2).

In this oracle is the first suggestion about the Servant's identity: "He said to me, 'You are my servant, Israel, in whom I will be glorified' " (49:3). The Servant protested that he had worked, but his strength was wasted. He realized that the LORD had his reward (49:3-4).

After the identification in verse 3, verses 5 and 6 take away some of the certainty. After restating that he was "formed from the womb to be his servant," the LORD went on to state that one of the Servant's responsibilities would be to bring Jacob and Israel back to the LORD. But that was not a big enough job. The Servant was also given the responsibility of being "a light to the nations," so that the LORD's salvation might "reach to the ends of the earth" (49:4-6).

Because verse 7 also refers to "the servant of rulers," some people take it also to be a part of the second Servant Song. According to verse 7, the role would be reversed, the kings serving the one who had once been their servant (49:7).

The return of the people (Isa. 49:7-13). This seems, with verse 7, to be a response to the second Servant poem. The reference to "you" would seem to refer to the Servant, who has been helped by the LORD and given "as a covenant to the people." They were called upon to come forth as the LORD would lead them from exile, seeing to their physical needs along the way (49:8-12). The prophet interrupted to sing a song of praise because the LORD had comforted the people (49:13).

Zion shall be comforted (Isa. 49:14–50:3).   This is the first of what are sometimes called the "Zion poems," which make up much of chapters 50–55. They deal with the restoration of Jerusalem, frequently called Zion in the Old Testament. This poem begins with a charge by Zion (as though it were a person), claiming that she had been forgotten by the LORD. The response was that the LORD could no more forget Zion than a mother could forget her suckling child (49:15). The LORD would not forget her. His plans were for her rebuilding, her enemies becoming as her ornaments for a bridal dress (49:14-18).

The time would come when the land would not hold the people. Then the people would have to live in other kingdoms simply because there would not be enough room in Palestine. No power, however, could keep the LORD's people captive; he would take the side of Israel in court and win the case. The opponent would be punished by death (49:19-25).

> Then all flesh shall know
>   that I am the LORD your Savior.
>   and your Redeemer, the Mighty One of Jacob (49:26).

Some would think that because the LORD had divorced his bride (Israel) this meant he could not redeem her again. Such was Israel's law of divorce (Deut. 24:1-4). But he was God, not man. He could forgive sin, and he could redeem what had been put away. After all, creation did his bidding (50:1-3).

The third Servant Song: the Servant's submission (Isa. 50:4-11).   The Servant again spoke, as in the second poem. He spoke of his God-given ability to comfort and encourage the weary and downtrodden. He was also open to the teaching that the LORD gave him day by day. But his work aroused opposition. He faced it with courage (50:4-5).

> I gave my back to the smiters,
>   and my cheeks to those who pulled out the beard;
> I hid not my face
>   from shame and spitting (50:6).

With God's help he had not been discouraged by the insults and persecution. He depended upon God, who would stand up for him in court. No one could bring a charge against him when the Supreme Judge of all the universe was on his side. His opponents would wear out before they would be successful (50:7-9).

He urged all who feared God to keep up their courage. Those who were trying to plot against others ("all you who kindle a flame") would answer to the LORD in the end (50:10-11).

284

Joy for Jerusalem and beyond (Isa. 51:1–52:12). Those who were wanting the LORD's salvation only had to be reminded how he had blessed Abraham. When it seemed that there was no hope, Isaac, his son and heir, was born. He would bring joy and gladness to Jerusalem. It would become a new garden of Eden (51:1-3).

But that would not be all. The LORD would extend his teaching to the nations. He would extend his rule over them. The heavens would disappear, but the LORD's deliverance would last forever. So, the one who was in the right should endure taunts and insults because the deliverance the LORD would bring was everlasting (51:4-8).

Verses 9-11 call for the LORD to wake up and deliver his people as he had done in the exodus from Egypt. If he would do so, those who were traveling back to Jerusalem would reach it "with gladness, singing and shouting for joy."

The LORD responded by assuring them that he was the same one who had created heavens and earth. Yet, they lived in constant fear of the Babylonians, from whom they had been freed. Those who were still prisoners would soon be freed. He was the Creator, and Jerusalem's inhabitants were his people whom he would teach and protect (51:12-16).

Jerusalem was called upon to awaken. Its punishment was over. It had experienced the double disasters of war and hunger. The anguish of the last days of Jerusalem would now be given to those who had caused them in Jerusalem (51:17-23).

Again Jerusalem was called to awaken and to put on its most beautiful garments, for the days of sadness and oppression were over.

> How beautiful upon the mountains
>   are the feet of him who brings good tidings,
> who publishes peace, who brings good tidings of good,
>   who publishes salvation,
>   who says to Zion, "Your God reigns" (52:7).

Watchmen, who usually raised their voices in alarm, were to "sing for joy" as they watched "the return of the LORD to Zion" (52:8). Even the waste places were to break forth in singing, for the LORD had redeemed his people. Even the ends of the earth would see the LORD's salvation. In preparation for the return, they were to purify themselves. They did not have to leave Babylon in a hurry. They were not fugitives, but they were a people led and guarded by the LORD (52:1-12).

The fourth Servant Song: the Servant's trial and death (Isa. 52:13–53:12). most important With this poem, the Servant Songs reach their climax. Unlike poem 1, where the LORD was the speaker; poem 2, where the Servant describes his call from the LORD; and poem 3, where the Servant talks of his initial suffering; poem 4 has at least two different speakers.

The poem was divided into five stanzas of three verses each (52:13-15; 53:1-3; 53:4-6; 53:7-9; and 53:10-12). In stanza 1, the LORD speaks *about* the Servant. In stanzas 2–5, another speaks about the Servant.

1. *The appearance of the Servant (Isa. 53:13-15)*.   The LORD introduced the Servant as one who had been given a high place. Yet his physical appearance was shocking because he had been disfigured. When the kings of the earth saw him, they were astonished. Somehow all of this seems to tie in to the Servant's commission to be a "light to the nations" (49:6).

2. *The rejection of the Servant (Isa. 53:1-3)*.   The things reported about the Servant were unbelieveable, especially since the LORD's power was said to have been revealed through him. He was like a dried-up, scrubby desert plant.[17] Men were not attracted to him, for he really was not compelling in his manner. Indeed, he was hated and shunned—a lonely man who knew deep sorrow.

3. *The Servant suffering for others (Isa. 53:4-6)*.   The narrator became personally involved as he described the Servant's suffering for "us." This kind of suffering, in which an innocent person suffers for another, is called "vicarious" suffering. In this section, the personal pronouns "we," "us," and "our" are used ten times to emphasize that the Servant had suffered for the narrator and those with him.

> All we like sheep have gone astray;
>   we have turned every one to his own way;
> and the LORD has laid on him
>   the iniquity of us all (53:6).

4. *The death and burial of the Servant (Isa. 53:7-9)*.   The Servant was like a lamb about to be slaughtered or a sheep about to be sheared. The sheep is not noted for its intelligence. It will stand still and mute as it is being killed. So the Servant offered no defense as he was unjustly condemned to death. He was "cut off out of the land of the living." When he died, he was buried along with the wicked (which he was not) and the rich (which he was not).

5. *The vindication of the Servant*[18] *(Isa. 53:10-12)*.   The LORD had permitted the Servant's suffering on behalf of the sins of others. The Servant would see his reward because his action would lead many to be counted as righteous. Instead of physical children, he would have children of righteousness—those who owed their right relationship to God to him. Then the astonishing thing would happen. The one who was despised

---

[17]John L. McKenzie, "Second Isaiah," *Anchor Bible*, Vol. 20 (New York, Doubleday and Co., 1968), p. 131.

[18]The basic idea for this outline is from J. Leo Green, Professor of Old Testament, Southeastern Baptist Theological Seminary.

and rejected would be classed with the great and the strong because of the unselfish act he had done for others.

6. *Who was the Servant?*[19] This is a problem that has intrigued interpreters for centuries. The answers can be divided up into two groups: (1) those who identify the Servant in a group or collective sense and (2) those who identify the Servant as an individual.

Those who argue for the first option point out that the Old Testament writers frequently spoke of a group as an individual. Throughout Second Isaiah, as well as the other prophets, all the people of Israel were spoken of as Israel, Jacob, Jerusalem, or Zion. Furthermore, Israel (the nation) is identified as the Servant in Isaiah 49:3, as well as in several other places in Second Isaiah (41:9; 43:10; 44:1). Both Jewish and non-Jewish interpreters argue for Israel as the Servant.

There are those who identify Israel as the Servant; not Israel as a whole, but the remnant (or ideal) Israel. The Servant would not be Israel as it was, but Israel as it ought to be.

Many are convinced that the fourth song indicates that the Servant had to be an individual. A number of historical persons have been suggested—among them the prophet Jeremiah himself or King Jehoiachin. Even Moses has been suggested since Second Isaiah speaks so often of the new Exodus.[20]

As there are those who identify the Servant with the ideal Israel, so there are those who identify him with an ideal person. Such a person would show Israel the revolutionary idea that through his suffering the door was open for the guilty to repent and to enjoy the LORD's salvation.[21]

Christian interpreters, beginning with the early church, have looked upon the Servant as Jesus Christ. There can be little doubt that Jesus interpreted his own life in terms of the Servant, more than he did in terms of the kingly Messiah of Isaiah 9 and 11. When one does this, however, one must realize that, as a Christian, he is looking back into the Servant Songs through Christian eyeglasses. If such a person had been in the position of Second Isaiah, would that person have been so positive in his identification? Perhaps the safer estimate is that found in the statement: "The Servant is the climactic figure in the prophetic line, who will proclaim the way of salvation and be himself the medium of salvation."[22]

Israel is assured (Isa. 54:1-17). This song of assurance reminds one of the picture of the "lonely widow" of Lamentations 1, who had lost her

---

[19]An excellent discussion of this problem can be found in McKenzie, "Second Isaiah," pp. xxxviii–lv.

[20]McKenzie, "Second Isaiah," p. xlvii.

[21]*Ibid.*, p. liv–lv.

[22]*Ibid.*, p. lv.

children but who now was assured that her children would be more than others who were married. It was a time to make enlargement plans, for prosperity was just around the corner (54:1-3).

The prophet goes back to the familiar husband-wife figure to speak of how the LORD had gone away from Israel for a while because of her unfaithfulness. But now he had taken her back because of his great love for her (54:4-8).

It was like Noah's time when he had destroyed the earth. As he had promised Noah never to destroy the earth, so he made a covenant with Israel that would not be removed (54:9-10).

The new Jerusalem would be built, many sons would be born, and enemies would be defeated. Since he made the weapon makers, he would see that no weapon would be made that could destroy Israel (54:11-17).

The great invitation (Isa. 55:1-13).   The climax of Isaiah 40–55 comes in an invitation for all to come and accept the LORD's free banquet. He would make an everlasting covenant, for this banquet would be a covenant-making meal. Israel would call nations that did not know the LORD. They would come to "the LORD your God, and . . . the Holy One of Israel" (55:1-5). The invitation was to

> Seek the LORD while he may be found,
>   call upon him while he is near;
> let the wicked forsake his way,
>   and the unrighteous man his thoughts;
> let him return to the LORD, that he may have mercy on him,
>   and to our God, for he will abundantly pardon (55:6-7).

God's thinking and way of doing things are far beyond man's. When his word was sent out, it accomplished the purpose for which he sent it out.

So Israel would "go in joy" and "be led forth in peace" (55:12). Even nature would break out in celebration of the happy times. Where thorns grew before would be trees as a sign that this was the LORD's doing (55:8-13).

Oracles to a restored people (Isa. 56:1–66:24).   These oracles no longer had the unbroken note of comfort found in Isaiah 40–55. Instead, there were mingled notes of comfort and rebuke, suggesting that the ideal conditions and conduct anticipated by the prophet had given way to the harsh realities of living once more in the land. When the exiles returned, they were confronted by at least two major problems: (1) Most of them were not prepared for the barrenness of the land compared with the lush, well-watered valleys along the Tigris and Euphrates rivers. (2) They encountered the people who had remained, who (a) looked upon the land as theirs by right of possession, and (b) looked upon themselves as still being true followers of the God of Israel. The returning exiles were not willing to agree on either point, thus setting a troublesome conflict that would continue for more than several hundred years. So the oracles in this section differ a great deal, even from one oracle to the next. If they are from one prophet, they may reflect a variety of moods. Some suggest that more than one prophet was involved and, furthermore, that he was not Second Isaiah. However, a changed situation could account for many of the changes found here.

The LORD's salvation is for all (Isa. 56:1-8).   In light of a later movement in Judaism, known as particularism, which rigidly held to the belief that Jewish people were the only people of the LORD, this oracle that extended the LORD's salvation and deliverance to such outcasts as eunuchs and foreigners showed a universal spirit in keeping with Isaiah 40–55. The eunuch, a man who through surgery had lost his ability to function sexually, was forbidden in the law to ever be a part of the congregation of Israel. The book of Deuteronomy required kind treatment for foreigners, but it did not include them in the congregation of Israel. The prophet foresaw, however, a time when even the most extreme outcasts would be received by the LORD on the basis of their faithfulness to him.

The beast and bad leaders (Isa. 56:9-12).   The leaders were beastly in their behavior, so the LORD called for the beasts of the field to come and devour them.

The idol worshipers are back (Isa. 57:1-13).   Not all who came back remained faithful. Some were drawn away again by the lust-filled fertility cults. They soon were participating in the Baal cult and the cult of Molech, which, among other things, involved child sacrifice. But the LORD would not stand for such to go on. Only those who followed him would possess the land.

Peace to all but the wicked (Isa. 57:14-21).   The call came to prepare the way for the people. The LORD was with the person who had "a contrite and humble spirit" (57:15). It was true he had punished Israel because Israel continually backslid. But he would heal the backslider and give peace "to the far and near." Only the wicked would not have peace.

Holy day religion (Isa. 58:1-14).   The LORD could not fault the people for their Temple attendance. They were conscientious in keeping the law and sacrificing and fasting. But it did not affect their relations with their workers or their neighbors. Kindness and justice did not increase when worship increased. The hungry were still just as hungry, and the naked had no clothes. When the worship was translated into action, then the presence of the LORD would be near (58:1-9). Only then could God's blessing flow like a spring of cold water and the cities be rebuilt. Worship and service were twins—one must accompany the other (58:10-14).

Call for repentance (Isa. 59:1-21).   This oracle complains about a lack of justice in the land. For this reason, a wall had separated God and the people. It was not the LORD's ability to save that had created the situation; rather, it was the people's sin (59:1-13).

> Justice is turned back,
>   and righteousness stands afar off;
> for truth has fallen in the public squares,
>   and uprightness cannot enter (59:14).

God would give justice, both to the just and the unjust. He would subdue the enemy and redeem his people. His spirit would come upon them and upon their children to follow them (59:15-21).

Poems about Zion (Isa. 60:1–62:12)

1. *Jerusalem's glorious future (Isa. 60:1-22).*   Jerusalem had been in darkness for many years, but now the light of the LORD would once more shine in it as his presence was felt. Its people would return, along with the nations bringing gifts to the LORD from the desert countries, from the Mediterranean countries. Jerusalem would be open to all nations as the Temple would arise in new splendor.

> The sun shall be no more
>   your light by day,
> nor for brightness shall the moon
>   give light to you by night;
> but the LORD will be your everlasting light,
>   and your God will be your glory (60:19).

2. *Good tidings to the lowly of Zion (Isa. 61:1-11).*   This oracle, made even more famous by Luke's account of Jesus' sermon at Nazareth (Luke 4:16-30), originally was a word of assurance to the poor and oppressed of the land of Palestine. The poor rarely had a champion, one who would protect their rights. The reference to the "day of vengeance of our God" meant the day when God would right those things that were wrong. The mourners would become rejoicers. The nation that had been poor and oppressed would be restored, and those who had mistreated the people would know the sting of justice just as Zion would know the joy of justice. This would come about because the LORD loved justice and hated wrong (61:1-9). The oracle ends with a call to praise God (61:10-11).

3. *New days and new names for Jerusalem (Isa. 62:1-12).*   Jerusalem's restoration would not only bring a new day but also new names that stood for its changed condition. Before, it had been called "Forsaken" and

"Desolate" (62:4); but now it would be called Hephzibah ("my delight is in her") and Beulah ("married"). It would be like a newly married woman (62:1-5).

The watchman's responsibility would be to remind the LORD of his obligations to Jerusalem until all he had promised was done. He had promised that hunger would no longer be a problem for them (62:6-9).

Jerusalem was under obligation also to prepare the way for the returning exiles. They, too, would share in the new names, being called "The Holy People, the redeemed of the LORD," "Sought Out, a city not forsaken" (62:10-12).

The day of the LORD's vengeance (Isa. 63:1-6). This rather gory oracle pictured the LORD as a fierce warrior. The metaphors are mixed somewhat, since he was also a winemaker treading the grapes in the winepress. The nations were the grapes being trodden down by the LORD, who was giving them the punishment they deserved. Redemption would come because justice was done.

A prayer and its answer (Isa. 63:7–65:25). As a sort of prologue to the prayer that follows, the prophet reminded the people of the LORD's past blessings as opposed to the people's failures. They were reminded once again how the LORD had led the patriarchs in their wanderings and the people in the exodus (63:7-14).

The prophet then prayed, addressing him as "our Father" and "our Redeemer from of old" (63:16). He asked for help to keep from erring. He prayed that the LORD would give aid against Israel's enemies. He was unlike any God man had seen. He helped the good and punished evil men. Israel had come to him polluted, and he had hidden his face from them (63:15 to 64:7).

He pleaded that the LORD not be angry, for he was their father. Their land was wilderness, their Temple was burned, and the beautiful places ruined (64:8-12).

The LORD answered that he was ready to answer prayer, but no one had sought him. While he waited, they had rebelled against him by sacrificing to pagan gods. They pretended to be so holy that others could not touch them, but the One who was really holy was angry at their lack of holiness. He would punish them as they deserved. He would not destroy all of them, however, for the tribe of Judah would be chosen to receive his blessings. The Plain of Sharon, which really never had been usable to Israel because it was covered with forests, would become a pasture for sheep. The Valley of Achor, symbol of everything bad because of the incident involving Achan (Josh. 7), would be a place of rest for flocks (65:1-11).

Those who were rebellious would be destined for the sword for the evil they had done; nothing would turn out right for them. In contrast, the LORD's servants would prosper in everything. The rebellious would be under the curse, while the chosen would know the blessing of the LORD (65:12-16).

An ideal age with a new heaven and a new earth would come to be (this is an apocalyptic idea). Jerusalem and its inhabitants would prosper with long and good life and prosperity and peace (65:13-24).

> The wolf and the lamb shall feed together,
>   the lion shall eat straw like the ox;
>   and dust shall be the serpent's food.
> They shall not hurt or destroy
>   in all my holy mountain, says the LORD (65:25).

The final words (Isa. 66:1-24).   The LORD who had his throne in heaven and earth as his footstool had no need of a house that men could build. What he looked for in man was who was "humble and contrite in spirit" and who trembles at the LORD's will. Sacrifices that were made by men who did not do the LORD's will were an insult to him. He would punish them for their false religion (66:1-6).

Jerusalem would be reborn even though it did not seem possible because the LORD would do it. Those who loved it could rejoice with it. They could be nourished by it as a mother cared for and fed her children (66:7-12). It would carry them around like a baby on its hip. They would be comforted by the LORD and would prosper like grass in a rainy time.

On the other side of the coin, the LORD would come in judgment upon those who defiled the land by idol worship. The survivors would be scattered to the nations of the world. They would carry the message of what the LORD had done. The people of Israel would be gathered, coming by every means of transportation to Jerusalem. As the new heavens and new earth would remain, so the people of Israel would remain before the LORD and worship him, while the rebels would die (66:13-24).

Summary on Second Isaiah.   Some of the major ideas found in Second Isaiah are as follows:

1. The LORD, the God of Israel is the Creator of the universe and Redeemer of his people.
2. The LORD was about to bring about a new Exodus through Cyrus, the Persian king.
3. Redeemed Israel had a mission to the world as shown by the Suffering Servant. The Servant, variously identified as Israel or as an individual, was to bring God's light to the nations through his suffering.

1. What makes the book of Lamentations distinctive?
2. What does Lamentations tell us about conditions in Jerusalem during the Babylonian siege?
3. What changes did Israel experience as the result of the Babylonian Exile?
4. How was the work of Ezekiel in the exile like that of Jeremiah in Jerusalem?
5. How did the vision associated with Ezekiel's call affect him?
6. What symbolic actions did Ezekiel act out and what was their significance?
7. What symbolized for Ezekiel the inevitable doom of Jerusalem?
8. What was Ezekiel's view of individual responsibility?
9. Why did Ezekiel not mourn his wife's death?
10. Name four allegories that Ezekiel used.
11. What was the meaning of Ezekiel's vision in the valley of the dry bones?
12. What was the basic message of the Gog of Magog oracles?
13. How did apocalpytic literature differ from the message of the prophets?
14. What is the theme of Ezekiel chapters 40–48?
15. What happened to the Babylonian empire?
16. How is Isaiah 40–66 related to Isaiah 1–39?
17. What are the major themes of Isaiah 40–55?
18. What are the Servant Poems?
19. How has the Suffering Servant been identified?
20. How do the oracles in Isaiah 56–66 differ from those in Isaiah 40–55?

FOR FURTHER STUDY

Ezekiel

EICHRODT, WALTER. *Ezekiel*. Trans. by Cosslett Quin. Old Testament Library. Philadelphia: Westminster, 1970.
MAY, H. G. "Ezekiel: Introduction and Exegesis." *Interpreter's Bible*, IV. New York: Abingdon, 1956.

Isaiah 40–66

ANDERSON, BERNHARD W. "Exodus Typology in Second Isaiah." *Israel's Prophetic Heritage.* New York: Harper & Row, 1962.

KNIGHT, GEORGE A. F. *Deutero-Isaiah: A Theological Commentary on Isaiah 40–55.* New York: Abingdon, 1965.

McKENZIE, JOHN L. *Second Isaiah.* Anchor Bible. Garden City. N.Y.: Doubleday, 1968. Excellent discussion of the identity of the Servant.

MUILENBURG, JAMES. "Isaiah 40–66: Introduction and Exegesis." *Interpreter's Bible,* V. New York: Abingdon, 1956.

ROWLEY, H. H. *The Servant of the Lord and Other Essays on the Old Testament,* 2nd ed. Oxford: Blackwell, 1965.

SMART, JAMES D. *History and Theology in Second Isaiah: A Commentary on Isaiah 35, 40–66.* Philadelphia: Westminster, 1965.

ZIMMERLI, WALTER, and J. JEREMIAS. *The Servant of God.* Studies in Biblical Theology, no. 20. Naperville, Ill.: Alec R. Allenson, 1957. Found also in Kittel's *Theological Dictionary of the Old Testament.*

CHAPTER TWELVE

The Postexilic Period: Judah Revived

In Thomas Wolfe's novel *You Can't Go Home Again* the author spoke of how home could never be what we thought it was. When we try to return, the home we knew is no longer there. Such must have been the experience of the Jews who returned to Palestine in 538. They came with big plans and high hopes, only to see them dashed on the hard rocks of reality.

The International Situation: 538–522

CYRUS THE GREAT

Israel's return to the land was made possible by Cyrus the Great's conquest of Babylon. Nabonidus, the ruler of Babylon, had managed to antagonize a large number of his subjects by his neglect of the kingdom and especially by his neglect of the national religion. When the armies of Cyrus came to Babylon, Nabonidus had already fled. The city, without any resistance, fell like an overripe plum. Many citizens welcomed the conqueror, who promptly declared that Marduk, the chief god of Babylon, had sent him. As his local ruler, he appointed his son Cambyses. By 538 Cyrus controlled all of western Asia as far as the frontier of Egypt.[1]

---

[1] Martin Noth, *The History of Israel,* pp. 300–302.

THE REIGN OF CAMBYSES (530–522)

In 530, Cyrus was killed and his son Cambyses succeeded him. Cambyses conquered Egypt in 525, completing the establishment of an empire that would dominate the Near East for 200 years.

DARIUS I (522–486)

In 522, there was a rebellion in the eastern part of Cambyses's empire. Cambyses, for some reason, committed suicide. Darius, one of his officers, immediately claimed the throne. He further strengthened his claim by defeating Gaumata, the rebel leader in the eastern provinces. Revolts sprang up like wildfire throughout the empire, with the result that it took Darius two years to gain full control of the throne. By 520, however, he had put down all the rebels and begun a long and stable reign.[2]

The Restored Community

The day the prophets had preached about and that the pious Jews had dreamed about for so long finally came in 538. The Jews were permitted to return to Palestine and to rebuild their Temple, which had lain in ruins for over 40 years.

CYRUS'S DECREE (EZRA 1:1-4)

The restoration was the result of the policies of Cyrus the Great. Cyrus reversed the policies of the previous kings who had dominated the Near East. Where they had deported people to help keep down rebellion, Cryus permitted as many of the exiles who wanted to, to return to their original homes. Where previous kings had tried to destroy such religious shrines as the Temple, Cyrus encouraged the subject peoples to rebuild their shrines. He even gave money to subsidize the cost of rebuilding such shrines.

In 538 Cyrus issued a decree that permitted exiled persons to return to their homelands.[3] The Jewish version of that decree is found in Ezra 1:2-4. In it, Cyrus declared that the LORD had given him the responsibility of seeing that the Temple was rebuilt. The exiles were to be given help in

---

[2]John Bright, *A History of Israel*, p. 369ff.

[3]The Persian version can be found in Pritchard, *The Ancient Near East*, pp. 206–208.

Figure 12–1. The Persian Empire.

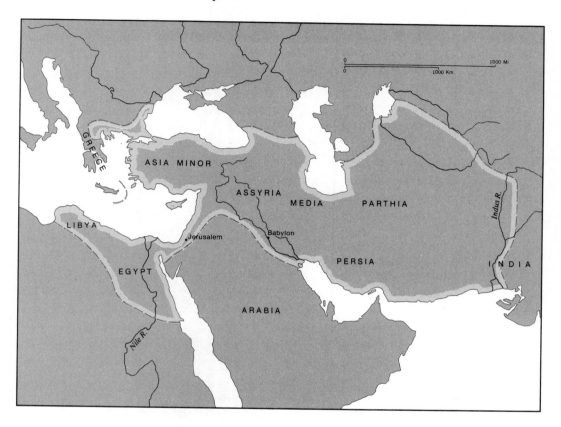

"silver and gold with goods and with beasts besides freewill offerings" (1:4). If one reads the biblical version of this decree, it would appear that only the Jews were given such help. It seems, however, that this was the kind of thing Cyrus did for peoples of all religions.

THE RETURNERS (EZRA 1:5–2:70)[4]

From 538 on for the next several years, groups of Jews returned to Palestine. The first group was led by Sheshbazzar, "the prince of Judah," who was the son of Jehoiachin. They carried with them some of the

---

[4]Unlike previous books where an attempt has been made to follow the order of the material as closely as possible, the order of Ezra and Nehemiah is somewhat confusing. References will be made to the material as nearly as possible in chronological order.

Figure 12–2. "The LORD stirred up the spirit of Cyrus King of Persia so that he made a proclamation throughout all his kingdom and also put it in writing" (Ezra 1:1). The Cyrus Cylinder reveals that Cyrus' policy of returning exiles to their native lands extended to people other than the Jews.

Courtesy of the Religious News Service.

Temple treasures Nebuchadnezzar had taken away. The most Sheshbazzar was able to accomplish was to lay the foundations to the temple (Ezra 5:14-16). Then the doldrums seem to have hit the community.

This condition evidently came from several major sources: (1) the harsh realities of coming into a land still bearing many of the marks of the Babylonian conquest; (2) the opposition of the people left in the land who felt that it was theirs by virtue of the fact that they had lived there undisturbed for more than 40 years; (3) those people of the old northern territories who looked upon themselves as still being faithful to the religion of Israel. Those who returned looked down upon them as being heretics.

Making a living turned out to be quite a chore since there seem to have been less than ideal agricultural conditions in those early years (Hag. 1:6). In contrast, Babylon, with its well-irrigated fields and busy cities, offered money and food in abundance. Conditions were so attractive that many Jews chose to remain there because of their prosperity. Babylon records indicate that some Jews became prominent bankers, businessmen, and high government officials. Some of those who went back to Palestine probably wished many times that they had not done so.

No word is given about the fate of Sheshbazzar. He is mentioned only in scattered references. He may have died and was replaced by Zerubbabel, who probably returned with another group of exiles in 520. The spiritual leader was Joshua, who was the high priest.

Haggai: Promoter of Temple-building (Hag. 1:1–2:23).
In four oracles dated in the late summer of 520, Haggai challenged the people to get on with the job of rebuilding the Temple.

If you expect the LORD's blessings, then do his will (Hag. 1:1-15).   In reaction to the people's excuse that the time had not "yet come to rebuild the house of the LORD" (1:2), Haggai reminded them that they had not let anything stop them from building their own houses. Yet, despite all efforts to meet their own needs, they were still not prosperous. Their efforts at agriculture had brought little produce, and they never seemed to have enough to eat and drink. Inflation had also taken its toll. Haggai's picturesque way of saying it was that "he who earns wages earns wages to put them into a bag with holes" (1:6). They needed to rebuild the Temple if they expected the LORD to bless them. Otherwise, drought would continue to devastate their crops (1:1-15).

There will be a greater Temple than Solomon's (Hag. 2:1-9).   To encourage the builders, the prophet asked if there was anyone who remembered Solomon's Temple. Since there must have been people present who had, the prophet went on to assure them that, regardless of the somewhat unpromising beginnings of the new building, "The latter splendor of this house shall be greater than the former." Such a promise would only be realized many centuries later, when Herod the Great rebuilt the Temple for the second time.

If the Temple is built, you will prosper (Hag. 2:10-19).   Haggai pointed out once more how poor their lot had been since they had returned to Palestine. If they wanted to prosper, the Temple had to be completed.

Zerubbabel, you are the chosen one (Hag. 2:20-23).   The uproar in the

Persian Empire undoubtedly caused Haggai's enthusiasm to outrun his judgment. In reference to the problems of Darius I, Haggai promised that this meant that Israel would be freed and Zerubbabel would be the Messiah.

Zechariah: Man of visions.   Zechariah was the second of the prophets who helped stir up the people to work on the Temple. His messages were of a different type from those of Haggai, however. Haggai might be said to have dealt with the bread-and-butter issues–that is, he saw completing the Temple a necessary condition for receiving the LORD's blessings in a practical form, such as food, clothing, and an improved standard of living. He only briefly mentioned the possibility of the coming of a messianic age.

Not so with Zechariah. First of all, the form of his messages was radically different. Instead of oracles like those of Haggai and most of the pre-exilic prophets, he, like Ezekiel, experienced numerous visions. In the second place, these visions dealt almost exclusively with the coming of the messianic age. This means that Zechariah was as much of an apocalyptist as he was a prophet. He delivered his messages like a prophet; their content was apocalyptic. He preached to encourage the people as they tried to do a hard job in a difficult time. That he and Haggai succeeded in inspiring the people to rebuild their ruined house of worship is a tribute to their faith and perserverance. They were not among the greatest prophets of Israel, but they served a useful function in their own day.

The dates of Zechariah's oracles range from 520 to 518. It is assumed by many interpreters that chapters 1–8 contain the genuine materials from Zechariah. Chapters 9–14 are also apocalyptic, but the internal historical references indicate that they originated in the Greek period.

Return from your evil ways (Zech. 1:1-6).   This first oracle was a call for repentance, reminding the listeners of earlier prophets with their calls for the people, "Return from your evil ways and from your evil deeds" (1:4). They did not listen, and so they died. Others, however, repented. Following this oracle were the visions of Zechariah. These visions were like Ezekiel's allegories, in which the vision was presented and then followed by an explanation. The problem is that the explanations were not always as clear as one would wish.

The first vision: the four horsemen (Zech. 1:7-17).   In this vision, a man was seen on a red horse, accompanied by three others riding red, sorrel, and white horses. These were described as a sort of earth patrol for the LORD sent out to check on conditions. The earth was at peace, but Jerusalem still lay in ruins. Other nations had added to her sufferings. The LORD promised that the city and the Temple would be rebuilt.

The second vision: the four horns and four smiths (Zech. 1:18-21).   The horn was used throughout the Old Testament as a symbol of strength and power. In this vision, the four horns stood for the four great powers that had had such an influence on the destiny of the Israelite peoples: Assyria, Media (which had joined with Babylon to destroy Assyria), and the Persians. The smiths were metal workers who made the weapons that gave the great nations their power. If the smiths could give power, in like manner they could take it away.

The third vision: the man with the measuring line (Zech. 2:1-5).   In modern society such a man would be called a surveyor. He was marking out property lines, a practice only appropriate for land that was about to be occupied. The vision meant that Jerusalem's population would increase so that it would spill over any walls built around the city.

A call to flee from Babylon (Zech. 2:6-13).   Many Jews remained in Babylon. The prophet said the LORD was going to let Babylon be plundered. Many nations would be drawn to the LORD and his people. Here was a prophet proclaiming a day of the LORD like the popular view of Amos's time. Zechariah assumed that the Jews' day of judgment was over. The time of Israel's glory was about to begin.

The fourth vision: Satan and Joshua (Zech. 3:1-10).   In one of the two places in the Old Testament where Satan was specifically named (the other was Job 1–2) Satan stood up as an accuser against Joshua.[5] Obviously, there were those who had tried to discredit Joshua as high priest. Thus he is pictured as wearing dirty clothes. The prophet saw that this was the action of Satan. The LORD knew the truth and changed Joshua's dirty clothes for clean clothes (3:1-5).

Joshua was promised that if he would follow the LORD wholeheartedly, he would "rule my house and have charge of my courts" (3:6). Furthermore, the LORD would bring his "servant the Branch." This probably referred to Zerubbabel. When this happened, "Everyone of you will invite his neighbor under his vine and under his fig tree" (3:10).

The fifth vision: the golden lampstand and the two olive trees (Zech. 4:1-14).   This vision of a gold lampstand with branches for seven lamps represented the presence of God. The lamps were small clay lamps containing olive oil and a string that served as a wick. In later Judaism the seven-branched lampstand became a seven-branched candlestick. It is called a *menorah* and is still a common Jewish religious symbol. The light, the gold lampstand, and the number seven all represented attributes of God (4:1-5; 10-14).

On either side were two olive trees representing Joshua as spiritual leader and Zerubbabel as the messiah figure. There followed a word of

[5]Satan is actually called *the* Satan. It would probably be more accurate to translate the phrase as "the accuser" or "the adversary."

assurance to Zerubbabel that he would be successful in completing the Temple. It would be "not by might nor by power, but by my Spirit, says the LORD" (4:6).

The sixth vision: the flying scroll (Zech. 5:1-4).   The flying scroll was a written curse that would afflict the thieves and those who took false oaths. This reflects the commonly held belief that a curse had the power within to destroy whatever or whoever it was directed toward. It was not a flying saucer!

The seventh vision: the woman in an ephah (Zech. 5:5-11).   The ephah was a dry measure similar to a wicker basket. This particular basket had a lead cover on it so that its contents would not escape easily. A woman whose name was "Wickedness" was in the basket. Two winged women carried her off to Shinar (Babylon), the "sin city" of Zechariah's day. This wickedness was removed from the land in preparation for the messianic kingdom.

The eighth vision: the four chariots (Zech. 6:1-8).   The final vision was of four chariots pulled by red, black, white, and gray horses. They were sent out to the "four winds of heaven," although only three directions (north, south, and west) are mentioned. The vision seems to be incomplete since no explanation was given. It undoubtedly had something to do with the announcement of the coming of the messianic kingdom.

Concluding oracles (Zech. 7:1–8:23).   Zechariah was approached by some northerners who had been observing a fast commemorating the fall of Jerusalem in 587. They asked if they should continue to observe such fasts. Zechariah gave an oracle by which he exhorted them "to put away the fasts which the exile had made necessary, and address themselves, as of old to the virtues and duties of civic life."[6] Like the earlier prophets he called upon the people to

> Render true judgments, show kindness and mercy each to his brother, do not oppress the widow, the fatherless, the sojourner, or the poor; and let none of you devise evil against his brother in your heart (7:9-10).

Failure to live by these principles had brought about the exile in the first place (7:1-14).

In the closing oracle, Zechariah saw Jerusalem restored and prosperous, a city where the elderly could live in peace and the children could play in freedom. The exiles in every land would be returned, the Temple would be rebuilt, and the Jews would no longer be the doormat to their enemies (8:1-13).

[6]George A. Smith, *The Book of the Twelve Prophets* (London: Hodder and Stoughton), II, p. 320.

While the LORD had good purposes in mind for Jerusalem, it did not mean that they were to forget the basic rules of justice and love toward one another. The fasts once had been for mourning; the fate of Jerusalem would become feasts of joy and celebration. The nations of the world would be drawn to the Jews, whose LORD had so blessed them (8:14-23).

Chapters 9–14 of Zechariah will be discussed in another chapter.

The effect of Haggai and Zechariah's work (Ezra 5:1–6:22). The prophets, along with Zerubbabel and Joshua, inspired the people to return to the Temple building with vigor. Trouble was not long in coming, however. The ruler of the province of which Jerusalem was a part sent someone to investigate what was going on. He found out who was responsible and sent an inquiry to the Persian capital to see if the work had indeed been authorized by Cyrus, as the Jews claimed. When the answer came back, not only was the right to rebuild the Temple confirmed, but also the governor Tattenai was instructed to pay the building costs out of royal revenues. The building was finished and dedicated with joyful ceremonies in the year 515.[7]

The Time of Silence

With the completion of the Temple, a curtain was drawn over events in Palestine for more than 50 years. What happened no one knows. Zerubbabel's hopes of bringing in the messianic kingdom most certainly did not come to pass. In fact, his hopes and the efforts of the prophets to promote him as the Jewish ruler may well have had fatal results. The Persians, while remarkably tolerant in their policy toward conquered people, were so highly organized that revolt was kept at a minimum. It could well be that Zerubbabel was removed because of the hopes that he would be the promised Messiah.

Ezra and Nehemiah

With the fading away of Zerubbabel, the messianic hope also faded. When the Jews once more appeared on the stage of history, there was no mention of a king. Instead, the dominant figure in Jewish life was the priest. In the hands of the high priest would come to rest both the chief religious and political powers among the Jewish people.

---

[7]For a fuller discussion, see Jacob M. Myers, "Ezra-Nehemiah," *Anchor Bible.* (Garden City, N.Y.: Doubleday, 1965), pp. 50–54.

EZRA THE PRIEST

In the person of Ezra, we meet perhaps the most influential person in the postexilic Jewish community. His activities have earned him the title "Father of Judaism."

The date of Ezra. Ezra led a group of immigrants from Babylonia to Jerusalem "in the seventh year of Artaxerxes the king" (Ezra 7:7). Given the dates of the reign of Artaxerxes I (465–424), it would seem a simple matter to conclude that Ezra arrived in Jerusalem in 458. But things are not quite that simple; there were two kings named Artaxerxes. Artaxerxes II ruled from 404 to 358. Ezra could have arrived in Jerusalem in 397 instead of 458.

A third date that has been suggested is 428, based on the belief that Ezra came in the thirty-seventh year of Artaxerxes I. This would mean that the word "thirty" would have to be added to the biblical text. There is little evidence to support such an addition.

Recent evidence has given new support to the first date 458. One of the major arguments against that date is that Ezra started some important reforms, of which Nehemiah found little evidence when he came in 445. As one scholar has pointed out, however, reformers in biblical history were not noted for their success. Good examples were King Hezekiah and King Josiah, whose reforms died rather quickly.[8] It is assumed here, therefore, that Ezra returned in 458, the seventh year of the reign of Artaxerxes I.

The work of Ezra (Ezra 7:1–10:44; Neh. 8:1–9:37)

The return to Jerusalem (Ezra 7:1–8:36). The picture given of Ezra is that he, like many Jews, had achieved a place of some respect in the Persian Kingdom. This was shown by the fact that not only did King Artaxerxes permit him to gather a group of immigrants to return to Jerusalem, but he also gave a rather generous amount of money to subsidize the immigrants (7:1-24). Furthermore, Ezra was "to appoint magistrates and judges who may judge all the people in the province beyond the River" (7:25).

In Ezra 7:27 the narrative switches to a first-person account of what happened on Ezra's trip to Jerusalem in 458 (7:7-9). First, there was a prayer of thanksgiving for the undertaking (7:27-28). Then, in true priestly fashion, there was a listing of those who made the trip (8:1-14). Finding that there were not sufficient priests, Ezra sent some eloquent

[8]Frank Moore Cross, "A Reconstruction of the Judean Restoration," *Interpretation*, XXIX, 2 (April 1975), 198. The article has a good summary of the three basic dates (pp. 187–203).

and influential men to the Levites to persuade some of them to go along on the trip (8:15-20).

They were successful. After Ezra gave a selected group of the priests responsibility for looking after the money and sacred vessels given for use in the Temple, the pilgrims set out on the long trip to Jerusalem. Finally, they arrived safely. The money and vessels were turned over to the Temple officials for safekeeping. Then, the proper calls of respect were paid to the local Persian officials, who were given letters of instruction from Artaxerxes as to their part in aiding Ezra (8:21-36).

Ezra's reforms (Ezra 9:1–10:44; Neh. 8:1–9:37).   Ezra did not lose any time making his presence felt in the community of Jerusalem.

1. *The problem of foreign wives (Ezra 9:1–10:44).*   Discovering that many of the Jews, including priests, had married non-Jewish women, like the holy men of old, Ezra tore his clothes, pulled his hair, and went in to a state of mourning (9:1-5).

At the time of the evening sacrifice, he prayed an eloquent prayer of confession about this condition, which to him represented a great sin by the people (9:6-15). By the time his prayer had ended, he was joined by many others who also were confessing that they had sinned by marrying non-Jewish wives. In the emotion of the moment, they had a covenant that they would divorce all non-Jewish wives. Ezra swore all the Levites and others present to an oath to do as they had promised (10:1-5).

After a night of prayer and fasting, Ezra called a meeting within three days of all Jews at Jerusalem. To impress on the people the importance of being present, any person who failed to appear would lose his property. Needless to say, a large crowd was present, even though a heavy rain was falling. It was decided that a council of the leading men would be set up to deal with the matter. The council was formed. Those who had married non-Jewish women divorced them and sent them away with any children born to them (10:6-44).

2. *The renewing of the covenant (Neh. 8:1–9:38).*   Again Ezra called the people together. The purpose was a ceremony of covenant renewal, recalling an ancient custom going back to the years following Israel's covenant at Sinai (Josh. 24). First, there was the reading of the Torah, or Law. By this time, that probably included essentially what is known as the Pentateuch today (Gen.-Deut.). As Ezra read the law, it had to be put into the language of the people, which now was Aramaic, not Hebrew. This, then, was the first recorded attempt to paraphrase the Scriptures (8:1-7).

The Aramaic paraphrase in later years was known as the Targums. They included the Torah (Gen. through Deut.), the Prophets (Josh.-2 Kings, Isa., Jer., Ezek., and the Twelve), and the Writings (except for Daniel and Ezra-Nehemiah).

While reading the law, it was discovered that the seventh month (when this was taking place) was also the time for the celebration of the Feast of Tabernacles or Booths. The people went out into the hills, cut tree limbs, and built shelters. They lived in the shelters for seven days to remind them of Israel's wilderness years. During those days they spent their time studying the law (8:9-18).

The festival was followed by a great day of repentance and confession. Some suggest that this may have come before the celebration of the Feast of Tabernacles.[9] The Jews "separated themselves from all foreigners" and confessed not only their sins but also those of their ancestors (9:2). They alternated hearing the law read with confession of sin. The solemn day was climaxed by Ezra's prayer of confession. In it, in a style common to the Old Testament, he first praised God. Then, the reason for the praise was stated by telling again the story of the LORD's mighty act in delivering the people from Egyptian bondage and his mercy on them even, though they had sinned so gravely against him (9:1-31).

Finally, he confessed the sins of the generation then present. Like their fathers, they, too, had sinned. As token of their repentance they entered into a solemn covenant, signed by the princes, Levites, and priests (9:32-38). This was the last mention of the work of Ezra.

NEHEMIAH THE BUILDER (NEH. 1:1-7:73; 13:1-31)

The time of Nehemiah's return is not so debated as that of Ezra. He said in his memoirs that he returned to Jerusalem in the twentieth year of Artaxerxes. There is general agreement that Artaxerxes I (465–424) is meant, thus dating Nehemiah's return in 445.

Events leading to Nehemiah's return (Neh. 1:1–2:8). Nehemiah, a devout Jewish layman, was cupbearer to the Persian king. The cupbearer's position was one of great honor since it involved great trust on the part of the king of the person who held the job.[10] Messengers came from Jerusalem, telling how the walls and gates of the city were in ruins. Either they had never been rebuilt since the Babylonian invasion or they had been destroyed by the Persians for some unknown reason. Nehemiah undertook a period of fasting and prayer when he heard the news (1:1-11).

Several months passed. One day while Nehemiah was performing his duties as cupbearer, the king noticed his haggard looks and questioned

---

[9]Myers, "Ezra-Nehemiah," *Anchor Bible,* p. 165.
[10]*Ibid.,* pp. 93—96, discusses the location of Susa and the role of the cupbearer.

him about it. When Nehemiah told him the reason, the king made Nehemiah governor of Jerusalem and gave him money and materials to repair the city walls (2:1-8).

The rebuilding of the walls (Neh. 2:9–7:73; 12:44-47). Nehemiah was not welcomed by everyone. Sanballat, governor of Samaria who had dominated Judah for some time; Tobiah, governor of Ammon in Transjordan; and Geshem (Gasmu), an Arab king, immediately took exception to Nehemiah's presence. They would cause much trouble in the days ahead (2:9-10,19).[11]

Nehemiah's first action was to make a nighttime survey of the broken walls. Afterward, he called the Jewish leaders together and told them of his plans to rebuild the walls. He received an enthusiastic response from them. The response from Sanballat, Tobiah, and Geshem was to suggest that he really was trying to stir up a rebellion against the emperor (2:11-20).

Organizing the people into construction gangs, Nehemiah proceeded with his plans (3:1-32). When Sanballat and Tobiah heard that construction was in progress, they immediately began to make threats about what they would do. Nehemiah responded by dividing the Jews into two groups—one to stand guard against an attack and another to carry on the construction (4:1-23).

Then, problems arose within the Jewish community. Many of the Jews had abandoned their villages and farms to aid in the construction. They had borrowed from their rich fellow Jews to have food for their families. When they could not pay their debts because of their contributions to the project, those to whom they owed money began to foreclose on them. Some even had to give their children as slaves to pay their debts.

Nehemiah called the leaders and told them that such practices must stop immediately. Anyone who was a slave must be freed. He threatened to call the wrath of God down on them if they did not do as he had ordered. They believed him and did so (5:1-13).

To show that he would not ask anyone else to do what he would not do himself, never in his first twelve-year term as governor did Nehemiah take a salary paid for by tax money. Instead, he supported himself and 150 other Jews from his own resources (5:14-19).

Sanballat and Tobiah kept trying to undermine Nehemiah. They invited him to several meetings outside Jerusalem to discuss matters. Each time, Nehemiah refused to go. In an open letter sent to Nehemiah, Sanballat suggested that the reasons the wall was being built were that the Jews intended to revolt and Nehemiah was going to have himself declared

[11]Cross, "A Reconstruction," *Interpretation*, XXIX, p. 200.

king by some of the prophets. He threatened to tell Artaxerxes about what was going on. Nehemiah denied all charges and continued his work. He also refused any special kind of precautions for his own safety (6:1-14).

After fifty-two days the construction was finished. Tobiah's sympathizers started a campaign to convince Nehemiah that Tobiah was a nice fellow after all. He had a Jewish father-in-law and a Jewish daughter-in-law. Nehemiah was still unconvinced. He posted trustworthy guards on the city gates with strict instructions about opening and closing hours (6:15–7:4).

When the building was completed, dedicatory services were held, the central feature being a service of sacrifice after a march around the walls. The march ended in the Temple area, where the service of thanksgiving was held (12:27-43).

> And they offered great sacrifices that day and rejoiced, for God had made them rejoice with great joy; the women and children also rejoiced. And the joy of Jerusalem was heard afar off (Neh. 12:43).

To climax his work, Nehemiah made arrangements for regular services to be carried on by people who were paid by the offerings given, as had been the case in the time of the great kings. The priests, then, could attend to the services instead of working at other jobs for a living since provisions were made for the regular collection of Temple revenues (12:44-47).

These were the major accomplishments of Nehemiah's first term as governor, which covered twelve years (445–433). In the thirty-second year of Artaxerxes, he returned to Persia (13:6).

Nehemiah's second term as governor (Neh. 13:1-31).   After some time Nehemiah returned to Jerusalem to find some rather disturbing developments. His old nemesis Tobiah had been given a room in the Temple itself. That an Ammonite would even be permitted within the Temple precincts was a shock to Nehemiah. The Deuteronomic Code contained a law that no Ammonite or Moabite ever be allowed to become a part of Israel since those peoples had opposed Israel's peaceful passage through their territory in the Exodus (Deut. 23:3-5). By the time of Nehemiah, the Torah (Gen.-Deut.) was already the written law (13:1-3).

When Nehemiah discovered that the high priest Eliashib had allowed Tobiah a room in the Temple, he ordered Tobiah thrown out, along with his furniture. A special cleansing of the room took place. It was then restored to its normal use (13:4-9).

He found, furthermore, that the support of the Levites who had been paid for conducting the services in the Temple had failed because offerings had fallen off. The Levites had to return to farming to make a living. Nehemiah immediately began collecting the tithes again for the support of Temple worship (13:10-14).

A third situation that confronted him in his second governorship was the fact that many people were no longer observing the sabbath. Instead, they were working on the sabbath as though it was just another day. He ordered the city gates closed on the sabbath so the foreign traders and farmers could not bring in their goods to sell on that day. He issued a warning that anyone who violated the sabbath would be punished (13:15-22).

Finally, in a rather severe manner he dealt with the still troublesome problem of mixed marriage. He physically beat Jews who were married to foreign wives, including the son of the high priest Eliashib. He made a decree that no such marriages would be permitted and rooted out other foreign influences from Jewish life (13:23-31).

Ezra and Nehemiah had played a vital role in preserving the religious life and culture of the Jews who returned from exile when the community was about to be swallowed up by its neighbors. The zeal they inspired would be carried over into a period which, in Jewish historical records, is almost blank. Around 200 the curtain would be lifted again, when Palestine once again became the battleground between two powers who were trying to gain control of its territory.

FOR FURTHER STUDY

ACKROYD, PETER. *Exile and Restoration: A Study of Hebrew Thought of the Sixth Century B.C.* Philadephia: Westminster, 1968.

MYERS, JACOB M. *Ezra-Nehemiah.* Anchor Bible. Garden City, N.Y.: Doubleday, 1965.

———. *I and II Chronicles.* 2 vols. Anchor Bible. Garden City, N.Y.: Doubleday, 1965.

OLMSTEAD, A. T. *History of the Persian Empire.* Chicago: University of Chicago Press, 1948.

SNAITH, NORMAN. *The Jews from Cyrus to Herod.* Walling, England: The Religious Education Press, 1949.

STUDY QUESTIONS

1. How did Cyrus's conquest of the Babylonians affect the Jews in exile?
2. What happened to the Jews who returned from the exile to Palestine?
3. What was Haggai's contribution to the postexilic Jewish community in Palestine?

4. What was the purpose of Zechariah's visions?
5. When did Ezra return from exile?
6. What was his function in the Jerusalem community?
7. What is the significance of the reading of the Law as described in Nehemiah 8?
8. What did Nehemiah accomplish as governor of Judah the first term? The second term?

CHAPTER THIRTEEN

A Legacy of Israel: Wise Men and Psalm Singers

Israel contributed many things to the world, even as its modern descendants (the Jews) are still making invaluable contributions to human society. Of all its literature, the most admired must be the words of its wise men and the songs of its singers. Its proverbs and metaphors spice the speech of many lands. Its greatest literary masterpiece, the book of Job, ponders the mystery of some of life's deepest questions. Its psalms reflect the full range of human emotion, from abject misery to ecstatic praise. Its love songs, the explicitness of which challenge both Jewish and Christian interpreters alike, sing of the "way of a man with a maiden" (Prov. 30:19).

Matters of Mechanics in Poetry

While poetic and wisdom literature are classed separately for discussion, they were alike in that both used poetic form.[1]

PARALLELISM

Hebrew poetry, unlike English poetry, was not so concerned with rhyme as it was with the balancing of ideas within a line. Each line of Hebrew poetry had at least two or three parts, but rarely did it have more

[1]An excellent brief discussion of the characteristics of Hebrew poetry is found in the second edition of *The New Oxford Annotated Bible with the Apocrypha*, RSV (New York: Oxford University Press, 1973), pp. 1523–1529.

than three. As a general rule, when a line of Hebrew poetry is translated into English, each part forms a separate line in English. Each part contained an idea. The other parts of the line either repeated the idea in a slightly different manner, stated a contrary or opposite idea, or added to the original idea. This way of relating ideas to each other is called *parallelism*. While there are many types of parallelism, three basic types discovered by a scholar named Lowth will be discussed here.

Synonymous parallelism.   In synonymous parallelism, the idea in the first part of the line was duplicated more or less in the second part of the line, using different language. Some examples are these:

> A good name is to be chosen
>   rather than great riches,
> and favor is better than silver or gold (Prov. 22:1).

> For the righteous will never be moved;
>   he will be remembered for ever (Ps. 112:6).

> He raises the poor from the dust,
>   and lifts the needy from the ash heap (Ps. 113:7).

Antithetical parallel.   In antithetical parallel, the idea in the second part of the line was the opposite of the idea in the first part. Proverbs 10–14 contain many examples of antithetical parallel:

> A wise son hears his father's instruction,
>   but a scoffer does not listen to rebuke (Prov. 13:1).

> A righteous man has regard for the life of his beast,
>   but the mercy of the wicked is cruel (Prov. 12:10).

Formal or synthetic parallel.   Formal parallel actually was not parallel at all; it was simply that the second part of the line added to the idea in the first part of the line.

> Come and hear, all you who fear God,
>   and I will tell what he has done for me (Ps. 66:16).

> So I looked upon thee in the sanctuary,
>   beholding thy power and glory (Ps. 63:2).

Other types of parallelism—such as emblematic, which involves comparisons; stairlike, in which the second part of the line repeats part of the first idea but then adds to it; and introverted, which extends over several lines—can also be found. They will not be discussed further here, however.

METER

Meter has to do with the rhythm of poetry. Hebrew poetry had a strong emphasis on rhythm, thus making it easy to remember. Each part of a line had either 2 or 3, and on rare occasions 4, strong accents or beats. If the line had 2 parts and each part had 3 strong beats, the rhythm was 3:3. This was the most common rhythm. If the poet wanted to express quickness or excitement, often he would use 2 strong beats for each part of the line. The meter then would be 2:2. Sadness was expressed by an uneven number of beats —3 in the first part and 2 in the second part. This 3:2 meter was called *qinah,* which means a dirge or sad song. The book of Lamentations was almost exclusively written in this meter. Finally, if there were 3-part lines, the meter could be 3:3:3 or 2:2:2.

It is not always easy to tell from English translations what the meter was in Hebrew poetry. Only by a knowledge of the Hebrew language itself can one know for certain what it was. As a general rule, however, the nouns and verbs (except forms of the verb "to be") indicate where the strong accents were.

Wise Men and Wisdom Literature

WISE MEN AND THEIR WORK

The teacher of wisdom was seldom mentioned in the Old Testament outside the wisdom literature. The prophet Jeremiah complained that among those who were persecuting him were the priests, the prophets, and the wise men (Jer. 18:18). This would seem to indicate that in Jeremiah's time the wise men were considered alongside the priest and prophet as leaders in Israelite religious life.

Interest in wisdom in Israel was much older than the time of Jeremiah, however. The Deuteronomic historian spoke frequently of Solomon's wisdom, telling how he prayed for wisdom instead of wealth (1 Kings 3:1-14); how he used it in settling disputes (1 Kings 3:15-28); how he "uttered three thousand proverbs" (1 Kings 4:32,34); and how he impressed the queen of Sheba (1 Kings 10:1-3,23). As a result, wisdom became associated with Solomon as the Law or Torah became associated with Moses and the psalms became associated with David.

But wisdom knows no political or national boundaries. This was true especially when those boundaries really did not act as barriers to travel as they do today. Israel's wisdom was a part of the larger pool of wisdom of the Near East. The book of Proverbs is a good illustration of this fact. In addition to collections of Israelite wisdom, it contains other materials that had been brought into Israel from other countries. For example, Proverbs

22:17–24:22 has thirty sections similar to the Instruction of Amen-em-opet, an Egyptian wisdom text from a time somewhere between the tenth to sixth centuries. There are numerous parallels between the two texts, suggesting that the Hebrew writer knew the Egyptian text. This would not be unlikely since Solomon had close relations with Egypt. His scholars, who were concerned with collecting and developing Israelite literature, were undoubtedly influenced by others.[2]

Other examples can be found in Proverbs 30–31. The former is said to have been "the words of Agur son of Jakeh of Massa" (30:1), while the latter chapter is attributed to "Lemuel, king of Massa" (31:1). Massa was not in Israelite territory but was located in northwestern Arabia (Gen. 25:14).[3]

Wisdom teachings were of two types. Practical wisdom was concerned with the problems of everyday living. The form of this wisdom was such so that much of it was easily taught. The use of easily remembered literary forms—such as proverbs, fables, and short poetic discourses on some human problem—could be committed to memory. The proverb was a short, easily remembered saying that contained one main point. It could take the form of a comparison or a contrast. The fable (such as Jotham's fable in Judg. 9:7-15) was a story that had a moral usually giving human characteristics to plants or animals. The short poetic discourses were actually just longer proverbs, still designed to make one main point. This kind of wisdom took a simple and orthodox view of life.

In the postexilic period the wise men became the schoolmen in Israel. Perhaps the most famous was Ben Sirach, whose teachings were collected in the apocryphal book of Ecclesiasticus or the Wisdom of Ben Sirach. Practical wisdom was the chief concern of the schoolmen.

Wisdom of a different kind was found in Ecclesiastes (not to be confused with the Wisdom of Ben Sirach) and the book of Job. These books belonged to the realm of philosophical, or speculative, wisdom. These were extended discussions involving many of the deepest questions that confront man as he tries to live in the world. They challenged many of the most widely held ideas of the time. They questioned things that most people would never dare to question. For them, life was far from simple. Indeed, they posed many unanswerable questions and challenged many traditional values.

WISDOM BOOKS

Proverbs.   Proverbs contains a diverse collection of orthodox wisdom. Life was viewed in a very simple manner—the man who followed the path of wisdom would prosper, while the man who ignored wisdom

[2]Pritchard, *The Ancient Near East,* pp. 237–243.
[3]*Oxford Annotated Bible,* RSV, notes on Prov. 30:1 and 31:1.

would fail. The first was wise; the second was the fool—there was no middle ground.

The wise man's purpose (Prov. 1:1-7).   Solomon's place in the wisdom movement is indicated by Proverbs 1:1, where the whole book was credited to him, even though later parts of the book indicate clearly that he was not the author of all the proverbs. Since Solomon was the most famous of all Israel's wise men, he was looked upon as the father of Israelite wisdom.

Verses 2-6 state the purpose of the book of Proverbs. Three groups were mentioned—men who needed "wisdom and instruction," men who needed "words of insight," and men who "receive instruction in wise dealing righteousness, justice, and equity" (1:2-3). The simple needed prudence, while youths needed "knowledge and discretion" (1:4). Even the wise man needed to "increase in learning" and to "acquire skill" to understand proverbs, figures of speech, and the words and riddles of the wise (1:5-6). The section ends with the theme:

> The fear of the LORD is the beginning of knowledge;
> fools despise wisdom and instruction (1:7).

The way to the good life (Prov. 1:8–9:18)

1. *Son, listen to your elders (Prov. 1:8-19).*   A father pleaded with his son to turn a deaf ear to bad companions. He warned him to avoid their ways. In following the way of robbery, violence, and bloodshed, he would be setting a trap for himself because violence breeds violence.

2. *Wisdom's sermon to the simple (Prov. 1:20-33).*   Wisdom was given human characteristics. She went into the busy places in the city to act as a prophet. Her sermon was addressed to the simple—those who had no wisdom. It was a warning to accept her leadership. If they did not, she would mock them when calamity came. She would ignore their pleas for help, for the judgment had fallen.

3. *Son, listen to wisdom (Prov. 2:1-22).*   The father called on his son to actively seek wisdom, for it came from the LORD. Because the LORD was the source, wisdom had great benefits for those who lived by it. To follow the path of integrity and justice was to be led by the LORD. Increased understanding of righteousness and justice would result. The ability to make right decisions would help him who followed wisdom to avoid evil men and evil ways. Most of all, he would avoid loose women who would lead him to the grave.

His companions would be good men. His life would be blessed, while the wicked would be destroyed. Here was a common theme of this type of wisdom literature: Personal goodness brought blessing; bad conduct brought judgment. There was no allowance for the prosperity of evil men or the poverty of a good man.

4. *Son, let the LORD lead you (Prov. 3:1-35).*   Loyalty and faithfulness

characterized the good life. Loyalty to the LORD was supreme. To trust the LORD and to follow his way was the simplest and best way of life. When the LORD corrected a person, it was because of his love. Those who understood this were the wise. Such wisdom made life pleasant and meaningful. Fear would be removed from life, for the LORD would keep his own safe, regardless of the disaster.

In relation to neighbors, one should live in peace and do whatever was promised promptly. One should not be contentious, nor should one be jealous of evil people. They would come to a bad end.

5. *Son, get wisdom and insight (Prov. 4:1-27).* The father told of his father's teaching that the supreme aim in life was to get wisdom. With it one could have protection and great honor. The wise person lived a long life, for with wisdom one learned how to avoid the pitfalls of life. In contrast, the wicked would only lead one astray. The wise man would stay away from the wicked men because they could not sleep unless they had done wrong.

The road the righteous traveled got lighter, but the road of the wicked led into darkness. Life should be lived with care and planning. It should be characterized by truth and honesty. A person who lived in this fashion could hold up his head without shame.

6. *Son, beware of that wild woman (Prov. 5:1-22).* One of the most vivid passages in Proverbs contains the warning against consorting with an adultress. Her smooth and seductive speech sounded sweet, but it led to death. The best thing to do was to keep as far away from her as possible, for she could only bring ruin.

Instead, a man should "drink water" from his own well and love the wife of his youth. The LORD's eyes were on men, so the wicked man could not escape the consequences of his sin.

7. *Son, remember four important things (Prov. 6:1-19).* (1) A man should be careful about giving security for another person's debt (6:1-5). (2) The diligence of the ant in its work should be an example to the lazy man (6:6-11). (3) A man should beware of a wicked man's words and ways. They would bring him to disaster (6:12-15). (4) The final warning was a numbers proverb using seven examples of the kinds of disgusting things that the LORD hated. They included:

> haughty eyes, a lying tongue,
>> and hands that shed innocent blood,
> a heart that devises wicked plans,
>> feet that make haste to run to evil,
> a false witness who breathes out lies,
>> and a man who sows discord among brothers (6:17-19).

8. *Son, wisdom will keep you safe from wicked women (Prov. 6:20-35).* A man who listened to the wisdom of his parents would be able to avoid

loose women. The adultress was even more dangerous than the harlot, for a harlot would only take a man's money while the adultress would take his life. A jealous husband would take no payment to soothe his anger. Instead, in his rage he would take a man's life.

9. *Son, let's talk some more about wicked women (Prov. 7:1-27).* Wisdom could keep a man from trouble, especially trouble involving someone else's wife. The father told of a personal observation. He saw a naive young man passing the house of an adulterous woman. She came up to him, kissed him boldly, and told him that she had plenty of delicious food, a waiting bed, and an absent husband.

> With much seductive speech she persuades him;
>   with her smooth talk she compels him.
> All at once he follows her,
>   as an ox goes to the slaughter,
>   or as a stag is caught fast
>   till an arrow pierces its entrails;
> as a bird rushes into a snare;
>   he does not know that it will cost him his life (7:21-23).

10. *Wisdom's sermon to men (Prov. 8:1-36).* Wisdom was personified as a woman standing in the city gate addressing the passersby. In the sermon she spoke of her value to mankind (8:1-11); the high position she held in the affairs of life (8:12-16); the rewards that came to those who sought her (8:17-21); and her role in creation as first of created things and companion of God in creation (8:22-31). The prudent person would eagerly seek wisdom (8:32-36).

11. *The two ways: the wise and the foolish (Prov. 9:1-18).* To the ancients prosperity was a sign of the LORD's blessings. So wisdom was pictured as having a beautiful house, vast flocks from which to choose animals of sacrifice, and an overflowing table to which she could invite those who lacked her blessings (9:1-6). There followed verses that compare the most foolish of the foolish with the wise men. The prize for the most foolish of men went to the scoffer who thought he knew something, but actually he knew nothing. One could rebuke a scoffer, and it would only make him worse. Rebuke a wise man, and he would become wiser. He knew that the fear (awe) of the LORD was the real beginning of wisdom (9:7-12). A final word about the foolish woman ends this section (9:13-18).

The proverbs of Solomon (Prov. 10:1–22:16). This section entitled "Proverbs of Solomon" (10:1) is made up exclusively of what modern comedians call "one-liners;" not in the sense that they are jokes, but in the sense that their message is contained in one line of Hebrew (two lines in English translation). These short, pointed sayings each contain a simple truth designed to tell any person who hears them some lesson about how to live in relation to his fellow man. They are strung together like beads, each one different; but each one is concerned with how to live a good life in human society.

As was pointed out previously, the fact that these were called the "proverbs of Solomon" did not mean necessarily that all of them were from Solomon. They were probably from many lands and many sources. The fact that Solomon collected proverbs and was noted for his wisdom made it natural that his name would be attached to such collections.

There was no attempt made to put these proverbs in any sort of logical order. Indeed, it would have been difficult to do so. While many proverbs in this section have antithetical parallelism, there are others which do not. Of those that are antithetical, some examples of the contrasts made are as follows:

> *The wise and the foolish:*
> A wise son makes a glad father,
> but a foolish son is a sorrow to his mother (10:1).
>
> *The proud and the humble:*
> It is better to be of a lowly spirit with the poor
> than to divide the spoil with the proud (16:19).
>
> *The righteous and the wicked:*
> The righteous has enough to satisfy his appetite,
> but the belly of the wicked suffers want (13:25).
>
> *Good and bad wives:*
> A good wife is the crown of her husband,
> but she who brings shame is like rottenness in his bones (12:4).
>
> *Truth and falsehood:*
> A truthful witness saves lives,
> but one who utters lies is a betrayer (14:25).

Not all these proverbs were stated as contrasts. Many were of a synonymous nature or used formal parallelism.

> A just balance and scales are the LORD's;
> all the weights in the bag are his work (16:11).
>
> He who states his case first seems right,
> until the other comes and examines him (18:17).

The book of thirty sayings (Prov. 22:17–24:22. This probably was a teacher's book of instructions to a pupil about some of life's important relationships. By it, the pupil could see what was "right and true." Then he could give a "true answer" to whomever questioned him (22:17-21). While some of its admonitions follow the one-line pattern of the previous section, for the most part they cover several lines. For instance, there were instructions on eating with a ruler (23:1-3); how to discipline children

(23:13-14); the inevitable warning about wicked women (23:26-28); a rather long warning against excessive wine drinking; and a warning to "fear the LORD and the king" (24:21-22). One piece of advice was repeated twice, the second time being somewhat longer than the first (22:28):

> Do not remove an ancient landmark
>   or enter the fields of the fatherless;
> for their Redeemer is strong;
>   he will plead their cause against you (23:10-11).

The sayings of the wise ended with an appendix which contained condemnation on showing favoritism in judgment (24:23-25), a word on getting ready for work (24:27), a warning against bearing false witness and spite actions (24:28-29), and a description of the lazy man (24:30-34).

More "Proverbs of Solomon" (Prov. 25:1–29:27). This section (like Prov. 10:1–22:16) was composed mostly of individual one-line (Hebrew) sayings. The title suggests that King Hezekiah's time was a time when interest in wisdom was blossoming since these were said to be Solomonic proverbs collected by the "men of Hezekiah" (25:1). After two longer sections on the power of the king (25:2-7) and one on conduct in court (25:7-10), there follows a mixture of proverbs using *comparison;*

> Like clouds and wind without rain
>   is a man who boasts of a gift he does not give (25:14).

contrasts;

> Better is a poor man who walks in his integrity
>   than a rich man who is perverse in his ways (28:6).

as well as other poetic forms.

> If a king judges the poor with equity
>   his throne will be established for ever (29:14).

The words of Agur (Prov. 30:1-33). This chapter was made up of two types of material. Verses 1-9 were presented as a conversation. "The man" (v. 1), who may have been Agur, told two men named Ithiel and Ucal that he had seen no evidence of God (30:2-4). He was told in return that God's every word is true and that he protects those who "take refuge in him" (30:5). In 30:6-9 a speaker looks on life's highest gifts as being food and truth.

The second part of the chapter begins with a series of statements beginning "There are those who." In those groups were those who cursed their fathers (30:11), who were "pure in their own eyes" (30:12), who were proud (30:13), and who were greedy (30:14).

There followed a series of "numbers proverbs" that sound like the formula in the oracles of the prophet Amos: "For three transgressions and for four" (Amos 1:3). Most of them use the "three–four" formula, although one (30:15-16) uses two, three, and four and another lists only four things that "are small but they are exceedingly wise" (30:24). Three shorter proverbs were mixed in with the numbers proverbs.

The words of Lemuel (Prov. 31:1-31).   This chapter contains a mother's advice to her son (31:1-9) and the Old Testament's highest tribute to a woman—the description of a good wife (31:10-31). The first part is about a queen's advice to her son on how to rule wisely. The tribute to the ideal wife pictured her as being of good reputation, diligent about her work, prudent in her decisions, concerned for her family, compassionate toward the needy, wise in speech, and honored by her family.

The book of Proverbs would be followed in later Judaism with other books that imitated it somewhat, the most famous being the Wisdom of Solomon and the Wisdom of Ben Sirach or Ecclesiasticus. Proverbs was orthodox in theology and practical in its view of life.

Job: when orthodoxy fails.

Job: when orthodoxy fails.   Job represents the struggle of a person who had accepted orthodox answers to all of life's questions, but found them useless when the bottom fell out of his world. To compound his problem, his friends sat around still giving the same old answers, never hearing the entirely new set of questions Job was raising.

Who wrote Job, and when did he do it?   While the traditional interpreters of Job have viewed the book as the work of a single author, in recent years the emphasis has been upon the book as a composite work. The story of the suffering righteous man is found in other literatures and indeed, the story of Job may well have originated outside Israel, possibly in Edom. That the story is an old one is shown by Ezekiel 14:14,20, where he speaks of "Noah, Daniel and Job" as great righteous men of the past. The patient, long-suffering Job of Job 1 and 2 is quite different from the Job of chapters 3–42:6, who skates right up to the edge of blasphemy as he complains bitterly to God about his lot in life. This Job is brutally honest, but he is anything but patient.

What we seem to have then is this: An ancient folk tale, possibly Edomite in origin, about a good and patient man named Job, who very early became a part of Israelite tradition. Sometime just before or during the Babylonian Exile, an Israelite wisdom writer used the old story to introduce a poetic masterpiece in which he examines the problem of a righteous man's relationship to God in the context of great physical and emotional suffering. Either the author of the poetic discourse (or someone else who wished to make the book sound more orthodox) added the ending from the older folk tale (Job 42:7-17).

Chapter 28, a discourse on wisdom, and the Elihu speeches (chapters 32–37) add little to the overall arguments of the book and thus do not seem to have been a part of the original work. The Elihu speeches could have been added later by the original author after further reflection on the problem.

Some things one needs to know to help in understanding Job.   Some basic ideas common in early Israel were in the background of the book of Job. Certain basic assumptions had been made in theology: (1) God was just and gave justice to men. (2) This life was all there was. When a man died he went to Sheol, the abode of the dead. There was no real life after death with rewards and punishments. (3) If justice was to be done, it had to be done in this life.

These assumptions led to certain conclusions: (1) The good man prospered, while the wicked man failed. (2) Sickness was a sign that a person had sinned. It was a part of God's judgment on sinners. These views of orthodox religion formed the basis of the arguments in the book of Job.

The book.

1. *Job, the righteous man: the prose story (Job 1:1–2:13).*   According to the old tradition, Job was an extremely wealthy man from the land of Uz. No one really knows where Uz was, although it could have been in Edom. He had seven sons and three daughters and vast herds of livestock. He was a faithful worshiper of God (*Elohim*) (1:1-5).

But such bliss could not continue. Satan (as in Zech. 3:2, he was *the Satan*) challenged God about Job, accusing him of giving Job special protection. God agreed to let Satan do what he would to Job, but he was not to touch Job's body (1:6-12). Disaster after disaster struck Job causing him to lose all his children, as well as his livestock. But through it all, Job did not criticize God in the least (1:13-22).

Satan appeared before the LORD again. The LORD proudly reminded him that Job was still faithful. Satan replied that every man had his limits and that included Job. When the LORD permitted Job to be afflicted personally, he would break under the pressure and curse the LORD. The LORD took up the challenge. He permitted Satan to do anything to Job except kill him (2:1-6).

Job's troubles really began. He was covered with painful sores from head to foot. He sat on an ash heap and used a piece of broken pottery to scrape the tops off the sores. His wife urged him to curse God and die so as to be out of his misery. But Job refused. Then three friends came to see him. When they saw him, they began to wail and to mourn over his condition. Then they sat and looked at him for seven days without uttering a single, solitary word (2:7-13).

This prose version of the story of Job pictured Satan as having easy access to the heavenly realms. He came when the "sons of God came to present themselves before the LORD" (1:6). In later theology, Satan was in violent opposition to the LORD, not someone who came to visit the LORD when he took a notion to do so.

Job's wife's advice to curse God and die revealed that there was not a developed doctrine of life after death in that time. The dead all went to Sheol (or the grave), so this life was all there was. There was a kind of existence after death; but the only thing that could disturb it was when (1) a body was not properly buried, or (2) a person had been murdered and his death was unavenged.[4]

2. *Job, the frustrated sufferer: the poetic discourse (Job 3:1–42:6).* This section of Job was cast in the form of a dialogue between Job and his three friends Eliphaz, Bildad, and Zophar. There were three cycles or sets of speeches, except that the third cycle was incomplete.

a. *Job's complaint (Job 3:1-26).* In contrast to Job's refusal to complain in the prose story, the poetic version began with Job cursing the day he was born. In an extended example of synonymous parallelism (3:1-10), Job piles up phrase after phrase to say what was said in 3:2:

> Let the day perish wherein I was born,
>   and the night which said,
>   "A man-child is conceived."

If he had died at birth, then he would have gone to the grave, where he would "have lain down and been quiet" (3:13). Sheol was where "the wicked cease their troubling" (3:17) for "the small and great are there, and the slave is free from his master" (3:19). But God had hedged Job in so that he had trouble, not peace and quiet (3:26).

b. *The debate: round one (Job 4:1–14:22)*

(1) *Eliphaz, the man who has visions (Job 4:1–5:27).* The core of the arguments of Job's friends was found in the first Eliphaz speech:

> "Think now, who that was innocent ever perished?
>   Or where were the upright cut off?
> As I have seen those who plow iniquity
>   and sow trouble reap the same.
> By the breath of God they perish,
>   and by the blast of his anger they are consumed" (4:7-9).

That Job was a sinner was evidenced by his sickness. Why else would he be suffering if he had not sinned? Eliphaz's authority for his opinion was that he had a vision in the night, which told him that God did not trust his angels, much less mortal man, who was "born to trouble as the sparks fly upward" (4:1–5:7).

What Job needed to do was to seek God and commit himself to him.

---

[4]John H. Tullock, *Blood-Vengeance,* p. 141ff.

Though God had afflicted Job, he could also heal him if Job had the proper attitude. Then he would have the traditional blessings of peace, prosperity, a large family, and a long life (5:8-27).

Perhaps the most distinctive mark of the argument of Eliphaz was his view of God. For him, God did not trust anyone, even those who were closest to him. God was just waiting for one of his creatures to do wrong so he could destroy the wrongdoer.

(2) *Job to Eliphaz: round one (Job 6:1–7:21).* Ignoring Eliphaz's charges, Job complained that God had become his enemy, filling him with arrows and lining up all his terrors against him. All Job wanted was for God to crush him so he would be out of his misery (6:1-13).

As for his friends, they were like wet weather springs that had promised cool water all year long but had dried up when the hot days of summer came. He had not asked any of them for money. If they could teach him anything, he was willing to listen. Instead of being honest, they were talking nonsense. They did not know the difference between right and wrong (6:14-30).

Since life for him was so trying and tedious, he decided that there was no need to be reluctant to say how he felt:

> Therefore I will not restrain my mouth;
>   I will speak in the anguish of my spirit;
>   I will complain in the bitterness of my soul (7:11).

When he sought comfort, he got terror. He had terrifying dreams. He was tired of living under such circumstances. But his God would not leave him alone even long enough to swallow his saliva. God was using him for "target practice" (7:20, TEV). Soon he would die and then God would not find him (7:1-21).

(3) *Bildad, the traditionalist (Job 8:1-22).* Bildad vigorously defended the justice of God. He suggested that Job's suffering was caused by the sins of his children. All that Job had to do, if he were "pure and upright" (8:6), was to seek God and everything would be just fine (8:1-7). Anyone who knew the teachings of the fathers (as Job surely did) would realize the truth of what Bildad was saying. The law of God was that the bad men were destroyed and the good men prospered. If Job would follow that philosophy, happiness would be his (8:8-22).

(4) *Job to Bildad: round one (Job 9:1–10:22).* Job would not argue about God's power and ability to do what he chose. No man could stand up against God and hope to win. Even if a man were innocent, God could take that man's words and condemn him. Job questioned a basic tenet of orthodox religion, for he had begun to doubt that God really was just:

> It is all one; therefore I say,
>   he destroys both the blameless and the wicked.

. . .

> The earth is given into the hand of the wicked;
>   he covers the faces of its judges—
>   if it is not he, who then is it? (9:22-24)

Job's days were passing swiftly. With them, his hope of receiving justice was also passing. He and God were in separate realms, and there was no mediator who could bridge the gap between them (9:1-35).

He was tired of living. Ignoring Bildad, he spoke to God. God had made him. Was he now going to destroy him? He was sure God had a purpose in making him, but now life was so confusing. He could not win for losing. He just wished he had never been born. Since he had to live, he just wanted to be left alone so he could possibly find a little comfort before he died (10:1-22).

(5) *Zophar, God's right-hand man (Job 11:1-20).* Zophar was tired of Job's nonsense. If Job would just listen, Zophar would give him God's point of view about his problems. God knew all things, but Job knew very little. Job just needed to get rid of his sin, and everything would be all right.

(6) *Job to Zophar: round one (Job 12:1–14:22).* Job was tired of his friend's advice:

> No doubt you are the people,
>   and wisdom will die with you.
> But I have understanding as well as you;
>   I am not inferior to you.
> Who does not know such things as these? (12:2-3)

Anyone could see that his condition was brought on by the LORD. Anyone knew that when God decided to do something, there was no way to stop him (12:1-25). His friends' defense of God's honor was self-serving. They lied for God, hoping he would overlook their sins. But that would not work. They could not deceive God by their actions (13:1-12).

Job, therefore, was going to speak his mind even if it cost him his life. He fully expected God to kill him for being so bold, but that would not stop him. He had prepared his case. He only wanted two concessions from God: (1) that God would hear him and (2) that God would not terrify him while he was speaking (13:13-22).

Job then presented his case to God. He wanted to know why God had ignored him and attacked him as though he were an enemy. Since man's time was so brief on earth, why was he not allowed to enjoy it? If a tree was cut down, it could sprout again. Not so with a man. If man had hope for life after death, it would make life's misery bearable. This yearning for life after death represented a reaching out for what later became accepted teaching in Judaism and Christianity. When life was seen to be unjust, then the doctrine of the justice of God demanded a future life in which God's justice could be carried out fully. The only other choice was to declare God to be unjust, an idea both Judaism and Christianity rejected.

But even as Job reached out for the hope of a future life, he turned back to despair. The situation was hopeless. This life was all there was (13:23–14:22).

c. The debate: round two (Job 15:1–21:34)

(1) *Eliphaz speaks again (Job 15:1–35).* Job's failure to agree with his friends led to increasingly sharp words being flung at him. Eliphaz charged him with undermining religion by assuming that he knew more than his friends, the elders, or even God himself (15:1-14). He returned to his theme of a God who did not trust anybody:

> Behold, God puts no trust in his holy ones,
>   and the heavens are not clean in his sight;
> how much less one who is abominable and corrupt,
>   a man who drinks iniquity like water! (15:15-16)

He then proceeded to tell Job what his fate as a wicked man would be. Such a person would suffer great pain and terror since he had defied God himself. His wealth would melt away, and destruction would come to him (15:17-35).

(2) *Job lambasts his friends and questions God (Job 16:1–17:16).* Job's patience wore out with the carping of his friends. They were "miserable comforters" who would sing a different tune if they were in Job's place. Everybody was against him, and God especially was against him. God had worn him out, dried him up, and "gnashed his teeth" at him. He was at ease before, yet God had attacked him, even though he had done violence to no one and had been innocent (16:1-17).

Job 16:18–17:2 represents one of the low places in the book of Job. The afflicted man cried out for the earth not to cover his blood when he died.[5] His unburied blood, which carried his life, would cry out to be avenged. This was a plea for justice to be done. God knew he deserved justice even though his friends scorned him. But death was closing in on him, and justice was not yet done. His friends, so sure of their own wisdom, really did not have a wise man among them (17:3-14). Added to their insults was his lack of hope of recovery:

> Where then is my hope?
>   Who will see my hope?
> Will it go down to the bars of Sheol?
>   Shall we descend together into the dust? (17:15-16)

(3) *Bildad plays the same record (Job 18:1-21).* Bildad really added little to what had been said.

---

[5]See Gen. 4:10; Ezek. 24:7.

(4) *Job reaches the bottom (Job 19:1-29).*   Continuing his rebuke of his friends, Job pointed out that even if he had sinned, it had been a personal fault, not a public one. God had put him "in the wrong" (19:6), stripped him of everything, and loosed his troops against Job. If that were not enough, even his closest friends and relatives now shunned him, including his wife. He pleaded with friends:

> Have pity on me, have pity on me, O you my friends,
>   for the hand of God has touched me!
> Why do you, like God, pursue me?
> Why are you not satisfied with my flesh? (19:21-22)

Job wanted his words to be written in a permanent record. He had confidence that one would come who would prove him right. The "redeemer" of whom he spoke (19:25) would be the one who cleared his name. To biblical man, one's honor and reputation were of supreme importance. Job desired that his name be cleared above all, and somehow he believed God would see that justice was done. At the lowest point, there came a glimmer of hope, another instance of reaching out to the later doctrine of life after death.

(5) *Zophar knows the answer (Job 20:1-29).*   Zophar was insulted by what Job had said. He knew how to reply, however, since he was one of those persons who always had an answer even if he did not know what the question was. He proceeded to lecture Job on the fate of the wicked according to traditional wisdom. No matter how he prospered, it would only be temporary. God would wash him away in the flood of his wrath.

(6) *Job replies to Zophar: round two (Job 21:1-34).*   Job replied that his quarrel was not with them. After all, look what had happened to him. When he compared his condition to some of the evil men he know, they were prospering while he, a righteous man, was suffering. With this argument, Job went completely counter to traditional theology. As his friends had overstated their case to prove him wrong, Job now overstated the case the other way. His so-called friends were just liars.

d. *The debate: round three (Job 22:1–27:23).*   The third cycle of speeches is incomplete. Perhaps the text was scrambled over the years. In part of one speech Job sounded like Zophar.

(1) *Eliphaz gets nasty (Job 22:1-30).*   Eliphaz began to make wild charges against Job. According to him, there was no end to Job's sins. He had oppressed his brothers, starved the hungry, and oppressed widows and orphans. His only hope lay in turning to God before it was too late. He could only be delivered if his hands were clean.

(2) *Job searches for God (Job 23:1–24:25).*   Ignoring Eliphaz's charges, Job complained of his inability to find God. He believed God would give him a fair hearing if he could only get a chance to lay his case before him. But wherever he sought God, he was not to be found. The terrifying thing

was, however, that God knew where Job was. He could do to Job whatever he chose, and no one could stop him (23:1-17).

Job again cited instances in which the wicked had seemingly escaped God's judgment while the righteous had suffered. Men stole property by moving line markers and oppressed the poor, who, though they were righteous, continued in their poverty. Yet the murderer and the adulterer sinned and went free.

Job 24:18-25 sounds more like Zophar than Job since it argued that the wicked were punished, in contrast to the arguments just stated that sinners escaped their just punishment.

(3) *Bildad contrasts God and man (Job 25:1-6).* In a short speech, Bildad spoke of God's rule over man, "Who is a maggot, and the son of man, who is a worm!" (25:6).

(4) *Job replies to Bildad: round three (Job 26:1-4).* In an abbreviated reply, Job lambasted Bildad for his arrogant attitude toward Job.

(5) *The continuation of Bildad's speech on God and man (Job 26:5-14).* This section obviously was part of Bildad's third speech since it continued to speak of God's rule over the universe. Its theme was God's mastery of the created order of things.

(6) *Job ends his part of the debate (Job 27:1-12).* To the end, Job defended his point of view, yielding nothing to his friends. He wished that those who opposed him would get the punishment they deserved.

(7) *Zophar again? (Job 27:13-23).* In another speech that sounded like Zophar's bombastic style, the debate was ended. He spoke as God's supposed authority on the fate of the wicked, which he described in loving detail.

e. *The wisdom poem (Job 28:1-28).* This poem, which separates the speech cycles from Job's final statement of his innocence, would fit well into the book of Proverbs. Its theme is the value of wisdom. Men dug deep into the earth for minerals and precious metals (28:1-11). Wisdom, however, could not be found in the depths of earth; nor could it be bought with man's most precious material possessions. Nothing could compare with it in value. Only God knew where wisdom could be found. It was with him in creation—he tested it and proved its worth. He declared:

> Behold, the fear of the LORD, that is wisdom;
> and to depart from evil is understanding (28:28).

f. *Job presents his case (Job 29:1–31:40).* Job's final arguments fell into three divisions: (1) his past prosperity, (2) his present problems, and (3) his code of ethics.

Looking back over his life, Job yearned for the good days he had enjoyed. His family had been around him, his flocks had prospered, and he had had an honored place in the community (29:1-10). He had been known in the community for his kindness and generosity toward the poor and oppressed. He had been praised by those around him. They had come to him for advice because he was a leader among men (29:11-25).

But things had changed. He was ridiculed by people who were on the very lowest levels of human society, people whom once he would not trust to care for his flocks. Now they spat on him. They made him the butt of their ridicule and harassed him at every turn. He was in pain—both in body and in spirit—for God had cast him down into the dirt (30:1-19).

Turning to God, Job charged him with treating him cruelly and shutting his ears to Job's pleas. His skin turned black and fell away. He mourned his fate (30:20-31).

As a climax to his speeches, Job set forth his code of conduct. It has been described as the "code of an Old Testament gentleman."[6] Except for the first, each common breach of conduct in human society was introduced by the formula "If I have . . ." followed by a sort of self-curse: "Let my [me] . . ." with the appropriate punishment. By this means, he declared himself innocent of each item. (1) He had not looked at a virgin with lust in his heart (31:1-4). (2) He had not lied, nor had he coveted the possessions of others (31:5-8). (3) He had not committed adultery (31:9-12). (4) He had been sensitive of the needs and rights of his servants (31:13-15). (5) He had seen to the needs of the less fortunate (31:16-23). (6) He had not put his trust in his wealth, nor had he worshiped the sun or moon (31:24-28). (7) He had not gloated over another man's ruin, failed to be kind to strangers, nor sinned any secret sins (31:29-34). If an indictment against him were written down, he would carry it to God like a prince wore a crown (31:35-37). Finally, he had taken care of his land (31:38-40).

g. *The Elihu speeches (Job 32:1–37:24).*   These speeches seem not to be a part of the original poetic section of Job. Elihu was mentioned nowhere, in either the prose or poetic sections. The language of this part is different from the rest. These speeches, furthermore, add very little to what has already been said. Elihu comes through as a brash young man who had more wind than he had wisdom. He constantly urged Job and the friends to speak up and refute what he was saying. He kept plowing ahead with such a massive outpouring of words that they never had a chance to get in anything. Perhaps the passage that catches the flavor of Elihu better than any other is 36:3-4:

> I will fetch my knowledge from afar,
>   and ascribe righteousness to my Maker
> For truly my words are not false;
>   one who is perfect in knowledge is with you.

[6]I am indebted to the late J. Philip Hyatt of Vanderbilt University for this phrase.

h. *The divine speeches (Job 38:1–41:34).*   God spoke from the whirlwind, chiding Job for questioning his wisdom. Then followed a series of divine test questions on the mysteries of nature. Beginning with creation, they were concerned with various aspects of the creation and the natural order but were especially concerned with water in nature (38:1-38). Then the questions turn to Job's knowledge of animal life, ranging from wild animals to domestic animals, such as the horse. The answer to all the questions was, "Only God knows these things." Job admitted his ignorance and vowed to speak no more (38:39–40:5).

God was not through with his speech, however. He challenged Job to use his power to bring down all the proud men of the earth. Then God would acknowledge Job's power and wisdom (40:6-14).

The divine speeches were concluded by the description of two legendary animals—Behemoth, which was an exaggerated description of the hippopotamus, and Leviathan, a legendary creature of the sea and rivers that was modeled on the crocodile (40:15–41:34).

i. *Job's submission (Job 42:1-6).*   Job was overwhelmed by the divine outpouring. He admitted God's power and wisdom far exceeded his own puny efforts:

> Therefore I have uttered what I did not understand,
>> things too wonderful for me, which I did not know (42:3).

But all that did not matter. His obsession with his sufferings was now superseded by a new and different experience with the divine:

> I had heard of thee by the hearing of the ear,
>> but now my eye sees thee;
> therefore I despise myself,
>> and repent in dust and ashes (42:5-6).

Job's previous knowledge of God had been a second-hand knowledge. What he had known of God had been passed on by tradition. Now, he had experienced God personally. That personal encounter with the divine had changed his view of himself and his problems.

The traditional ending of the story (Job 42:7-17).   The unorthodox ending of the poetic portions of Job was too much for the traditionalists. To bring it in line with orthodoxy, the ending of the older Job story was added. In it, Job's friends had to have Job to sacrifice for them because they had misrepresented God.

As for Job himself, his health and wealth were restored. His family, who had shunned him in his illness, now gathered to comfort him once the ordeal was over. He lived a long life, accumulated twice as many animals as before his illness, and once again had the perfect number of children, seven sons and three daughters. The names of the daughters were Jemimah, ("Dove"), Keziah ("Cinnamon"), and Keren-happuch ("Horn of eye paint").

problem of human suffering

Job: a summary.   Job has been long conceded to be one of the great literary masterpieces of all time. The question with which it deals still intrigues and baffles thoughtful people of our age—the problem of human suffering and, more specifically, the suffering of righteous or innocent people. The problem is especially crucial in the context of the belief in a just and all-wise God. Job did not really solve the problem. Instead, Job's vision of God changed his focus from his own problems to faith in a personal God. The air of mystery surrounding Job and the problem with which the book deals remains. Perhaps that is part of the reason the book is still so fascinating.

Ecclesiastes: skeptical wisdom.   Ecclesiastes illustrates how far some Jewish thinkers had strayed from orthodox theology in the postexilic period. Except for occasional orthodox corrections, the book voiced the skeptical, pessimistic feelings of a man who had tried everything but had found nothing satisfying or meaningful in which to invest his life. The main speaker in the book was the "Preacher, the son of David, King in Jerusalem" (1:1). "Preacher" is but one possible translation of the Hebrew title *Koheleth*. It was used to refer to a schoolmaster, or one who was in charge of an assembly of people.

The reference to the son of David, King in Jerusalem, has led to Solomon's being identified as the author of Ecclesiastes. In reality, Solomon's relation to this book was probably the same as Ruth's relation to the book of Ruth—that is, he was the main character portrayed by the book rather than the author. The language and thought of the book suggest that it was postexilic in its origin. Like Proverbs, it probably was used as a schoolbook.

Vanity of vanities (Eccl. 1:1–2:26.   "Vanity of vanities! All is vanity" (1:2). With these words, the writer of Ecclesiastes announced his opinion of the world and life in it. Nothing was lasting—nothing was of real value. While he was not an atheist (one who denied the existence of God), he was a deist, one who believed in God but who believed that God had little or nothing to do with what went on in the world.

The Preacher had tried many things. He had tried work, but he concluded that it was for nothing. The world was going in circles. Life had no purpose.

> What has been is what will be,
>   and what has been done is what will be done;
>   and there is nothing new under the sun (1:9).

So work did not satisfy (1:2-11).

Next he tried wisdom. He acquired great wisdom, but it too was emptiness, for "he who increases knowledge increases sorrow" (1:12-18). Pleasure was tested without restraint; but it, too, proved to be worthless (2:1-11). When he considered wisdom and folly, he realized that both the wise men and the fool died with no lasting memory of their accomplishments and failures (2:12-16). This thought led him to despair when he realized that what a man gained in this life had to be left for someone else to enjoy (2:17-23). So he concluded:

> There is nothing better for a man than that he should eat and drink, and find enjoyment in his toil. . . . For to the man who pleases him God gives wisdom and knowledge and joy (2:24-26).

The latter verse sounds more like the voice of orthodoxy speaking.

"For everything there is a season" (Eccl. 3:1-15).   These famous lines, a setting out of opposites to stress the paradoxical nature of life, represented a view of history that was strange to the rest of the Old Testament. The general Old Testament view was that history had a beginning and it will have an end. It was moving to a goal under the expert direction of God himself.

A philosophy of history that saturated the book of Ecclesiastes— history moves in circles, going nowhere, having no purpose or goal—was clearly expressed in 3:1-15. It was like a dog chasing its tail but never catching it. Essentially, this was a Greek, not a Hebrew, conception of history. This seems to suggest that Ecclesiastes was influenced by the Hellenistic culture that blossomed across the Near East following the conquests of Alexander the Great (3:1-8).

While God had given man a sense of time as past and future, he had not given him ability to look at life as a whole. The best he could do, then, was to take life as it came while doing his best (3:9-15).

The question of justice (Eccl. 3:16–4:3).   As far as justice was concerned, it was a matter of chance, too. Wickedness triumphed just as often as righteousness did. Man had no advantage over the animals. The oppressed cried out, but no one comforted them. Power was behind the oppressors. As a result, the dead were better off than the living. The unborn were even more fortunate since they had not had to experience life.

The futility of working alone (Eccl. 4:4-16).   Man worked out of a sense of rivalry with his fellow man. It was better to work with someone so as to have the protection a partner could give. It was better to be young, poor, and wise than to be an old and foolish ruler. Being a hero was also just temporary, since heroes were soon forgotten.

Do not fool around with God (Eccl. 5:1-7).   The Preacher warned that a person should avoid calling God's attention to himself. God should be obeyed without question. If one could not keep a vow, it would be better not to make it. Silence was better than chatter that might make God become angry.

Life has problems (Eccl. 5:8–6:12).   If the government oppressed a man, he had no hope for justice since every official was protected by the one above him (5:8-9). Kings and rich men had money, but life was not a bed of roses for the rich. More riches meant that one was responsible for more people. A rich man lost sleep worrying about his money, while the laborer slept peacefully. If a man saved money, he would lose it and leave his work as he came into it—with nothing. The best thing to do was to accept what God gave and not worry about it (5:10-20).

There was no justice in the Preacher's way of looking at life. A man could be wealthy and lose it all. He could have a large family and a long life and still be disgraced by not having a proper burial. If a man could not be happy while he lived, he would have been better off not to have been born. The best thing to do was take what one saw rather than to desire the unseen thing. Things were already predetermined for a man, so there was no profit in arguing about it (6:1-12).

Thinking about life (Eccl. 7:1–8:1).   These reflections on life saw life's end as more important than its beginning. Mourning was better than joy, and sorrow was better than laughter. Only a fool laughed. The wise rebuked the fool. Wisdom was the best guarantee that a man would keep what he had. The key to life was moderation. Wisdom had shown the Preacher "the wickedness of folly and the foolishness which is madness" (7:25). But the worst of all things was woman. A very few men could be trusted, but no woman was worthy of his trust.

Watch out for the ruler (Eccl. 8:2-9).   The only safe thing to do in regard to rulers was to stay out of their way. If man were wise enough, he could make the right choices about what to do and when to do it. Unfortunately, no man had that kind of wisdom.

There is no justice in life (Eccl. 8:10–9:12).   The wicked prospered as though he were righteous. There was just no way the Preacher could understand the ways of God. Even those wise men who made such a claim to know God's way really did not know them. The Preacher had decided that the wise and righteous were controlled by God, however (8:10–9:1).

The righteous and the wicked suffered the same fate. A sinner was just as well off as a saint. Of course, while there was life there was hope. While one was living, he should enjoy life with his wife. He should do what he did with diligence, for there would be no chance to do anything once he went to the grave. His time would come before he knew it (9:2-12).

Wisdom and foolishness (Eccl. 9:13–10:20). This section contains a number of illustrations about wisdom and foolishness. According to the Preacher, a little wisdom would go a long way; but a little foolishness could cancel the effects of a great deal of wisdom. Foolishness was especially bad when it infected those who had power.

The actions of the wise (Eccl. 11:1-6). A man wise in business spreads his investments around. One who always worried about the weather would never reap a crop. That was just the risk of living.

Advice to the young (Eccl. 11:7–12:8). Long life should be appreciated, but such a life would have its dark days. A young man should relish his youth, but he should still remember that he had to account to God for it. For that reason, he should take God into account in his youth before the problems of age and death overtook him.

The end of it all (Eccl. 12:9-14). Another person summarized the Preacher's life. He had taught what he had discovered about life with honest conviction. A final word was given to students:

> Of making many books there is no end, and much study is a weariness of the flesh (12:12).

A final orthodox word was added:

> Fear God, and keep his commandments; for this is the whole duty of man (12:13).

What about Ecclesiastes? Ecclesiastes revealed that postexilic Jews were not all orthodox in their views of God. The writer of Ecclesiastes believed in God. For him, however, God was not actively involved in the everyday events of life—or, if he were, one could not discover how he was involved. He did not accept the orthodox view that righteousness was always rewarded with blessing and that sin was always punished.

The Sweet Singers of Israel

Any complete discussion of Israel's poets and singers would involve almost every book in the Old Testament. A major portion of the materials in the books of the prophets was in poetic form. Jeremiah and Nahum, especially, excelled as poets. The historical works abound in poetic passages. Two notable examples of such passages were the Song of Deborah (Judg. 5) and David's lament over Jonathan and Saul (2 Sam. 1:19-27). As has been indicated previously, the wisdom materials made extensive use of poetic forms.

Song

There was a reason for this extensive use of poetry. Poetry was much more easily remembered than prose. Putting words in a rhythmic pattern gave an additional device for aiding the memory of a people who had to depend on it as the most common method of preserving and passing along traditions they valued. The words plus the rhythm were easier to commit to memory, just as words sung to a tune are easier to remember than just words by themselves.

Two books in the Old Testament were devoted exclusively to preserving Israel's greatest poetry. One of them deals with what we would call a secular theme—human love—and, more specifically, love between a man and a woman. It should be pointed out that to the Israelite this was not a secular theme. All of life and its relationships were of concern to the LORD of Israel, a biblical view that somehow has been lost over the centuries.

The second book, the Psalms, represented Israelite worship, both on the personal and the community level. In it all areas of life were touched, from going to war to praising God. In it were placed poems expressing the Israelite's violent expressions of hatred to his most joyous sense of praise for God's blessings.

THE SONG OF SONGS

This book has long been a source of embarrassment to Judaism and to the Christian church. It does not mention God anywhere. This failure has caused its place in the canon to be debated perhaps as no other Old Testament book has. Judaism and Christianity both solved the problem by interpreting it allegorically. The "husband" was the LORD and Israel was his "bride." For Christians, Jesus was the "husband" and the church was the "bride."

SONG OF SOLOMON

The nature of the book.   In reality, the book was a collection of love songs, celebrating the joys of physical love making. Its lesson was that sex was God's gift to mankind. Like all such gifts, it could be used properly or abused. But because some abused it, this did not lessen its value or beauty.

The poems cover a wide span of years. They were brought together in their present arrangement in the postexilic period. Solomon was not only noted for his wisdom but he also seemed to enjoy a reputation for his way with women. He was reputed to have had 700 wives and 300 concubines (1 Kings 11:3). So this book, like Proverbs, was attributed to him. The collector and arranger of the poems thought of Solomon as one of the main characters.

Interpretations of the book.   There are two basic interpretations of the characters in the book. Some hold that there were two characters:

Solomon and the maiden. Others argue that three characters were involved: Solomon, the maiden, and her home-town boyfriend. For the purposes of this discussion, it will be assumed that only two characters were involved.

A look in the book

The bride is prepared for her lover (Song 1:1-6).   Before a bride was brought to her husband for the first time, she was carefully bathed and perfumed for the occasion. The poet has skillfully caught the thoughts of the bride as she approaches the time she will first be brought to the groom. As she was anointed with oils, she anticipated his kisses. Her manner had charmed the maidens who waited on her (1:2-4).

She looked at herself. She was tanned by the sun. She wondered if this would make her less attractive. For this reason, she explained why she was so dark—she had been forced to work in the vineyards by her brothers.

The bride and the groom together (Song 1:7–2:5).   She asked where he was. He answered in a teasing manner that since she did not know, he was following the flock. He praised her beauty, comparing her to "a mare of Pharaoh's chariots" (1:9)! She, in turn, praised him. He was like "a cluster of henna blossoms in the vineyards of Ein-gedi" (1:14), an oasis on the Dead Sea. His next compliment was more appropriate:

> Behold, you are beautiful, my love;
>   behold, you are beautiful;
>   your eyes are doves.
> Behold, you are beautiful, my beloved.
>   truly lovely (1:15-16).

Compliments continued to pass back and forth between the lovers as he brought her to the banqueting house and fed her the finest delicacies (2:1-5).

The bride's memories of love (Song 2:6-17).   She remembered their love making and longed for him to wake up from his sleep. She thought of how he had come to her and how he had used such beautiful words to woo her in that springtime season:

> Arise, my love, my fair one,
>   and come away;
> for lo, the winter is past,
>   the rain is over and gone.
> The flowers appear on the earth,
>   the time of singing has come,
> and the voice of the turtledove
>   is heard in our land (2:10-12).

With those memories, she rested, assured of his love for her.

The bride has a bad dream (Song 3:1-5). She dreamed that he was gone. She went out to search for him. She had just asked the watchman if he had seen her lover when she found him. She took him home so he would be safe with her.

The king's wedding procession (Song 3:6-11). The king was borne to the wedding in an elaborate litter or palaquin, preceded by 60 soldiers in battle dress as a guard of honor.

The groom describes the bride (Song 4:1–5:1). This was a twofold description: What the bride looked like to the groom (4:1-8), and how she had devastated his heart (4:9-15). While the groom's description of the bride's features might not suit a modern maid, they were the highest compliments he could give a girl of his time. Her eyes were doves (4:1); her hair "like a flock of goats" (4:1); her neck was "like the tower of David" (4:4); her breasts were "like two fawns" of a gazelle (4:5). In short, there was no flaw in her (4:7). She had so captured him that she was like a garden of the most fragrant flowers and spices (4:9-15). The thoughts of her caused him to call her to him (4:16–5:1).

The bride has another dream (Song 5:2–6:3). In her dream, the bride heard her lover call at her door in the night. She ran to open it; but when she did, he was gone. When she went to look for him, she was attacked by the city's watchmen (5:2-8).

Her dream changed. She was describing her lover to the women of Jerusalem. He was tall, dark, and rugged. They asked her where he had gone. She answered that he had "gone down to his garden . . . to pasture his flock in the gardens and to gather lilies (6:2). The garden probably was an exaggerated expression for the open pasture lands (5:9–6:3).

The groom describes the bride (Song 6:4-10). Using many of the same terms found in 4:1-7, the groom described the bride. Of all his wives, she was the only perfect one. Even the other wives in the harem praised her beauty.

An invitation to dance (Song 6:11–7:9). She visited the garden where the fruit and nut trees blossomed. The next she knew she was in her lover's chariot (6:11-12). Then she was invited to dance (6:13). Her dance evoked the poetry in the soul of her lover as once again he tried to describe her charms (7:1-9).

The bride invites the groom to a garden tryst (Song 7:10-13). The bride invites the groom into the garden where she will give herself to him. There grew the mandrake, a fruit which was believed to promote fertility (see Gen. 30:14-15).

A poem in anticipation of the wedding (Song 8:1-4).   This poem reflected the protected status of women. Strange men were not permitted to have any dealings with them. The bride-to-be wished that her lover were like a brother. Then he would have access to her tent as a member of the family.

Please be faithful (Song 8:5-12).   Here were some of the Song's most famous lines as she pleads for him to be faithful to her:

> Set me as a seal upon your heart,
>   as a seal upon your arm;
> for love is strong as death,
>   jealousy is cruel as the grave.
> Its flashes are flashes of fire,
>   a most vehement flame.
> Many waters cannot quench love,
>   neither can floods drown it.
> If a man offered for love
>   all the wealth of his house,
>   it would be utterly scorned (8:6-7).

She had been chaste as a young girl. Now she was a mature woman ready for the fulfillment of love. She had kept herself for this special time.

A final call (Song 8:13-14).   The lovers call to each other as the book ends.

THE BOOK OF PSALMS

No book in the Old Testament is better known than Psalms because no other Old Testament book mirrors human emotions better than Psalms. There are psalms for times of meditation, psalms for times of despair, psalms for times of worship, and psalms for times of joy. Unlike other Old Testament literature—which describes what had happened to Israel, contained messages to Israel from the LORD through the prophets, or was the distilled wisdom of society—the psalms were man's expressions of his feelings to God. They were directed toward God, not toward other men. As a result, they run the gamut of human emotions.

Who wrote the psalms and when were they written?   There is no simple answer to this question. David, called the psalmist in Jewish and Christian tradition, undoubtedly wrote some of the psalms. But even the book itself—if the introductory comments found in some of the psalms are to be taken literally—indicates that David did not write all the psalms. Many names were attached to the psalms by the earliest commentators on psalms—those men who attached the titles to the individual psalms many years after a psalm was written. Thus the names of Asaph (Psalms 73–83), the sons of Korah (84,85,87), Heman the Ezrahite (88), Ethan the Ezrahite (89), and Moses (90) were attached to the psalms.[7] Many psalms had no one's name attached to them.

In reality, the book of Psalms was more like a modern church hymnal in that it was a collection of songs that came into existence over a long span of time. A church hymnal today may have hymns whose words go back to the early Christian centuries, while at the same time it will have hymns that were written especially for that hymnal. Psalm 29, for instance, was a "Yahwistic adaptation of an older Canaanite hymn to the storm-god Baal"[8]—that is, the Israelites liked the hymn so much that they removed Baal's name and inserted the personal name of the God of Israel. Psalm 29 then went back in its original form to at least the fourteenth century. Similar adjustments are made in songs today when words to popular tunes are changed slightly to give them a religious meaning. On the other hand, psalms such as Psalm 137 clearly reflect an exilic background, and some psalms probably even came from postexilic times.

Within the book of Psalms, there are other evidences that the psalms come from different periods in Israel's history. The book, for example, had five divisions, to correspond to the five books of the Torah or Law (1–41; 42–72; 73–89; 90–106; 107–150). Each of these divisions has its own benedictions, Psalm 1 serving as an introduction to the whole book and Psalm 150 serving as the benediction for the whole book. Book 2 (42–72) ends with the statement that "the prayers of David, the son of Jesse, are ended" (72:20). There are some psalms in the other sections which are titled "a psalm of David," but it is generally agreed that most of the psalms that might have come from David are in chapters 1–72 and most likely in chapters 1–41.

The title "a psalm of David," furthermore, does not necessarily mean Davidic authorship. The Hebrew language allows it to be translated "in the style of David," or "to David"—that is, "dedicated to David." These and similar titles indicate that there were several smaller collections of psalms before the final edition that we know as the book of Psalms.

Another evidence of such collections is that there are duplications in the book of Psalms. The most notable example of this duplication is Psalms 14 and 53. They are identical for all practical purposes except for their references to God. Psalm 14 refers to God as *Yahweh* (the LORD), while Psalm 53 uses *Elohim* (God). This must have been a popular psalm that

---

[7]The sons of Korah and Asaph were professional singing guilds connected with the Temple (1 Chron. 25).

[8]Mitchell Dahood, "Psalms I," *Anchor Bible,* vol. 16, p. 175.

was known in different parts of the country. Since the psalms were collected at local worship centers (shrines), this psalm got into two different collections. When the book was put together, the two collections were put together without noticing that there were duplicate psalms in them. To conclude: While David was called the psalmist, the psalms actually came from different periods of Israelite history. Before the present book of Psalms there were a number of smaller collections. Sometime in the postexilic period they were brought together into one large collection that we call the book of Psalms.

The study of the psalms. Psalms studies have changed much in the last 50 years. Archaeological discoveries, especially of Canaanite materials, have opened up many new avenues of study. Whereas 50 years ago the tendency was to date the psalms late in Israelite history, now the trend is toward a much earlier dating. Many words and phrases in the poems which once were obscure now have been clarified by the discovery of the Ugaritic materials. One of the latest commentaries on the book of Psalms made extensive use of those materials.[9]

The most important influence on the study of the psalms was the work of Hermann Gunkel, a German scholar of the Old Testament. Before Gunkel's time, each psalm was studied individually. Scholars tried to discover its historical setting by connecting it with some person or event in Israelite history. Since the book of Psalms contains few historical references, scholars based their interpretations more on guesswork than on evidence.

Gunkel, however, made an important discovery. He concluded that the psalms had to be looked at in light of their association with Israelite worship services. By looking at the literary form of the individual psalms, he discovered that they could be separated into classes. He concluded that there were five groups (or classes) into which more than two-thirds of the psalms would fit. There were five other subclasses which would accommodate the rest of the psalms.

Gunkel said that each psalm had a specific setting in life—it was used for a particular kind of worship service. Thus, when a person who had been ill and who had recovered wanted to offer a sacrifice to show gratitude, he did not compose a psalm. There were already psalms for that purpose. Or, when a psalm such as a hymn was composed, it followed a rather fixed pattern, so that all hymns shared certain basic likenesses.

While there have been modifications to Gunkel's classifications, they still are accepted today as the basis for most modern study of the psalms. For that reason—and because the length of the book of Psalms makes a

---

[9]Mitchell Dahood, "Psalms I, II, and III," *Anchor Bible,* vol. 16, pp. 17a, 17b.

comment on every psalm somewhat difficult—selected psalms following the Gunkel classification will be studied as examples for all the psalms.[10]

Hymns.   The key word for the hymns was "Hallelujah," which means praise the LORD. Hymns usually had three basic parts: (1) a call to praise God; (2) the reason for praising him, and (3) a call once again to praise God. Other than Individual Laments, this was the largest class.[11]

There were two subclasses of the hymn: Songs of Zion (46, 48, 76, 87), which were hymns praising Jerusalem; and Enthronement Songs (47, 93, 97, 99), which were used in connection with the crowning of the king. This latter group was called New Year's Psalms by Sigmund Mowinckel, a Scandinavian scholar. Mowinckel argued that the Hebrews in postexilic times had a New Year's festival in which the king portrayed the role of God in creation. Psalms 47, 93, 95, 96, 97, 98, 99, and 100 were used, according to Mowinckel, as a part of such a festival because they contain the phrase "the LORD reigns" (Ps. 47:7).

Communal Laments.   These were prayers of petition to God to bring deliverance to the community in time of such disaster as war, famine, or epidemic. The laments usually contained (1) a cry to God for help, (2) a description of the situation which brought on the appeal, (3) a prayer for deliverance, and (4) sometimes an oracle from a prophet or an expression of confidence that the LORD would answer. All these elements were not always present, nor did they necessarily follow the same order.[12]

Individual Laments.   The lament of the individual had the same basic form that communal laments had. They were used in services in which individuals were asking God to deliver them from personal disaster. This was the largest class.[13]

Since laments often contained an expression of confidence that the LORD would answer the plea of the sufferer, a subclass of the Individual Lament was the Psalms of Confidence. Psalms 4, 11, 16, 23, 27:1-6, 62, and 131 made up this subclass.

Individual Songs of Thanksgiving.   These were hymns used by an individual to praise the LORD for deliverance from trouble. They had (1) an introduction; (2) a narration which told of his trouble, his cry to God,

---

[10]A compact presentation of Gunkel's views can be found in Hermann Gunkel, "The Psalms," No. 19 in *Facet Books* (Philadelphia: Fortress Press, 1967).

[11]It includes Psalms 8, 19, 33, 65, 68, 96, 98, 100, 103, 104, 105, 111, 113, 114, 115, 117, 135, 136, 145–150.

[12]Among the Communal Laments are Psalms 44, 58, 60, 74, 79, 80, 83, 106, and 125.

[13]It included Psalms 3, 5, 6, 7, 13, 17, 22, 25, 26, 27:7-14, 28, 31, 35, 38, 39, 42–43, 51, 52, 54, 55, 56, 57, 59, 61, 63, 64, 69, 70, 71, 86, 88, 102, 109, 120, 130, 139, 140, 141, 142, and 143.

and his deliverance; (3) an acknowledgment of his deliverance; and (4) the announcement of an offering of thanks.[14]

The Royal Psalms.   These psalms were used for special occasions in the religious services for the king. No major activity could be carried out by the king without the proper religious ceremony. Later, when Israel had no king, these psalms began to be interpreted as applying to God's anointed king of the future, the Messiah.[15]

The other psalms.   Not all psalms could be fitted into the five major classes. There were five.other classes: (1) songs of pilgrimage (84, 122); (2) community songs of thanksgiving (67, 124); (3) wisdom poetry (1, 37, 49, 73, 112, 127, 128); (4) two types of liturgies—Torah liturgies (15, 24, 121, 134); and prophetic liturgies (12, 14, 50, 53, 75, 81, 82, 85, 91, 95, 132); and (5) mixed poems, the largest group outside the major classes. These psalms often combined characteristics of the major classes (9–10, 36, 40, 77, 89, 90, 94, 107, 108, 119, 123, 129, 137, 144, 78).

A look at selected psalms.   Since not all psalms can be examined, representative psalms from each category will be studied.

Psalm 1 (a wisdom psalm).   This psalm seems to have been written to introduce the book of Psalms. Its theme is "the two ways." The psalm tells what the righteous man is (1:1); what he does (1:2); and what he is like (1:3). In contrast, the wicked were like wheat husks that can be blown away by the wind (1:4). They cannot endure the judgment (1:5). The conclusion is given here:

> The LORD knows the way of the righteous,
>   but the way of the wicked will perish (1:6).

Psalm 8 (a hymn on the glory of the LORD and the dignity of man).   While not opening with a call to praise as was typical of the hymns, Psalm 8 does open with praise to the LORD (8:1). The greatness of the LORD's presence can be seen in the heavenly bodies he has created (8:2-3). They made the psalmist consider man, whom the LORD had made as the highest of his creatures. Man had been given dominion or authority over all other creatures—whether the land animals, the birds of the air, or the sea creatures (8:4-8). The psalm closes with a repeat of the psalmist's praise to the LORD.

Psalm 117 (a short hymn).   The shortest psalm is a classic example of a hymn. The call to praise (117:1) begins with one of the few Hebrew

---

[14]Psalms 18 (a Royal Psalm as well), 30, 32, 34, 41, 66, 92, 116, and 138.
[15]They include Psalms 2, 18, 20, 21, 45, 72, 101, 110, and 132.

Figure 13–1. "The wicked are not so, but are like chaff which the wind drives away" (Psalm 1:4). Threshing floors, such as this one in the Judean hill country, were established where the threshers could take advantage of the late afternoon breeze to separate the husks, or chaff, from the grain.

Photograph by John H. Tullock.

words which has been transliterated into English—"Hallelujah," which means "praise the LORD." Verse 2 gives the reason for praising the LORD:

> For great is his steadfast love toward us;
>   and the faithfulness of the LORD endures forever!

The renewed call to praise, "Hallelujah," ends the psalm.

Psalm 74 (a communal lament). The condition that gave rise to this psalm was an attack on the Temple. As a lament, it begins with a complaint to God. He had cast off his people. He had forgotten the congregation of Israel, because the Temple, God's dwelling place in Zion, was destroyed (74:1-3). The complaint was renewed later in verses 10-11.

The psalmist described how the enemy destroyed the Temple wood-work and burned the Temple. There was no prophet to give a word from the LORD (74:4-9).

It was not a lack of ability that had caused God not to deliver Israel from the enemy. He had created the heavens and the earth. He had defeated the great sea monster Leviathan. He had set the heavenly bodies in place and had established the seasons (74:12-17).

On the basis of the need of God to defend his own honor, the psalmist called on him to

> Arise, O God, plead thy cause;
>   remember how the impious scoff at thee all the day!
> Do not forget the clamor of thy foes,
>   the uproar of thy adversaries which goes up continually! (74:22-23)

When God punished his foes for scoffing at him, he would also be destroying Israel's enemies. Thus, two needs could be met by one activity.

Psalm 22 (an individual lament). The largest class of the psalms was the individual lament. The opening words of this lament are familiar to Christians, because, according to Matthew and Mark, they were quoted by Jesus on the cross (Matt. 27:46; Mark 15:34). The opening cry (22:1-2) complains that God has forsaken the sufferer. Instead of an account of his condition, the psalmist recalled God's activity on behalf of the fathers (22:3-5). He had a low opinion of himself, for he said, "But I am a worm, and no man." Men mocked and scorned him. They also scoffed at God for not delivering him (22:6-8).

He recalled that he had depended on God from birth. For this reason he still called on God. His enemies were like raging bulls. He was weak from illness, his strength was all gone, his mouth felt dry, and death seemed near. This encouraged his enemies to circle him like a pack of vicious dogs, ready to snap and bite him, exposing his bones (22:9-18).

From the depths of despair, he moved upward toward assurance that God would hear him. He repeated his cry for help (22:19-21) and promised that he would praise God to his brethren. He exhorted those near him to stand in awe of the LORD. The LORD would hear the cry of the afflicted (22:22-24).

Addressing God again, he pledged to praise him in the assembly (22:25-26). The remainder of the psalm was an expression of confidence in God. This type of ending, while not present in all laments, did appear frequently (22:27-31).

Psalm 23 (a psalm of confidence). The psalms of confidence grew out of the individual laments. This, the most famous of all the psalms, is often referred to as "the Shepherd Psalm." While the figure of the shepherd does introduce the psalm, there are two other figures in the psalm—the guide and the host.

The psalmist thought of the LORD as a shepherd to lead his flock to the best pastures where there was tender grass and plenty of water (23:1-3a). The LORD was like a guide who led the traveler through the deep, dark ravines so common in the Palestinian hill country. There lurked thieves and wild animals ready to pounce on the unsuspecting traveler. The guide carried both a heavy stick and a weighted club to defend the one he was guiding. The traveler could proceed with assurance that the guide would protect him (23:3*b*-4).

The LORD was like a Bedouin sheik who took in a man fleeing from his enemies. The law of hospitality in the Near East, especially among the nomadic and seminomadic groups, was to take in any stranger, to give him the best of food, and to protect him at the cost of the host's own life, if necessary.[16] The practice of anointing the guest's head with oil was an act of hospitality, as was the filling of the cup to overflowing. As the servants of the host would serve the stranger, so goodness and mercy followed the one blessed of the LORD throughout his days (23:5-6).

Psalm 51 (an individual lament).   This is perhaps the most famous of the individual laments. Early Jewish interpreters connected it with David's seduction of Bathsheba and the child born from that act. Its appeal, however, like that of the psalms in general, is that it mirrors the inner conflict of any moral man who has committed a grievous sin of immorality. It contains a varied vocabulary describing sin and repentance.

Verses 1 and 2 contain a plea for forgiveness based on God's mercy, his "steadfast love" and his "abundant mercy." Sin was described in a threefold manner as "transgression" (or rebellion), "sin" (which basically means failing to come up to the accepted standard), and "iniquity" (meaning moral distortion). God's forgiveness also was described as a threefold action: blotting out or erasing, washing thoroughly, and cleansing as in a ceremonial sense (51:1-2).

The psalmist had a deep sense of guilt. He felt that he had sinned against God and that the troubles he had been enduring were just punishment for his failures (51:3-5). He asked God to teach him wisdom. The cleansing he desired was both outward cleansing of a ceremonial act and inward cleansing through repentance and forgiveness. He wanted a sense of inner joy. This could only come with the assurance of sins forgiven (51:6-9).

He pleaded with God to create a clean heart within him, for God to keep him in his presence, and for God to restore him to the joy of the salvation which was God's (51:10-12). If these things were done, he promised to proclaim God's ways to sinners (51:13-14). Unlike some psalms, in which animal sacrifices were offered, this one speaks of "a broken and contrite heart" as the sacrifice most acceptable to God. (51:15-17). A later addition by a priestly hand tried to bring it back to priestly

[16]See the story of Abraham and the two men (Gen. 18:1-33). Also, Lot's attempt to protect the same men (Gen. 19:1-11).

orthodoxy by mentioning "burnt offerings and whole burnt offerings" (51:18-19).

Psalm 32 (an individual song of thanksgiving).   This psalm, like others of its class, was used in a service to offer thanks to the LORD when one had recovered from a severe illness. After speaking about the blessedness of being forgiven of his sins, the psalmist told about the effects of his sense of guilt before he confessed his sins. It had made him physically ill so that his "strength was dried up like the heat of summer" (32:3-4). But he had confessed his sins, and his happiness was restored (32:5). He would recommend that the godly pray to the LORD.

An oracle, probably spoken by a Temple prophet, interrupted the psalmist:

> I will instruct you and teach you the way you should go;
>   I will counsel you with my eye upon you (32:8).

He was not to be like the horse or mule that had to be controlled with "bit and bridle" in order to get it to obey (32:9).

The psalm closes with a call for joy over the love which the LORD had given to those who trusted him (32:10-11).

Psalm 116 (an individual song of thanksgiving).[17]   This psalm, more clearly than most, gives directions for worship. The individual had been healed of a devastating illness. He came to the Temple to make a sacrifice of thanksgiving. The service opened with an address to the other worshipers, in which he described what had happened to him (116:1-4). Praise to the LORD followed because the LORD had delivered him from almost certain death (116:5-11).

Next, the offerings were made. They were introduced by the question, "What shall I render to the LORD for all his bounty to me." There followed the drink offering. The cup containing the wine was lifted to the LORD while he recited his vows and commitment (116:12-16). Then, the animal sacrifice was made with the proper comments (116:17-19). The service was ended with the shout "Hallelujah!"

Psalm 45 (a royal psalm).   This was a psalm for a royal wedding. It was sung by the court minstrel to celebrate the happy event that was about to take place. First, the singer addressed the king, using exaggerated language to describe him. In verses 6-7 especially there appears the kind of language that led later interpreters to see this as a messianic psalm, particularly in those days when Israel had no king. The king was told that

---

[17]The idea for what follows in the discussion of this psalm came from Flanders, Crapps and Smith, *The People of the Covenant,* 2nd ed. (New York: The Ronald Press, 1973), p. 443ff.

his "divine throne" would "endure forever and ever" (45:1-9). In another royal psalm the king was called "God's son" (Pss. 2:7).

Next the queen-to-be was addressed. She was told how fortunate she was to be marrying the king of Israel. She was to forget the people and submit to the king as her lord (45:10-12). As though he were a writer of the bridal column in the Jerusalem *Gazette,* the psalmist described the queen's bridal attire as she was led by her escort to the wedding chamber (45:12-15).

The psalm ends with a forecast that the king will be succeeded by sons more famous than their forefathers. This could cause the king's name to be remembered for many generations because of the illustrious sons born to him and his queen (45:16-17).

Psalm 139 (a lament of the individual). This great psalm reflects a more developed theology than some of the earlier poems. It falls into four stanzas of six verses each. In the first stanza, the psalmist speaks of God's knowledge of the psalmist's everyday activities and thoughts. He was awed by such intimate knowledge as the LORD possessed (139:1-6).

In the second stanza, he spoke of God's all-pervading presence in the universe. No matter where he might go in the future, God would be there, even in the grave. This was a new idea (139:7-12).

In the third stanza, he spoke of God's knowledge of him before he was even born. God had seen his creation in the womb. God knew what he would be before he ever was. The thoughts of God were beyond his comprehension (139:13-18).

In the fourth stanza (139:19-24), he turned to his enemies, who were also God's enemies. Since he was powerless to overcome them, he called on God who had all power to do so. Then, the thought struck him that his thoughts might not be what they should. He closed with a plea:

> Search me, O God, and know my heart!
>   Try me and know my thoughts!
> And see if there be any wicked way in me,
>   and lead me in the way everlasting! (139:23-24)

Special groups of psalms. There are a number of psalm groupings and special psalms that need to be mentioned. One such group is Psalms 113–118. These psalms are still used today in the celebration of the Jewish feast of Passover. They are known as the Egyptian Hallel. Another such special group is Psalms 120–134. Each psalm in this group bears the title "A Song of Ascents." They were used in the great pilgrimage festivals. As devout Jews went up to Jerusalem, they sang these "Songs of Ascents" as they moved toward the Holy City.

While they are not distinct groups as such, certain psalms have unique characteristics. Among these were the acrostics, the most famous of which is Psalm 119. It contains 22 sections of stanzas, each containing 8 verses. All 8 verses in a stanza begin with the same Hebrew letter, and all 22 stanzas begin with a different letter in alphabetical order. Certain of the psalms were antiphonal psalms. They were written so that a leader spoke lines that told a story while a choir or the people answered with a refrain. Thus, in Psalm 136 the speaker told the story of the Exodus while the congregation or choir interrupted each line with the refrain, "For his steadfast love endures forever." When the refrain is removed, the words of the leader tell the story.

The vengeance psalms.   One of the major problems that face interpreters of the psalms are those psalms which express violent hatred toward the enemies of the nation or of the psalmist. Psalm 137 is an example of such attitudes. After lamenting the conditions that the exiles had to endure, the psalm turns to a violent denunciation of the Babylonians. It ends with the bitter words:

> O daughter of Babylon, you devastator!
> Happy shall he be who requites you
> with what you have done to us!
> Happy shall he be who takes your little ones
> and dashes them against the rock! (137:8-9)

One must admit that this attitude was a far cry from that expressed by a great teacher of a later time who said: "Let the children come to me, and do not hinder them, for to such belongs the kingdom of heaven" (Matt. 19:14). How does one deal with these psalms and what value, if any, do they have? Certain things must be understood before these questions can be answered. In the background were certain ideas:

1. They were grounded in ideas from the practice of blood-vengeance. Blood-vengeance was justice in its most primitive form. It arose in a time when there was no state to see that justice was done. Because of this lack of a neutral party to administer justice, the family or clan had that responsibility. The more specific responsibility fell upon the nearest of kin of the person who had been wronged. Thus, if A^1 killed B^1, then A^1 could expect B^2 to try to avenge the death of B^1. This avenger (or redeemer as he was called) was judge, jury, and executioner. (See Gideon's revenge for the death of his brothers in Judg. 8.)

2. Closely allied with these ideas was the idea of corporate personality. The individual was so bound up with the group that whatever affected him affected the group.

3. The concept of the covenant also was at work in these psalms. The LORD and Israel were bound together in covenant. In that covenant relationship, the LORD had become a part of Israel's "family," so to speak.

4. The belief in the justice of God and that justice had to come in this life led to the plea for God to destroy the enemy.

With these ideas in mind, the vengeance psalms reflect a condition in which Israel (or an individual) had been devastated by an enemy. There was no avenger who had survived the devastation or who had strength enough to see that justice was done. God, as Israel's covenant partner, was the only one left who could see that justice was done. Thus, basically, these rather brutal-sounding psalms really came from a people so brutalized themselves that God was their only hope. So, in a rather obscene way, they cry for justice just as oppressed groups still do today.

Summary on the psalms.   The psalms are the hymns of a people. They represent individual and group worship. For the most part, they reflect the kind of orthodox theology that the book of Proverbs and the friends of Job reflect: (1) God is just. (2) This life is all there is of real life. (3) Since God is just, the good will prosper and the wicked will suffer. Despite their simple view of life, they continue to speak to every generation because they mirror the full range of human emotion.

STUDY QUESTIONS

1. What is parallelism?
2. Name and define three kinds of parallelism in Hebrew poetry.
3. What is meter? Give examples.
4. How was Israelite wisdom related to wisdom in other countries?
5. How did the Egyptian "Instruction of Amen-en-opet" influence the Jewish book of Proverbs?
6. Name and define two types of wisdom teachings.
7. What was the theme of the book of Proverbs?
8. How does Proverbs chapters 1–9 differ from chapters 10–31?
9. What distinctive proverb form in Proverbs 30 reminds one of the prophet Amos?
10. What does Proverbs 31:10-31 tell us about the status of some women in ancient Israel?
11. What are the evidences that the book of Job is the work of more than one author?
12. What are some things one needs to know to help in the understanding of the book of Job?
13. What is the role of Satan in Job 1 and 2?
14. How does Job in chapters 1 and 2 differ from Job in chapters 3:1–42:6?

15. Who are Job's friends and what are their basic arguments to Job?
16. What are Job's arguments to his friends? to God?
17. Why is Job 31 called the "code of an Old Testament gentlemen"?
18. What do the Elihu speeches add to the book?
19. How does God answer Job?
20. What is the conclusion that Job reaches about the meaning of his suffering?
21. Why is Ecclesiastes called "skeptical wisdom"?
22. How does the view of God taken by Ecclesiastes differ from that taken by the book of Job?
23. What sort of philosophy of life does Ecclesiastes advocate?
24. What does Ecclesiastes tell us about the theological views of at least some Jews in postexilic times?
25. What was the purpose of the Song of Songs?
26. How has the Song of Songs been interpreted?
27. Who are the characters in the Song of Songs?
28. What basic difference in the nature of the psalms helps to explain some of the attitudes they contain?
29. How do we know that the book of Psalms is a collection of songs covering a long period of time?
30. How is the book of Psalms arranged?
31. What does the expression "a psalm of David" mean?
32. What did Hermann Gunkel contribute to our understanding of the Psalm?
33. What are Gunkel's five major classes of psalms?
34. What does Psalm 116 tell us about worship?
35. What was the purpose of Psalm 45?
36. How is one to interpret the vengeance psalms?
37. What is the basic theology of the psalms?

FOR FURTHER STUDY

Wisdom

BLANK, SHELDON H. "Wisdom." *Interpreter's Dictionary,* IV, 852-860.
McKANE, WILLIAM. *Prophets and Wise Men.* Oxford: Clarendon, 1960.
RAD, GERHARD VON. *Wisdom in Israel.* Trans. by James D. Martin. New York: Abingdon, 1973.

RANKIN, O. S. *Israel's Wisdom Literature.* New York: Schocken Books, 1969. Paperback.

SCOTT, R.B.Y. *The Way of Wisdom in the Old Testament.* New York: Macmillan, 1971.

Proverbs

FRITSCH, CHARLES T. "Proverbs: Introduction and Exegesis." *Interpreter's Bible,* IV. New York: Abingdon, 1955.

McKANE, WILLIAM. *Proverbs: A New Approach.* Old Testament Library. Philadelphia: Westminster, 1970.

SCOTT, R. B. Y. *Proverbs and Ecclesiastes.* Anchor Bible. Garden City, N.Y.: Doubleday, 1965.

Job

GORDIS, ROBERT. *The Book of God and Man: A Study of Job.* Chicago: University of Chicago Press, 1965.

POPE, MARVIN H. *Job.* Anchor Bible. Garden City, N.Y.: Doubleday, 1965.

ROBINSON, H. WHEELER. *The Cross in the Old Testament.* Philadelphia: Westminster, 1965. Also in paperback by S.C.M. Press, 1960.

TERRIEN, SAMUEL. "Job: Introduction and Exegesis." *Interpreter's Bible,* III. New York: Abingdon, 1954. One of the best commentaries on Job.

———. *Job: Poet of Existence.* Indianapolis: Bobbs-Merrill, 1958. Less technical than the IB volume.

WATTS, JOHN D. W., JR., J. OWENS, and MARVIN TATE. "Job." Broadman Commentary, IV. Nashville: Broadman Press, 1970.

Ecclesiastes

GORDIS, ROBERT. *Koheleth, the Man and His World.* New York: Jewish Theological Seminary of America Press, 1951. A revised edition has been issued as a Schocken paperback, 1967.

RANKIN. O. S. "Ecclesiastes: Introduction and Exegesis." *Interpreter's Bible,* V. New York: Abingdon, 1956.

The Song of Songs

MEEK, T. J. "The Song of Solomon." *Interpreter's Bible,* V. New York: Abingdon, 1956.

MURPHY, ROLAND E. "Form Critical Studies in the Song of Songs" in *Interpretation,* XXVII (1973), pp. 413–422.

ROWLEY, H. "The Interpretation of the Song of Songs" in *The Servant of the Lord and Other Essays.* Oxford: Blackwell, 1965, pp. 195–245.

Psalms

ANDERSON, BERNHARD W. *Out of the Depths: The Psalms Speak to Us Today.* Philadelphia: Westminster, 1974, Paperback.

BARTH, CHRISTOPH. *Introduction to the Psalms.* Trans. by R. A. Wilson. New York: Chas. Scribner's Sons, 1966. Paperback.

DAHOOD, MITCHEL. *Psalms: I, II, III.* Anchor Bible. New York: Doubleday, 1966–1970.

DURHAM, JOHN I. "Psalms" in *Broadman Bible Commentary.* Nashville: Broadman, 1971.

GUNKEL, HERMANN. The Psalms: *A Form-critical Introduction.* Trans. by T. M. Horner. Philadelphia: Fortress Press, 1967. This is a Facet paperback giving the essentials of Gunkel's pioneer work on the Psalms.

MOWINCKEL, SIGMUND. *The Psalms in Israel's Worship,* I–II. Trans. by D. R. Ap-Thomas. New York: Abingdon, 1962. Mowinckel is second only to Gunkel in his influence on modern studies of the Psalms.

TERRIEN, SAMUEL. *The Psalms and Their Meaning Today.* Indianapolis: Bobbs-Merrill, 1952.

WEISER, ARTUR. *The Psalms.* Old Testament Library. Trans. by Herbert Hartwell. Philadelphia: Westminster, 1962.

WESTERMANN, CLAUS. *The Praise of God in the Psalms,* 2nd ed. Richmond: John Knox, 1965.

CHAPTER FOURTEEN

The Time of Silence: Judah in Eclipse

It was as though someone had suddenly put out all the lights on a stage and cut off the sound while a play was in progress. The actors continued to act out their parts, but the audience could not see or hear, for there were neither lights nor sound. Things happened in Palestine between 400 and 200 B.C., but our knowledge has to be based largely on what was evident in 200 and what can be gleaned from sources outside of Israel.

The Historical Situation: 400–150

PERSIA'S LAST DAYS

The Persian Empire continued to control Palestine for the next century and a half. Persia was not without its trouble, however. From the time of Nehemiah on, Persia faced constant problems—first from an Egyptian revolt, then from the Greeks, and finally from the rulers from the western part of the empire.

Real trouble came, however, during the reign of Darius III Codomannus (336–331). When Philip II of Macedon (359–336) came to power, Macedonia gained control of the Greek states in 338. Although he was assassinated in 336, that tragedy was not to Persia's advantage because it put Alexander, Philip's son, on the throne of Macedonia.[1]

---

[1]John Bright, *A History of Israel,* pp. 409–410.

THE CAMPAIGNS OF ALEXANDER THE GREAT

The young Alexander (336–323) was a military genius. In 334 he invaded Asia Minor and quickly gained control of the entire area. At the battle of Issus (333) he routed the main Persian army, even capturing Darius's wife and family. Moving down the Mediterranean coast, he quickly captured Phoenicia (except Tyre) and Palestine. He was welcomed with open arms by the Egyptians in 332. From there he moved eastward until he reached the Indus River. In his wake he left centers of Greek learning and culture, as he required his older soldiers to retire and live in the conquered lands. Over a period of several hundred years, the effects of Alexander's action changed the course of civilization because of the influence of Greek culture.

PTOLEMIES AND SELEUCIDS IN PALESTINE

When Alexander died in 323, his empire was divided among four of his generals. Ptolemy (an Egyptian) was given control of Palestine, while Syria was given to Seleucus. For a century, the Ptolemies dominated Palestine. During that time, Egypt became a center of Jewish population. It has been estimated that 1 million Jews lived in Alexandria in the first century B.C.

But Egyptian domination of Palestine came under direct challenge from the Seleucids when Antiochus the Great (223–187) came to the Seleucid throne. After a number of battles, Antiochus finally prevailed in a battle of Panium (Baniyas), where the later city of Caesarea Philippi (of New Testament fame) was to be located.[2]

While Antiochus the Great was welcomed by the Jews—especially since he gave special favors to the Jewish priests and other leaders—the honeymoon ended when Antiochus IV Epiphanes came to the throne.

Antiochus Epiphanes was determined that all his subjects worship Greek gods, speak the Greek language, and follow Greek customs. He infuriated pious Jews by his actions, especially when he interfered in the selection of the high priest. He threw out Onias III, the ruling high priest, and sold the office to Onias's brother Jason. Before long, Menelaus (a priest who did not even belong to a high priestly family) paid Antiochus a larger sum of money. Antiochus deposed Jason in favor of Menelaus.

The high priest then became the promoter of Hellenization—the adoption of Greek religion and culture. There followed a number of outrages by Antiochus against the Jews. Among other things he forbade

---

[2]John Bright, *A History of Israel,* pp. 414–418. See also Martin Noth, *The History of Israel,* pp. 346–351.

Figure 14–1. Alexander's Empire.

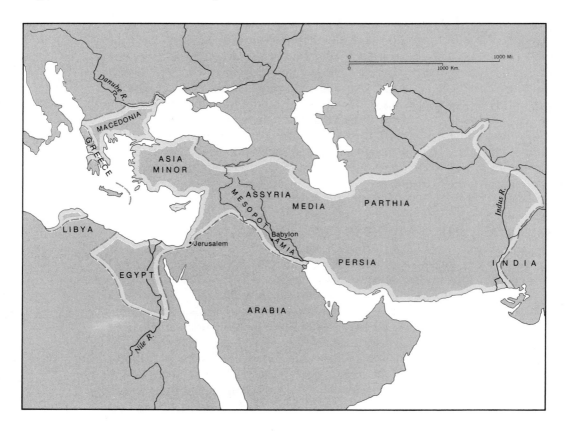

Jewish religious practices (including circumcision), set up an altar to the Greek god Zeus in the Temple, and sacrificed a hog on the sacred altar. Those Jews who resisted him were slaughtered without mercy. When he ordered all Jews to sacrifice to Zeus, he provoked a revolt that would bring Jewish independence for the first time in many centuries.

The Maccabean Revolt

In 168 a representative of the king went to the little village of Modein to enforce the Hellenization decree. He called on a village leader, a priest named Mattathias, to set the example by sacrificing to Zeus. Instead, Mattathias killed the king's officer, as well as a Jew who had offered to make the sacrifice. Having done that, he fled into the Judean wilderness with his five sons.

Mattathias soon died, but his son Judas Maccabeus took leadership of the revolt his father's action had inspired. Judas and his brothers were joined by pious Jews called the *Hasidim*. Their revolt was so successful that by 165 they had recaptured Jerusalem. In December 165, the Temple was cleansed and rededicated to the worship of the LORD.

Later, Judas was killed. His brother Jonathan succeeded him. Jonathan, recognizing the political power of the high priest, took over that office for himself in 150. Simon, another brother, would lead the Jews to complete independence from the Seleucids in 142 and would found the Hasmonean Dynasty that would rule Palestine until the Roman takeover in 63.

The Word of the LORD in Difficult Times

The period from the end of Nehemiah's governorship until the Maccabean revolt saw a good bit of the literature of the Old Testament reach the form in which we now know it. As has been previously indicated, we actually know little about what was going on in Palestine.

There were large Jewish communities outside Palestine, however. Such a community existed in Babylon, where Jews were deeply involved in the business life of the area. In Egypt, the Persians had a Jewish military colony located at Elephantine in southern Egypt. This colony even had its own temple, where regular sacrifices were offered. It was somewhat unorthodox in its doctrine of God, saying that he had a wife—among other things. A third god seemingly also was worshiped.[3]

From the community records it was learned that attempts were made to communicate with the Temple officials in Jerusalem. The Elephantine temple was destroyed by the Egyptians around 410, and the colony appealed to Jerusalem for help in rebuilding. When no help came, they then appealed to Bagoas (the governor of Judah) and the sons of Sanballat (who ruled Samaria). They got the help they requested. This colony was still in existence as late as 399.[4]

THE LAST OF THE PROPHETS

From this time in Jewish history came the last of the prophets and their successors, the apocalyptists.

Obadiah: a hymn of hate against Edom (Obad. 1:1-21). Nothing is known about the author of this short book. The name means "the LORD's servant," which may not be a name at all but just a title. Part of the book

[3]Martin Noth, *The History of Israel,* p. 294–295.
[4]John Bright, *A History of Israel,* p. 408ff.

almost duplicates a section of Jeremiah (vv. 1-9 are quite similar to Jer. 49:7-22).

The animosity between Israel and Edom was long-standing. It obviously continued as long as both countries existed. The time of these oracles could be almost any period of Israelite history, but they were more likely to have come after the fall of Jerusalem in 587.

The main theme of the book was that Edom was doomed. Petra (for Sela), its capital, was so secure that the prophet compared it to an eagle's nest built on a lofty peak. But the LORD would bring it down (1:1-4). As Edom gloated over the rape and pillage of Jerusalem, so the Jews would have the opportunity to gloat over the ruin of Edom. The day of the LORD was going to be directed toward his enemies, and they would receive just punishment for their actions. The Jews would be triumphant over such enemies as Edom and Philistia when the LORD's kingdom came to pass (1:5-21).

Malachi: the LORD questions the community.   Since none of the Israelite historical material mentions Malachi, nor does the book give any sort of biographical information, this prophet, like Obadiah, is anonymous. The name means "my messenger." Malachi 1:1 could be translated "the oracle of the word of the LORD to Israel by my messenger." The content of the book suggests a time not too far removed from that of Ezra and Nehemiah. Many of the same problems were the concern of the prophet with which Ezra and Nehemiah had to deal. It was a time when the hopes of the returned exiles had turned bitter. The people had grown cynical and were careless in their acts of worship. The prophet was trying to arouse a disillusioned community, grown cynical with the continued delay of the glorious future Second Isaiah had talked about.

The nature of the book is that of a dialogue. The LORD, through the prophet, made a statement. It provoked a question which, in turn, was answered by the LORD.

1. The Statement: "I have loved you."
   The Question: "How have you loved us?"
   The Answer: "I chose Jacob instead of Esau to be my people. The Edomites (Esau) will be punished" (1:1-5).

2. The Statement: "You have not shown proper respect to me."
   The Question: "How have we disrespected you?"
   The Answer: "By offering blemished animals. The priests have failed in their responsibilities to see that the proper kinds of sacrifices were made" (1:6–2:9).

3. The Statement: "The LORD no longer accepts your offerings."
   The Question: "Why does he not?"
   The Answer: "Because you have been faithless to your wives as

you have been faithless to the LORD's covenant. The LORD hates divorce" (2:10-16).

4. The Statement: "You have wearied the LORD with your words."
   The Question: "How have we wearied him?"
   The Answer: "By saying that God is unjust. The LORD is coming in judgment upon such sinners" (2:17-3:5).

5. The Statement: "Return to me, and I will return to you."
   The Question: "How shall we return?"
   The Statement: "You are robbing me."
   The Question: "How are we robbing you?"
   The Answer: "In tithes and offerings."
   (This series of questions and answers suggests something of the same kind of condition Nehemiah found at the beginning of his second term as governor of Judah) (3:6-12).

6. The Statement: "Your words have been stout against me."
   The Question: "How have we spoken against you?"
   The Answer: "By saying that those who do evil will not be punished for their sins. But the LORD keeps a record of the righteous and will reward them according to their righteous deeds. In the judgment, evildoers will be punished" (3:13–4:4).

The book closes with a promise to send the LORD's messenger, before the day of the LORD comes to call people to repentence (4:5-6).

Joel: prophecy and apocalyptic. Joel combines characteristics of both prophetic and apocalyptic literature. For many years this book was regarded as one of the early books of the prophets, but in recent years its relationship to apocalyptic literature has caused it to be put in the postexilic era. Its exact date is far from certain, but it does share common themes with Zechariah 9-14 and Daniel. Because of that, it is discussed here.

The locusts are coming! (Joel 1:1–2:27). The prophet was "Joel, the son of Pethuel" (1:1). Beyond that, nothing personal is known about him. The outstanding feature of this book is its vivid description of one of the most frightening plagues known to ancient man—the locusts. Locusts are a kind of large and voracious grasshopper, destructive beyond description (1:4). When they would descend by the millions on an area, they would literally devour every living plant.

> It [the locust] has laid waste my vines,
>   and splintered my fig trees;
> it has stripped off their bark and thrown it down;
>   their branches are made white (1:7).

But the locust plague was only a way to introduce a bigger and more important idea, for Joel was really talking about the day of the LORD. (See Amos 5:18.)

> Alas for the day!
> For the day of the LORD is near,
>   and as destruction from the Almighty it comes.
> Is not the food cut off before our eyes,
>   joy and gladness from the house of our God? (1:15-16)

Using words sounding as if they were borrowed directly from the prophet Amos, Joel spoke of the day of the LORD as a "day of darkness and gloom, a day of clouds and thick darkness" (2:2). The locusts, who were the LORD's agents for bringing in the great day of the LORD, were like a conquering army sweeping over the land:

> Like warriors they charge,
>   like soldiers they scale the wall.
> They march each on his way,
>   they do not swerve from their paths (2:7).

The locusts were everywhere, even in the houses.

The whole universe got involved. There was an earthquake, the sun and moon could not be seen, and the stars disappeared (2:10-11). The LORD called on the people to repent and return to him. As in times of calamity, a solemn fast was to be observed, where everyone, regardless of what he was doing, gathered. The priest led the people in prayer for a lifting of the plague (2:12-17).

The LORD heard and would return his blessings on the land. A time of unequaled prosperity would come when food would be plentiful, peace would prevail, and the LORD would rule his people (2:18-27).

The great day of the LORD (Joel 2:28-3:21). A part of this passage (2:28-32) is well known to Christians because it was quoted in Peter's sermon at Pentecost in Acts 2:17-21. It shows the characteristics of apocalyptic in its references to the darkening of the sun, and the moon turning to blood as a sign of the approaching judgment. Now the other nations would be subject to judgment, but Judah and Jerusalem would be restored to a place of glory. Tyre, Sidon, and Philistia were used as examples of nations which had oppressed Judah. The reference to the Greeks (3:6) would seem to give a hint about the time of this prophet's work. If so, the time would be somewhere in the fifth or fourth centuries (3:1-8).

The nations would be called to judgment in the valley of Jehoshaphat, a valley whose name meant "the LORD judges." Like a farmer harvesting grain, the nations would be cut down. It would be a time of decision with the multitudes gathered (3:9-15). The words of Amos were quoted:

> And the LORD roars from Zion,
>   and utters his voice from Jerusalem, [see Amos 1:2]
>   and the heavens and the earth shake.
> But the LORD is a refuge to his people,
>   a stronghold to the people of Israel (3:16).

For Judah and Jerusalem, the day of the LORD would bring in a time of unparalleled prosperity. For Egypt and Edom, which long had been thorns in Judah's side, the day would mean drought and desolation for the crimes committed against Judah. The LORD would see that justice was done (3:17-21).

THE APOCALYPTIC WRITERS

Joel marked the transition from prophecy to apocalyptic. Discouraging times produced such men, whose purpose was to give the people hope when the situation seemed hopeless.

Zechariah 9–14.   This part of the book of Zechariah differs radically in form from the rest of the book. While chapters 1–8 consist of a series of visionary experiences in which Zechariah plays a major role, no mention was made of the prophet in these chapters. The mention of the Greeks, furthermore, suggests a later time than that of the prophet Zechariah. These matters have led to the conclusion that chapters 9–14 of the book that bear Zechariah's name were from an apocalyptic writer sometime before the Greek or Hellenistic period of Judah's existence (332–63), since Tyre was still uncaptured (9:3-4). It fell to Alexander the Great in 333 after a seven months' siege.

The day of the LORD means new life for Israel (Zech. 9:1–11:17).   With the boundaries of Israel in the days of David and Solomon in mind, the writer envisioned the triumph of the LORD over Israel's enemies. From northern Syria to the southernmost borders of David's kingdom, the restored kingdom would stretch (9:1-8). Yet, its king would not be warlike. He would ride a small burro, the symbol of peace, instead of the prancing stallion of a warlord (9:9-10).

The Jews would be gathered from the ends of the earth. Judah would even be triumphant over powerful Greece (9:11-13). The reason for this turn of events would be the LORD's leadership:

> Then the LORD will appear over them,
>   and his arrow go forth like lightning;
> the LORD God will sound the trumpet,
>   and march forth in the whirlwinds of the south (9:14).

The people would be saved. They would prosper in a well-watered land. The idols, on the other hand, and their prophets were powerless to deliver on their promises. God's anger would be directed toward such false leaders (9:14–10:5). But the LORD would raise up leaders for Judah:

> Out of them shall come the cornerstone,
>   out of them the tent peg,
> out of them the battle bow,
>   out of them every ruler (10:4).

Israel would be strong once again because the LORD would gather the people from among the nations where they had been scattered. Egypt and Assyria, representative of the nations that had scattered the LORD's people, would be destroyed (10:6-12). Others who had oppressed the LORD's people would be burnt out like a fire raging in a forest (11:1-3).

As the shepherd had life-and-death control over his sheep, so the Jews' rulers had life-and-death control over them. The prophet, acting for the LORD, took the role of the shepherd of the people. Symbolizing their one-time condition as a united people (Israel and Judah), he took two shepherd's staffs and held them together as one. Three rulers (shepherds) came and went in rapid succession. To express the LORD's unhappiness at the situation, the staff named "Grace" was broken. As a wage, the prophet was given 30 shekels of silver for being the shepherd. These he gave to the Temple treasury. Then the second staff (Union) was broken, symbolizing the separation of Israel and Judah. The LORD was going to raise up a shepherd (leader) who did not care for the people (11:4-17).

The day of the LORD and the triumph of Jerusalem (Zech. 12:1–14:21). As part of the apocalyptic vision of the day of the LORD, Jerusalem and the cities of Judah would be attacked by their enemies. But they would fall, for Jerusalem would be like an immovable rock straining the back of anyone who tried to lift it. The tide of battle would turn, with Judean's clans destroying the enemy while Jerusalem's people stayed safely within the city (12:1-6).

Since the descendants of David were among Jerusalem's citizens, Judah's warfare on their behalf would assure that all Judah, not just Jerusalem, would receive praise for their success. Any nation that tried to attack Jerusalem would be destroyed. Its defense would be led by descendants of David. The Jerusalemites and the Davidic descendants would also take on a new spirit of mercy and prayer. They would mourn someone whom they had stabbed to death, possibly because too late they realized he was not guilty of what he was accused of. It would be like Baal worshipers mourning in the annual fertility rites in Megiddo. All the Jerusalem families would be mourning (12:7-14).

In the day of the LORD, idols would be banished and false prophets sent out to do useful work, such as farming. Even their former friends would attack them if they tried to prophesy again. The people who were false would be destroyed to purify the land (13:1-9).

But Jerusalem's troubles would not be over. Its enemies would attack again and it would be taken. Then the LORD himself would intervene. He would stand on the Mount of Olives, east of the city. A great earthquake would cleave an east-west valley through the mountain. The LORD with his angels would come, bringing in the ideal age (14:1-5).

The age would bring marvelous changes. There would be ideal weather (24-hour sunshine) and perpetual rivers flowing east and west from Jerusalem to the Dead Sea and the Mediterranean. Over this the LORD would reign in triumph (14:6-9).

To the south, the land would become a plain, with only Jerusalem on a hill, dominating the land. Jerusalem's enemies would suffer horrible diseases. Judah would loot its enemies, becoming immensely wealthy. The enemy would realize that the God of the Jews was to be the LORD of all and would come to worship him in Jerusalem each year during the Feast of Booths or Tabernacles. Those who refused would be wiped out by an epidemic.

Everything would be dedicated to the LORD, even the harnesses on the horses. Jerusalem would become one big worship center, with every pot in town set apart for use in the services of sacrifice (14:10-21).

Daniel: an encouraging word for a dark time.   For the Old Testament, Daniel is the most apocalyptic book of all. The name Daniel was well known in ancient Palestine. In Canaanite literature there was a hero Dan'el.[5] Ezekiel mentioned Noah, Daniel, and Job. He said that if these three men were in Palestine, their righteousness would only be sufficient to deliver them and no one else (Ezek. 14:14,20). He said:

> Even if Noah, Daniel, and Job were in it, as I live, says the LORD God, they would deliver neither son nor daughter; they would deliver but their own lives by their righteousness (14:20).

According to Daniel 1:1-7, Daniel was taken to Babylon by Nebuchadnezzar in 606. Ezekiel's oracle was from the period before Jerusalem's fall in 587. While it cannot be said with certainty, Ezekiel spoke of Daniel as though he was a figure of the distant past since he was classed with Noah and Job, both names from ancient Israelite tradition. That he could have been speaking of the Daniel of the book by the same name is not an impossibility, of course.

[5]See "The Tale of Aqhat," in Pritchard, *The Ancient Near East,* pp. 118–132.

The book: its form.   The book of Daniel was not included among the prophets in the Jewish canon. Instead, it was classed as one of the Writings, the last books to be accepted as Scripture. It was found among the Dead Sea Scrolls; but the way it was copied indicated that the Essenes, who were responsible for the Scrolls, did not consider it to be Scripture. Those books they considered sacred were copied in a special way.

While the stories in the book were set in the background of the Babylonian exile, as it stands now, evidence suggests that it was put in its present form during the persecutions of Antiochus Epiphanes to encourage those who were under persecution. Just as the LORD had delivered Daniel, so he would deliver the righteous ones who were being persecuted by the tyrant Antiochus IV.

One other note of interest about the book—a major portion of it was written in Aramaic (2:4–7:8), the language the Jews adopted in Babylon. Only one other book (Ezra 7:12-26) used Aramaic to any extent, and it was a postexilic product.

The book: its contents.   The book has two major divisions: (1) stories about Daniel, and (2) apocalyptic visions of a brighter future for those under persecution.

1. *Stories about Daniel (Dan. 1:1–6:28).*   The first story (1:1-21) concerns the captivity of Daniel and three of his friends of the Jerusalem nobility. Each of the friends were given Babylonian names. Daniel was called "Belteshazzar," while the other three friends were called Shadrach, Meshach, and Abednego. The king ordered that they were to be educated for three years for court service. As such they were to be fed from the king's table. "But Daniel resolved that he would not defile himself with the king's rich food, or with the wine that he drank" (1:8). Thus, he and his friends resolved to be faithful to the laws of their Jewish faith.

When the servant brought them the rich food, they asked instead for vegetables since there would be no danger in violating Jewish laws concerning food if they ate no meat or milk products. When the three years were up, the Jewish youths were as healthy as any others and much more skilled in wisdom. This would say to those whom Antiochus was trying to force to follow Hellenistic customs to be faithful to the law and they would prosper just as Daniel and his friends did.

As in the story of Joseph, in which the pharaoh's dreams had such an important place, so the second story about Daniel concerns the dreams of King Nebuchadnezzar (2:1-49). Nebuchadnezzar had dreams his wisest men could not interpret. Daniel told him the dream had to do with things that would come to pass "in the latter days" (2:28). This emphasis on the last days of history is known as eschatology (2:1-30).

In Nebuchadnezzar's dream he had seen a great image with a head of gold, "breasts and arms of silver," belly and thighs of bronze, legs of iron, and feet "partly of iron and partly of clay" (2:33). The image was broken by a stone that became "a great mountain and filled the whole earth" (2:35). The image represented kingdoms that had dominated the Near East, beginning with Nebuchadnezzar. Others were the Medes and Persians, the empire of Alexander. But Alexander's kingdom, the one made of iron, was divided so that part of it was mixed with clay. It (the Seleucids and Ptolemies) would crumble. Then, the kingdom of God would come in and replace all earthly kingdoms (2:31-45). Because of Daniel's success in interpreting the dream, he was given a place of honor in the king's court (2:46-49).

The third story concerned Daniel's companions Shadrach, Meshach, and Abednego. When the king set up an idol and demanded that everyone worship it, the three young men refused. Nothing was said about where Daniel was when all this was going on. When news of the Jews' refusal to worship reached the king, they were ordered thrown into a fiery furnace. When the king looked in to see what had happened to them, he saw not three, but four, one of whom was like "a son of the gods" (3:25). It was a word of assurance to those who were undergoing the fiery trials of persecution by Antiochus Epiphanes (3:1-30).

Next came the story of another dream by the king. He dreamed of a mighty tree that covered the earth; but, on God's orders, a heavenly being descended and cut down the tree. When Daniel was asked to interpret the dream, he told the king that he was the tree. He would suffer temporary insanity, during which he would act like an animal because he exalted himself above God. When a year passed, the king suffered as Daniel had said. Then he acknowledged the power of the Most High God (4:1-37). In this story, the apocalyptist was saying what Second Isaiah had said many years before:

> By myself I have sworn,
>   from my mouth has gone forth in righteousness
>   a word that shall not return:
> "To me every knee shall bow,
>   every tongue shall swear" (Isa. 45:23).

That even included the tyrant Antiochus who called himself "God manifest" (Epiphanes).

Chapter 5 tells the story of Belshazzar's feast. Belshazzar was the son and coregent of Nabonidus (he was called the son of Nebuchadnezzar in 5:2). Nabonidus was an amateur archaeologist who was more interested in old ruins than he was with breakdown in his kingdom. While Belshazzar was having a wild drinking bout using sacred vessels from the Jerusalem Temple, he saw a message written on the wall. The words were *MENE, MENE, TEKEL, PARSIN*. Daniel, when called to interpret them, explained that they pronounced Belshazzar's doom. His days were numbered, for he had been found lacking in leadership qualities. Now, his kingdom would be divided among the Medes and Persians. According to Daniel, the kingdom was taken by "Darius the Mede." According to Persian records, it was Cyrus. Darius the Persian ruler came to the throne succeeding Cambyses (530–522) in 522 (5:1-30).

The final story is the most famous of the Daniel stories. Exalted to position of satrap or governor over a province in the Persian Empire, Daniel was still the faithful worshiper of Jewish law. His fellow governors persuaded the king to make a decree that no one could pray to any god for thirty days. Only the king could be petitioned. Daniel ignored the edict and continued to worship three times a day as was his custom. The result was that he was thrown to the lions.

The king realizing what a mistake he had made, worried all night about Daniel. But in the morning, Daniel walked out of the lion's den unharmed. Those who had set the trap for him were fed to the lions.

The object of all these stories was to tell the people who were suffering under persecution that as the LORD delivered Daniel, Shadrach, Meshach, and Abednego, so he would deliver them. This was a common theme in apocalyptic literature—the delivery of the righteous from the fire of persecution and the human animals who were trying to devour them (6:1-28).

2. *Daniel's visions (Dan. 7:1–12:12).*   In the visions recorded in Daniel, there was typical apocalypse. Unusual beasts, the use of numbers, and the view of the last days including a messianic figure were all common themes in apocalyptic writing. Despite any persecution the saints might have been undergoing, the apocalyptic writer brought a message of hope whose theme was that God would win out over the forces of evil.

a. *The four beasts from the sea (Dan. 7:1-28).*   In the first vision, four beasts arose out of the sea. For Jews, the sea always represented a place of awe and mystery. It was a fearsome place, which had great monsters who swallowed up men who dared to venture out into it. Thus, it was not unusual for them to conceive of evil creatures coming from the sea. The beasts in the vision represented the strong empires of the time: the Babylonian; the Median, which lay east of the Mesopotamian region; the Persian; and finally the Greek or Hellenistic empire of Alexander and his successors. The ten horns represented the ten kings who followed Alexander. The horn was symbolic of power, so the writer described Antiochus Epiphanes as a little horn, a button with a big mouth "that spoke great things" (7:20). But God ("the Ancient of Days," 7:22) would put an end to his persecution and his mouthings.

> And the kingdom and the dominion
> > and the greatness of the kingdoms under the whole heaven
> > shall be given to the people of the saints of the Most High;
> > their kingdom shall be an everlasting kingdom,
> > and all dominions shall serve and obey them (7:27).

b. *The ram and the he-goat (Dan. 8:1-27).*   The ram was the Persian Empire, which owed much of its strength to an alliance with the Medes. Alexander (the he-goat) defeated the Medo-Persian empire. At his death, four of his generals (the four horns) inherited his empire (8:22). Antiochus (a king of bold countenance, 8:23) persecuted the Jews. The 2300 "mornings and evenings" were three-and-a-half years of the period from the beginning of the Maccabean revolt until the cleansing of the Temple in December, 165.

c. *The seventy weeks (Dan. 9:1-27).*   Numerology came into full play in this vision, along with the introduction of the angel Gabriel as the chief messenger for God. Daniel was pondering Jeremiah's prophecy of the seventy weeks in Jeremiah "in the first year of Darius, the son of Ahasuerus . . . who became King over the realm of the Chaldeans" (9:1). This verse holds problems, since Persian records presently available know nothing of such a king. Furthermore, the Chaldeans were the Babylonians, not the Persians.

After a long prayer of repentance and confession, both of his sins and the sins of the people (9:3-19), Daniel was visited by the angel Gabriel. Gabriel's purpose was to reveal the meaning of the seventy weeks, which were explained as "seventy weeks of years," or 490 years. Unfortunately, the meaning of what was revealed to Daniel has not been passed on to us, either by written or oral tradition, making this passage one that has brought forth interpretations over the centuries ranging from something less than the sublime to the ridiculous. Seemingly, if the historical context is of any value, it referred to the period from the return (538) to the Maccabean era (about 168). It would end when one would come (the Messiah) who "makes desolate, until the decreed end is poured out on the desolator" (9:27). Again, there seems to be a reference to Antiochus Epiphanes, who profaned the altar by sacrificing a hog on it. That this interpretation is widely disputed can be readily admitted. One can find all sorts of contrary interpretations, including some current best-sellers, applying this to some future event. History is full of such interpretations (9:20-27).

d. *The last days (Dan. 10:1–12:13).*   A favorite theme of the apocalyptists was the last days when the LORD would bring an end to evil and bring in the kingdom of God. It has always been tempting, especially in trying times, for Jewish and Christian interpreters to apply this passage to their own time. A notable example occurred in the 1840s, when a sincere preacher convinced thousands of people that the end would come in 1843. When it did not come, he changed the date to 1844. There were still many who believed him. But when the end did not come, he died a disillusioned and broken man. This vision, like the others, seems to be best understood as referring to the events from 538 to the Maccabean period. References such as 11:31 "Forces from him [Antiochus Epiphanes] shall appear and profane the Temple and fortress, and shall take away the continual burnt offering," seem to point to Antiochus and his atrocities against the Jews. For Daniel, this was the prelude to the coming of the Messiah who would deliver the righteous Jews. After a clear reference to a belief in life after death, with rewards and punishment (12:1-4), Daniel closed the veil so that what came after was hidden from view.

THE GREAT DEBATE: HOW TO DEAL WITH THE WORLD

In the postexilic period there developed a strong conflict among the Jews over how to deal with the non-Jewish world. Second Isaiah had spoken glowingly of Israel's responsibility to be a "light to the nations" (Isa. 49:7). Two poles of opinion grew up on that subject. One said that the Jews' responsibility was to be closed to the world around them, to be exclusively the people of God. Such people undoubtedly would have argued that the nations would be drawn to Israel's God if Israel was faithful to him. This view has been designated as particularism.

On the opposite end of the spectrum was the view that the Jews were to be the people of God, but that they were to actively seek to bring others to the knowledge of their God. This missionary outlook encompassed all men and, as such, is known as universalism.

Expressions of these contrasting viewpoints are stated nowhere more clearly than in three short books: Esther, Ruth, and Jonah.

Esther: Jews should look after themselves.   This book, set in the background of the Persian Kingdom in the mid-fifth century B.C., was a strongly nationalistic tract of the times. God was not mentioned in the book. Its purpose seems to be to explain the origin of the Jewish feast of Purim.

According to the story, Ahasuerus (Xerxes I 485–464), king of Persia, had a banquet for his friends. When he asked his queen Vashti, to appear at the banquet, she refused. In retaliation, Ahasuerus deposed her as queen and set up a national search for a replacement (1:1–2:4).

At this point, Esther, the heroine of the story, was introduced. She was a beautiful Jewish girl who had been reared by her elderly cousin, Mordecai. When the national beauty contest was conducted, Esther (who had concealed her Jewish background) was chosen to be the new queen. Not long afterward, Mordecai heard of a plot against the king and, through Esther, was able to warn him. The conspirators were punished, but Mordecai was not rewarded; although his action was noted in the king's chronicles (2:5-23).

Figure 14–2. "In the days of Ahashuerus . . ." (Esther 1:1). This was Xerxes I (485–464) of the book of Esther. These ruins of Xerxes Porch are at his capitol, Persepolis.

Courtesy of H. Armstrong Roberts.

The villain of the story appeared when Haman the Agagite was made prime minister to Ahasuerus. Mordecai refused to bow to Haman when he went out the palace gate, so Haman decided that he would get rid of Mordecai. While Haman was doing that, he would get rid of all the Jews in the land, since he hated Jews (3:1-6).

Casting lots (Purim)[6] to determine the best time for getting rid of the

[6]*Oxford Annotated Bible,* note on Esther 3:7.

Jews, Haman finally felt that the time was right to approach the king. To further convince the king of the rightness of his cause, Haman offered the king an enormous bribe when he asked him to make a decree that all Jews were to be killed. The king gladly obliged Haman, still not realizing that Esther was a Jewess (3:7-15).

Mordecai immediately went into mourning when the decree was published. Esther heard about his mourning and sent to ask him why he was doing so. Since she stayed in the king's harem, she would not have known about the decree. Mordecai sent a copy of the decree to Esther with the request that she go to the king and ask him to lift the death sentence from the Jews. She was reluctant, but she finally agreed to do so, even though she was risking her life (4:1-17).

When she went to the king, he granted her the privilege to speak to him. She asked him to invite Haman to a dinner for the three of them. The king granted her wish. Haman, sure that his moment of glory had arrived, rejoiced until he happened to see Mordecai at the palace gate. He went home and ordered carpenters to build a gallows in his garden so that he could personally hang the Jew he hated most (5:1-14).

Meanwhile, the king was having a sleepless night. Looking for something to read, he happened to read in his chronicles that Mordecai had saved his life but had never been properly rewarded. The next morning, when Haman arrived, he asked him what would be a proper reward to be given to a man the king wanted to honor. Thinking that he was the one the king intended to honor, Haman suggested that such a man should be clad in the king's robes, put on the king's own horse, led through the streets of the capital, and have it proclaimed that the man was being honored by the king. The king liked the suggestion. He ordered Haman to find Mordecai and do as he had described. Naturally, Haman did it; but that did not mean he enjoyed it. To the contrary, he felt rather sick about the whole affair (6:1-14).

The day of Haman's invitation to dine with the king and queen came. Ahasuerus asked Esther what was it that she had wanted him to do. Then she revealed that she was Jewish. She pleaded for her own life, as well as for the lives of her people. When the king (who seemed to have problems with his memory) asked who had caused all this trouble, she pointed an accusing finger at Haman. In anger the king left the room for the cool of the garden. Haman fell at the queen's feet as she lay on the dining couch. The king returned to the room "as Haman was falling on the couch where Esther was" (7:8). He took what he saw as an attempt of Haman to rape the queen. That did it. Haman was hanged on the gallows that he had built for Mordecai (7:1-10).

Since he could not revoke his decree about the slaughter of the Jews, once it was written, he sent out another decree that gave the Jews the right to defend themselves against anyone who might attack them (8:1-

17). The Jews took it as an opportunity to rid themselves of their enemies throughout the kingdom. The tenth day of the month of Adar was designated the day for celebrating the event (9:1-32). Mordecai was made prime minister in Haman's place (10:1-3).

Ruth and Jonah: the Jews have an obligation to others.   Two other books carry the arguments of the universalists.

The book of Ruth (Ruth 1:1–4:18).   The setting for Ruth was the period of the Judges. A postexilic author composed a beautiful short story about Ruth, King David's grandmother, to say that the Jews had no right to be narrow in their view of other nations.

Naomi, a Jewess, had been taken by her husband, Elimelech, to live in Moab during a time of famine in Israel. Elimelech died in Moab, leaving Naomi with two sons, Mahlon and Chilion. Eventually, the sons married two Moabite women, Orpah and Ruth. Then the sons died, leaving the three widowed women with no one to look after them (1:1-5).

Naomi decided to return to Israel to be among her own people. The daughters-in-law were determined to go with her, but she tried to persuade them to return to their own people. Orpah did so, but Ruth insisted on going with Naomi:

> Entreat me not to leave you or to return from following you; for where you go I will go, and where you lodge I will lodge; your people shall be my people, and your God, my God (1:16).

These words, often used as a bride's vow to her husband in a wedding ceremony, were addressed to a mother-in-law, not a husband (1:6-18)!

The women arrived in Bethlehem where Naomi's husband had rights to ancestral property. As a widow, she had no rights to the property, since, in reality, she was part of the property rather than owner of it. Whoever got the property had to assume responsibility for Naomi and Ruth. They arrived in Bethlehem in time for the barley harvest (1:19-22).

Elimelech's property was to go to his nearest male relative. Boaz, a wealthy landowner at Bethlehem, was a relative of Elimelech; but there was another who was closer kin than Boaz. Naomi took Ruth out in the barley fields to gather scattered heads of grain that had been left by the reapers so that the poor could find them for their meager food supply. Ruth happened to be gleaning in Boaz's field when he noticed her. When told who she was, he ordered that extra grain be scattered where she could find it. Calling her to him, Boaz told her to follow his reapers closely so she would not miss the extra grain. She was allowed, furthermore, to drink water from the vessels of Boaz. When she asked why she was so favored, she was told it was because of her kindness to her mother-in-law Naomi (2:1-14).

After being fed by Boaz, she gathered a large amount of grain because of his generosity. When Naomi heard what had happened, she was pleased to hear what Boaz had done (2:15-23).

Naomi began to plan. She told Ruth to clean up and put on her nicest perfume and prettiest clothes. Then, she was to go down to the threshing floor where Boaz was threshing his grain. Such work was done late in the afternoon when the breezes arose. When Boaz had finished eating and had lain down to sleep, Ruth was to go up and lie down at his feet, pulling his cover over her. In those days, that was a woman's way of proposing to a man (3:1-5).

Ruth did as she was told. When Boaz awoke to find her lying at his feet, he was pleasantly surprised, especially since she was a beautiful young woman and he was an older man. As if to answer her proposal, he gave her a sackful of grain to carry home the next morning (3:6-18).

There were complications, however. Since Boaz was not the nearest relative, he had to get the right to inherit Elimelech's property. He found the nearest relative in the town gate, where all legal transactions took place. He told him of the property, and the man said that he would claim his right of inheritance. When he found out about the two women who went with the property, he changed his mind, however. Since he would have had to marry Ruth, the first son born to her would have been credited to her first husband and thus would have the right to inherit Ruth's first husband's property.[7]

Boaz then claimed the right of inheritance since he was the next in line. He married Ruth and they, according to the story, were the grandparents of King David. The point of the story was the the Jews could not claim to be an exclusive and pure-blooded people when the grandmother of their greatest king had been a foreigner (4:1-22).

The book of Jonah (Jonah 1:1–4:11). The tragedy of the book of Jonah is that a great missionary plea is known largely as a fish tale! The fish was not a major character—he played only a supporting role!

The historical character Jonah was a fiercely nationalistic prophet who lived in the days of Jeroboam II (2 Kings 14:25). The book that bears his name was written by Jonah, not by him. Unlike the other prophetic books that contain the oracles of the prophet, the book of Jonah contains only one oracle of Jonah which has only five Hebrew words.

The importance of this book did not lie in what the prophet said. Instead, the important thing was what the book said. Arguments about whether a man could survive three days in the belly of a fish, while they may be interesting, really miss the point of the book. It is tragic that most people get so fascinated by the story of the fish that they never get to chapter 4, where the real purpose of the book was unfolded.

---

[7]This was the law of the levirate marriage (Deut. 25:5-6).

1. *Jonah, the stubborn prophet (Jonah 1:1-17).*   There were interesting parallels between Jonah and Israel. In chapter 1, Jonah, called of God to go to Nineveh, was stubborn and rebellious. He decided he would do things his way, so he went down to Joppa to board a ship to Tarshish. Tarshish possibly was Spain, and it was the extreme opposite to where Jonah was supposed to be going. The next thing he knew, a storm was tossing the ship. Jonah ended up being tossed into the sea where a great fish swallowed him.

As it was with Jonah, so it had been with Israel. Her prophets had constantly called on her to do as the LORD's will, but Israel had been stubborn and rebellious. The Babylonians, to use Isaiah's figure about the Assyrians (Isa. 8:7), had overflowed the land; and Israel had been swallowed up in the exile.

2. *Jonah, the prophet in the depths (Jonah 2:1-10).*   To symbolize Jonah's despair over his condition, a psalm of lament comprises Jonah 2. Such psalms undoubtedly were common in the exile as the Israelites poured out their feelings of despair. These psalms often ended with a note of renewed commitment and with praise to the LORD. As Jonah came out of the depths, so Israel came out of Babylon.

3. *Jonah, the reluctant prophet (Jonah 3:1-10).*   When Jonah funally decided to do what he was called to do, he met with unusual success. The king ordered that even the animals should wear sackcloth as a symbol of mourning and repentance. With high hopes Israel had returned to the land. The people of the land had offered to join with them to rebuild the Temple, but the particularistic Jews had rejected all such offers. They did not want to contaminate their faith, which had been purified by the exile in Babylon.

4. *Jonah, the angry prophet (Jonah 4:1-11).*   God's failure to destroy Nineveh was frustrating to Jonah. He wanted his problem solved by God's annihilation of Nineveh, not by his transformation of it. Particularistic Jews wanted their enemies wiped out rather than taken in by God's grace. There was stinging satire in the description of Jonah's vigil on the hill overlooking Nineveh as he waited for its hoped-for destruction. The LORD who had already "appointed a great fish to swallow up Jonah" (1:17) now "appointed a plant" to shade Jonah's head (4:6). Just as Jonah was beginning to relax in its shade, "God appointed a worm" whose attack on the plant caused it to wither (4:7). If that were not enough, he "appointed a sultry east wind," which combined with the sun beaming down on his head and added to his inner turmoil. This drove Jonah to beg to die so he would not be so miserable (4:8). In return the LORD chided Jonah for being more concerned with plants than he was with people, even the hated Ninevehites.

The universalists felt that the particularists were more concerned with their own "plants" than they were concerned about people, the most important of God's living creatures. They could not be a "light to the nations" by the Jonah method. Instead, they had to be concerned enough about other peoples to gladly carry the word to them. In short, the book of Jonah was a missionary tract that proclaimed the views of postexilic Jews who believed that they had to be active examples in a non-Jewish world.

STUDY QUESTIONS

1. Describe the conquests of Alexander the Great.
2. Who were the Ptolemies and the Seleucids?
3. Why did many of the Jews dislike Antiochus Epiphanes so intensely?
4. What caused the Maccabean revolt and who were its leaders?
5. What was Elephantine?
6. What was the theme of the book of Obadiah?
7. What does the book of Malachi tell us about religious conditions in that day?
8. What is unique about the form of the book of Malachi?
9. What natural catastrophe did Joel use to describe the coming Day of the Lord?
10. Why is Zechariah 9–14 described as apocalyptic literature?
11. What evidence does Ezekiel present to show that Daniel was a character from ancient times?
12. What seems to have been the purpose for the book of Daniel?
13. What are the two major divisions of the book of Daniel?
14. How is Antiochus Epiphanes symbolized in the stories about Daniel?
15. Who were the "universalists" and the "particularists" in postexilic Judaism?
16. What does the book of Esther argue for?
17. What is the main point of the book of Ruth?
18. Who was the original Jonah?
19. What was the book of Jonah designed to say?

FOR FURTHER STUDY

Judaism

BICKERMAN, E. *From Ezra to the Last of the Maccabees.* New York: Schocken Books, 1962.

CHARLES, R. H. *Apocrypha and Pseudepigrapha of the Old Testament.* 2 vols. New York: Oxford, 1913, but reprinted in 1963. Here one can see how there was much literary activity among Jews, the products of which never became scripture.

FOERSTER, WORNER. *From the Exile to Christ: A Historical Introduction to Palestinian Judaism.* Trans. by Gordon E. Harris. Philadelphia: Fortress, 1964.

RUSSELL, D. S. *Between the Testaments.* London: SCM Press, 1960.

Apocalyptic

FROST, STANLEY. *Old Testament Apocalyptic.* London: Epworth Press, 1952.

HANSON, PAUL. *The Dawn of Apocalyptic: The Historical and Sociological Roots of Jewish Apocalyptic Eschatology.* Philadelphia: Fortress, 1967.

HEATON, E. W. *The Book of Daniel.* London: S.C.M. Press, 1956.

JEFFREY, ARTHUR. "Daniel: Introduction and Exegesis." *Interpreter's Bible,* VI. New York: Abingdon, 1956.

KLAUSNER, JOSEPH. *The Messianic Idea in Israel from Its Beginning to the Completion of the Mishnah.* New York: Macmillan, 1955.

MOWINCKEL, SIGMUND. *He That Cometh.* Trans. by G. W. Anderson. New York: Abingdon, 1956. A classic work on eschatology.

PORTEOUS, NORMAN. *Daniel.* Old Testament Library. Philadelphia: Westminster, 1965.

RINGGREN, HELMER. *The Messiah in the Old Testament.* London: SCM Press, 1956.

RUSSELL, D. S. *The Method and Message of Jewish Apocalyptic.* Philadelphia: Westminster, 1964.

For the prophets of the period see the books on the prophets cited in chapter 8.

CHAPTER FIFTEEN

Epilogue: The Continuing Story

The Old Testament story comes to an end, but it would be a grave error to suppose that religious men ceased to write. Indeed, if the literature that has survived is any indication, there were numerous religious literary works some of which never became a part of any canon of Scripture. Their work, nevertheless, played an important role in the lives of religious people of their times. All that remains for us is to examine briefly some important changes in the religious life of the Jewish community, to discuss the rise of some factions within Judaism that were to play important roles in later history, and to look at some of the more important other religious literature from the time between the Babylonian exile and the beginning of the Christian era.

Life in the Jewish Community

Except for the freedom they gained during the Maccabean revolt, Palestinian Jews, as well as their brothers outside of Palestine, were the pawns of foreign rulers. Most Jews, in fact, did not live in Palestine. The Babylonian, Persian, and Greek conquests of Palestine had had the effect of scattering Jews all over the middle East. Babylonia and Egypt in particular had large Jewish communities. Those Jews who lived outside of Palestine were said to be a part of the *Diaspora*.

While Israel was no longer a nation, it was still a people, spread from Babylon to Alexandria to Rome, yet bound together by a love for God, a love for his teaching (TORAH), and a love for his city (Jerusalem). No matter how far he lived from Jerusalem, every devout Jew vowed to go to that city to worship at least once in his lifetime. This love for Jerusalem is expressed in the words of a lonely poet during the Babylonian exile:

> How shall we sing the LORD's song
>   in a foreign land?
> If I forget you, O Jerusalem,
>   let my right hand wither!
> Let my tongue cleave to the roof of
>   my mouth
> if I do not remember you,
>   if I do not set Jerusalem
> above my highest joy (Psa. 137:4-6).

As a consequence of their loss of political independence, certain important changes took place in the Jewish community that had their effects not only in Palestine but also in the Jewish communities of the Diaspora. First, the chief priest increasingly assumed both religious and political roles in the Palestinian Jewish community, his power in many ways extending to Jewish communities everywhere. An important step in this rise in political power came when Jonathan, the brother of Judas Maccabeus, officially combined the office of political ruler and high priest (circa 150 B.C.).

Secondly, the voice of the prophet, so powerful in Israelite life before and during the Babylonian Exile, faded to a whisper as the written Torah gradually became the standard of life and conduct. Since Torah basically means teaching, the teacher or rabbi became a major force in Jewish life. More and more the synagogue was where the teaching took place. While the Temple, located in Jerusalem, was Judaism's most sacred shrine, every Jewish community where there were ten Jewish men had its synagogue as the very center of community life. Since the synagogue was a lay institution and the rabbi was a layman, the lay interpreters of the Torah became the most important religious influence in the life of the ordinary Jew, whether he lived in Palestine, Egypt, or Babylonia. So while the political power of the high priest was increasing, the religious influence of the priesthood as a group was decreasing.

Two important things grew out of this situation. First, since teaching became primarily a function of laymen, by 200 B.C. there were two great lay interpreters in each generation whose authority in scriptural interpretation became preeminent. The second thing was that oral tradition came to have equal status with the written Torah. This was based on the belief (1) that it, like the written Torah, had its origins in the time of Moses and (2) that it had been passed along over the centuries by word of mouth until it came to be entrusted to the *zugoth*, the pair of great rabbis whose word was law for that day.

The Rise of Parties and Sects

This period also saw the rise of numerous parties within Judaism that were to have major roles in its future. Before the Maccabean revolt, the Samaritans, descendants of the inhabitants of the territory of the northern kingdom which Assyria had conquered in 722/21 B.C., became a distinct group. Assyria had brought in foreign colonists who intermarried with the poor Israelites left in the land. In the Babylonian conquests, the poor also were left in the land while the upper classes were carried into exile. Open hostility developed between those who remained in the land and the Jews who returned after the Babylonian exile. The people of the land still looked upon themselves as true followers of the God of Israel, but the Jews felt that those who had stayed in the land had a corrupted faith and that their mixed heritage disqualified them from being a part of Judaism. Eventually, the Samaritans, so named because Samaria was their chief city, built a temple on Mt. Gerizim, one of the mountains that overlook the site of the old Israelite capital of Shechem. Later, John Hyrcanus, the Hasmonean ruler, forcefully converted the Samaritans to his version of Judaism, destroyed their temple, and earned their undying enmity both for himself and Judaism of the Jerusalem variety.[1]

The extremely orthodox *Hasidim* who had supported the Maccabean revolt in its beginnings became disenchanted when the revolt became more of an attempt to gain political power than a struggle for freedom. It is likely, though not proved, that two groups important in later Judaism had roots in this movement. They were the Pharisees and the Essenes. The Pharisees were predominately a group made up of laymen who wanted to interpret the law so that its meaning was clear to each generation. They were the party that emphasized oral tradition and that produced the great rabbis who were to dominate later Judaism. The Pharisees accepted the Pentateuch (*Torah*), the Prophets (*Nebi'im*), and the Writings (*Kethub'im*) as authoritative. While they would have strongly affirmed their religious orthodoxy, they were in fact the religious liberals of their day, introducing into Judaism such ideas as the belief in the resurrection of the dead and the belief in angels.

The Essenes, whose best known settlement was the Qumran community near the Dead Sea, produced the now famous Dead Sea Scrolls. Many interpreters believe that the Essenes withdrew from Jerusalem initially when Jonathan, the brother of Judas Maccabeus, seized the high priesthood (circa 150 B.C.). Frequent reference is made in their literature to the "wicked priest." Of the known historical personages, Jonathan best fits this description.

---

[1]R. J. Coggins, *Samaritans and Jews*, rev. ed. (Garden City, N.Y.: Doubleday, 1964) is a good up-to-date discussion of the Samaritans and their relationship to the Jews. The Samaritan temple was destroyed circa 128 B.C.

Their theology was similar to that of the Pharisees in many respects but had some important differences. The Essenes believed they were to prepare for the coming of the end of the age. Their literature was dominated with the idea that a great final struggle was approaching, the war of the "Sons of Light" (themselves) and the "Sons of Darkness" (all who opposed them). Everything they did was aimed at preparing for the day when God would intervene on their behalf and make them victorious over their enemies. They were attempting to make real the things about which apocalyptic writers wrote.[2]

Jonathan's attempt to combine the office of the high priest and ruler was further carried out by the Hasmoneans, who ruled the country after the Maccabean revolt gained freedom for the Jewish people in 142 B.C. The priestly party, the Sadducees, dominated the political and economic life of the country but lost much of their religious influence with the common people. They were quite conservative religiously, accepting only the first five books of the Bible as Scripture, those books that describe the responsibilities of the priests. In contrast, since the prophets frequently attacked the priesthood, this would not have endeared their books to the Sadducees. The Sadducees' political and economic power as well as their religious views led to a struggle between them and the Pharisees. This situation, in turn, lead to severe persecution of the Pharisees during the early days of the Hasmonean rule.

While there would be other parties and sect groups that would arise later in Judaism, these were the most important. Their existence illustrates that as the Old Testament story closes, Judaism was not a unified religion in which everyone believed the same doctrines and interpreted God's will for their lives in the same way. Instead the Jews were a diverse people whose society and religion mirror that diversity.

Literary Activity

As the period that produced the Old Testament came to a close, literary activity did not cease among religious men. Four major groups of literature need to be examined briefly: the Apocrypha, the Pseudepigrapha, the Dead Sea Scrolls, and the oral tradition of the Jews which eventually produced the Talmud.

THE APOCRYPHA

To speak of the Apocrypha as extrabiblical literature is not entirely accurate since the Roman Catholic canon accepts these books as sacred

---

[2]T. H. Gaster, *The Dead Sea Scriptures*, rev. ed. (Garden City, N.Y.: Doubleday, 1964).

Scripture. This is because the Roman Catholic canon basically follows the Alexandrian canon. The Apocrypha may be defined as those books accepted by the Jews of Alexandria as part of their sacred writings that were not accepted as part of the Hebrew Canon. They may be grouped as follows:[3]

1. Additions to biblical books

Apocryphal book	*Related biblical book*
1 Esdras	2 Chronicles, Ezra, Nehemiah
Baruch	Jeremiah
The Letter of Jeremiah	Jeremiah
The Prayer of Azariah and the Song of the Three Young Men	Daniel
Susanna	Daniel
Bel and the Dragon	Daniel
The Prayer of Manasseh	2 Chronicles

2. An apocalypse—2 Esdras
3. Two stories of Jewish Piety
   Tobit
   Judith
4. Two books of wisdom
   The Wisdom of Solomon
   Ecclesiasticus, or the Wisdom of Jesus, the Son of Sirach
5. Historical books
   1 Maccabees
   2 Maccabees

The books that are supposed to be additions to biblical books are varied. 1 Esdras essentially duplicates portions of the biblical books of 2 Chronicles (35:1–36:23), all of Ezra, and that part of Nehemiah that tells of Ezra reading the Torah to the Jews (7:38–8:12). The only original part of the book is a delightful story of three guards in the palace of the Persian King who compete for a prize by giving their answers to the question "What one thing is the strongest?" (1 Esdras 3:5). One argues for wine; the second for the king himself; and the third, who is identified as Zerubbabel, wins the argument and the prize by praising women and truth. As his reward, he is allowed to return to Jerusalem to rebuild the

---

[3]For the most part this classification scheme is that of Robert C. Dentan, *Apocrypha: Bridge of the Testaments* (The Seabury Press, 1954, 1964).

Temple (1 Esdras 4:61-63). Of the other books listed in the first category, Baruch, the Letter of Jeremiah, and The Prayer of Manasseh also can be classified as wisdom literature.[4]

2 Esdras differs drastically from 1 Esdras in that it is an apocalypse. The introduction and conclusion show evidence of being the work of Christian editors while the core of the book is from a Jewish writer. While it wrestles with the problem of how a just God can permit such an evil world (as do some wisdom books), its emphasis on revelations, angels, and the final judgment puts it into the category of the apocalyptic.

Tobit and Judith are contrasting stories that illustrate Jewish piety in postexilic times. Tobit is a man who is unusually sensitive to the hurts of his fellow Jews. He even risks the wrath of the governing authorities because of his concern to see that the dead receive proper burial. After many reverses, including blindness, his faithful service to God is rewarded. Tobit's son Tobias carries out a mission for his father that secures the family's wealth, cures his father's blindness, and frees a beautiful woman from domination by a demon. The woman, Sarah, also becomes the wife of Tobias.

The story of Judith, on the other hand, is not nearly so romantic. When her native city is surrounded by the Assyrian army, she follows God's guidance and uses her feminine wiles to cut off the head of the enemy general. The siege is lifted and the people are freed. Internal evidences within both books confirm that both Judith and Tobit are fictional characters.

The Wisdom of Solomon and Ecclesiasticus are two of the finest books in the Apocrypha. Had they come from an earlier time, they undoubtedly would have been included in the Hebrew canon. The Wisdom of Solomon is from the Alexandrian Jewish community, probably from the first century B.C. It deals with the themes of the righteous and the wicked, immortality, the judgment of the wicked, and the importance of wisdom as the guide for life. In this book wisdom takes on even more of the characteristics of a person than it does in earlier wisdom books. Chapters 10–12 illustrate how wisdom guided the great persons and events in Israel's history.

Ecclesiasticus or the Wisdom of Jesus the Son of Sirach is the work of a Jewish schoolmaster who lived about 200 B.C. It sets out rules for getting along in this world. Unlike the book of Proverbs, in which the sayings are not grouped according to subject matter, Ecclesiasticus tends to group material in a topical arrangement.

Of the two historical books, 1 Maccabees is the more valuable as history. It is an unusually reliable history that begins with the reign of Antiochus Epiphanes (175 B.C.) and ends with the beginning of the reign

[4]Robert C. Dentan, *Apocrypha*, pp. 76–92.

of John Hyrcanus, the first Hasmonean ruler (135 B.C.). Its major concern is the Maccabean revolt. 2 Maccabees covers a shorter time period and primarily concerns itself with the exploits of Judas Maccabeus. Its writer has a strong bias against the Hasmonean rulers.

The earliest books in the Apocrypha probably come from the late third century B.C., while the latest would be dated as late as the first century A.D. They came from a time when many changes were taking place in the Near East and did their part to encourage the faithful during unsettled days.

THE PSEUDEPIGRAPHA

Pseudepigrapha literally means "false writing." They were written under the names of famous persons who were long since dead. None of the writings classed as pseudepigraphical are found in either of the major canons of Scripture. It does not mean that they are of no value. As evidence of the regard with which some were held, the New Testament book of Jude quotes the Assumption of Moses (Jude 8) and Enoch (Jude 14–15). Another pseudepigraphical work, the Psalms of Solomon, was included among one of the more important collection of biblical manuscripts.[5]

What is to be included in the Pseudepigrapha is uncertain, especially now that in recent years much ancient extrabiblical material is coming to light. Some of the prominently mentioned writings are: The Letter of Aristeas, The Book of Jubilees, The Martyrdom of Isaiah, The Psalms of Solomon, 4 Maccabees, The Sibylline Oracles, The Book of Enoch, The Assumption of Moses, 4 Ezra, The Apocalypse of Baruch, The Testaments of the Twelve Patriarchs, The Life of Adam and Eve, Pirke Abot (The Sayings of the Fathers), and the Damascus Document. The major value of the Pseudepigrapha lies in showing the many currents of religious thought that were present at the end of the Old Testament era.[6]

THE DEAD SEA SCROLLS

In 1947, a young goat herder's curiosity led to one of the greatest archaeological discoveries of all time. A Bedouin boy threw a rock into a hole in a cliff overlooking the Dead Sea. When he heard the sound of

---

[5]The Sinaiticus manuscripts.

[6]For a brief summary of each of the books of the Apocrypha and the Pseudepigrapha see Leonhard Rost, *Judaism Outside the Hebrew Canon: An Introduction to the Documents,* translated by David Green (Nashville: Abingdon, 1976). For translations of the various writings see R. H. Charles, *The Apocrypha and Pseudepigrapha of the Old Testament* (Oxford: at the Clarendon Press, 1913).

something breaking, he climbed up the cliff to investigate. Inside the cave were clay jars filled with manuscripts. Most of these manuscripts eventually fell into the hands of biblical scholars, who recognized their great value. This led to the investigation of a number of other caves in the area and the excavation of a nearby ruin. The result of these investigations was the finding of a large number of manuscripts and manuscript fragments from almost every Old Testament book, as well as manuscripts of numerous religious writings. The latter finds furnished a wealth of new information about the people known as the Essenes, a Jewish sect that existed in the early part of the Christian era and about whom little was previously known. The community that produced the manuscripts existed at Qumran, on the northwestern shore of the Dead Sea from Maccabean times off and on until the Roman conquest of Palestine around A.D. 70.

The most famous biblical manuscript found at Qumran is commonly known as the St. Mark's Isaiah Scroll. It is at least 1000 years older than any previously known manuscript of Isaiah, yet its discovery led to no major changes in the translations of the book of Isaiah. Of the nonbiblical manuscripts, the best known are The Manual of Discipline, a rulebook for the conduct of the members; The Thanksgiving Scroll, which contains songs similar to the Book of Psalms; The War of the Sons of Light and the Sons of Darkness, a book describing a great battle that was to take place between the community members (the Sons of Light) and the Kittim or Romans (the Sons of Darkness). The latter work illustrates the apocalyptic nature of the community. Another major manuscript, the Temple Scroll, was published for the first time in 1978.[7]

The Dead Sea Scrolls and the people who produced them are just another illustration of the diverse character of Judaism as it was developing.

Judaism's Oral Tradition

The final body of literature we must mention is the growing body of oral tradition being developed by the rabbinic interpreters of the Hebrew scriptures. The aim of the great rabbis was to translate the principles in the Torah and the Prophets into rules for everyday living. Because of this felt need, a pair (zugoth) of outstanding rabbis, one representing a more orthodox or conservative viewpoint and one of a more liberal persuasion, interpreted the Scriptures for the men of their day. As was mentioned previously, they believed that this oral tradition extended all the way back to Moses, who, according to their view, received both an oral and a written Torah.

[7]Jacob Milgram, "The Temple Scroll," Biblical Archaeologist (Vol. 41, No. 3, 1978), pp. 105–120.

The time of the great rabbis began around 200 B.C. and would continue until A.D. 500. There was two types of oral literature: (1) *halakah* or rules for living based on the interpretation of the legal portions of the Old Testament and (2) *haggadah*, a more sermonic and illustrative kind of material that consisted of such things as fanciful expansions of the narrative parts of the Old Testament. It was designed to encourage the ordinary Jew to be diligent in observing *halakah*. By the end of the second century A.D. this material would be collected and organized into six divisions by the great rabbi Judah ha Nasi. This was the *Mishnah*. Following this, a commentary on the *Mishnah* was developed that would be known as the *Gemara*. The *Mishnah* and the *Gemara* were then joined to form the *Talmud*. There eventually would be two Talmuds—a Palestinian and a Babylonian Talmud. The truly amazing thing about this was that each generation of rabbis memorized the interpretations of the previous generations, added their own interpretations, and passed them on to the succeeding generation. Nothing was preserved in writing until about the fifth century A.D.! But these developments were only in their beginnings as the Old Testament story closes.

THE END OF THE MATTER

This version of the Old Testament story comes to an end. Perhaps it has opened a few eyes to the treasures of the Old Testament. If so, the telling has been worth it. It may even inspire some to look again at the story and to try to make it theirs so they can experience the thrill of walking in the steps of its characters; experiencing their joys, sorrows, and frustrations; tasting their foods; and smelling some of the smells of that world. If so, then that is even better. But this version of the story closes with the hope that even those who may never look at it again will in some way be a bit richer than before because they came this way to listen to the story.

STUDY QUESTIONS

1. Identify:
   a. *Diaspora*
   b. *zugoth*
   c. synagogue
   d. rabbi
2. What event symbolized the increasing political involvement of the High Priest?
3. Why were laymen increasingly influential in religious matters in postexilic Jewish communities?

4. How were the Samaritans related to Judaism?

5. What were the distinct beliefs of the Pharisees?

6. Why is it said that the Essenes were an apocalyptic group?

7. What best illustrates the diverse nature of Judaism as it was developing?

8. Why is it not completely accurate to speak of the Apocrypha as extrabiblical literature?

9. Briefly state the nature of the following books of the Apocrypha:
   a. I Esdras
   b. II Esdras
   c. Tobit
   d. The Wisdom of Solomon
   e. Ecclesiasticus or the Widsom of Jesus, the Son of Sirach
   f. I Maccabees

10. What illustrates the importance of the pseudepigraphical literature?

11. What do the Dead Sea Scrolls contribute to our knowledge of the Bible and of the Essenes?

12. How did the Talmuds develop?

FOR FURTHER STUDY

The Dead Sea Scrolls

CROSS, FRANK M. *The Ancient Library of Qumran and Modern Biblical Studies.* Garden City, N.Y.: Doubleday, 1961. One of the best books on the Dead Sea Scrolls. Also in a Doubleday Anchor paperback.

DRIVER, G. R. *The Judean Scrolls: The Problem and the Solution,* rev. ed. New York: Schocken Books, 1965.

GASTER, T. H. *The Dead Sea Scriptures,* rev. ed. Garden City, N.Y.: Doubleday, 1964. A representative collection of the nonbiblical materials from Qumran. Paperback.

VERMÈS, GÉZA. *The Dead Sea Scrolls in English.* Baltimore: Penguin Books, 1962. Paperback.

The Samaritans

COGGINS, R. J. *Samaritans and Jews: The Origins of Samaritanism Reconsidered.* Growing Points in Theology. Atlanta: John Knox, 1975. A thorough look at the evidences concerning the development of Samaritanism.

Judaism

MOORE, G. F. *Judaism in the First Centuries of the Christian Era,* Vol. 1. New York: Schocken Books, 1927 and 1971. Read especially the first few chapters.

NEUSNER, JACOB. *From Politics to Piety: The Rise of Pharisaic Judaism.* Englewood Cliffs, N.J.: Prentice-Hall, 1972.

The following is a select list of more technical introductions to the Old Testament, each taking a different approach to the subject than the one taken here.

ANDERSON, BERNHARD W. *Understanding the Old Testament,* 3rd ed. Englewood Cliffs, N.J.: Prentice-Hall, 1975. This undoubtedly is the most widely used introduction to the Old Testament. An excellent book.

FLANDERS, H. J., JR., R. W. CAPPS, and D. A. SMITH. *The People of the Covenant: An Introduction to the Old Testament,* 2nd ed. New York: Ronald Press, 1973.

FOHRER, GEORG. *Introduction to the Old Testament. Introduction to the Old Testament.* Trans. by David Green. Nashville: Abingdon, 1968. The revision of an earlier work by E. Sellin (1910).

GOTTWALD, NORMAN K. *A Light to the Nations.* New York: Harper & Row, 1959.

HARRELSON, WALTER. *Interpreting the Old Testament.* New York: Holt, Rinehart, and Winston, 1964. This book follows the order of the Hebrew Canon.

HARRISON, R. F. *Introduction to the Old Testament.* Grand Rapids: Eerdmans, 1969. An encyclopedic introduction by a leading conservative scholar.

KAISER, OTTO. *Introduction to the Old Testament: A Presentation of Its Results and Problems.* Trans. by John Sturdy. Minneapolis: Augsburg, 1975.

PFEIFFER, CHARLES F. *Old Testament History.* Grand Rapids: Baker Book House, 1973. Very conservative but comprehensive introduction.

PFEIFFER, ROBERT H. *Introduction to the Old Testament,* rev. ed. New York: Harper & Row, 1949. Another encyclopedic work, but one whose author would be on the opposite end of the theological spectrum from Harrison.

ROWLEY, H. H. *The Growth of the Old Testament.* London: Hutchinson, 1950. Also in a Harper Torchbook, 1963. Brief, but packed with information.

WEISER, ARTHUR. *The Old Testament: Its Formation and Development.* Trans. from the 4th German ed. by Dorothea M. Barton. New York: Association Press, 1961.

For the overall message of the Old Testament the following theologies are recommended:

EICHRODT, WALTER. *Theology of the Old Testament.* 2 vols. Trans. by J. A. Baker. Philadelphia: Westminster, 1961 and 1967.

JACOB, EDMOND. *Theology of the Old Testament.* Trans. by A. W. Heathcote and P. J. Allcock. New York: Harper & Row, 1958.

MUILENBURG, JAMES. *The Way of Israel.* New York: Harper & Row, 1961.

RAD, GERHARD VON. *Old Testament Theology.* 2 vols. Trans. by D. M. G. Stalker. New York: Harper & Row, 1962 and 1965.

VRIEZEN, H. C. *An Outline of Old Testament Theology.* London: Blackwell, 1958.

COMPREHENSIVE CHRONOLOGICAL CHART

B.C.	EGYPT	PALESTINE AND SYRIA	MESOPOTAMIA (AND ASIA MINOR)
(Middle Bronze Age) 2000 to 1900	XII Dynasty	Egyptian Control	Third Dynasty of Ur (c. 2060-1950) Hurrian Movement Amorite Invasion
1900 to 1800	XII Dynasty		First Babylonian Dynasty (c. 1830-1530)
1800 to 1700	Hyksos Invasion (c. 1720)	Abraham	The Mari Age Hammurabi (c. 1728-1686)
1700 to 1600	Hyksos Rule (XV to XVI Dynasties) XVII (Theban Dynasty)	Hyksos Control Descent of Jacob family into Egypt	Decline of Babylonia
(Late Bronze Age) 1600 to 1500	XVIII Dynasty: Ahmose (c. 1552-1527) Expulsion of Hyksos	Egyptian Control	Old Hittite Empire (c. 1600-1500)
1500 to 1400	Thutmose III (c. 1490-1436)		Kingdom of Mitanni (c. 1500-1370)
1400 to 1300	Amenhotep III (c. 1403-1364) Amenhotep IV or Akhnaton (c. 1364-1347)	Amarna Age (c. 1400-1350) Egyptian Weakness	New Hittite Empire (c. 1375-1200) Rise of Assyria (c. 1356-1197)
1300 to 1200	XIX Dynasty: Seti I (c. 1305-1290) Rameses II (c. 1290-1224) Merneptah (c. 1224-1211)	Egyptian Revival (The Exodus, c. 1290) Israelite Conquest (c. 1250-1200) Merneptah's Victory (c. 1220)	Assyrian Dominance
(Iron Age) 1200 to 1100	XX Dynasty (c. 1185-1069) Sea Peoples defeated by Rameses III (c. 1175) Egyptian decline	Period of the Judges (c. 1200-1020) Philistines settle in Canaan Battle of Megiddo (c.1125)	Collapse of Hittite Empire Assyrian decline
1100 to 1000	XXI Dynasty (c. 1069-935) Egyptian decline	Philistine ascendancy Fall of Shiloh (c. 1050) Samuel and Saul (c. 1020-1000)	Brief Assyrian revival Tiglath-pileser I (c. 1116-1078)

B.C.	EGYPT	PALESTINE		PHOENICIA	MESOPOTAMIA
(Iron Age)	Decline	**THE UNITED KINGDOM** David, c. 1000-961 Solomon, c. 961-922		Hiram I c. 969-936	Assyrian Decline
	XXII Dynasty Shishak I (c. 935-914)				
1000 to 900		Division of the kingdom at death of Solomon, c. 922			

THE DIVIDED KINGDOM

B.C.	EGYPT	JUDAH	ISRAEL	PHOENICIA	MESOPOTAMIA
	Shishak invades Judah c. 918	DAVIDIC DYNASTY: Rehoboam, c. 922-915 Abijah (Abijam), c. 915-913 Asa, c. 913-873	Jeroboam I, c. 922-901 Nadab, c. 901-900		Assyrian Revival
900 to 850	Egyptian Weakness	Jehoshaphat, c. 873-849 Jehoram, c. 849-842 Ahaziah, c. 842	Baasha, c. 900-877 Elah, c. 877-876 Zimri, c. 876 (7 days) *Omri Dynasty:* Omri, c. 876-869 Ahab, c. 869-850 (*Elijah,* c. 850) Ahaziah, c. 850-849 Jehoram, c. 849-842	SYRIA Benhadad I, c. 880-842 Hazael, c. 842-806	Adad-nirari II, c. 912-892 Ashur-nasir-apal II, c. 884-860 Shalmaneser III, c. 859-825 Battle of Qarqar, 853
850 to 750	Decline	Athaliah, c. 842-837 Joash, c. 837-800 Amaziah, c. 800-783 Uzziah (Azariah), c. 783-742	*Jehu Dynasty:* Jehu, c. 842-815 Joahaz, c. 815-801 J(eh)oash, c. 801-786 Jeroboam II, c. 786-746 (*Amos,* c. 750) (*Hosea,* c. 745) Zechariah (6 mos.) c. 746-745		(Jehu pays tribute, 841) Shamshi-Adad V, c. 824-812 Adad-nirari III, c. 811-784 Decline

B.C.	EGYPT	PALESTINE		MESOPOTAMIA
		DIVIDED KINGDOM		
		JUDAH · ISRAEL	SYRIA	ASSYRIA

B.C.	EGYPT	JUDAH	ISRAEL	SYRIA	ASSYRIA
	Decline	Jotham (regent), c. 750-742 Jotham (king), c. 742-735 (*Isaiah*, c. 742-700) Jehoahaz (Ahaz), c. 735-715 Invasion by Syro-Israelite Alliance, 735	Shallum (1 mo.), c. 745 Menahem, c. 745-738 Pekahiah, c. 738-737 Pekah, c. 737-732 SYRO-ISRAELITE ALLIANCE	Rezin, c. 740-732	Tiglath-pileser III, c. 745-727 EXPANSION OF ASSYRIAN EMPIRE
750 to 700		(*Micah*: before 722 to c. 701)	Hoshea, c. 732-724 FALL OF SAMARIA 722-721	FALL OF SYRIA, 732	Siege of Damascus, 732 Shalmaneser V, 726-722 Siege of Samaria, 722/721
	XXV Dynasty (Ethiopian) c. 716-663	JUDAH Hezekiah, c. 715-687			Sargon II, 721-705 Siege of Ashdod, 712 Sennacherib, 704-681 Invasion of Palestine, 701
	Tirhakah, c. 685-664 Invasion by Assyria, 671 Sack of Thebes, 663, by Ashurbanapal	Manasseh, 687/6-642 Amon, 642-640 Josiah, 640-609 First show of Judean independence, 629 (*Zephaniah*, c. 628-622) (*Jeremiah*, c. 626-587)			Esarhaddon, 680-669 Invasion of Egypt, 671 Ashurbanapal, 668-627 RISE OF BABYLONIA Nabopolassar, 626-605
700 to 600	XXVI Dynasty, c. 664-525 Psammetichus I c. 664-610	Josiah's "Deuteronomic Reform," 621			
	Necho II, 609-594	Death of Josiah at Megiddo, 609 Jehoahaz II (Shallum), 609 (3 mos.) Jehoiakim (Eliakim), 609-598 (*Habakkuk*, c. 605)			Fall of Ashur to Medes, 614 Fall of Nineveh to Medes and Babylonians, 612 Babylonian defeat of Assyrians and Egyptians at Haran, 609 Battle of Carchemish, 605 FALL OF ASSYRIA

B.C.	EGYPT	PALESTINE	MESOPOTAMIA

B.C.	EGYPT	PALESTINE	MESOPOTAMIA
		THE BABYLONIAN EMPIRE	BABYLONIA
		Jehoiachin (Jeconiah), 3 mos., 598-597 First Deportation to Babylonia, 597	Nebuchadrezzar, 605-562
	Apries (Hophra), 589-570	Zedekiah (Mattaniah), 597-587 FALL OF JERUSALEM SECOND DEPORTATION, 587	
		BABYLONIAN EXILE Ezekiel, c. 593-573	
			Nabonidus, 556-539 (his son: Belshazzar) RISE OF PERSIA Cyrus II, 550-530 Defeat of Media, c. 550 Invasion of Lydia, c. 546
600 to 500		(*Second Isaiah*, c. 540) Edict of Cyrus, 538	FALL OF BABYLON, 539
		THE EMPIRE OF PERSIA	
	Conquest by Persia 525	THE RESTORATION JUDAH Return of exiles Rebuilding of Temple, 520-515 (*Haggai*) (*Zechariah*)	Cambyses, 530-522 Darius I, 522-486
500 to 400	Egypt under Persian rule, 525-401	(*Malachi*, c. 500-450) Ezra's mission, 458(?) Nehemiah arrives, 445 Ezra's mission, c. 428(?)	Persia Xerxes I (Ahasuerus), 486-465 Artaxerxes I (Longimanus), 465-424 Xerxes II, 423 Darius II, 423-404
		Ezra's mission, c. 398(?)	Artaxerxes II (Mnemon), 404-358 Artaxerxes III, 358-338 Arses, 338-336 Darius III, 336-331

425

B.C.	EGYPT	PALESTINE	MESOPOTAMIA
		EMPIRE OF ALEXANDER THE GREAT, 336-323	
400 to 300	*Ptolemaic Kingdom* Ptolemy I, 323-285	Egyptian Control	*Seleucid Kingdom* (Mesopotamia and Syria) Seleucus I, 312/11-280
300 to 200	Ptolemy II, 285-246 Ptolemy III, 246-221 Ptolemy IV, 221-203	Egyptian Control	Antiochus I, 280-261 Antiochus II, 261-246 Seleucus II, 246-226 Seleucus III, 226-223 Antiochus III, 223-187
200 to 100	Ptolemy V, 203-181 Ptolemy VI, 181-146 Ptolemy VII, 146-116	Syrian Conquest, 198-200 MACCABEAN REVOLT, 168 (167) Judas, 166-160 Jonathan, 160-143 Simon, 143-134 John Hyrcanus, 134-104 Conquest of Shechem, 128	Seleucus IV, 187-175 Antiochus IV (Epiphanes), 175-163 Antiochus V, 163-162 Demetrius I, 162-150 Alexander Balas, 150-145 Demetrius II, 145-138 Antiochus VI, 145-141 Antiochus VII, 138-129
100 to A.D.	Roman Conquest, 30	Pompey captures Jerusalem, 63	Roman occupation of Syria, 63
		THE EMPIRE OF ROME	

Source: Bernhard W. Anderson, *Understanding the Old Testament*, 3rd ed., copyright 1975, pp. 602–606. Reprinted by permission of Prentice-Hall, Inc.

Index